W9-BGK-809

CASES IN COLLECTIVE BARGAINING
AND INDUSTRIAL RELATIONS

A Decisional Approach

CASES IN COLLECTIVE BARGAINING AND INDUSTRIAL RELATIONS

A Decisional Approach

STERLING H. SCHOEN
Professor of Management

RAYMOND L. HILGERT
*Professor of Management
and Industrial Relations*

*Both of the Graduate School
of Business Administration
Washington University,
St. Louis, Missouri*

1986 FIFTH EDITION

IRWIN
Homewood, Illinois,   60430

ISBN 0-256-03503-2

Library of Congress Catalog Card No. 85–80613

Printed in the United States of America

2 3 4 5 6 7 8 9 0 K 3 2 1 0 9 8 7

PREFACE

This fifth edition provides a convenient but extensive set of cases in a variety of union-management problem situations. The book is probably most appropriate as a supplementary book in basic or survey courses in collective bargaining, labor economics, and industrial relations. The cases vary in length, complexity, and numbers of issues. Therefore, the collection of cases is of sufficient magnitude and depth that the book would be suitable for advanced courses or case courses in the field of collective bargaining and labor relations.

A major objective is to provide a means by which students can apply principles, concepts, and legal considerations that they have learned to realistic decision situations and confrontations between labor and management. We have used the cases in seminars and classes and have found them to be challenging and fascinating learning instruments.

The cases are representative of the types of problems that continue to confront management and labor unions. Cases such as these test analytical ability in dealing with challenging human relations and union-management situations in a way useful even for students who do not have a management or labor relations career in mind.

In an effort to reflect the impact of recent trends, we have collected representative cases dealing with problems that focus upon current and contemporary issues. Some 25 percent of the cases in the fifth edition are new to this collection. The cases we have retained from previous editions provide continuity and balance, and these cases are "timeless" in the evaluation of union-management relations.

Part One of the book presents a collection of National Labor Relations Board cases as restructured from published reports of the NLRB and court decisions. Our intent has been to describe each situation from the perspective of impartial writers reporting the facts and issues of the case. The case format has been developed as follows: the background information of the case is first presented, including relevant legal issues; the position of the union(s) or person(s) is stated; and the position of the management or company is

v

stated. An introductory discussion and important and substantive sections of the Labor Management Relations Act (as amended) are included at the outset of Part One to enable students to become familiar with the provisions of the Act which are applicable throughout the cases.

We believe that the legal obligations and responsibilities of unions and management under the Labor Management Relations Act continue to be among the most dynamic and important areas of collective bargaining today. Case studies such as those in the first section enable the student to appreciate the nature of this Act, its application in numerous union-management situations, and the duties and legal obligations of management and union representatives to carry out their bargaining responsibilities in good faith.

Part Two consists of cases adapted from grievance-arbitration decisions. We are grateful to the Bureau of National Affairs, Inc., for permission to adapt certain published cases from *Labor Arbritration Reports*. Here, too, the approach has been to restructure these actual arbitration cases in a convenient format. The highlights and issues of each case are provided through relevant background information, including the contractual clauses, rules, practices, and the like, which are pertinent. Principal arguments of the union and management sides are then presented. Cases in this part demonstrate complexities and controversial areas, which continue to manifest in the ongoing relationships between management and union personnel. We also have included a brief introductory discussion of the major considerations involved in grievance-arbitration procedures from which these cases emanate.

For both the NLRB and labor arbitration cases—which have not been selected with any intent of presenting "good" or "bad" or "right" or "wrong" union-management practices—the student should ask, "What are the problems or principal issues?" "What is at stake between the parties?" "What is justice or equity in the situation?" "What does the law require?" "What does the contract say on the issue(s)?" "How have previous NLRB decisions or previous labor arbitration decisions handled similar circumstances?" These types of questions, and the more specific questions we have developed at the conclusion of each case, urge students toward a depth analysis of issues. Decisions of the NLRB, the courts, and labor arbitrators for these cases are included in an Instructor's Manual. It has been the authors' experience that most students want to compare their decisions and approaches with those of authorities in the field.

Index and classification tables are included in each section of the book prior to the cases. These tables briefly cite the major issues of each case; for the NLRB cases, legal provisions are indicated. Selected bibliographies are also provided for more detailed reading in areas that either directly or indirectly are involved in the cases and materials in both sections of the book.

Although we cannot recognize everyone who has had a part in developing this book, we wish to acknowledge the cooperation of Karl Sauber of the St. Louis office of the National Labor Relations Board, whose assistance in developing several cases for Part One was invaluable. The cooperation of Charles Riley of the St. Louis office of the Federal Mediation and Conciliation Service in providing us with FMCS materials is similarly acknowledged.

Our research assistants at Washington University, William Robards and Robert McElroy, were involved in researching case materials. We also acknowledge the cooperation of Dean Robert Virgil who provided support for our endeavors, principally through the services and assistance of the Business School word processing staff: Ruth Scheetz, Mary Blair, Phyllis Koerner, Linda Young, and Carla Stricklin.

Sterling H. Schoen
Raymond L. Hilgert

CONTENTS

PART ONE

Legal Aspects of Collective Bargaining

NATIONAL LABOR RELATIONS BOARD CASES

Introduction to

THE LABOR MANAGEMENT RELATIONS ACT (LMRA)

This introductory section will briefly introduce the principal provisions of the Labor Management Relations Act (LMRA) of 1947 as amended. A partial text of this act follows this introductory section. For even more analytical understanding of the provisions of the Act and its applications, a selected bibliography for reading is included at the end of this introductory section. It also is recommended that the student of collective bargaining and industrial relations contact a regional or national office of the National Labor Relations Board (NLRB) to obtain various NLRB publications which explain detailed principles and procedures involved in administration of the law. For example, a publication included in the bibliography entitled, *A Guide to Basic Law and Procedures under the National Labor Relations Act*, is prepared by the Office of the General Counsel of the NLRB; this booklet is very helpful in understanding many of the day-to-day activities of the Board and some of its most recent thinking. Parts of this publication have been excerpted and included in this introductory section.

The LMRA of 1947, also known as the Taft-Hartley Act in recognition of the principal congressional authors of the law, is the principal labor legislation governing the "rules of the game" of collective bargaining for the private sector of the U.S. economic system.[1] The

[1] The Railway Labor Act of 1926 (as amended) governs collective bargaining in the rail and airline industries. Although the Railway Labor Act is not widely applicable and some of its provisions are considerably different from those in LMRA, its premises and procedures were drawn upon by the framers of the National Labor Relations (Wagner) Act of 1935, upon which the Act of 1947 subsequently was based. The student is encouraged to study the provisions of the Railway Labor Act, as well as a history of labor laws in the railroad industries, which led to the passage of the Railway Labor Act of 1926.

3

LMRA of 1947 constituted a major amendment and revision of the National Labor Relations (Wagner) Act of 1935. The Act since has been amended a number of times (1951, 1958, 1959, 1969, 1973, 1974, and 1980); the 1974 amendments primarily focused upon health care institutions. As it stands today, the Act is the fundamental legislative basis for the majority of union-management relationships in the United States.[2] The LMRA is an extremely complex document in and of itself. Of even greater complexity, however, is the body of administrative laws and decisions which has evolved over the years of its existence in hundreds of thousands of union-management case situations. The Act is constantly being tested, evaluated, and reevaluated by the NLRB, the courts, and by the Congress of the United States, in the light of changing times, new confrontations, and new decisions. It is not the purpose of this section to completely interpret the Act nor to present it in its entirety. Rather, selected parts of the Act will be discussed to underscore the major elements of the Act governing the collective bargaining process. An understanding of these parts of the Act should provide sufficient insights on which various aspects of specific union-management cases may be analyzed.

EXCERPTS AND COMMENTS ON THE TEXT OF THE LABOR MANAGEMENT RELATIONS ACT, 1947, AS AMENDED

Section 1. The Statement of Findings and Policy

The LMRA begins with a statement to the effect that industrial strife interferes with the normal flow of commerce. The purpose of the Act is to promote the full flow of commerce by prescribing and

[2] One of the major developments in contemporary labor relations has been at the federal government employee level. Executive Order 10988, originally signed by President Kennedy in 1962, was replaced by Executive Order 11491 issued by President Nixon in 1970. (Executive Orders 11616 and 11636 issued by President Nixon in 1971 and Executive Order 11838 issued by President Ford in 1975 amended Executive Order 11491.) These orders provided for federal employees union representation and collective bargaining rights. Subsequently, in 1978, Title VII of the Civil Service Reform Act replaced these Executive Orders and consolidated into law provisions for civilian federal government employees to govern collective bargaining in the federal sector. Title VII of the Civil Service Reform Act (Public Law 95–454) closely parallels the LMRA in many fundamental areas, with many of its provisions similar to various provisions in LMRA governing union-management relations in the private sector. Of course, federal government employees do not have the right to strike nor to have a "union shop," and a number of key areas remain outside of the scope of bargaining in the federal sector. For example, most wages and certain working conditions are set by Congress, and a number of areas of employee concern are handled under federal and civil service regulations. Nevertheless, this law which replaced amended Executive Order 11491 is a major development in collective bargaining in the United States. The authors have included only one case from the federal sector in this part of the text. However, numerous cases have been decided in the federal sector which have drawn heavily for precedent and policy from decisions of the NLRB in

protecting rights of employers and employees and by providing orderly and peaceful procedures for preventing interference by either with the legitimate rights of the other.

Also included in this statement of public policy is that the labor law of the land is designed to regulate both unions and employers in the public interest. The Act encourages the right of employees to organize labor unions and to bargain collectively with their employers as a means of balancing bargaining power. At the same time, the Act encourages union and employer practices which are fundamental to the friendly adjustment of industrial disputes, with the objective of eliminating some union and employer practices which impair the public interest by contributing to industrial unrest and strikes.

The NLRB, which is the federal agency administering the Act, has consistently interpreted this section to mean that the public policy of the United States is to promote and encourage the principle of unionism.

Section 2.   Definitions

This section of the Act defines various terms used in the course of the Act, and also outlines the coverage of the Act. By its terms, the Act does not apply to employees in a business or industry where a labor dispute would not affect interstate commerce. In addition, the Act specifically states that it does not apply to the following:

Agricultural laborers, as defined by the Fair Labor Standards Act (Wage-Hour Law).

Domestic servants.

Any individual employed by one's parent or spouse.

Government employees, including those of government corporations or the Federal Reserve Bank, or any political subdivision such as a state or school district.[3]

---

the private sector. Included in the bibliography at the end of this introductory section are a number of sources to consult for public sector bargaining law, cases, and decisions.

The U.S. Postal Service was brought under partial coverage of the LMRA through enactment of the Postal Reorganization Act of 1970 (Public Law 91–375). This law granted the NLRB jurisdiction over the U.S. Postal Service for various aspects of bargaining unit determination, unfair labor practices, and related matters.

[3] A number of states have laws—which vary widely in scope and coverage—to provide collective bargaining rights and procedures for state and local government employees, including teachers and employees of government operated health care facilities. In 1984, Illinois became the most recent state to enact a comprehensive labor relations law for its public employees.

The following sources are recommended for a review of legislation governing collective oargaining for state, local, and municipal government employees: Alan Edward Bent and T. Zane Reeves, *Collective Bargaining in the Public Sector* (Menlo Park, Calif.: Benjamin/ Cummings, 1978); and Marvin J. Levine, *Labor Relations in the Public Sector: Readings and Cases*, 2d ed., (Columbus, Ohio: Grid, 1985).

Independent contractors who depend upon profits, rather than commissions or wages, for their income.

Exempted also are employees and employers who are subject to provisions of the Railway Labor Act.

Supervisors are excluded from the definition of employees covered by the Act. Whether or not a person is a supervisor is determined by authority rather than by title. The authority required to exclude an employee from coverage of the Act as a supervisor is defined in Section 2(11) of the Act.

All employees properly classified as "managerial," not just those in positions susceptible to conflicts of interest in labor relations, are excluded from the protection of the Act. This was the thrust of a decision of the Supreme Court in 1974.

The 1974 amendments to LMRA (Public Law 93-360) brought all private health care institutions, whether or not operated for a profit, under the coverage of the Act. Section 2(14) defines a private health care institution as, "any hospital, convalescent hospital, health maintenance organization, health clinic, nursing home, extended care facility, or other institution devoted to the care of sick, infirm, or aged person."

An *employer* is defined in the law as including "any person acting as an agent of employer, directly or indirectly." A *person* is defined to include "one or more individuals, labor organizations, partnerships, associations, legal representatives, trustees, trustees in bankruptcy, or receivers."

The term *labor organization* means any organization, agency, or employee representation committee or plan in which emloyees participate and which exists for the purpose, in whole or in part, of dealing with employers concerning grievances, labor disputes, wages, rate of pay, hours of employment, or conditions of work.

Section 2(12) defines the meaning of the term *professional employee* for which specific organizational rights are guaranteed in a later section.

Sections 3, 4, 5, 6. The National Labor Relations Board

Section 3 creates the NLRB as an independent agency to administer the Act. The NLRB consists of five members appointed by the President of the United States.

Section 3 also authorizes the appointment of a General Counsel of the Board, who is given supervisory authority over the Board attorneys and officers and employees in the regional offices of the board.

Sections 4 and 5 outline certain compensation, procedural, and administrative authorities granted to the NLRB by the Congress.

However, the key section is Section 6, which gives the Board authority to establish rules and regulations necessary to carry out provisions of the LMRA. *In effect, this section empowers the NLRB to administer and interpret the labor law in whatever manner it deems appropriate to the situations encountered.*

In order to do this, the Board has developed various standards— for the most part, dollar sales or volume standards— by which it determines whether or not a business enterprise is deemed to be interstate commerce and thus covered under the provisions of the Act.[4] The Board has developed detailed rules, policies, and pro-

---

[4] For example, the NLRB has used a standard of $500,000 total annual volume of business to determine if a *retail enterprise* was considered interstate. For *nonretail businesses* the Board uses two tests:*(a)* direct sales to consumers in other states or indirect sales through others called outflow of at least $50,000 a year; or *(b)* direct purchases of goods from suppliers from other states or indirect purchases through others called inflow of at least $50,000 a year.

Among the NLRB jurisdictional standards in effect since July 1, 1976, are the following:

Office buildings: Total annual revenue of $100,000 of which $25,000 or more is derived from organizations which meet any of the standards except the indirect outflow and indirect inflow standards established for nonretail enterprises.

Public utilities: At least $250,000 total annual volume of business, or $50,000 direct or indirect outflow or inflow.

Newspapers: At least $200,000 total annual volume of business.

Radio, telegraph, television, and telephone enterprises: At least $100,000 total annual volume of business.

Hotels, motels and residential apartment houses: At least $500,000 total annual volume of business.

Transit systems: At least $250,000 total annual volume of business.

Taxicab companies: At least $500,000 total annual volume of business.

Privately operated health care institutions: At least $250,000 total annual volume of business for hospitals; at least $100,000 for nursing homes, visiting nurses associations, and related facilities; and at least $250,000 for all other types of private health care institutions defined in the 1974 amendments to the Act.

Associations: These are regarded as a single employer in that the annual business of all association members is totaled to determine whether any of the standards apply.

Enterprises in the territories and the District of Columbia: The jurisdictional standards apply in the territories; all businesses in the District of Columbia come under NLRB jurisdiction.

National defense: Jurisdiction is asserted over all enterprises affecting commerce when their operations have a substantial impact on national defense, whether or not the enterprises satisfy any other standard.

Private universities and colleges: At least $1 million gross annual revenue from all sources (excluding contributions not available for operating expenses because of limitations imposed by the grantor).

Symphony orchestras: At least $1 million gross annual revenue from all sources (exclud-

(continued on next page)

cedures by which it determines appropriate collective bargaining units, holds representational elections, investigates labor disputes, and other such matters. *The NLRB by its policies and rulings in effect can and does reshape the Act, subject only to review of the federal courts.* The Appendix to this introductory section will provide an overview to the general operations of the NLRB and the magnitude of those operations.

Section 7. Rights of Employees

This section is perhaps one of the most significant in the Act. It guarantees employees the right to self organization; to form, join, or assist labor organizations; to bargain collectively through representatives of their own choosing; and to engage in (or refrain from) certain other concerted activities for the purpose of collective bargaining or other mutual aid or protection.

Examples of employee rights protected by Section 7 are:

Forming or attempting to form a union among the employees of a company.

Joining a union.

Assigning a union to organize the employees of any company.

Going out on strike for the purpose of attempting to obtain improved wages, hours, or other conditions of employment.

Refraining from joining a union in the absence of a valid union shop agreement.

---

ing contributions not available for operating expenses because of limitations imposed by the grantor).

Ordinarily if an enterprise does the total annual volume of business listed in the standard, it will necessarily be engaged in activities that "affect" commerce. The Board must find, however, based on evidence, that the enterprise does in fact "affect" commerce.

The Board has established the policy that where an employer whose operations "affect" commerce refuses to supply the Board with information concerning total annual business, and so on, the Board may dispense with this requirement and exercise jurisdiction.

Section 14(c) (1) authorizes the Board, in its discretion, to decline to exercise jurisdiction over any class or category of employers where a labor dispute involving such employees is not sufficiently substantial to warrant the exercise of jurisdiction, provided that it cannot refuse to exercise jurisdiction over any labor dispute over which it would have asserted jurisdiction under the standards it had in effect on August 1, 1959.

Finally, the NLRB has adopted other standards and policies which it uses in determining its jurisdiction depending upon various types of businesses and unique conditions involved. For example, in 1976 the NLRB changed its policy of exempting nonprofit, noncommercial, and charitable institutions from coverage of LMRA. The Board asserted that it would use the same general revenue standards for these types of institutions to determine if an employer's operations "substantially affect interstate commerce" and thus should be subject to provisions of the Act.

UNFAIR LABOR PRACTICES: EMPLOYERS

The unfair labor practices of employers are listed in Section 8(a) of the Act; those of labor organizations in Section 8(b). Section 8(e) lists an unfair labor practice that can be committed only by an employer and a labor organization acting together.

Section 8(a) (1).   Employers are forbidden from engaging in practices which would interfere with, restrain, or coerce employees in the exercise of rights guaranteed by Section 7.

Section 8(a) (1) constitutes a broad statement against interference by the employer; employers violate this section whenever they commit any unfair labor practices. Thus, a violation of Section 8(a) (2), (3), (4), or (5) also results in a violation of Section 8(a) (1).

Various acts of an employer may independently violate Section 8(a) (1). Examples of such violations are:

Threatening employees with loss of jobs or benefits if they should join or vote for a union.

Threatening to close down the plant if a union should be organized in it.

Questioning employees about their union activities or membership in such circumstances as will tend to restrain or coerce the employees.

Spying on union gatherings, or pretending to spy.

Granting wage increases deliberately timed to discourage employees from forming or joining a union.

Threatening to terminate credit at the company store or to force employees to move out of company housing if the union wins bargaining rights for the employees.

Circulating antiunion petitions among employees.

Section 8(a) (2).   Employers may not dominate or interfere with the formation or administration of any labor organization or contribute financial or other support to it.

In this regard, the Board distinguishes between "domination" of a labor organization and conduct which amounts to little more than illegal "interference." When a union is found to be "dominated" by an employer, the Board will normally order the organization completely disestablished as a representative of employees. But if the organization is found only to have been supported by employer assistance amounting to less than domination, the Board usually orders the employer to stop such support and to withhold recognition from the organization until it has been certified by the Board as a bona fide representative of employees.

In recent years, there has been a growth in various types of labor-management cooperative efforts such as, quality circles, quality-of-worklife programs, employee involvement groups, labor-management participation teams, and the like. In general, these types of efforts do not of themselves violate Section 8(a) (2), unless one becomes of such a nature that it leads to a circumvention of the negotiated labor agreement or some other interference with union or employee rights.

An employer violates Section 8(a) (2) by engaging in activities such as:

Assisting employees in organizing a union or an employee representation plan by providing financial support, legal counsel, or active encouragement.

Conducting a straw vote to determine whether employees favor an inside union, as opposed to one affiliated with one of the national unions.

Signing a union security contract with an inside union to forestall an organizing drive by an outside union.

Exerting pressure on employees to join a particular union.

Permitting a union to solicit dues checkoff authorizations from new employees as they go through the hiring process.

Permitting officers of one union to leave their machines to solicit union members while denying officers of a competing union these same privileges.

Section 8(a) (3). This section prohibits discrimination in hiring or tenure of employment or any term or condition of employment which tends to encourage or discourage membership in any labor organization. This provision, together with Section 8(b) (2), prohibits the closed shop, in which only persons who already hold membership in a labor organization may be hired. It also prohibits discriminatory hiring hall arrangements by which only persons who have "permits" from a union may be hired. However, a proviso of this section permits an employer and labor union to agree to a union shop where employees may be required to join a union after 30 days of employment.

Section 8(a) (3) provides that an employee may be discharged for failing to pay the required union initiation fees and dues uniformly required by the exclusive bargaining representative under a lawful union shop contract. The section provides further, however, that no employer can justify any discriminatory action against an employee for nonmembership in a union if the employer has reason to believe that membership in the union was not open to the employee on the same terms and conditions that apply to others, or that the employee was denied membership in the union for some reason other than failure to pay regular dues and initiation fees.

Some examples of types of discrimination in employment prohibited by Section 8(a) (3) would include:

Discharging employees because they urged other employees to join a union.

Refusing to reinstate employees when jobs they are qualified for are open because they took part in a union's lawful strike.

Granting of "superseniority" to those hired to replace employees engaged in a lawful strike.

Demoting employees because they circulated a union petition among other employees asking the employer for an increase in pay.

Discontinuing an operation at one plant and discharging the employees involved followed by opening the same operation at another plant with new employees because the employees at the first plant joined a union.

Refusing to hire qualified applicants for jobs because they belong to a union. It would also be a violation if the qualified applicants were refused employment because they did not belong to a union, or because they belonged to one union rather than another.

Section 8(a) (4). Employers may not discharge or otherwise discriminate against employees because they have filed charges or given testimony under this Act. Examples of violations of this section are:

Refusing to reinstate employees when jobs they are otherwise qualified for are open because they filed charges with the NLRB claiming their layoffs were based on union activity.

Demoting employees because they testified at an NLRB hearing.

Section 8(a) (5). It is an unfair labor practice for an employer to refuse to bargain collectively with the representatives of the employees. The meaning of "bargaining collectively" is more specifically outlined in Section 8(d) of the Act. Section 8(d) has been interpreted in many ways, and it might be considered as the cornerstone for the basic philosophy of the Act.

Examples of employer violations of this section are as follows:

Refusing to meet with representatives of a certified union because employees have threatened to go on strike.

Insisting that the union withdraw its demand for a union shop before the company would enter negotiations over a contract.

Insisting that members of the negotiating committee of the union be composed of employees of the company.

Refusing to discuss an increase in the price of coffee served in the company cafeteria.

Granting a wage increase without consulting the certified union.

Refusing to supply the union negotiators with information concerning the incentive system.

Subcontracting certain work to another employer without notifying the union that represents the affected employees and without giving the union an opportunity to bargain concerning the change in working conditions of the employees.

UNFAIR LABOR PRACTICES: LABOR ORGANIZATIONS

The 1947 and 1959 amendments to the Act made certain activities of labor unions unfair labor practices.

Section 8(b) (1) (A). A labor organization or its agents are forbidden "to restrain or coerce employees in the exercise of the rights guaranteed in section 7." The section also provides that it is not intended to "impair the rights of a labor organization to prescribe its own rules" concerning membership in the labor organization.

Examples of restraint or coercion that violate Section 8(b) (1) (A) when done by a union or its agents include the following:

Mass picketing in such numbers that nonstriking employees are physically barred from entering the plant.

Acts of force or violence on the picket line, or in connection with a strike.

Threats to do bodily injury to nonstriking employees.

Threats to employees that they will lose their jobs unless they support the union's activities.

Statement to employees who oppose the union that the employees will lose their jobs if the union wins a majority in the plant.

Entering into an agreement with an employer which recognizes the union as exclusive bargaining representative when it has not been chosen by a majority of the employees.

Fining or expelling members for crossing a picket line which is unlawful under the Act or which violates a no-strike agreement.

Fining employees for conduct in which they engaged after resigning from the union

Fining or expelling members for filing unfair labor practice charges with the Board or for participating in an investigation conducted by the Board.

Refusing to process a grievance in retaliation against an employee's criticism of union officers.

Section 8(b) (1) (B). A labor organization is prohibited from restraining or coercing an employer in the selection of a bargaining representative. The prohibition applies regardless of whether the labor organization is the majority representative of the employees in the bargaining unit. The prohibition extends to coercion applied by a union to a union member who is a representative of the employer in the adjustment of grievances. This section is violated by such conduct as the following:

Insisting on meeting only with a company's owners and refusing to meet with the attorney the company has engaged to represent the company in contract negotiations, and threatening to strike to force the company to accept demands.

Striking against several members of an employer association that had bargained with the union as the representative of the employers with resulting individual contracts being signed by the struck employers.

Insisting during contract negotiations that the employer agree to accept working conditions which will be established by a bargaining group to which it does not belong.

Fining or expelling supervisors for the way they apply the bargaining contract while carrying out their supervisory functions.

Section 8(b) (2). This section bars a union from causing or attempting to cause an employer to discriminate against an employee in violation of Section 8(a) (3). It also prohibits the union from attempting to cause an employer to discriminate against an employee to whom the union had denied or terminated membership, except where this action was taken by the union because the employee failed to "tender" the regular initiation fees and/or periodic dues uniformly required as a condition of acquiring or retaining membership in the union, where a union shop agreement is in effect.

Contracts or informal arrangements with a union under which an employer gives preferential treatment to union members are violations of Section 8(b) (2). It is not unlawful for an employer and a union to enter an agreement whereby the employer agrees to hire new employees exclusively through the union hiring hall so long as there is neither a provision in the agreement nor a practice in effect that discriminates against nonunion members in favor of union members or otherwise discriminates on the basis of union membership obligations. Both the agreement and the actual operation of the hiring hall must be nondiscriminatory; referrals must be made without reference to union membership or irrelevant or arbitrary considerations such as race.

Examples of violations of Section 8(b) (2) are:

Causing an employer to discharge employees because they circulated a petition urging a change in the union's method of selecting shop stewards.

Causing an employer to discharge employees because they made speeches against a contract proposed by the union.

Making a contract that requires an employer to hire only members of the union or employees "satisfactory" to the union.

Causing an employer to reduce employees' seniority because they engaged in antiunion acts.

Refusing referral or giving preference on the basis of race or union activities in making job referrals to units represented by the union.

Seeking the discharge of an employee under a union security agreement for failure to pay a fine levied by the union.

Section 8(b) (3). This section requires a labor organization to bargain in good faith with an employer about wages, hours, and other conditions of employment if it is the representative of that employer's employees. This section imposes on labor organizations the same duty to bargain in good faith that is imposed on employers by Section 8(a) (5). Both the labor organization and the employer are required to follow the procedure set out in Section 8(d) before terminating or changing an existing contract.

Section 8(b) (3) not only requires that a union representative bargain in good faith with employers but also requires that the union carry out its bargaining duty fairly with respect to the employees it represents. A union, therefore, violates Section 8(b) (3) if it negotiates a contract which conflicts with that duty, or if it refuses to handle grievances under the contract for irrelevant or arbitrary reasons.

Section 8(b) (3) is violated by any of the following:

Insisting on the inclusion of illegal provisions in a contract, such as a closed shop or a discriminatory hiring hall.

Refusing to negotiate on a proposal for a written contract.

Striking against an employer who has bargained, and continues to bargain, on a multiemployer basis to compel it to bargain separately.

Refusing to meet with the attorney designated by the employer as its representative in negotiations.

Terminating an existing contract and striking for a new one without notifying the employer, the Federal Mediation and Conciliation Service (FMCS), and the state mediation service, if any.

Conditioning the execution of an agreement upon inclusion of a nonmandatory provision such as a performance bond.

Refusing to process a grievance because of the race, sex, or union activities of an employee for whom the union is the statutory bargaining representative.

Section 8(b) (4). This section forbids secondary boycotts and certain types of strikes and picketing; it is an extremely complicated section. Secondary boycotts; sympathy strikes or boycotts to force recognition of an uncertified union; a strike to substitute another bargaining representative for one certified by the Board; strikes over so-called union jurisdictional disputes or work assignment disputes; and several other types of unfair acts—all are forbidden under this section.

More specifically, Section 8(b) (4) prohibits a labor organization from engaging in strikes or boycotts or taking other specified actions to accomplish certain purposes or "objects" as they are called in the Act. The actions are listed in clauses (i) and (ii); the objects are described in subparagraphs (A) through (D). A union commits an unfair labor practice if it takes any of the kinds of action listed in clauses (i) and (ii) as a means of accomplishing any of the objects listed in the four subparagraphs.

Clause (i) forbids a union to engage in a strike, or to induce or encourage a strike, work stoppage, or a refusal to perform services by "any individual employed by any person engaged in commerce or in an industry affecting commerce" for one of the objects listed in subparagraphs (A) through (D). Clause (ii) makes it an unfair labor practice for a union to "threaten, coerce, or restrain any person engaged in commerce or in an industry affecting commerce" for any of the proscribed objects.

Section 8(b) (4) (A) prohibits unions from engaging in actions specified in clause (i) or (ii) to compel an employer or self-employed person to join any labor or employer organization; or to force an employer to enter a hot cargo agreement prohibited by Section 8(e).

Section 8(b) (4) (B) contains the Act's secondary boycott provision. A secondary boycott occurs if a union has a dispute with Company A and in furtherance of that dispute causes the employees of Company B to stop handling the products of Company A, or otherwise forces Company B to stop doing business with Company A. The dispute is with Company A, called the primary employer; the union's action is against Company B, called the secondary employer; hence, the term *secondary boycott*. Section 8(b) (4) (B) also prohibits secondary action to compel an employer to recognize or bargain with a union that is not the certified representative of its employees.

Section 8(b) (4) (C) forbids a labor organization from using clause (i) or (ii) conduct to force an employer to recognize or bargain with a labor organization other than the one that is currently certified as the representative of its employees.

Section 8(b) (4) (D) forbids a labor organization from engaging in action described in clauses (i) and (ii) for the purpose of forcing any employer to assign certain work to "employees in a particular labor organization or in a particular trade, craft, or class rather than to employees in another labor organization or in another trade, craft, or class." The Act sets up a special procedure for handling disputes over work assignments under Section 10(K).

A proviso to Section 8(b) (4) makes clear that it is not unlawful for a person to refuse to enter the premises of an employer if the employees of that employer are engaged in a lawful strike ratified or approved by a representative of these employees. Another provision permits informational picketing in various circumstances, so long as such publicity and information picketing do not have the effect of inducing any individual employed by any person other than a primary employer to refuse to pick up, deliver, or transfer goods or not to perform services at the establishment of the employer involved in the dispute.

The following union activities are considered to be unfair labor practices under this section:

Picketing a company after three of its four partners refused to comply with the union's demand that they become members [8(b) (4) (A)].

Insisting that where final court action requires employees to handle goods at premises involved in a labor dispute, the employer must pay triple wages for the day or the entire tour of duty [8(b) (4) (A)].

Picketing the premises of an employer to compel him to cease doing business with another employer who has refused to recognize the union [8(b) (4) (B)].

Threatening an employer by telling him that his business will be picketed if he continues to do business with another employer whom the union has designated as "unfair" [8(b) (4) (B)].

A union's directing its members not to pick up and deliver products from a plant where the drivers had voted to be represented by a different union which had received certification from the NLRB [8(b) (4) (C)].

A union's engaging in a strike to attempt to force the employer to assign to it the job of installing metal doors when the employer had assigned the work to the members of another union [8(b) (4) (D)].

Section 8(b) (5). A union may not require employees under a union shop agreement to pay an initiation fee which the Board finds excessive or discriminatory. The section states that the Board shall consider in determination of these types of fees the practices and customs of labor organizations in the particular industry and the wages currently paid to employees affected.

For example, a union violated this section when it raised its initiation fee from $50 to $500 when other locals of the same union charged from $10 to $200 and the starting rate for the job was $90 per week.

Section 8(b) (6). This section prohibits what is commonly known as featherbedding. Unions may not force an employer to pay or deliver or to agree to pay or deliver, any money or thing of value for services which are not performed or not to be performed. This section has been narrowly interpreted by the board and does not include situations in which the work is performed, although it may be "unnecessary."

Section 8(b) (7). This is a complex provision prohibiting a union which has not been certified as the bargaining agent from picketing or threatening to picket an employer for the purpose of obtaining recognition by that employer or acceptance by his workers as their bargaining representative. Both recognitional and organizational picketing constitute unfair labor practices when: (*a*) the employer has recognized a certified union and a new representation election would be barred under the Act, (*b*) an NLRB election has been conducted during the previous 12 months, or (*c*) a representation petition has not been filed with the Board "within a reasonable period of time not to exceed 30 days from the commencement of such picketing."

However, this section does not prohibit picketing for the purpose of truthfully advising the public (including consumers) that the company does not employ union members, nor have a contract with a union, unless the effect of the picketing is to interfere with deliveries, pickups, and other services required by the picketed employer.

Section 8(e). This complicated provision forbids both labor organizations and employers to enter into agreements commonly known as hot cargo agreements. These are defined as agreements where the employer will not handle, use, sell, transport, or deal in any of the products of another employer as required or forced by the labor organization.

The Act exempts both the construction and garment industries from the conditions of this section. In the construction industry the parties may agree to a clause which restricts the contracting or subcontracting of work to be performed at the construction site. Typically, the union and the employer agree that subcontracted work will go to an employer who has a contract with the union. A union may strike, picket, or engage in any other lawful activity in order to obtain such an agreement with the employer. A labor organization in the garment industry may not only strike, picket, or engage in other lawful activity to obtain such an agreement, but it may also engage in such activities in order to enforce it.

Section 8(f). A union and employer in the construction industry may enter into an agreement whereby employees must join the union not later than 7 days after the date of hire, rather than 30 days, as provided in Section 8(a) (3) for all other employers. The parties may enter into such an agreement without having first established the majority status of the union, as required in Section 9.

FREE SPEECH

Section 8(c). This section of the Act provides that the expression of any views, argument, or opinion shall not constitute or be evidence of an unfair labor practice "if such expression contains no threat of reprisal or force or promise of benefit." Examples of situations which this provision does not protect, and which would be ruled as unfair labor practices, are:

Where an employer has made an implied threat that the organization of a union would result in the loss of certain benefits for employees.

Where an employer threatened to close down a plant to move to another location, in the event of a union's winning an election.

A statement by a management official to an employee that the employee will lose her job if the union wins a majority in the plant.

THE MEANING OF COLLECTIVE BARGAINING

Section 8(d). This section defines the meaning of collective bargaining as required from both parties by the Act. This definition imposes a mutual obligation upon the employer and the representative of the employees

> to meet at reasonable times and confer in good faith with respect to wages, hours, and other terms and conditions of employment or the negotiation of an agreement or any question arising thereunder and the execution of a written contract incorporating any agreement reached if requested by either party, but such obligation does not compel either party to agree to a proposal or require the making of a concession.

The duty to bargain thus covers all matters concerning rates of pay, hours of employment, or other conditions of employment. These are called mandatory subjects of bargaining about which the employer, as well as the employees' representative, must bargain in good faith, although the law does not require "either party to agree to a proposal or require the making of a concession." As determined by the NLRB, mandatory subjects of bargaining include but are not limited to such matters as pensions for present and retired employees, bonuses, group insurance, grievance procedure, safety practices, seniority, procedures for discharge, layoff, recall, or discipline, and the union shop. On nonmandatory subjects, that is, matters that are lawful but not related to "wages, hours, and other conditions of employment," the parties are free to bargain and to agree, but neither party may insist on bargaining on such subjects over the objection of the other party.

Section 8(d) also requires that the parties to a collective agreement follow certain steps in terminating or modifying the agreement. Among these requirements are that the party wishing to terminate or modify a labor contract must notify the other party to the contract in writing about the proposed termination or modification 60 days before the date on which the contract is scheduled to expire. This party also must, within 30 days after the notice to the other party, notify the FMCS of the existence of a dispute if no agreement has been reached by that time, and further notify at the same time any state or territorial mediation or conciliation agency in the state or territory where the dispute occurred.[5]

The NLRB has interpreted this section to mean that employees

---

[5] Procedures of the FMCS are described in Appendix B to this chapter.

who go on strike without following the prescribed steps for terminating or modifying the contract lose the protection of the law. They may not appeal to the Board if the employer disciplines or discharges them.

REPRESENTATIVES AND ELECTIONS

Section 9 of the Act is a lengthy section which governs the procedural and legal requirements for the designation of representatives and election of union representatives. It provides for three types of elections among employees:[6]

Representation elections to determine the employees' choice of a collective bargaining agent. These are held upon petition of an individual, employer, employees, or a labor organization. Typically, the NLRB will not hold an election unless the petitioner can show that at least 30 percent of the employees involved have indicated their support for the union, or for an election.

Decertification elections to determine whether or not the employees wish to withdraw the bargaining authority of the union. These are held upon the petition of the employees or a labor organization.

Deauthorization polls to determine whether or not the employees wish to revoke the authority of their union to enter into a union shop contract.

Section 9(a). This section provides that the union representative designated by a majority of employees appropriate for collective bargaining becomes the exclusive representative of the employees in bargaining. When a union majority representative has been chosen, it becomes illegal for an employer to bargain with anyone else.

Sections 9(b) and 9(c). These sections outline in general terms the "rules of the game" for the holding of NLRB elections. Included in 9(b) is the designation for the Board to determine what group of employees constitutes an appropriate unit for bargaining. The appropriate bargaining unit may extend to one or more employers, to one or more plants of the same employer, or it may be a subdivision of a plantwide unit such as a unit of skilled craftsmen. It is up to the Board to consider similarities of skills, wages, working conditions;

---

[6] The Board also conducts "expedited elections" in connection with Section 8(b) (7) (C), and employer last-offer elections in connection with Section 209 of the Act.

the history of collective bargaining in the company; the wishes of the employees; and any other factors which the Board may consider important in determination of the appropriate unit. In short, employees who possess common employment interests concerning wages, hours, and conditions of employment usually are grouped together in a bargaining unit. However, Section 9(b) specifically limits the Board in its determination of a bargaining unit in several ways. It may not include professional and nonprofessional employees in the same unit, unless a majority of the professional employees votes to be included in the unit. It also prohibits the Board from including plant guards in the same unit with other employees, and from certifying a union of guards if it also includes members who are not guards. The Board also may not use "the extent to which employees have organized" as the controlling factor in deciding the appropriate bargain unit [Section 9(c) (5)].

Section 9(c) (1) authorizes the NLRB to direct an election and certify the results thereof, provided the record shows that a question of representation exists.

An election may be held by agreement between the employer and the individual or labor organization claiming to represent the employees. In such an agreement the parties would state the time and place agreed on, the choices to be included on the ballot, and a method to determine who is eligible to vote. They would also authorize the NLRB Regional Director to conduct the election.

If the parties are unable to reach an agreement, the Act authorizes the NLRB to order an election after a hearing. The Act also authorizes the Board to delegate to its Regional Directors the determination on matters concerning elections. Under this delegation of authority the Regional Directors can determine the appropriateness of the unit, direct an election, and certify the outcome. Upon the request of an interested party, the Board may review the action of a Regional Director, but such review does not stop the election process unless the Board so orders. The election details are left to the Regional Director. Such matters as who may vote, when the election will be held, and what standards of conduct will be imposed on the parties are decided in accordance with the Board's rules and its decisions.

Section 9(c) (3) prohibits the holding of an election in any collective bargaining unit or subdivision thereof in which a valid election has been held during the preceding 12-month period.

In summary, Section 9 is one of the key sections which constantly confronts both unions and management in collective bargaining relationships, particularly in the formulative stages of a labor union in its efforts to gain representational status.

SPECIAL PROVISIONS FOR HEALTH CARE INSTITUTIONS

Representation election procedures are the same for health care facilities as for other establishments.[7] Similarly, as to unfair labor practices, the health care area is covered by the same statutory provisions such as those which forbid employer or union discrimination against employees, failure to bargain in good faith, certain unlawful union picketing, and employer domination or support of a labor organization.

But with a goal of minimizing work stoppages at health care institutions and providing continuity of patient care, Congress in 1974 wrote into the Act a new unfair labor practice—*Section 8(g)*. It prohibits a labor organization from striking or picketing a health care institution, or engaging in any other concerted refusal to work, without first giving the employer and FMCS a 10-day notice of such action. The section specifies, "The notice shall state the date and time that such action will commence. The notice, once given, may be extended by the written agreement of both parties."

Additionally, a series of special provisions for the health care industry were added to Section 8(d) of the Act. These health care amendments call for special dispute-settling procedures. A 90-day written notice must be served by employer or union of intent to terminate or modify a collective bargaining contract (30 days more than required by the Act elsewhere). If the dispute continues, the FMCS and similar state agencies must be notified at the 60-day point. If a dispute arises in bargaining for an initial contract, 30 days' notice must be given by the union to the employer, FMCS, and the appropriate agency. In either a contract termination-modification or initial contract dispute, under Section 213 of the Act, the FMCS may, if disagreement continues, invoke a 30-day no-strike, no-lockout period and set up a fact-finding board to make settlement recommendations, while continuing its mediation-conciliation efforts.

All else failing, the 10-day strike or picketing notice must be given as required by Section 8(g).

---

[7] In early 1975 the NLRB issued its guidelines for appropriate representational units in private health care institutions. In a series of cases—217 NLRB 131–138—these guidelines limit the number of bargaining units to avoid "proliferation" of units in health care organizations. However, in a recent case, the NLRB ruled that it was no longer going to be held to a "community of interest" standard and would begin using a "disparity of interest" standard in health care bargaining unit determination. See decision of the NLRB, St. Francis Hospital and IBEW Local 474, 271 NLRB No. 160. See also *White Collar Report*, August 15, 1984, pp. 213–219.

PREVENTION OF UNFAIR LABOR PRACTICES

Section 10 is very important in that it outlines the procedural requirements and limitations which are placed upon the Board and interested parties in processing unfair labor practice cases. The LMRA is not a criminal statute. The NLRB's actions are designed to stop unfair labor practices and to restore situations to their "original states" which prevailed before the violations occurred, insofar as possible. The orders of the Board serve basically to remedy the situation, not to punish persons who may have violated its provisions. The NLRB is authorized by Section 10(c) not only to issue a cease and desist order but "to take such affirmative action including reinstatement of employees with or without back pay, as will effectuate the policies of this Act."

Sections 10(a), 10(b), 10(c), 10(d). These sections of the Act outline the general procedures by which the NLRB and its regional offices investigate, attempt to prevent, and/or remedy unfair labor practices. Generally, an unfair labor practice charge must be filed with an office of the NLRB within six months of the date of the occurrence of the alleged unfair labor practice. (As of 1980, about 50 regional and other field offices of the NLRB were located in major cities in various sections of the country.) When a charge is received in the office of the Board, an agent will investigate to see whether formal proceedings are warranted.[8] If the regional office of the NLRB is unable to resolve the issue, and the complaint warrants a full hearing, an Administrative Law Judge (ALJ) from the Board's independent Division of Judges may be assigned to conduct a full, formal hearing to take testimony and examine the evidence. If the opinion of the ALJ is that the evidence presented is not sufficient to justify a finding that an unfair labor practice has been committed, the ALJ will issue an order dismissing the complaint. However, if the ALJ is of the opinion that an unfair labor practice(s) has occurred, he or she will make an appropriate finding and issue a remedial order. In effect, the findings and orders of the ALJ become recommendations to the NLRB. If there is no appeal of the ALJ's decision, the decision and remedial order (if any) of the ALJ become the decision and the order of the Board. If the case is appealed, the NLRB itself will review the determination made by the ALJ and either reverse, modify, or affirm the decision and order of the ALJ.

---

[8] In the event that the regional office refuses to issue a formal complaint, the person(s) who filed the charge may appeal this decision to the General Counsel of the NLRB who has final authority to determine whether to issue a formal complaint [Section 3(d)].

A remedial order issued by the NLRB usually will require the person, union, or company involved to cease and desist from the unfair labor practice(s) and to take affirmative action designed to remedy the effects of the unfair labor practice(s). Since the LMRA is not aimed at designating criminal penalties, these orders will be designed to restore equity to the situation on the assumption that such equity is necessary to guarantee rights protected under the Act. Examples of affirmative actions required of employers are:

Disestablish a union dominated by the employer.

Reopen a plant closed in an attempt to thwart the employees' attempts at self-organization.

Offer to hire employees denied employment because of their prounion attitudes or activities.

Offer to reemploy workers who were discharged for union activity; reimburse the employees for all lost wages, including interest; and restore full seniority and all other rights, including promotions, pay increases, pension privileges, and vacation rights that would have been received had the discriminatory discharges not occurred.

Upon request, bargain collectively with a certain union as the exclusive representative of the employees in a certain described unit and sign a written agreement if an understanding is reached.

Examples of affirmative actions required of unions are:

Notification to the employee and the employer that the union does not object to the reinstatement or employment of certain persons who were discharged or denied employment as a result of certain discriminatory actions by the union.

Order the union to refund dues and fees illegally collected, including interest.

Sign an agreement which had been negotiated with the employer.

Sections 10(e) and 10(f). These sections provide the machinery for the legal enforcement of Board orders and for appeal for relief from Board orders by an employer or union who believes that an order has been issued in error. Normally, the first appeal from an order of the regional office or ALJ will go to the full NLRB itself in Washington, D.C. The NLRB in order to seek enforcement of its orders may petition a federal district court or circuit court of appeals for appropriate relief or restraining order. Appeals from a Board or district court order may be made to a federal appeals court, and ultimate appeal can be made to the U.S. Supreme Court. The large majority of cases, however, are not appealed to the federal courts but are decided at Board regional office and/or national NLRB levels.[9]

Section 10(k). Special procedures for hearing and adjudicating jurisdictional disputes are provided for in this section.

Section 10(l). This section provides for special priority procedures, including court injunctions, so as to stop quickly certain acts, strikes, and boycotts which may result in "irreparable harm" to the employer. For the most part, these are directed against secondary boycotts and certain types of organizational picketing.

MISCELLANEOUS PROVISIONS

The remainder of the LMRA, although quite extensive in length, is not nearly so important to the duty to bargain collectively as are the provisions discussed to this point. Only brief mention will be made of the more salient miscellaneous provisions covered in the remaining sections which have not been mentioned previously.

Sections 11 and 12—Investigatory Powers and Penalties. As the name suggests, Section 11 outlines the legal powers of investigation given the NLRB by the Congress. Section 12 provides for penalties under the Act.

Sections 13 to 18—Limitations. Sections 13 through 18 state a series of limitations which the Act is not to be construed as interfering with or diminishing in any way. Section 13 guarantees that the right to strike is still a right not limited by the LMRA. Section 14(a) permits supervisors to be members of a labor organization, but states that employers are not required to bargain with supervisors as part of labor organizations. Section 14(b) permits so-called right-to-work laws in states where these laws are enacted. Specifically, Section 14(b) allows states to ban union shop contracts if they so choose. In early 1985, Idaho became the 21st state to have a right-to-work law on its statute books[10], and a number of other states were considering legislation in this area.

Section 19. As amended in legislation passed in 1980, this section provides that any employee who has conscientious objections to

---

[9] Statistically, about 65 percent of the unfair labor practice charges filed with the NLRB are dismissed by the regional offices of the Board or withdrawn by the parties. Of the remainder, over 90 percent usually are settled at the regional office level. Of the cases which are tried by an ALJ, about two thirds are appealed to the full NLRB. Some 25 to 35 percent of Board decisions are appealed to Courts of Appeal; typically the NLRB is sustained in whole or part in about 80 percent of these cases. Only a few cases are reviewed by the Supreme Court, usually some five or less annually.

[10] However, the application of the Idaho right-to-work statute was being challenged in the Idaho court system, and its final outcome may be determined by a statewide referendum on the issue.

joining or financially supporting a labor organization, based on the traditional tenets of a bona fide religion or sect, shall not be required to do so.[11]

However, such an employee may be required to make charitable contributions in an amount equal to union dues and initiation fees, and may be required to pay the costs incurred by the union of any requested grievance-arbitration procedure instituted on his/her behalf.

The language in this section defining conscientious objection is not to be construed in such a way as to discriminate among religions, or to favor any religious views.

Sections 201 through 205. These sections create and outline the functions of the FMCS and create a National Labor Relations Panel to advise the President on problems of industrial relations. The National Labor Relations Panel, consisting of representatives of management, labor, and the public, has not been active in recent years.

Sections 206 through 210. The National Emergency Strike provisions, giving the President power to intervene in those types of disputes which he deems to be national emergencies, are outlined in these sections.

Section 301. This section provides that suits for violation of contracts between an employer and a union may be brought into the federal district courts. Unions are made responsible for the acts of their agents; however, money judgments assessed against a labor organization in a district court are only enforceable against the organization as an entity and not against individual members per se.

Section 303. Strikes and boycotts enumerated in Section 8(b) (4) are made illegal, as well as their being unfair labor practices. Employers may sue to collect damages for injury resulting from such strikes.

SUMMARY

The remaining provisions of the Act are relatively minor in nature but should be studied by the student of industrial relations. Certainly, the complexity of the LMRA is one which the student recognizes from both study and application in case situations. Only by extensive analysis of labor-management cases can the student come to understand and appreciate the intent and effectiveness of the Act and its purpose to govern the duty to bargain collectively.

---

[11] Section 19 originally was added to the Act in the 1974 amendments solely for health care institutions, but without the grievance-arbitration proviso.

APPENDIX A

Edited Excerpts from the Informational Pamphlet, The NLRB—What It Is, What It Does*

Each fiscal year the NLRB receives some 45,000 cases of all kinds. Some two thirds are unfair labor practice charges. Over the years charges filed against employers have outnumbered those filed against unions by about 2 to 1. Charges are filed by individual workers, employers, and unions.

What is the structure of the NLRB? The NLRB has five Board Members and a General Counsel, each appointed by the President with Senate consent. The Board Members are appointed to five-year terms, the term of one Member expiring each year. The statute specifies that the President shall designate one Member to serve as Chairman of the Board. The General Counsel is appointed to a four-year term. Reappointments may be made.

Headquartered in Washington, the NLRB has 33 Regional Offices and 16 smaller field offices throughout the country.

The NLRB's judicial functions are separate by law from its prosecuting functions. The five-member Board acts primarily as a quasi-judicial body in deciding cases upon formal records, generally upon review from Regional Directors' or Administrative Law Judges' decisions. The General Counsel is responsible for the investigation and prosecution of charges of violations of the Act, and he has general supervision of the Regional Offices.

Who enforces Board orders? The NLRB has no statutory independent power of enforcement of its orders, but it may seek enforcement in the U.S. Courts of Appeals. Similarly, parties aggrieved by its orders may seek judicial review in the courts.

Annually, the U.S. Courts of Appeals hand down some 300 decisions related to enforcement and/or review of Board orders in unfair labor practice proceedings. Of these, about 80 percent affirm the Board in whole or in part.

How do NLRB procedures work? Upon the filing of an unfair labor practice charge with an NLRB Regional Office, members of the professional staff of that office investigate circumstances from which the charge arises, in order to determine whether formal proceedings are warranted. Approximately one third of the unfair labor practice allegations are found, after investigation, to require legal disposition.

---

* Published by the NLRB, Washington, D.C.

In such a case, the Regional Office works with the parties in an attempt to achieve a voluntary settlement adequate to remedy the alleged violation. A very substantial number of cases are settled at this stage. If a case cannot be settled, then a formal complaint is issued, and the case is heard before an Administrative Law Judge.

NLRB Administrative Law Judges conduct formal hearings and issue decisions, which may be appealed to the five-member Board; if they are not appealed, the Administrative Law Judges' recommended orders become orders of the Board.

The NLRB's traditional emphasis on voluntary disposition of cases at all stages means that only about 5 percent of the unfair labor practice charges originally filed with the Regional Offices are litigated all the way through to a decision of the Board. Yet, despite the small percentage, the Board is still called to decide on the order of 1,200 unfair labor practice cases and 700 representation cases each year.

In representation election cases, the 33 Regional Directors have the authority to process all petitions, rule on contested issues, and direct elections or dismiss the requsts, subject to review by the Board on limited grounds. The NLRB, through its Regional Offices, conducts thousands of representation elections a year in which hundreds of thousands of employees exercise their free choice by secret ballot.*

NATIONAL LABOR RELATIONS BOARD
OFFICE OF THE GENERAL COUNSEL
SUMMARY OF OPERATIONS†—FISCAL YEAR 1984

The information set forth below reflects the work of the various Divisions during this past fiscal year. These statistics are based on actions taken during the year.

Case Intake

Fiscal year 1984 saw an intake of approximately 43,426 cases, 11.1 percent fewer cases than the 48,840 cases docketed in FY 83 and 8.0 percent fewer than the 47,210 cases docketed in FY 82. It was also the lowest total case intake since 1974. During FY 84, unfair labor prac-

---

* Union representational elections conducted by NLRB offices during the early 1980s were averaging about 5,000 to 6,000 annually. Unions were winning certification in about 45 percent of these elections, down from 50 to 55 percent a decade earlier.

† From the "Summary of Operations," *Report of the Office of the General Counsel of the NLRB*, for the fiscal year ended September 30, 1984.

tices (C) case intake was 34,855 which represents a decrease of 12.9 percent from FY 83 and 8.5 percent from FY 82. There were 7,770 representation petitions filed in FY 84, a decrease of 3.3 percent from FY 83 and 6.1 percent from FY 82.

There were also 801 cases filed in other categories, such as union deauthorization, amendment of certification and unit clarification cases.

Remedies

In FY 84, $39,227,845 of backpay was distributed to employees, which was 19.5 percent less backpay distributed than in FY 83 when a *record* $48,707,609 was distributed. However, the FY 84 figure was the second highest amount ever distributed, and was 31.3 percent more backpay than the $29,886,550 distributed in FY 82. In addition, the amount of fees, dues and fines reimbursed in FY 84 was $656,692 which was 17.8 percent less than the *record* reimbursement in FY 83 of $798,853 but 27 percent more than the $517,067 reimbursed in FY 82. In addition, 6,249 offers of reinstatement were made in FY 84 which was 7.9 percent and 1.3 percent fewer offers than in FY 83 and FY 82, respectively.

Unfair Labor Practice Cases

ULP Merit Factor.   The percentage of unfair labor practice charges in which merit was found after investigation in the recent fiscal year was 34.1 percent compared to 34.8 percent in FY 83 and 34.1 percent in FY 82.

Complaints.   In FY 84, 3,610 unfair labor practice complaints were issued in a median time of 45 days. This figure represents a decrease of 20.5 percent in the number of complaints issued, compared to FY 83, when 4,543 complaints were issued, and a 13 percent decrease from FY 82, when 4,148 complaints were issued.

Litigation Results.   The 72 percent of Board and Administrative Law Judge decisions, won in whole or in part in FY 84, represents a decrease from the 79 percent and 80.9 percent litigation rates of FY 83 and FY 82, respectively.

Representation Cases

Elections.   The Regions held 5,181 elections, of which a *record* 84 percent were held pursuant to agreement of the parties. This compares with 5,196 elections and an 81.9 percent election agreement rate for FY 83 and 5,628 elections and 80.7 percent election agreement rate for FY 82. The time to proceed to an election from the filing of a petition was 47.6 days compared to the 47.2 and 48 day medians for FY 83 and FY 82 respectively.

Regional Director Decisions. Regional Directors issued 1,031 decisions in contested representation cases, after hearing, in a median of 41 days, which is well below our goal of 45 days. This compares with FY 83, when 1,056 decisions were issued in a median of 40 days and with FY 82, when 1,146 decisions were issued in a median of 41 days.

Representation and Union Deauthorization Hearings. In these categories, 1,393 initial hearings were held in FY 84, compared to 1,416 in FY 83 and 1,454 in FY 82.

APPENDIX B—THE FEDERAL MEDIATION AND CONCILIATION SERVICE (FMCS)

Excerpts from the Publication, *Securing Labor-Management Peace Through Mediation**

A strike or lockout is not the only answer when an employer and a union exhaust their bargaining talents and reach a stalemate. *Mediation* is the alternative.

A mediator can help bring reason and a fresh viewpoint to the dilemma, and often points the way to a solution. In fact, 9 out of 10 disputes receiving active mediation assistance are settled peacefully —without a strike. These are pretty good odds mediation is a course worth trying.

Even when there is no stalemate or imminent deadline—but mounting difficulties clearly signal real trouble ahead—the mediator can be helpful. The mediator's training and skill often can spot difficulties early and help develop a remedy.

Mediation is a free and voluntary process. It can be requested by either party to a dispute, or the mediator may volunteer to help. There is no cost to either side, and mediation is available not only to private industry but also in public employment situations.

The mediator is completely impartial, a confidential advisor who neither takes sides nor forces decisions. The only role that a mediator has is that of a constructive peacemaker who brings objectivity to disputed issues and opens new roads to problem solving and decision making.

Collective bargaining is an indispensable ingredient of a free in-

* Published by the FMCS, Washington, D.C.

dustrial society. Mediation is a time-tested and productive tool that helps preserve and strengthen our collective bargaining system.

What Is the Federal Mediation and Conciliation Service? The Federal Mediation and Conciliation Service is an independent agency of the Federal Government created by Congress with a Director appointed by the President. Its primary duty is to promote labor-management peace.

This responsibility is fulfilled by providing mediation assistance in preventing and settling collective bargaining controversies. For this purpose Federal mediators, known as commissioners, are stationed strategically throughout the country.

The Labor Management Relations Act requires that parties to a labor contract must file a dispute notice if agreement is not reached 30 days in advance of a contract termination or reopening date. The notice must be filed with the FMCS and the appropriate State or local mediation agency.

The notice alerts the Service to possible bargaining trouble. If the case falls within the jurisdiction of the Service, the regional office then assigns a mediator to check with the employer and union involved to see whether assistance is required.

It is a tribute to the Nation's free collective bargaining system that in more than 95 out of 100 cases in which notices are filed, the employers and unions reach agreements on their own without requiring mediation aid. Yet in those cases where third-party assistance is needed it makes good sense to call in the mediator.

Who Are the Mediators? Mediators are carefully selected and trained. About equal numbers have backgrounds with management and with labor, and many have had some experience with both.

Mediators are picked for the job because of their knowledge and demonstrated skill in collective bargaining. Regardless of background, they are required to maintain strict objectivity as representatives of the public interest.

How Does the Mediator Work? While methods and circumstances vary, the mediator generally will confer first with one of the parties involved and then with the other to get their versions of the pending difficulties. Then with these problems firmly in mind, the mediator usually will call joint conferences with the employer and union representatives.

Mediators function informally, meeting separately and jointly with the parties to help them find some mutually acceptable solutions.

It is part of the job to listen, review, analyze, suggest, advise, reason, and explore all possible means of reaching an agreement.

The mediator can get stalled negotiations going again, improve the bargaining atmosphere, encourage mutual discussions, explore alternative solutions, suggest specific contract clauses that have worked well elsewhere, and provide needed economic data and other information.

The mediator works hard to promote cooperation and understanding between management and labor not only during contract disputes but at other times as well in order to improve day-to-day relations in the workplace.

Through the use of FMCS technical services, unions and employers, with the assistance of the mediator, can improve the labor-management climate. The mediator can give advisory assistance on specific problems and encourage the use of joint labor-management committees. A skilled mediator can provide training and information to improve the knowledge and skill of both parties, can identify trends and developments, can encourage early bargaining to avoid deadline tensions, and will respond to the various needs of labor and management, including government employers and labor organizations, to improve their bargaining relationships.

In addition, the Service helps employers and unions in selecting arbitrators to adjudicate labor-management disputes by maintaining a large roster of qualified arbitrators. When an employer and a union need an arbitrator, they only need to notify the Service and the Service will provide at no charge a listing of qualified arbitrators in their area who are available to hear the dispute. When the parties have agreed on one name from the list, they notify FMCS and the Service notifies the arbitrator.*

SELECTED BIBLIOGRAPHY

A Guide to Basic Law and Procedures under the National Labor Relations Act. Washington, D.C.: Office of the General Counsel of the NLRB, U. S. Government Printing Office, 1978.

Allen, Robert E., and Timothy J. Keaveny. *Contemporary Labor Relations.* Reading, Mass.: Addison-Wesley Publishing, 1983.

Baderschneider, Jean A.; Richard N. Block; and John A. Fossum. *The Collective Bargaining Process—Readings and Analysis.* Plano, Texas: Business Publications, 1983.

Barrett, Jerome T., and Ira B. Lebel. "Public Sector Strikes—Legislative and Court Treatment." *Monthly Labor Review,* September 1974, pp. 19–23.

Bent, Alan, and T. Zane Reeves. *Collective Bargaining in the Public Sector.* Menlo Park, Calif.: Benjamin/Cummins, 1978.

* As of 1983, the FMCS maintained 72 field offices and 8 regional offices throughout the United States.

Bloom, Gordon F., and Herbert R. Northrup. *Economics of Labor Relations.* 8th ed. Homewood, Ill.: Richard D. Irwin, 1977.

Brinker, Paul A., and Benjamin J. Taylor. "Secondary Boycott Analysis by Industry." *Labor Law Journal* 24, No. 10 (October 1973).

Bunker, Charles S. *Collective Bargaining: Non-Profit Sector.* Columbus, Ohio: Grid, 1975.

Bureau of National Affairs, Inc. *Labor Relations Reference Manual.*

Chamberlain, Neil W.; Donald E. Cullen; and David Lewin. *The Labor Sector* 3d ed. New York: McGraw-Hill, 1980.

Clark, R. Theodore, Jr. *Coping with Mediation, Fact Finding, and Forms of Arbitration.* Chicago: International Personnel Management Association, 1974.

Cohen, Sanford. *Labor in the United States.* 4th ed. Columbus, Ohio: Charles E. Merrill, 1975.

Davey, Harold W.; Mario F. Bognanno; and David L. Estenson. *Contemporary Collective Bargaining* 4th ed. Englewood Cliffs, N.J.: Prentice-Hall, 1982.

Dilts, David A., and Clarence R. Deitsch. *Labor Relations.* New York: Macmillan, 1983.

Estey, Marten. *The Unions.* 3d ed. New York: Harcourt Brace Jovanovich, 1981.

Feldacker, Bruce. *Labor Guide to Labor Law.* 2d ed. Reston, Va. Reston Publishing, 1983.

Fisher, Roger, and William Ury. *Getting to Yes: Negotiating Agreement Without Giving In.* New York: Penguin Books, 1983.

Getman, Julius; Steven Goldberg; and Jeanne B. Herman. *Union Representation Elections: Laws and Reality.* New York: Russell Sage Foundation, 1976.

Gould, William. *A Primer on American Labor Law.* Cambridge: MIT Press, 1982.

Gregory, Charles O., and Harold H. Katz. *Labor and the Law.* New York: W. W. Norton, 1979.

Hagburg, Eugene C., and Marvin J. Levine. *Labor Relations: An Integrated Perspective.* St. Paul, Minn.: West Publishing, 1978.

Herman, E. Edward, and Alfred Kuhn. *Collective Bargaining and Labor Relations.* Englewood Cliffs, N.J.: Prentice-Hall, 1981.

Hilgert, Raymond L., and Sterling H. Schoen. *Labor Agreement Negotiations.* Cincinnati: South-Western Publishing, 1983.

Holley, William H., Jr., and Kenneth M. Jennings. *The Labor Relations Process.* 2d ed. Hinsdale, Ill.: Dryden Press–CBS College Publishing, 1984.

Imundo, Louis V., Jr. "Some Comparisons between Public Sector and Private Sector Collective Bargaining." *Labor Law Journal*, December 1973, pp. 810–17.

Kleingartner, Archie. "Collective Bargaining between Salaried Professionals and Public Sector Management." *Public Administration Review* 33, no. 2 (March-April 1973), 165–72.

34

Kochan, Thomas A. *Collective Bargaining and Industrial Relations.* Homewood, Ill.: Richard D. Irwin, 1980.

Krawlewski, John. "Collective Bargaining among Professional Employees." *Hospital Administration,* Summer 1974.

Labor Law Course. 26th ed. Chicago: Commerce Clearing House, 1983.

Levine, Marvin J. *Comparative Labor Relations Law.* Morristown, N.J.: General Learning Press, 1975.

Levine, Marvin J. *Labor Relations in the Public Sector: Readings and Cases.* 2d ed. Columbus, Ohio: Grid 1985.

Lumsden, Keith, and Craig Peterson. "The Effect of Right-to-Work Laws on Unionization in the United States." *Journal of Political Economy,* December 1975, pp. 1237–48.

McCulloch, Frank W., and Tim Bornstein. *The National Labor Relations Board.* New York: Praeger Publishers, 1974.

McKelvey, Jean T., ed. *The Changing Law of Fair Representation.* Ithaca: New York State School of Industrial Relations, Cornell University, 1985.

Mills, D. Quinn, and Janice McCormick. *Industrial Relations in Transition— Cases and Text.* New York: John Wiley & Sons, 1985.

Nesbitt, Murray B. *Labor Relations in the Federal Government Service.* Washington, D.C.: Bureau of National Affairs, 1976.

Reynolds, Lloyd G. *Labor Economics and Labor Relations.* 7th ed. Englewood Cliffs, N.J.: Prentice-Hall, 1978.

Richardson, Fred C. *Collective Bargaining by Objectives.* Englewood Cliffs, N.J.: Prentice-Hall, 1977.

Robinson, James W., and Roger W. Walker. *Introduction to Labor.* 2d ed. Englewood Cliffs, N.J.: Prentice-Hall, 1985.

Rosenbloom, David H. and Jay M. Shafritz. *Essentials of Labor Relations.* Reston, Virginia: Reston Publishing, 1985.

Rowan, Richard L. (editor). *Readings in Labor Economics and Labor Relations.* 5th ed. Homewood, Illinois: Richard D. Irwin, Inc., 1985.

Sloane, Arthur A., and Fred Witney. *Labor Relations.* 4th ed. Englewood Cliffs, N.J.: Prentice-Hall, 1981.

Smith, Russell A.; Leroy S. Merrifield; and Theodore J. St. Antoine. *Labor Relations Law: Cases and Materials.* 5th ed. Indianapolis: Bobbs-Merrill, 1974.

Stieber, Jack. *Public Employee Unionism: Structure, Growth, Policy.* Washington, D.C.: Brookings Institution, 1973.

Susser, Peter A. "National Labor Relations Board Reverses its Position on Midterm Relocations," *Personnel Administrator,* June, 1984, pp. 187–194.

Taylor, Benjamin J., and Fred Witney. *Labor Relations Law.* 2d ed. Englewood Cliffs, N.J.: Prentice-Hall, 1975.

The Federal Mediation and Conciliation Service. Washington, D.C.: Federal Mediation and Conciliation Service, U.S. Government Printing Office, 1979.

Twomey, David. *Labor Law and Legislation.* 6th ed. Cincinnati, Ohio: South-Western Publishing, 1980.

Weitzman, J. *The Scope of Bargaining in Public Employment.* New York: Praeger Publishers, 1975.

Williams, Robert E.; Peter A. Janus; and Kenneth C. Huhn. *NLRB Regulation of Election Conduct.* Labor Relations and Public Policy Series. Report no. 8. Philadelphia: University of Pennsylvania, Industrial Research Unit, 1974.

Young, Oran. *Bargaining: Formal Theories of Negotiations.* Urbana: University of Illinois Press, 1976.

Partial Text of

THE LABOR MANAGEMENT RELATIONS ACT, 1947*

as amended by the Labor-Management Reporting and Disclosure Act of 1959†, by Public Law 93-360, 1974, and by Public Law 96-593, 1980

[Public Law 101—80th Congress]
[Chapter 120—1st Session]

AN ACT

To amend the National Labor Relations Act, to provide additional facilities for the mediation of labor disputes affecting commerce, to equalize legal responsibilities of labor organizations and employers, and for other purposes.

Be it enacted by the Senate and House of Representatives of the United States of America in Congress assembled.

Short Title and Declaration of Policy

Section 1. (a) This Act may be cited as the "Labor Management Relations Act, 1947."

(b) Industrial strife which interferes with the normal flow of commerce and with the full production of articles and commodities for commerce, can be avoided or substantially minimized if employers, employees, and labor organizations each recognize under law one another's legitimate rights in their relations with each other, and above all recognize under law that neither party has any right in its relations with any other to engage in acts or practices which jeopardize the public health, safety, or interest.

It is the purpose and policy of this Act, in order to promote the full flow of commerce, to prescribe the legitimate rights of both employees and employers in their relations affecting commerce, to provide

---

* Also known as the Taft-Hartley Act.

† Also known as the Landrum-Griffin Act, Public Law 86-257.

orderly and peaceful procedures for preventing the interference by either with the legitimate rights of the other, to protect the rights of individual employees in their relations with labor organizations whose activities affect commerce, to define and proscribe practices on the part of labor and management which affect commerce and are inimical to the general welfare, and to protect the rights of the public in connection with labor disputes affecting commerce.

TITLE I—AMENDMENT OF NATIONAL LABOR RELATIONS ACT

Section 101.   The National Labor Relations Act is hereby amended to read as follows:

Findings and Policies

Section 1.   The denial by some employers of the right of employees to organize and the refusal by some employers to accept the procedure of collective bargaining lead to strikes and other forms of industrial strife or unrest, which have the intent or the necessary effect of burdening or obstructing commerce by (a) impairing the efficiency, safety, or operation of the instrumentalities of commerce; (b) occurring in the current of commerce; (c) materially affecting, restraining, or controlling the flow of raw materials or manufactured or processed goods from or into the channels of commerce, or the prices of such materials or goods in commerce; or (d) causing diminution of employment and wages in such volume as substantially to impair or disrupt the market for goods flowing from or into the channels of commerce.

The inequality of bargaining power between employees who do not possess full freedom of association or actual liberty of contract, and employers who are organized in the corporate or other forms of ownership association substantially burdens and affects the flow of commerce, and tends to aggravate recurrent business depressions, by depressing wage rates and the purchasing power of wage earners in industry and by preventing the stabilization of competitive wage rates and working conditions within and between industries.

Experience has proved that protection by law of the right of employees to organize and bargain collectively safeguards commerce from injury, impairment, or interruption, and promotes the flow of commerce by removing certain recognized sources of industrial strife and unrest, by encouraging practices fundamental to the friendly adjustment of industrial disputes arising out of differences as to wages, hours, or other working conditions, and by restoring equality of bargaining power between employers and employees.

Experience has further demonstrated that certain practices by some labor organizations, their officers, and members have the intent or the necessary effect of burdening or obstructing commerce by preventing the free flow of goods in such commerce through strikes and other forms of industrial unrest or through concerted activities which impair the interest of the public in the free flow of such commerce. The elimination of such practices is a necessary condition to the assurance of the rights herein guaranteed.

It is hereby declared to be the policy of the United States to eliminate the causes of certain substantial obstructions to the free flow of commerce and to mitigate and eliminate these obstructions when they have occurred by encouraging the practice and procedure of collective bargaining and by protecting the exercise by workers of full freedom of association, self-organization, and designation of representatives of their own choosing, for the purpose of negotiating the terms and conditions of their employment or other mutual aid or protection.

Definitions

Section 2.   When used in this Act—

(1) The term "person" includes one or more individuals, labor organizations, partnerships, associations, corporations, legal representatives, trustees, trustees in bankruptcy, or receivers.

(2) The term "employer" includes any person acting as an agent of an employer, directly or indirectly, but shall not include the United States or any wholly owned Government corporation, or any Federal Reserve Bank, or any State or political subdivision thereof, or any person subject to the Railway Labor Act, as amended from time to time, or any labor organization (other than when acting as an employer), or anyone acting in the capacity of officer or agent of such labor organization.

(3) The term "employee" shall include any employee, and shall not be limited to the employees of a particular employer, unless the Act explicitly states otherwise, and shall include any individual whose work has ceased as a consequence of, or in connection with, any current labor dispute or because of any unfair labor practice, and who has not obtained any other regular and substantially equivalent employment, but shall not include any individual employed as an agricultural laborer, or in the domestic service of any family or person at his home, or any individual employed by his parent or spouse, or any individual having the status of an indepedent contractor, or any individual employed as a supervisor, or any individual employed by an employer subject to the Railway Labor Act, as

amended from time to time, or by any other person who is not an employer as herein defined.

(4) The term "representatives" includes any individual or labor organization.

(5) The term "labor organization" means any organization of any kind, or any agency or employee representation committee or plan, in which employees participate and which exists for the purpose, in whole or in part, of dealing with employers concerning grievances, labor disputes, wages, rates of pay, hours of employment, or conditions of work.

(6) The term "commerce" means trade, traffic, commerce, transportation, or communication among the several States, or between the District of Columbia or any Territory of the United States and any State or Territory, or between any foreign country and any State, Territory, or the District of Columbia, or within the District of Columbia or any Territory, or between points in the same State but through any other State or any Territory or the District of Columbia or any foreign country.

(7) The term "affecting commerce" means in commerce, or burdening or obstructing commerce or the free flow of commerce, or having led or tending to lead to a labor dispute burdening or obstructing commerce or the free flow of commerce.

(8) The term "unfair labor practice" means any unfair labor practice listed in section 8.

(9) The term "labor dispute" includes any controversy concerning terms, tenure or conditions of employment, or concerning the association or representation of persons in negotiating, fixing, maintaining, changing, or seeking to arrange terms or conditions of employment, regardless of whether the disputants stand in the proximate relation of employer and employee.

(10) The term "National Labor Relations Board" means the National Labor Relations Board provided for in section 3 of this Act.

(11) The term "supervisor" means any individual having authority, in the interest of the employer, to hire, transfer, suspend, lay off, recall, promote, discharge, assign, reward, or discipline other employees, or responsibility to direct them, or to adjust their grievances, or effectively to recommend such action, if in connection with the foregoing the exercise of such authority is not of a merely routine or clerical nature, but requires the use of independent judgment.

(12) The term "professional employee" means

(a) any employee engaged in work (i) predominantly intellectual and varied in character as opposed to routine mental, manual, mechanical, or physical work; (ii) involving the consistent exercise of discretion and judgment in its performance; (iii) of such a character that the output produced or the result accomplished cannot be standardized in relation to a given period of time; (iv) requiring knowledge of an advanced type in a field of science or learning customarily acquired by a prolonged course of specialized intellectual instruction and study in an institution of higher learning or a hospital, as distinguished from a general academic education or from an apprenticeship or from training in the performance of routine mental, manual, or physical process; or

(b) any employee, who (i) has completed the courses of specialized intellectual instruction and study described in clause (iv) of paragraph (a), and (ii) is performing related work under the supervision of a professional person to qualify himself to become a professional employee as defined in paragraph (a).

(13) In determining whether any person is acting as an "agent" of another person so as to make such other person responsible for his acts, the question of whether the specific acts performed were actually authorized or subsequently ratified shall not be controlling.

(14) The term "health care institution" shall include any hospital, convalescent hospital, health maintenance organization, health clinic, nursing home, extended care facility, or other institution devoted to the care of the sick, infirm, or aged person.

National Labor Relations Board

Section 3. (a) The National Labor Relations Board (hereinafter called the "Board") . . . as an agency of the United States, shall consist of five . . . members, appointed by the President by and with the advice and consent of the Senate . . . for terms of five years each, excepting that any individual chosen to fill a vacancy shall be appointed only for the unexpired term of the member whom he shall succeed. The President shall designate one member to serve as Chairman of the Board. Any member of the Board may be removed by the President, upon notice and hearing, for neglect of duty or malfeasance in office, but for no other cause.

(b) The Board is authorized to delegate to any group of three or more members any or all of the powers which it may itself exercise. The Board is also authorized to delegate to its regional directors its powers under section 9 to determine the unit appropriate for the purpose of collective bargaining, to investigate and provide for hearings, and determine whether a question of representation exists, and to direct an election or take a secret ballot under subsection (c) or (e) of section 9 and certify the results thereof, except that upon the filing of a request therefore with the Board by any interested person, the

Board may review any action of a regional director delegated to him under this paragraph, but such a review shall not, unless specifically ordered by the Board, operate as a stay of any action taken by the regional director. A vacancy in the Board shall not impair the right of the remaining members to exercise all of the powers of the Board, and three members of the Board shall, at all times, constitute a quorum of the Board, except that two members shall constitute a quorum of any group designated pursuant to the first sentence hereof. The Board shall have an official seal which shall be judicially noticed.

(c) The Board shall at the close of each fiscal year make a report in writing to Congress and to the President stating in detail the cases it has heard, the decisions it has rendered, and an account of all moneys it has disbursed.

(d) There shall be a General Counsel of the Board who shall be appointed by the President, by and with the advice and consent of the Senate, for a term of four years. The General Counsel of the Board shall exercise general supervision over all attorneys employed by the Board (other than trial examiners and legal assistants to Board members) and over the officers and employees in the regional offices. He shall have final authority, on behalf of the Board, in respect of the investigation of charges and issuance of complaints under section 10, and in respect of the prosecution of such complaints before the Board, and shall have such other duties as the Board may prescribe or as may be provided by law. In case of a vacancy in the office of the General Counsel the President is authorized to designate the officer or employee who shall act as General Counsel during such vacancy, but no person or persons so designated shall so act (1) for more than 40 days when the Congress is in session unless a nomination to fill such vacancy shall have been submitted to the Senate, or (2) after the adjournment *sine die* of the session of the Senate in which such nomination was submitted.

*   *   *   *   *

[Omitted Sections 4 and 5—Compensation and offices of the NLRB.]

Section 6.   The Board shall have authority from time to time to make, amend, and rescind, in the manner prescribed by the Administrative Procedure Act, such rules and regulations as may be necessary to carry out the provisions of this Act.

Rights of Employees

Section 7.   Employees shall have the right to self-organization, to form, join, or assist labor organizations, to bargain collectively through representatives of their own choosing, and to engage in other concerted activities for the purpose of collective bargaining or other mutual aid or protection, and shall also have the right to refrain from any or all of such activities except to the extent that such right may be affected by an agreement requiring membership in a labor organization as a condition of employment as authorized in section 8(a) (3).

Unfair Labor Practices

Section 8. (a) It shall be an unfair labor practice for an employer—

(1) to interfere with, restrain, or coerce employees in the exercise of the rights guaranteed in section 7;

(2) to dominate or interfere with the formation or administration of any labor organization or contribute financial or other support to it: *Provided*, that subject to rules and regulations made and published by the Board pursuant to section 6, an employer shall not be prohibited from permitting employees to confer with him during working hours without loss of time or pay;

(3) by discrimination in regard to hire or tenure of employment or any term or condition of employment to encourage or discourage membership in any labor organization: *Provided*, that nothing in this Act, or in any other statute of the United States, shall preclude an employer from making an agreement with a labor organization (not established, or assisted by any action defined in section 8(a) of this Act as an unfair labor practice) to require as a condition of employment membership therein on or after the 30th day following the beginning of such employment or the effective date of such agreement, whichever is the later, (i) if such labor organization is the representative of the employees as provided in section 9(a), in the appropriate collective bargaining unit covered by such agreement when made, and (ii) unless following an election held as provided in section 9(e) within one year preceding the effective date of such agreement, the Board shall have certified that at least a majority of the employees eligible to vote in such election have voted to rescind the authority of such labor organization to make such an agreement: *Provided further*, that no employer shall justify any discrimination against an employee for nonmembership in a labor organization (A) if he has reasonable grounds for believing that such membership was not available to the employee on the same terms and conditions generally applicable to other members, or (B) if he has reasonable grounds for believing that membership was denied or terminated for reasons other than the failure of the employee to tender the periodic dues and the initiation fees uniformly required as a condition of acquiring or retaining membership;

(4) to discharge or otherwise discriminate against an employee because he has filed charges or given testimony under this Act;

(5) to refuse to bargain collectively with the representatives of his employees, subject to the provisions of section 9(a).

(b) It shall be an unfair labor practice for a labor organization or its agents—

(1) to restrain or coerce (A) employees in the exercise of the rights guaranteed in section 7: *Provided*, that this paragraph shall not impair the right of a labor organization to prescribe its own rules with respect to the acquisition or retention of membership therein; or (B) an employer in the selection of his representatives for the purposes of collective bargaining or the adjustment of grievances;

(2) to cause or attempt to cause an employer to discriminate against an employee in violation of subsection (a) (3) or to discriminate against an employee with respect to whom membership in such organization has been denied or terminated on some ground other than his failure to tender the periodic dues and the initiation fees uniformly required as a condition of acquiring or retaining membership;

(3) to refuse to bargain collectively with an employer, provided it is the representative of his employees subject to the provisions of section 9(a);

(4) (i) to engage in, or to induce or encourage any individual employed by any person engaged in commerce or in any industry affecting commerce to engage in, a strike or a refusal in the course of his employment to use, manufacture, process, transport, or otherwise handle or work on any goods, articles, materials, or commodities or to perform any services; or (ii) to threaten, coerce, or restrain any person engaged in commerce or in an industry affecting commerce, where in either case an object thereof is:

(A) forcing or requiring any employer or self-employed person to join any labor or employer organization or to enter into any agreement which is prohibited by section 8(e).

(B) forcing or requiring any person to cease using, selling, handling, transporting, or otherwise dealing in the products of any other producer, processor, or manufacturer, or to cease doing business with any other person, or forcing or requiring any other employer to recognize or bargain with a labor organization as the representative of his employees unless such labor organization has been certified as the representative of such employees under the provisions of section 9: *Provided*, that nothing contained in this clause (B) shall be construed to make unlawful, where not otherwise unlawful, any primary strike or primary picketing;

(C) forcing or requiring any employer to recognize or bargain with a particular labor organization as the representative of his employees if another labor organization has been certified as the representative of such employees under the provisions of section 9;

(D) forcing or requiring any employer to assign particular work to employees in a particular labor organization or in a particular trade, craft, or class rather than to employees in another labor organization or in another trade, craft, or class, unless such employer is failing to conform to an order or certification of the Board determining the bargaining representative for employees performing such work:

Provided, that nothing contained in this subsection (b) shall be construed to make unlawful a refusal by any person to enter upon the premises of any employer (other than his own employer), if the employees of such employer are engaged in a strike ratified or approved by a representative of such employees whom such employer is required to recognize under this Act: *Provided further,* that for the purposes of this paragraph (4) only, nothing contained in such paragraph shall be construed to prohibit publicity, other than picketing, for the purpose of truthfully advising the public, including consumers and members of a labor organization, that a product or products are produced by an employer with whom the labor organization has a primary dispute and are distributed by another employer, as long as such publicity does not have an effect of inducing any individual employed by any person other than the primary employer in the course of his employment to refuse to pick up, deliver, or transport any goods, or not to perform any services, at the establishment of the employer engaged in such distribution;

(5) to require of employees covered by an agreement authorized under subsection (a) (3) the payment, as a condition precedent to becoming a member of such organization, of a fee in an amount which the Board finds excessive or discriminatory under all the circumstances. In making such a finding, the Board shall consider, among other relevant factors, the practices and customs of labor organizations in the particular industry, and the wages currently paid to the employees affected;

(6) to cause or attempt to cause an employer to pay or deliver or agree to pay or deliver any money or other thing of value, in the nature of an exaction, for services which are not performed or not to be performed; and

(7) to picket or cause to be picketed, or threaten to picket or cause to be picketed, any employer where an object thereof is forcing or requiring an employer to recognize or bargain with a labor organization as the representative of his employees, or forcing or requiring

the employees of an employer to accept or select such labor organization as their collective bargaining representative, unless such labor organization is currently certified as the representative of such employees:

(A) where the employer has lawfully recognized in accordance with this Act any other labor organization and a question concerning representation may not appropriately be raised under section 9(c) of this Act.

(B) where within the preceding 12 months a valid election under section 9(c) of this Act has been conducted, or

(C) where such picketing has been conducted without a petition under section 9(c) being filed within a reasonable period of time not to exceed 30 days from the commencement of such picketing: *Provided,* that when such a petition has been filed the Board shall forthwith, without regard to the provisions of section 9(c) (1) or the absence of a showing of a substantial interest on the part of the labor organization, direct an election in such unit as the Board finds to be appropriate and shall certify the results thereof: *Provided further,* that nothing in this subparagraph (C) shall be construed to prohibit any picketing or other publicity for the purpose of truthfully advising the public (including consumers) that an employer does not employ members of, or have a contract with, a labor organization, unless an effect of such picketing is to induce any individual employed by any other person in the course of his employment, not to pick up, deliver or transport any goods or not to perform any services.

Nothing in this paragraph (7) shall be construed to permit any act which would otherwise be an unfair labor practice under this section 8(b).

(c) The expressing of any views, argument, or opinion, or the dissemination thereof, whether in written, printed, graphic, or visual form, shall not constitute or be evidence of an unfair labor practice under any of the provisions of this Act, if such expression contains no threat of reprisal or force or promise of benefit.

(d) For the purposes of this section, to bargain collectively is the performance of the mutual obligation of the employer and the representative of the employees to meet at reasonable times and confer in good faith with respect to wages, hours, and other terms and conditions of employment, or the negotiation of an agreement, or any question arising thereunder, and the execution of a written contract incorporating any agreement reached if requested by either party, but such obligation does not compel either party to agree to a proposal or require the making of a concession: *Provided,* that where there is in effect a collective bargaining contract covering employees in an industry affecting commerce, the duty to bargain collectively shall also mean that no party to such contract shall terminate or modify such contract, unless the party desiring such termination or modification—

(1) serves a written notice upon the other party to the contract of the proposed termination of modification 60 days prior to the expiration date thereof, or in the event such contract contains no expiration date, 60 days prior to the time it is proposed to make such termination or modification;

(2) offers to meet and confer with the other party for the purpose of negotiating a new contract or a contract containing the proposed modifications;

(3) notifies the Federal Mediation and Conciliation Service within 30 days after such notice of the existence of a dispute, and simultaneously therewith notifies any State or Territorial agency established to mediate and conciliate disputes within the State or Territory where the dispute occurred, provided no agreement has been reached by that time; and

(4) continues in full force and effect, without resorting to strike or lockout, all the terms and conditions of the existing contract for a period of 60 days after such notice is given or until the expiration date of such contract, whichever occurs later.

The duties imposed upon employers, employees, and labor organizations by paragraphs (2), (3), and (4) shall become inapplicable upon an intervening certification of the Board, under which the labor organization or individual, which is a party to the contract, has been superseded as or ceased to be the representative of the employees subject to the provisions of section 9(a), and the duties so imposed shall not be construed as requiring either party to discuss or agree to any modification of the terms and conditions contained in a contract for a fixed period, if such modification is to become effective before such terms and conditions can be reopened under the provisions of the contract. Any employee who engages in a strike within any notice period specified in this subsection, or who engages in any strike within the appropriate period specified in subsection (g) of this section shall lose his status as an employee of the employer engaged in the particular labor dispute, for the purposes of sections 8, 9, and 10 of this Act, as amended, but such loss of status for such employee shall terminate if and when he is reemployed by such employer. Whenever the collective bargaining involves employees of a health care institution, the provisions of this section 8(d) shall be modified as follows:

(A) The notice of section 8(d) (1) shall be 90 days; the notice of section 8(d) (3) shall be 60 days; and the contract period of section 8(d) (4) shall be 90 days;

(B) Where the bargaining is for an initial agreement following certification or recognition, at least 30 days' notice of the existence of a dispute shall be given by the labor organization to the agencies set forth in section 8(d) (3).

(C) After notice is given to the Federal Mediation and Conciliation Service under either clause (A) or (B) of this sentence, the Service shall promptly communicate with the parties and use its best efforts, by mediation and conciliation, to bring them to agreement. The parties shall participate fully and promptly in such meetings as may be undertaken by the Service for the purpose of aiding in a settlement of the dispute.

(e) It shall be an unfair labor practice for any labor organization and any employer to enter into any contract or agreement, express or implied, whereby such employer ceases or refrains or agrees to cease or refrain from handling, using, selling, transporting, or otherwise dealing in any of the products of any other employer, or to cease doing business with any other person, and any contract or agreement entered into heretofore or hereafter containing such an agreement shall be to such extent unenforceable and void: *Provided*, that nothing in this subsection (e) shall apply to an agreement between a labor organization and an employer in the construction industry relating to the contracting or subcontracting of work to be done at the site of the construction, alteration, painting, or repair of a building, structure, or other work: *Provided further*, that for the purposes of this subsection (e) and section 8(b) (4) (B) the terms "any employer," "any person engaged in commerce or in industry affecting commerce," and "any person" when used in relation to the terms "any other producer, processor, or manufacturer," "any other employer," or "any other person" shall not include persons in the relation of a jobber, manufacturer, contractor, or subcontractor working on the goods or premises of the jobber or manufacturer or performing parts of an integrated process of production in the apparel and clothing industry: *Provided further*, that nothing in this Act shall prohibit the enforcement of any agreement which is within the foregoing exception.

(f) It shall not be an unfair labor practice under subsections (a) and (b) of this section for an employer engaged primarily in the building and construction industry to make an agreement covering employees engaged (or who, upon their employment, will be engaged) in the building and construction industry with a labor organization of which building and construction employees are members (not established, maintained, or assisted by any action defined in section 8(a) of this Act as an unfair labor practice) because (1) the majority status of such labor organization has not been established under the provisions of section 9 of this Act prior to the making of such agreement, or (2) such agreement requires as a condition of employment, membership in such labor organization after the seventh day following the beginning of such employment or the effective date of the agreement, whichever is later, or (3) such agreement requires the employer to notify such labor organization of opportunities for employment with such employer, or gives such labor organization an opportunity to refer qualified applicants for such employment, or (4) such agreement specifies minimum training or experience qualifications for employment or provides for priority in opportunities for employment based upon length of service with such employer, in the industry or in the particular geographical area: *Provided,* that nothing in this subsection shall set aside the final proviso to section 8(a) (3) of this Act: *Provided further,* that any agreement which would be invalid, but for clause (1) of this subsection, shall not be a bar to a petition filed pursuant to section 9(c) or 9(e).

(g) A labor organization before engaging in any strike, picketing, or other concerted refusal to work at any health care institution shall, not less than 10 days prior to such action, notify the institution in writing and the Federal Mediation and Conciliation Service of that intention, except that in the case of bargaining for an initial agreement following certification or recognition the notice required by this subsection shall not be given until the expiration of the period specified in clause (B) of the last sentence of section 8(d) of this Act. The notice shall state the date and time that such action will commence. The notice, once given, may be extended by the written agreement of both parties.

Representatives and Elections

Section 9. (a) Representatives designated or selected for the purposes of collective bargaining by the majority of the employees in a unit appropriate for such purposes, shall be the exclusive representatives of all the employees in such unit for the purposes of collective bargaining in respect to rates of pay, wages, hours of employment, or other conditions of employment: *Provided,* that any individual employee or a group of employees shall have the right at any time to present grievances to their employer and to have such grievances adjusted, without the intervention of the bargaining representative, as long as the adjustment is not inconsistent with the terms of a collective bargaining contract or agreement then in effect: *Provided further*, that the bargaining representative has been given opportunity to be present at such adjustment.

(b) The Board shall decide in each case whether, in order to assure to employees the fullest freedom in exercising the rights guaranteed by this Act, the unit appropriate for the purposes of collective bargaining shall be the employer unit, craft unit, plant unit, or subdivision thereof: *Provided*, that the Board shall not (1) decide that any unit is appropriate for such purposes if such unit includes both professional employees and employees who are not professional employees unless a majority of such professional employees vote for inclusion in such unit; or (2) decide that any craft unit is inappropriate for such purposes on the ground that a different unit has been established by a prior Board determination, unless a majority of the employees in the proposed craft unit vote against separate representation or (3) decide that any unit is appropriate for such purposes, if it includes, together with other employees, any individual employed as a guard to enforce against employees and other persons rules to protect property of the employer or to protect the safety of persons on the employers' premises; but no labor organization shall be certified as the representative of employees in a bargaining unit of guards if such organization admits to membership, or is affiliated directly or indirectly with an organization which admits to membership, employees other than guards.

(c) (1) Wherever a petition shall have been filed, in accordance with such regulations as may be prescribed by the Board—

(A) by an employee or group of employees or any individual or labor organization acting in their behalf alleging that a substantial number of employees (i) wish to be represented for collective bargaining and that their employer declines to recognize their representative as the representative defined in section 9(a), or (ii) assert that the individual or labor organization, which has been certified or is being currently recognized by their employer as the bargaining representative, is no longer a representative as defined in section 9(a); or

(B) by an employer, alleging that one or more individuals or labor organizations have presented to him a claim to be recognized as the representative defined in section 9(a);

the Board shall investigate such petition and if it has reasonable cause to believe that a question of representation affecting commerce exists shall provide for an appropriate hearing upon due notice. Such hearing may be conducted by an officer or employee of the regional office, who shall not make any recommendations with respect thereto. If the Board finds upon the record of such hearing that such a question of representation exists, it shall direct an election by secret ballot and shall certify the results thereof.

(2) In determining whether or not a question of representation affecting commerce exists, the same regulations and rules of decision shall apply irrespective of the identity of the persons filing the petition or the kind of relief sought and in no case shall the Board deny a labor organization a place on the ballot by reason of an order with respect to such labor organization or its predecessor not issued in conformity with section 10(c).

(3) No election shall be directed in any bargaining unit or any subdivision within which, in the preceding 12-month period, a valid election shall have been held. Employees engaged in an economic strike who are not entitled to reinstatement shall be eligible to vote under such regulations as the Board shall find are consistent with the purposes and provisions of this Act in any election conducted within 12 months after the commencement of the strike. In any election where none of the choices on the ballot receives a majority, a runoff shall be conducted, the ballot providing for a selection between the two choices receiving the largest and second largest number of valid votes cast in the election.

(4) Nothing in this section shall be construed to prohibit the waiving of hearings by stipulation for the purposes of a consent election in conformity with regulations and rules of decision of the Board.

(5) In determining whether a unit is appropriate for the purposes specified in subsection (b) the extent to which the employees have organized shall not be controlling.

(d) Whenever an order of the Board made pursuant to section 10(c) is based in whole or in part upon facts certified following an investigation pursuant to subsection (c) of this section and there is a petition for the enforcement or review of such order, such certification and the record of such investigation shall be included in the transcript of the entire record required to be filed under section 10(e) or 10(f), and thereupon the decree of the court enforcing, modifying, or setting aside in whole or in part the order of the Board shall be made and entered upon the pleadings, testimony, and proceedings set forth in such transcript.

(e) (1) Upon the filing with the Board, by 30 per centum or more of the employees in a bargaining unit covered by an agreement between their employer and a labor organization made pursuant to section 8(a) (3), of a petition alleging they desire that such authority be rescinded, the Board shall take a secret ballot of the employees in such unit and ceritfy the results thereof to such labor organization and to the employer.

(2) No election shall be conducted pursuant to this subsection in any bargaining unit or any subdivision within which, in the preceding 12-month period, a valid election shall have been held.

Prevention of Unfair Labor Practices

Section 10.   (a) The Board is empowered, as hereinafter provided, to prevent any person from engaging in any unfair labor practice (listed in section 8) affecting commerce. This power shall not be affected by any other means of adjustment or prevention that has been or may be established by agreement, law, or otherwise: *Provided*, that the Board is empowered by agreement with any agency of any State or Territory to cede to such agency jurisdiction over any cases in any industry (other than mining, manufacturing, communications, and transportation except where predominantly local in character) even though such cases may involve labor disputes affecting commerce, unless the provision of the State or Territorial statute applicable to the determination of such cases by such agency is inconsistent with the corresponding provision of this Act or has received a construction inconsistent therewith.

(b) Whenever it is charged that any person has engaged in or is engaging in any such unfair labor practice, the Board, or any agent or agency designated by the Board for such purposes, shall have power to issue and cause to be served upon such person a complaint stating the charges in that respect, and containing a notice of hearing before the Board or a member thereof, or before a designated agent or agency, at a place therein fixed, not less than five days after the serving of said complaint: *Provided*, that no complaint shall issue based upon any unfair labor practice occurring more than six months prior to the filing of the charge with the Board and the service of a copy thereof upon the person against whom such a charge is made, unless the person aggrieved thereby was prevented from filing such charge by reason of service in the armed forces, in which event the six-month period shall be computed from the day of his discharge. Any such complaint may be amended by the member, agent, or agency conducting the hearing or the Board in its discretion at any time prior to the issuance of an order based thereon. The person so complained of shall have the right to file an answer to the original or amended complaint and to appear in person or otherwise and give testimony at the place and time fixed in the complaint. In the discretion of the member, agent, or agency conducting the hearing or the Board, any other person may be allowed to intervene in the said proceeding and to present testimony. Any such proceeding shall, so far as practicable, be conducted in accordance with the rules of evidence applicable in the district courts of the United States under the rules of civil procedure for the district courts of the United States, adopted by the Supreme Court of the United States pursuant to the Act of June 19, 1934 (U.S.C., title 28, secs. 723-B, 723-C).

(c) The testimony taken by such member, agent, or agency or the Board shall be reduced to writing and and filed with the Board. Thereafter, in its discretion, the Board upon notice may take further testimony or hear argument. If upon the preponderance of the testimony taken the Board shall be of the opinion that any person named in the complaint has engaged in or is engaging in any such unfair labor practice, then the Board shall state its findings of fact and shall issue and cause to be served on such person an order requiring such person to cease and desist from such unfair labor practice, and to take such affirmative action including reinstatement of employees with or without back pay, as will effectuate the policies of this Act: *Provided*, that where an order directs reinstatement of an employee, back pay may be required of the employer or labor organization, as the case may be, responsible for the discrimination suffered by him: *And provided further*, that in determining whether a complaint shall issue alleging a violation of section 8(a) (1) or section 8(a) (2), and in deciding such cases, the same regulations and rules of decision shall apply irrespective of whether or not the labor organization affected is affiliated with a labor organization national or international in scope. Such order may further require such person to make reports from time to time showing the extent to which it has complied with the order. If upon the preponderance of the testimony taken the Board shall not be of the opinion that the person named in the complaint has engaged in or is engaging in any such unfair labor practice, then the Board shall state its findings of fact and shall issue an order dismissing the said complaint. No order of the Board shall require the reinstatement of any individual as an employee who has been suspended or discharged, or the payment to him of any back pay, if such individual was suspended or discharged for cause. In case the evidence is presented before a member of the Board, or before an examiner or examiners thereof, such member, or such examiner or examiners, as the case may be, shall issue and cause to be served on the parties to the proceeding a proposed report, together with a recommended order, which shall be filed with the Board and if no exceptions are filed within 20 days after service thereof upon such parties, or within such further period as the Board may authorize, such recommended order shall become the order of the Board and become effective as therein prescribed.

(d) Until the record in a case shall have been filed in a court, as hereinafter provided, the Board may at any time, upon reasonable notice and in such manner as it shall deem proper, modify or set aside, in whole or in part, any finding or order made or issued by it.

(e) The Board shall have power to petition any court of appeals of the United States, or if all the courts of appeals to which application may be made are in vacation, any district court of the United States, within any circuit or district, respectively, wherein the unfair labor practice in question occurred or wherein such person resides or transacts business, for the enforcement of such order and for appropriate temporary relief or restraining order, and shall file in the court the record in the proceedings, as provided in section 2112 of title 28, United States Code. Upon the filing of such petition, the court shall cause notice thereof to be served upon such person, and thereupon shall have jurisdiction of the proceeding and of the question determined therein, and shall have power to grant such temporary relief or restraining order as it deems just and proper, and to make and enter a decree enforcing, modifying, and enforcing as so modified, or setting aside in whole or in part the order of the Board. No objection that has not been urged before the Board, its member, agent, or agency, shall be considered by the court, unless the failure or neglect to urge such objection shall be excused because of extraordinary circumstances. The findings of the Board with respect to questions of fact if supported by substantial evidence on the record considered as a whole shall be conclusive. If either party shall apply to the court for leave to adduce additional evidence and shall show to the satisfaction of the court that such additional evidence is material and that there were reasonable grounds for the failure to adduce such evidence in the hearing before the Board, its member, agent, or agency, the court may order such additional evidence to be taken before the Board, its member, agent, or agency, and to be made a part of the record. The Board may modify its findings as to the facts, or make new findings, by reason of additional evidence so taken and filed, and it shall file such modified or new findings, which findings with respect to questions of fact if supported by substantial evidence on the record considered as a whole shall be conclusive, and shall file its recommendations, if any, for the modification or setting aside of its original order. Upon the filing of the record with it the jurisdiction of the court shall be exclusive and its judgment and decree shall be final, except that the same shall be subject to review by the appropriate United States court of appeals if application was made to the district court as hereinabove provided, and by the Supreme Court of the United States upon writ of certiorari or certification as provided in section 1254 of title 28.

(f) Any person aggrieved by a final order of the Board granting or denying in whole or in part the relief sought may obtain a review of such order in any circuit court of appeals of the United States in the circuit wherein the unfair labor practice in question was alleged to have been engaged in or wherein such person resides or transacts business, or in the United States Court of Appeals for the District of Columbia, by filing in such court a written petition praying that the order of the Board be modified or set aside. A copy of such petition shall be forthwith transmitted by the clerk of the court to the Board, and thereupon the aggrieved party shall file in the court the record in the proceeding, certified by the Board, as provided in section 2112 of title 28, United States Code. Upon the filing of such petition, the court shall proceed in the same manner as in the case of an application by the Board under subsection (e) of this section, and shall have the same jurisdiction to grant to the Board such temporary relief or restraining order as it deems just and proper, and in like manner to make and enter a decree enforcing, modifying, and enforcing as so modified, or setting aside in whole or in part the order of the Board; the findings of the Board with respect to questions of fact if supported by substantial evidence on the record considered as a whole shall in like manner be conclusive.

(g) The commencement of proceedings under subsection (e) or (f) of this section shall not, unless specifically ordered by the court, operate as a stay of the Board's order.

(h) When granting appropriate temporary relief or a restraining order, or making and entering a decree enforcing, modifying, and enforcing as so modified, or setting aside in whole or in part an order of the Board, as provided in this section, the jurisdiction of courts sitting in equity shall not be limited by the Act entitled "An Act to amend the Judicial Code and to define and limit the jurisdiction of courts sitting in equity, and for other purposes," approved March 23, 1932 (U.S.C., Supp. VII, title 29, secs. 101–115).

(i) Petitions filed under this Act shall be heard expeditiously, and if possible within 10 days after they have been docketed.

(j) The Board shall have power, upon issuance of a complaint as provided in subsection (b) charging that any person has engaged in or is engaging in an unfair labor practice, to petition any district court of the United States (including the District Court of the United States for the District of Columbia), within any district wherein the unfair labor practice in question is alleged to have occurred or wherein such person resides or transacts business, for appropriate temporary relief or restraining order. Upon the filing of any such petition the court shall cause notice thereof to be served upon such person, and thereupon shall have jurisdiction to grant to the Board such temporary relief or restraining order as it deems just and proper.

(k) Whenever it is charged that any person has engaged in an unfair labor practice within the meaning of paragraph (4) (D) of section 8(b), the Board is empowered and directed to hear and determine the dispute out of which such unfair labor practice shall have arisen, unless, within 10 days after notice that such charge has been filed, the parties to such dispute submit to the Board satisfactory evidence that they have adjusted, or agreed upon methods for the voluntary adjustment of, the dispute. Upon compliance by the parties to the dispute with the decision of the Board or upon such voluntary adjustment of the dispute, such charge shall be dismissed.

(l) Whenever it is charged that any person has engaged in an unfair labor practice within the meaning of paragraph (4) (A), (B), or (C) of section 8(b), or section 8(e) or section 8(b) (7), the preliminary investigation of such charge shall be made forthwith and given priority over all other cases except cases of like character in the office where it is filed or to which it is referred. If, after such investigation, the officer or regional attorney to whom the matter may be referred has reasonable cause to believe such charge is true and that a complaint should issue, he shall, on behalf of the Board, petition any district court of the United States (including the District Court of the United States for the District of Columbia) within any district where the unfair labor practice in question has occurred, is alleged to have occurred, or wherein such person resides or transacts business, for appropriate injunctive relief pending the final adjudication of the Board with respect to such matter. Upon the filing of any such petition the district court shall have jurisdiction to grant such injunctive relief or temporary restraining order as it deems just and proper, notwithstanding any other provision of law: *Provided further*, that no temporary restraining order shall be issued without notice unless a petition alleges that substantial and irreparable injury to the charging party will be unavoidable and such temporary restraining order shall be effective for no longer than five days and will become void at the expiration of such period: *Provided further*, that such officer or regional attorney shall not apply for any restraining order under section 8(b) (7) if a charge against the employer under section 8(a) (2) has been filed and after the preliminary investigation, he has reasonable cause to believe that such charge is true and that a complaint should issue. Upon filing of any such petition the courts shall cause notice thereof to be served upon any person involved in the charge and such person including the charging party, shall be given an opportunity to appear by counsel and present any relevant testimony: *Provided further*, that for the purposes of this subsection district courts shall be deemed to have jurisdiction of a labor organization (1) in the district in which such organization maintains its principal office, or (2) in any district in which its duly authorized officers or agents are engaged in promoting or protecting the interests of employee members. The service of legal process upon such officer or agent shall constitute service upon the labor organization and make such organizations a party to the suit. In situations where such relief is appropriate the procedure specified herein shall apply to charges with respect to section8(b) (4) (D).

(m) Whenever it is charged that any person has engaged in an unfair labor practice within the meaning of subsection (a) (3) or (b) (2) of section 8, such charge shall be given priority over all other cases except cases of like character in the office where it is filed or to which it is referred and cases given priority under subsection (1).

* * * * *

[Omitted: Sections 11 and 12—Investigatory powers of the NLRB.]

Limitations

Section 13.   Nothing in this Act, except as specifically provided for herein, shall be construed so as either to interfere with or impede or diminish in any way the right to strike, or to affect the limitations or qualifications on that right.

Section 14.   (a) Nothing herein shall prohibit any individual employed as a supervisor from becoming or remaining a member of a labor organization, but no employer subject to this Act shall be compelled to deem individuals defined herein as supervisors as employees for the purpose of any law, either national or local, relating to collective bargaining.

(b) Nothing in this Act shall be construed as authorizing the execution or application of agreements requiring membership in a labor organization as a condition of employment in any State or Territory in which such execution or application is prohibited by State or Territorial law.

(c) (1) The Board, in its discretion, may, by rule of decision or by published rules adopted pursuant to the Administrative Procedure Act, decline to assert jurisdiction over any labor dispute involving any class or category of employers, where, in the opinion of the Board, the effect of such labor dispute on commerce is not sufficiently substantial to warrant the exercise of its jurisdiction: *Provided,* that the Board shall not decline to assert jurisdiction over any labor dispute over which it would assert jurisdiction under the standards prevailing upon August 1, 1959.

(2) Nothing in this Act shall be deemed to prevent or bar any agency or the courts of any State or Territory (including the Commonwealth of Puerto Rico, Guam, and the Virgin Islands), from assuming and asserting jurisdiction over labor disputes over which

the Board declines, pursuant to paragraph (1) of this subsection, to assert jurisdiction.

*   *   *   *   *

[Omitted: Sections 15, 16, 17, and 18 relating to limitations.]

Individuals with Religious Conviction

Section 19.   Any employee who is a member of and adheres to established and traditional tenets or teachings of a bona fide religion, body, or sect which has historically held conscientious objections to joining or financially supporting labor organizations shall not be required to join or financially support any labor organization as a condition of employment; except that such employee may be required in a contract between such employees' employer and a labor organization in lieu of periodic dues and initiation fees, to pay sums equal to such dues and initiation fees to a nonreligious, nonlabor organization charitable fund exempt from taxation under section 501(c) (3) of title 26 of the Internal Revenue Code, chosen by such employee from a list of at least three such funds, designated in such contract or if the contract fails to designate such funds, then to any such fund chosen by the employee. If such employee who holds conscientious objections pursuant to this section requests the labor organization to use the grievance-arbitration procedure on the employee's behalf, the labor organization is authorized to charge the employee for the reasonable cost of using such procedure.

*   *   *   *   *

[Omitted: Sections 102, 103, and 104 concerning effective dates of certain changes.]

TITLE II—CONCILIATION OF LABOR DISPUTES IN INDUSTRIES AFFECTING COMMERCE; NATIONAL EMERGENCIES

Section 201.   That it is the policy of the United States that—

(a) sound and stable industrial peace and the advancement of the general welfare, health, and safety of the Nation and of the best interest of employers and employees can most satisfactorily be secured by the settlement of issues between employers and employees through the processes of conference and collective bargaining between employers and the representatives of their employees;

(b) the settlement of issues between employers and employees through collective bargaining may be advanced by making available full and adequate governmental facilities for conciliation, mediation, and voluntary arbitration to aid and encourage employers and the representatives of their employees to reach and maintain agreements concerning rates of pay, hours, and working conditions, and to make all reasonable efforts to settle their differences by mutual agreement reached through conferences and collective bargaining or by such methods as may be provided for in any applicable agreement for the settlement of disputes; and

(c) certain controversies which arise between parties to collective bargaining agreements may be avoided or minimized by making available full and adequate governmental facilities for furnishing assistance to employers and the representatives of their employees in formulating for inclusion within such agreements provision for adequate notice of any proposed changes in the terms of such agreements, for the final adjustment of grievances or questions regarding the application or interpretation of such agreements, and other provisions designed to prevent the subsequent arising of such controversies.

Section 202. (a) There is hereby created an independent agency to be known as the Federal Mediation and Conciliation Service (herein referred to as the "Service") . . . The Service shall be under the direction of a Federal Mediation and Conciliation Director (hereinafter referred to as the "Director"), who shall be appointed by the President by and with the advice and consent of the Senate. . . .

(b) The Director is authorized, subject to the civil-service laws, to appoint such clerical and other personnel as may be necessary for the execution of the functions of the Service. . . .

(c) The principal office of the Service shall be in the District of Columbia, but the Director may establish regional offices convenient to localities in which labor controversies are likely to arise. The Director may by order, subject to revocation at any time, delegate any authority and discretion conferred upon him by this Act to any regional director, or other officer or employee of the Service. The Director may establish suitable procedures for cooperation with State and local mediation agencies. The Director shall make an annual report in writing to Congress at the end of the fiscal year.

* * * * *

[Omitted: Section 202(d) which relates to the original creation of the FMCS.]

Functions of the Service

Section 203. (a) It shall be the duty of the Service, in order to prevent or minimize interruptions of the free flow of commerce growing out of labor disputes, to assist parties to labor disputes in industries affecting commerce to settle such disputes through conciliation and mediation.

(b) The Service may proffer its services in any labor dispute in any industry affecting commerce, either upon its own motion or upon the request of one or more of the parties to the dispute, whenever in its judgment such dispute threatens to cause a substantial interruption of commerce. The Director and the Service are directed to avoid attempting to mediate disputes which would have only a minor effect on interstate commerce if State or other conciliation services are available to the parties. Whenever the Service does proffer its services in any dispute, it shall be the duty of the Service promptly to put itself in communication with the parties and to use its best efforts, by mediation and conciliation, to bring them to agreement.

(c) If the Director is not able to bring the parties to agreement by conciliation within a reasonable time, he shall seek to induce the parties voluntarily to seek other means of settling the dispute without resort to strike, lockout, or other coercion, including submission to the employees in the bargaining unit of the employer's last offer of settlement for approval or rejection in a secret ballot. The failure or refusal of either party to agree to any procedure suggested by the Director shall not be deemed a violation of any duty or obligation imposed by this Act.

(d) Final adjustment by a method agreed upon by the parties is hereby declared to be the desirable method for settlement of grievance disputes arising over the application or interpretation of an existing collective bargaining agreement. The Service is directed to make its conciliation and mediation services available in the settlement of such grievance disputes only as a last resort and in exceptional cases.

Section 204.   (a) In order to prevent or minimize interruptions of the free flow of commerce growing out of labor disputes, employers and employees and their representatives, in any industry affecting commerce, shall—

(1) exert every reasonable effort to make and maintain agreements concerning rates of pay, hours, and working conditions, including provision for adequate notice of any proposed change in the terms of such agreements;

(2) whenever a dispute arises over the terms or application of a collective bargaining agreement and a conference is requested by a party or prospective party thereto, arrange promptly for such a conference to be held and endeavor in such conference to settle such dispute expeditiously; and

(3) in case such dispute is not settled by conference, participate fully and promptly in such meetings as may be undertaken by the Service under this Act for the purpose of aiding in a settlement of the dispute.

* * * * *

[Omitted: Section 205 which creates a national labor-management panel to advise the Director of FMCS.]

National Emergencies

Section 206. Whenever in the opinion of the President of the United States, a threatened or actual strike or lockout affecting an entire industry or a substantial part thereof engaged in trade, commerce, transportation, transmission, or communication among the several States or with foreign nations, or engaged in the production of goods for commerce, will, if permitted to occur or to continue, imperil the national health or safety, he may appoint a board of inquiry to inquire into the issues involved in the dispute and to make a written report to him within such time as he shall prescribe. Such report shall include a statement of the facts with respect to the dispute, including each party's statement of its position but shall not contain any recommendations. The President shall file a copy of such report with the Service and shall make its contents available to the public.

Section 207. (a) A board of inquiry shall be composed of a chairman and such other members as the President shall determine, and shall have power to sit and act in any place within the United States and to conduct such hearings either in public or in private, as it may deem necessary or proper, to ascertain the facts with respect to the causes and circumstances of the dispute.

* * * * *

Section 208. (a) Upon receiving a report from a board of inquiry the President may direct the Attorney General to petition any district court of the United States having jurisdiction of the parties to enjoin such strike or lockout or the continuing thereof, and if the court finds that such threatened or actual strike or lockout—

(i) affects an entire industry or a substantial part thereof engaged in trade, commerce, transportation, transmission, or communication among the several States or with foreign nations, or engaged in the production of goods for commerce; and

(ii) if permitted to occur or to continue, will imperil the national health or safety, it shall have jurisdiction to enjoin any such strike or lockout, or the continuing thereof, and to make such other orders as may be appropriate.

*   *   *   *   *

Section 209.(a) Whenever a district court has issued an order under section 208 enjoining acts or practices which imperil or threaten to imperil the national health or safety, it shall be the duty of the parties to the labor dispute giving rise to such order to make every effort to adjust and settle their differences, with the assistance of the Service created by this Act. Neither party shall be under any duty to accept, in whole or in part, any proposal of settlement made by the Service.

(b) Upon the issuance of such order, the President shall reconvene the board of inquiry which has previously reported with respect to the dispute. At the end of a 60 day period (unless the dispute has been settled by that time), the board of inquiry shall report to the President the current position of the parties and the efforts which have been made for settlement, and shall include a statement by each party of its position and a statement of the employer's last offer of settlement. The President shall make such report available to the public. The National Labor Relations Board, within the succeeding 15 days, shall take a secret ballot of the employees of each employer involved in the dispute on the question of whether they wish to accept the final offer of settlement made by their employer as stated by him and shall certify the results thereof to the Attorney General within 5 days thereafter.

Section 210.   Upon the certification of the results of such a ballot or upon a settlement being reached, whichever happens sooner, the Attorney General shall move the court to discharge the injunction, which motion shall then be granted and the injunction discharged. When such motion is granted, the President shall submit to the Congress a full and comprehensive report of the proceedings, including the findings of the board of inquiry and the ballot taken by the National Labor Relations Board, together with such recommendations as he may see fit to make for consideration and appropriate action.

*   *   *   *   *

[Omitted: Section 211 which covers authorization for collection and dissemination of collective bargaining information by federal agencies, and Section 212 which exempts persons covered by provisions of the Railway Labor Act from the provisions of the LMRA.]

Conciliation of Labor Disputes in the Health Care Industry

Section 213. (a) If, in the opinion of the Director of the Federal Mediation and Conciliation Service a threatened or actual strike or lockout affecting a health care institution will, if permitted to occur or to continue, substantially interrupt the delivery of health care in the locality concerned, the Director may further assist in the resolution of the impasse by establishing within 30 days after the notice to the Federal Mediation and Counciliation Service under clause (A) of the last sentence of section 8(d) (which is required by clause (3) of such section 8(d), or within 10 days after the notice under clause (B), an impartial Board of Inquiry to investigate the issues involved in the dispute and to make a written report thereon to the parties within 15 days after the establishment of such a Board. The written report shall contain the findings of fact together with the Board's recommendations for settling the dispute, with the objective of achieving a prompt, peaceful and just settlement of the dispute. Each such Board shall be composed of such number of individuals as the Director may deem desirable. No member appointed under this section shall have any interest or involvement in the health care institutions or the employee organizations involved in the dispute.

* * * * *

[Omitted: Section 213(b) which provides for compensation for members appointed to a Board formed under Section 213(a).]

(c) After the establishment of a board under subsection (a) of this section and for 15 days after any such board has issued its report, no change in the status quo in effect prior to the expiration of the contract in the case of negotiations for a contract renewal, or in effect prior to the time of the impasse in the case of an initial bargaining negotiation, except by agreement, shall be made by the parties to the controversy.

(d) There are authorized to be appropriated such sums as may be necessary to carry out the provisions of this section.

TITLE III

Suits by and against Labor Organizations

Section 301. (a) Suits for violation of contracts between an employer and a labor organization representing employees in an industry affecting commerce as defined in this Act, or between any such labor organizations, may be brought in any district court of the United States having jurisdiction of the parties, without respect to the amount in controversy or without regard to the citizenship of the parties.

(b) Any labor organization which represents employees in an industry affecting commerce as defined in this Act and any employer whose activities affect commerce as defined in this Act shall be bound by the acts of its agents. Any such labor organization may sue or be sued as an entity and in behalf of the employees whom it represents in the courts of the United States. Any money judgment against a labor organization in a district court of the United States shall be enforceable only against the organization as an entity and against its assets, and shall not be enforceable against any individual member or his assets.

(c) For the purposes of actions and proceedings by or against labor organizations in the district courts of the United States, district courts shall be deemed to have jurisdiction of a labor organization (1) in the district in which such organization maintains its principal offices, or (2) in any district in which its duly authorized officers or agents are engaged in representing or acting for employee members.

(d) The service of summons, subpena, or other legal process of any court of the United States upon an officer or agent of a labor organization, in his capacity as such, shall constitute service upon the labor organization.

(e) For the purposes of this action, in determining whether any person is acting as an "agent" of another person so as to make such other person responsible for his acts, the question of whether the specific acts performed were actually authorized or subsequently ratified shall not be controlling.

*   *   *   *

[Omitted: Section 302—Restrictions on payments to employee representatives.]

Boycotts and Other Unlawful Combinations

Section 303. (a) It shall be unlawful, for the purpose of this section only, in an industry or activity affecting commerce, for any labor organization to engage in any activity or conduct defined as an unfair labor practice in section 8(b) (4) of the National Labor Relations Act, as amended.

(b) Whoever shall be injured in his business or property by reason of any violation of subsection (a) may sue therefor in any district court of the United States subject to the limitations and provisions of Section 301 hereof without respect to the amount of the controversy, or in any other court having jurisdiction of the parties, and shall recover the damages sustained by him and the cost of the suit.

* * * * *

[Omitted are the following sections: Section 304—Restrictions on political contributions; Title IV—Creation of a joint committee to study and report on basic problems affecting labor relations and productivity.]

TITLE V

Definitions

Section 501. When used in this Act—

(1) The term "industry affecting commerce" means any industry or activity in commerce or in which a labor dispute would burden or obstruct commerce or tend to burden or obstruct commerce or the free flow of commerce.

(2) The term "strike" includes any strike or other concerted stoppage of work by employees (including a stoppage by reason of the expiration of a collective bargaining agreement) and any concerted slowdown or other concerted interruption of operations by employees.

(3) The terms "commerce," "labor disputes," "employer," "employee," "labor organization," "representative," "person," and "supervisor" shall have the same meaning as when used in the National Labor Relations Act as amended by this Act.

Saving Provision

Section 502. Nothing in this Act shall be construed to require an individual employee to render labor or service without his consent, nor shall anything in this Act be construed to make the quitting of his labor by an individual employee an illegal act; nor shall any court issue any process to compel the performance by an individual employee of such labor or service, without his consent; nor shall the quitting of labor by an employee or employees in good faith because of abnormally dangerous conditions for work at the place of employment of such employee or employees be deemed a strike under this Act.

Separability

Section 503. If any provision of this Act, or the application of such provision to any person or circumstance, shall be held invalid, the remainder of this Act, or the application of such provision to persons or circumstances other than those as to which it is held invalid, shall not be affected thereby.

Index to Cases for Part One

Index to Cases for Part One (concluded)

1. DISCHARGE FOR VIOLATION OF THE NO-SOLICITATION RULE

Company: W. W. Grainger, Inc., Niles, Illinois

Union: International Brotherhood of Teamsters, Chauffeurs, Warehousemen and Helpers of America, Local 714

BACKGROUND

W. W. Grainger, Inc., was engaged in the business of wholesale distribution of electrical products and operated a distribution warehouse in Niles, Illinois. Approximately 90 people were employed.

For several years the company had experienced attempts at union organization of its employees. During the first week of April 1975, two employees, Lou Bommarito and Carlos Gomez,[1] solicited employees to sign Teamsters union authorization cards at the warehouse entrance. Bommarito and Gomez were both brothers-in-law of Martin Tolman, another employee. Their relationship to Tolman and their union activity were also known to Raymond Nolan, the company personnel manager.

On several days prior to work, Tolman gave union authorization cards to some of the employees at the warehouse, and handed out some ball-point pens imprinted with the name of the union. On several occasions, Tolman discussed the union with several employees during work time. In May 1975, Nolan indicated to Tolman that he had heard that Tolman was soliciting for the union on working time. Tolman denied the charge and stated that he was merely telling the employees that "the union was good." Nolan then warned Tolman that "any further soliciting on working time" would result in his termination. Later the same day, Nolan confronted another employee, Walt Pulsifer, with a similar accusation. Pulsifer denied that he had been soliciting for the union, and stated that it was Tolman

---

[1] The names of all individuals have been disguised.

who was soliciting. Nolan then warned Pulsifer that soliciting during working time could be punished by discharge. In neither interview did Nolan reveal any of the details concerning the alleged solicitations, or tell them who had reported that they had been soliciting during working time.

On June 2, Ralph Macon, the company's warehouse operations manager, issued a written warning to Pulsifer, advising him that employee Bill Cheek had told Macon that Pulsifer had solicited Cheek during working time. Although Pulsifer denied the accusation, he signed the written warning. Pulsifer then told Macon that it was Tolman who had been soliciting. Later the same day, Macon asked Pulsifer whether Tolman had solicited others. Pulsifer said that Tolman had solicited him during the prior week in regard to a meeting to be held in June. Pulsifer further stated that Tolman had solicited employees Mort Polanski and Marty Donald, although he gave no details about this solicitation nor was he asked to do so. A couple of days later Macon handed Pulsifer a statement which read: "I was approached during working hours by Martin Tolman. My work was interrupted by Tolman's solicitation activity. I have brought this to the attention of my supervisor."

Upon Macon's request, Pulsifer signed the statement. Macon showed the document to the company's vice president, Stanley Lincoln, with a recommendation that Tolman be fired. Lincoln remarked that this "written documentation" constituted evidence of "flagrant multiple violations" of the company's no-solicitation rule during working time.

On June 9, as Tolman was reporting for work, he was escorted by a foreman to Macon's office. Macon told Tolman that he was being terminated for soliciting for a union, and that the company had evidence in its files that he was soliciting on company time. Tolman denied the accusation and asked to see the evidence in the files. His request was refused; Tolman was escorted off the premises.

Subsequently, on behalf of Martin Tolman, the union filed unfair labor practice charges against the company, claiming that the company had violated Sections 8(a) (1) and 8(a) (3) of the Labor Management Relations Act (LMRA) by maintaining a vague, "overbroad" no-solicitation rule, and then by issuing disciplinary warnings to two employees and later discharging one of them for alleged violations of this rule.

POSITION OF THE UNION

The union claimed that Martin Tolman's open distribution of union authorization cards and ball-point pens and discussion of the union with employees, as well as his familial relationship to others doing the same, were well known to company management. According to the union, most all of Tolman's actual soliciting occurred before and after work or during breaks and lunch periods. At the first meetings with Pulsifer and Tolman, Nolan accused the two of soliciting during working time on the basis of what he had heard. The record contained no evidence of what acts led Nolan to believe that Tolman and Pulsifer had solicited on company time. According to Tolman, he merely had been remarking to other employees that the union was good—an act which can hardly amount to soliciting; especially since company supervisors allowed virtually unrestricted discussion among employees as long as they continued to work.

With respect to the June 2 meeting between Pulsifer and Macon, Pulsifer told Macon that Tolman had solicited him on company time. Macon did not inquire of Pulsifer or anyone else as to the details concerning when, where, what was done, and so on, but rather drafted a conclusory statement which Pulsifer later signed. Further, the substance of what Pulsifer told Macon was far from clear. According to Pulsifer, the solicitation consisted of a conversation with Tolman lasting about five minutes during working time, which ended with him signing an authorization card and receiving a ball-point pen. According to Macon, Pulsifer told him that Tolman "solicited" about a meeting to be held at Tolman's house. After Pulsifer stated to Macon that Tolman had also solicited Marty Donald and Mort Polanski during working time, an effort was made to confirm the solicitation of Polanski. Other than the conclusion that Tolman had solicited Polanski during working time, the company offered no evidence that the facts underlying the conclusion were investigated. Apparently no effort was made to contact Donald to check out whether Tolman had actually solicited him during working time.

In essence, the union claimed the company's no-solicitation rule was not valid, since it was "overbroad" and lacking in specifics as to intent. All of the company management's actions were a pretext to discourage union organization activity. By issuing improper warnings to Tolman and Pulsifer, the company had violated Section 8(a)(1) of the Act. By preparing a statement for Pulsifer to sign which was not supported by specific evidence, the company deliberately sought to create a reason for terminating Martin Tolman. The real reason for terminating Tolman was not for violating a no-solicitation rule, but to discourage union organizational activity.

The union requested that Martin Tolman be reinstated and made whole for all lost pay and benefits, and that the company be ordered to cease and desist from issuing warnings and attempting to enforce an invalid no-solicitation rule.

POSITION OF THE COMPANY

The company first of all claimed that its no-solicitation rule was quite valid and a legitimate management right under the Act. Company managers had clearly conveyed to employees who were sympathetic to the union that any solicitation during working time was prohibited. These employees understood that the intent of this rule was to limit any union solicitation to the employee's own time, such as breaks and during lunch periods.

The company further contended that Pulsifer and Tolman were adequately warned that soliciting on company time for the union was punishable by dismissal. Nevertheless, Tolman persisted in soliciting during working time. His discharge, therefore, was consistent with the company's right to maintain discipline at its business.

The company maintained that it had supporting evidence to show that Tolman had violated the no-solicitation rule. A fellow employee, Walt Pulsifer, signed a statement attesting to this fact. Other employees had reported that Tolman had solicited them during working time. This could not be tolerated by the company. Even though the amounts of time involved in the union solicitation on company time were small, the employees had been specifically warned that any such solicitation during working hours could lead to their dismissal. The company in discharging Tolman exercised its managerial rights in order to prevent a potential wholesale breakdown in employee discipline.

The company claimed that it had not violated the Act, and that the unfair labor practice charges should be dismissed in totality.

QUESTIONS

1. Was the company's no-solicitation rule overbroad and lacking in specifics? Why should a company be very careful in any efforts to prohibit solicitation of employees on company time?
2. Evaluate the union's argument that company management's actions in this case were a "pretext" designed to discourage union organizational activity.
3. Were the company's disciplinary and discharge actions consistent with the company's right to maintain discipline at its business?
4. Why is it unusual—and of questionable merit—for a company to try to pit one employee against another employee in gathering information related to union organizing efforts and violation of company rules?

2. SHOULD THE EDITORIAL WRITERS BE INCLUDED IN THE BARGAINING UNIT?

Company: Wichita Eagle & Beacon Publishing Company, Inc., Wichita, Kansas

Union: Wichita Newspaper Guild, affiliated with the Newspaper Guild, AFL-CIO

BACKGROUND

The company is engaged in the publishing, sale, and distribution of daily newspapers in Wichita, Kansas. In August 1970 the Wichita Newspaper Guild, affiliated with the Newspaper Guild, AFL-CIO, filed a petition with the National Labor Relations Board (NLRB) seeking certification as the collective bargaining agent of the newspaper's news department employees. The regional office of the Board conducted a hearing on the petition and ordered an election to be held. In connection therewith, the Board found that two editorial writers, Alice Sanford and Hazel Jaeger,[1] should be included in the proposed news department bargaining unit.

An election was conducted by the Board among the unit that it had determined was appropriate, and the union was certified as the collective bargaining agent for the unit. The newspaper filed an exception to the election under Sections 9(b) and 9(c) of the Act, challenging the inclusion of Alice Sanford and Hazel Jaeger in the bargaining unit.

About the time of the election, the newspaper transferred Sanford to the Sunday magazine department from the editorial page department. The union claimed that this transfer was in reprisal for Sanford's part in helping organize the union, and the union filed unfair labor practice charges against the newspaper on her behalf. An Administrative Law Judge (ALJ) of the Board conducted a hearing on this matter and found that the newspaper had violated Sections 8(a)

---

[1] The names of all individuals have been disguised.

(1) and (3) of the Act by transferring Alice Sanford against her will from the editorial page department to the Sunday magazine department "because of her union activities," and because she had been told by her employer that "consequences of her union membership and activity might be severe." The ALJ recommended that she be reinstated in the editorial page department and that she be awarded any back pay she would have been entitled to, including increases in salary, but for her transfer. The newspaper filed an appeal to this decision, which was part of its continuing challenge to the original inclusion of both Sanford and Jaeger in the bargaining unit.

POSITION OF THE UNION

According to the union, Sanford's position prior to her transfer to the Sunday magazine department was that of an editorial writer. The editorial page department of the newspaper consisted of three people. Arthur Jackson, editor of the editorial page, was the supervisor of the two employees in the editorial page department, Sanford and Jaeger. Jackson was not included in the collective bargaining unit. Martin G. Patrick, editor and publisher of the newspaper, was also part of the editorial page department, but more in an "ex officio" capacity.

According to testimony presented at the hearing, normal day-to-day procedure in the editorial page department included a midmorning conference, with Patrick, Jackson, Sanford, and Jaeger participating. At these conferences, each person in turn would be asked what he or she had in mind for an editorial. Sanford, for instance, when thus asked, might say that she had in mind writing a piece on ecology. Patrick or Jackson would say, "We had an editorial on air and water pollution last week, so we will not go on ecology again at this time." That would dispose of Sanford's proposal. Or, for instance, Patrick might have responded to Sanford's proposal in the following vein: "What particular aspect of ecology do you have in mind?" Sanford would respond with some details and elaboration; the matter would then be discussed by those present. Patrick might then say to Sanford, "All right, give it a try." On some other subject thus raised, Patrick might make it clear that there were certain specific things that he wished to be stated in the particular proposed editorial, for example, "The theme of the editorial should be that, on balance, after weighing the arguments pro and con, the government should proceed with the development of the supersonic transport plane because of the need to maintain leadership in the field of air transportation and because of the need to maintain a viable aerospace industry and the tens of thousands of jobs involved in that and in satellite industries." The editorial writer would follow such a directive.

Following the foregoing type of daily conference with Patrick, the other three would return to their offices. They would then get together in Jackson's office and discuss at greater length topics that had received tentative approval at the conference with Patrick. Views and possibly conflicting contentions would be exchanged and argued. In most instances it would be at this tripartite conference that definite editorial topics would be assigned by Jackson to Sanford and Jaeger.

After a writer drafted or wrote an editorial, it was then submitted to Jackson. He might approve it, disapprove it, or prescribe changes or revisions. If the editorial cleared Jackson, it would then go to Patrick. Again, the editorial might be approved, rejected, or rejected subject to some particular revision being made.

The union claimed that the editorials of the newspaper functioned as the voice of the newspaper's ownership and management. What appeared in an editorial was the subjective viewpoint of management, that is, of Jackson and Patrick. In the union's view, neither Sanford nor Jaeger could exercise much independent judgment in their work as editorial writers. Nor were they responsible for the supervision of any other employees, and they had no part in determining wages, hours, and working conditions for other employees.

The union claimed, therefore, that both Sanford and Jaeger were employees within the meaning of Section 2(3) of the LMRA, and they should properly be included in the newspaper's bargaining unit. Consequently, the finding of unfair labor practices against the newspaper for transferring Sanford because of her union activities should not be dismissed on grounds that she was not covered by provisions of the Act.

POSITION OF THE NEWSPAPER

The newspaper contended that editorial writers have the essential characteristics of managerial and confidential employees, and therefore the two editorial writers in question, Sanford and Jaeger, were improperly included in the collective bargaining unit. Therefore, the newspaper's action in transferring Sanford was not properly subject to the Act's coverage.

Although the term *managerial employee* is not used in the LMRA, nor is provision made in the Act for the inclusion or exclusion of such employees in bargaining units, the newspaper pointed out that the NLRB has long followed the practice of excluding employees designated as "managerial" from bargaining units in representation elections. It does so on the premise that certain nonsupervisory employees are so closely allied with management that they should be excluded from employment bargaining units.

In this case, according to the newspaper, Sanford and Jaeger were directly responsible to the editorial page editor, Jackson, and in turn to the editor and publisher of the newspaper, Patrick, concerning the content and direction of the newspaper's editorials. Both were active participants in "formulating, determining, and effectuating" the newspaper's journalistic policies. The daily conferences between Patrick, Jackson, Sanford, and Jaeger attested to this relationship. Although subject to supervision in writing by the editorial page editor and the editor and publisher, both Sanford and Jaeger could and did propose topics for editorials, and they offered their own viewpoints in an effort to influence editorial policy on various subjects. They were "integral participants in the newspaper's subjective voice, its editorials." Whether termed a managerial employee, a confidential employee, or whatever, the relationship of Sanford and Jaeger to the newspaper and its staff placed them in a position where they were directly involved in "formulating, determining, and effectuating" the policies of the paper.

In the newspaper's view, for the NLRB to hold that a person who was involved in the formulation of editorial content of a newspaper is not aligned with the newspaper's management would come "perilously close to infringing upon the newspaper's First Amendment guarantee of freedom of the press."

In summary, the newspaper argued that Sanford and Jaeger should not have been classified as employees within the meaning of Section 2(3) of the Act. In line with long-standing Board policy, editorial writers such as Sanford and Jaeger should be excluded from the newspaper's news department bargaining unit, since their duties were essentially managerial and confidential in nature. The unfair labor practice charges against the newspaper in connection with its transfer of Sanford correspondingly should be dismissed, since she was not covered by provisions of the Act.

QUESTIONS

1. Evaluate the argument of the union and management concerning the managerial and confidential nature of the work of the editorial writers.
2. What is the difference between an editorial writer who is involved in "formulating, determining, and effectuating" the policies of the newspaper as compared to simply writing material at the direction of the owner of the newspaper? Why is this a gray area on which the determination of this case depends?

3. Evaluate the newspaper's argument that to include the editorial writers in a bargaining unit would possibly infringe upon constitutional guarantees of freedom of the press.

4. If a person does not supervise any other employees and has no part in determining wages, hours, and working conditions for other employees, does this mean that the NLRB must classify such a person as a nonmanagerial employee eligible for inclusion in a bargaining unit? Discuss.

3. SHOULD THE DEPARTMENT MANAGERS, SECURITY RECEIVERS, AND BOOKKEEPERS BE INCLUDED IN THE BARGAINING UNIT?

Company: Big Y Foods, Inc., Springfield, Massachusetts
Union: Retail Clerks Union, Local 1459

BACKGROUND

The company operated a chain of 16 retail food stores. Eleven of these stores, employing approximately 850 to 900 people, were involved in the case at hand. The other 5 stores had been organized in whole or part by the Meat Cutters Union, which also was involved in efforts to organize the remaining 11 stores. A representational campaign to organize the remaining 11 stores was conducted by both the Retail Clerks Union and the Meat Cutters Union beginning in 1976. A number of questions and issues developed concerning the appropriate storewide bargaining unit and who should be included in this unit. These issues had not been fully resolved at the time of this case in early 1978. However, the NLRB had determined that the 11 stores constituted an appropriate storeswide collective bargaining unit.

In the course of filing for a representational election to be conducted by the Regional Office of the Board and the litigation that arose out of the petition for an election, three separate disputes arose between the Retail Clerks Union and the company concerning the appropriate status of the stores' department managers, security receivers, and bookkeepers.

THE DEPARTMENT MANAGERS

The company's entire chain of stores was centrally operated. Personnel policies were developed and administered by the central office. Full-time employees were hired by the central office. All stores had the same job classifications, such as store managers, department managers, head meatcutters, meatcutters, wrappers, and clerks, which covered the same job functions.

Each store was divided into five departments: front-end, grocery, meat, delicatessen, and produce. Consequently, there were five classifications of department managers at each store, that is, front-end manager, grocery manager, meat manager, delicatessen manager, and produce manager. All of these department managers reported directly to the overall store manager of each store.

Additionally, the central office employed specialists for each department who coordinated purchasing. The specialists also visited the stores in order to supervise merchandising, and in general to oversee the operations of the various departments. In this respect, the specialists worked in support of and in conjunction with the department managers and store managers.

The company claimed that the department managers were supervisors, while the Retail Clerks Union claimed that they were employees under the Act.[1] In seeking to determine whether these positions were supervisory within the meaning of Section 2(3) and Section 2(11) of the Act, testimony and evidence were presented concerning the actual responsibilities that were assigned to the department managers who occupied these positions and not on their job titles.

In the case of the produce department managers and delicatessen department managers, their respective departments were quite small. For the most part, other employees, either full or part time, were not present when these managers were at work. Produce department and delicatessen department managers did prepare the work schedule for employees who worked when the department managers were not present. However, these managers could participate in disciplining of unit employees. On one occasion, a delicatessen manager was involved in the discharge of an employee who had failed to report for work. The company argued that these department managers were responsible for decisions concerning their respective products and the profitability of each department. However, other evidence showed that the central office department specialists were primarily responsible for these functions for the produce and delicatessen departments.

Concerning the grocery department managers, their responsibilities were similar to the produce department and delicatessen department managers. However, the grocery departments were considerably larger in size; normally other grocery department employ-

---

[1] During the proceedings at hand, the Meat Cutters Union took the position that the meat department manager was a supervisor under the Act. The Meat Cutters Union expressed no view on the status of the other department managers at issue, nor concerning the security receivers and bookkeepers.

ees were present at the same time that the grocery department managers would be working. Similarly, the meat department managers and the front-end managers directed a substantial number of employees in their departments. The meat department managers supervised the head meatcutters, meatcutters, apprentice meatcutters, and meat clerks. These managers could impose discipline, interview prospective employees, adjust grievances, attend supervisory meetings, and prepare schedules. Similarly, the front-end managers supervised the cashiers, summoned additional employees from other parts of the stores when help was needed to package customers' purchases, and disciplined employees regarding shortages.

The union argued that all of the department managers were really "working straw bosses" or "lead people," not supervisors within the meaning of Section 2(11) of the LMRA. In reality, the department managers were tightly controlled by the store specialists and the store managers and could exercise little independent judgment. Similarly, the central office specialists and the store managers were responsible for most of the stores' operating results, not the department managers. The union urged that the department managers should be included in the bargaining unit and be eligible to vote in the representational election. The company, however, claimed that all of the department managers exercised supervisory authority as defined under Section 2(11) of the Act, and that they should thus be excluded from the proposed bargaining unit as specified in Section 2(3) and be ineligible to vote in the representation election.

THE SECURITY RECEIVERS

The company and union also disputed concerning the status of the security receivers. The company argued that they were guards, and pursuant to Section 9(b) (3) of the Act, they should not be included in the bargaining unit.[2] The Retail Clerks Union argued that the security receivers were not guards, and they should appropriately be included in the unit and be eligible to vote in the representational election.

Testimony indicated that security receivers spent approximately

---

[2] Section 9(b) (3) of the Act states in relevant part: "(b) The Board shall decide in each case whether, in order to assure to employees the fullest freedom in exercising the rights guaranteed by this Act, the unit appropriate for the purposes of collective bargaining shall be the employer unit, craft unit, plant unit, or subdivision thereof: *Provided,* that the Board shall not . . . (3) decide that any unit is appropriate for such purposes, if it includes, together with other employees, any individual employed as a guard to enforce against employees and other persons rules to protect property of the employer or to protect the safety of persons on the employer's premises."

60-70 percent of their time actually receiving goods. This involved determining the quantity of each item that the store received each week and completing a computer form with that information. During their remaining time at work, security receivers performed such tasks as opening and pricing goods, sweeping and washing floors, pulling cardboards from shelves, and picking up carriages from the parking lots, in addition to delivering and recording merchandise. Security receivers were not uniformed or armed, did not wear badges, and did not have police powers. Security receivers were paid according to a separate wage schedule, but they had the same benefits as other company employees. The company engaged an outside security service to provide surveillance related to shoplifting and parking lot checks during the business day as well as at night and on Sundays. This outside security service also had responsibility for apprehending employees suspected of thefts.

The union claimed that the security receivers were little more than inventory control clerks who performed clerical and physical job functions. The company, however, claimed that the security receivers primarily were involved in protecting the property of the company, and thus they were properly classified as guards as defined in Section 9(b) (3) of the Act.

THE BOOKKEEPERS

A third disagreement between the company and union was whether the bookkeepers in each store should be included in the storeswide bargaining unit. The company would exclude them, and the Retail Clerks Union would include them.

Under the union's petition for a representational election, the Regional Office of the Board had determined that central office clerical employees employed by the company were not to be included in the storeswide unit of 11 stores sought by the union. However, under Section 9(b) of the Act, the status of each store's bookkeeper came into dispute. Each store had a courtesy booth where a bookkeeper worked along with a "booth person," but each in separate rooms. The bookkeepers received the same pay and benefits as cashiers. Some of the stores trained a regular cashier to serve as a backup bookkeeper whenever the regular bookkeeper was absent. Bookkeepers wore the same smocks as cashiers, and they occasionally substituted for the cashiers. Job progression was normally from cashier to bookkeeper. Bookkeepers took their breaks in the same area as other employees, and they reported to the store manager for supervision. Technical problems were handled over the telephone by the main office. The bookkeepers' primary responsibility was to handle money and process lottery tickets and money orders that were received by the front end of the store. They also had to be familiar with the operation of a cash register.

The company contended that these employees primarily performed an accounting function, since they were responsible for maintaining the financial records for each store. The company stressed the financial and clerical nature of the bookkeepers' job and argued that they should be excluded from a unit of store employees. The company claimed that store bookkeepers could be included in a separate clerical employees' bargaining unit along with central office clerical employees in the eventuality that these employees sought some form of union representation. But store bookkeepers should not be included in a storeswide unit of store employees whose primary functions were associated with the selling of merchandise to customers in stores.

The Retail Clerks Union, however, argued that the bookkeepers were merely "senior experienced cashiers and booth persons" who were responsible for one facet of front-end store duties. Their jobs were essentially store and customer related, and thus bookkeepers should be included and eligible to vote in the stores' representational election.

QUESTIONS

1. Which—if any or all—of the department managers should be classified as supervisors within the meaning of the Act? Discuss.
2. Were the security receivers guards within the meaning of the Act? Discuss.
3. Should the bookkeepers be excluded from the proposed storeswide bargaining unit? Why, or why not?
4. Why is the resolution of the status of these persons of crucial significance both to the company and union?

4. ELECTION INTERFERENCE, OR PERMISSIBLE CAMPAIGN PROPAGANDA?

Company: Cafe Tartuffo, Inc., and Fiorello's Roman Cafe, Inc., New York, New York

Union: Local 6, Hotel and Restaurant Employees Union

BACKGROUND

In late 1980, Local 6 of the Hotel and Restaurant Employees won a representational election to represent certain employees at Fiorello's Roman Cafe, Inc. In the spring of 1981, Fiorello's Roman Cafe and the union signed a collective bargaining agreement covering employees of Fiorello's Roman Cafe.

Fiorello's was owned by the same management which also operated Cafe Tartuffo, another restaurant located several blocks from Fiorello's on the west side of New York City. In 1981, the union began an organizing campaign among employees of Cafe Tartuffo, and an election was ordered by the regional office of the NLRB to be held on July 9, 1981.

Prior to the election date, the company on June 25, 1981, sent a letter to the home address of all its employees. This letter contained the following statements (which are designated for reference purposes by paragraph numbers):

Dear Fellow Employees:

1. As you know, there will be a Union Election on July 9. At that Election each of you will have the opportunity to vote to determine whether or not you want to be represented by the restaurant workers' union.

2. You are much luckier than the employees at Fiorello's, our restaurant on the west side. Some time ago those employees voted to be represented by the restaurant workers' union. They were led down the primrose path by union promises of increased wages and benefits. In fact, after the election the Union negotiated a contract with the

restaurant management which, in my opinion, gave the employees at Fiorello's no more than they would have gotten had there been no union—and probably gave them less. In addition, I believe many of these employees will be hurt by the inflexibility of the Union contract.

3. On the other hand, you know from the experience of the Fiorello's employees exactly the kind of contract the Union would negotiate if it became your collective bargaining representative. A contract which produces nothing more than you would expect to receive were there no union in the picture. For that, you are afforded the privilege of paying Union dues.

Paragraph 6 of the letter stated:

6. The restaurant does not want a union at Fiorello's! Our experience on the west side has shown that we can negotiate an agreement with the Union which does not cost us any more in wages and benefits than without the Union and may even cost less. But our experience on the west side has also shown us that the presence of the Union results in a tense working relationship with extreme disharmony among the employees. This is a real cost to everyone. It can result in a loss of customers and a loss of income to our employees who serve those customers, as well as to the restaurant itself. The Union benefits no one but itself.

The union lost the representational election at Cafe Tartuffo. Immediately thereafter, the union filed unfair labor practice charges and exceptions to the election under Section 9(c) of the Labor Management Relations Act, requesting that the results of the election be set aside.

POSITION OF THE UNION

The union contended that the company letter of June 25, 1981, went far beyond permissible employer statements allowed by Section 8(c) of LMRA.

First of all, with respect to paragraph 2 of the letter, there was reference to the election and the union's collective bargaining agreement with Fiorello's Roman Cafe. While the letter indicated that Fiorello's employees had "probably" received "less" with the union, Fiorello's Roman Cafe employees had in fact gained a wage increase that was greater than that obtained previously and also had acquired various additional benefits. Similarly, paragraph 6 of the letter and that paragraph's second sentence stated that the company could negotiate an agreement with the union that would not cost the company any more money than without a union and might cost it less. The language in paragraphs 2 and 6 of the letter thus meant that the company was saying it would provide its employees with the

84

same planned benefits whether or not they chose a union. And taken together, paragraphs 2 and 6 constituted a promise of benefit if employees rejected the union and suggested the futility of selecting a union.

The union also protested the language in paragraph 3 of the letter to the effect that the company could negotiate "a contract which produces nothing more than you would expect to receive were there no union in the picture. For that you are afforded the privilege of paying union dues." This language conveyed the impression that not only would no new benefits come to the employees with a union, but that the employees would lose benefits because they would have the additional requirement of paying union dues.

Finally, the union protested the language of paragraph 6 which indicated that the "presence of the union results in a tense working relationship" and "this is a real cost to everyone," which "can result in a loss of customers and a loss of income to our employees." The union claimed that this was an obvious threat to employees designed to put employees in fear of losing money and possibly their jobs if they voted for the union.

In summary, the union claimed that since the company letter contained both promises of benefits and threats of loss of benefits, the company had violated Section 8(c) of the Act and thus had coerced and interfered with employees' rights in violation of Section 8(a) (1) and Section 7 of the Act. The union requested that a new election should be held, and that the company should be ordered to cease and desist in interfering and coercing employees in their selection of a collective bargaining representative.

POSITION OF THE COMPANY

The company claimed that all of the language within its letter of June 25, 1981, was legitimate and permissible "campaign propaganda" within the protected limits of Section 8(c) of the Labor Management Relations Act.

Concerning paragraph 2 of the letter, the company claimed it simply was stating its opinion relative to a union contract at its other location. The letter cannot be read fairly to state or imply that the company acting independently would grant the same wages and benefits to its employees that were negotiated at Fiorello's Roman Cafe. In this regard, the company claimed that it had held a general meeting with its employees on June 15, at which time it distributed copies of the collective bargaining agreement between the union and Fiorello's Roman Cafe. At this meeting, company management informed the employees that a union business agent had offered management to sign the same basic agreement for Cafe Tartuffo employees if the company would agree to forego an election; alternatively, if the election were held, the union was willing to negotiate a collective bargaining agreement for Cafe Tartuffo based on the one formulated for Fiorello's Roman Cafe.

Similarly, the company contended that paragraph 6 of the letter did not constitute or contain a promise of benefits. It was only the company's opinion of the outcome of negotiations at Fiorello's Roman Cafe, and the company's further opinion that based on those negotiations the union would likely be willing to negotiate a contract which would not result in significant increases for employees at Cafe Tartuffo. Such comments are protected by Section 8(c) of the Act.

For essentially the same reasons, the company argued that there were no impermissible statements in paragraph 3 of the letter. Here, too, the company reiterated its perception of the contract that the union had negotiated at Fiorello's Roman Cafe. The paragraph did not indicate what the company's position would be if the union won the election; it only indicated management's interpretation of what the union's position in negotiations would be. The company was not prohibited from making such statements. Further, the company did not say that voting for the union indicated to the employees that a union would be futile. The company did not indicate that it had a fixed position with regard to what it would offer in negotiations and only expressed an opinion of what the union would seek in negotiations.

Finally, the company contended that the last four sentences of paragraph 6 were not designed to place employees in fear of losing money or possibly their jobs if they voted for the union. These statements constituted nothing more than an employer's permissible predictions of the effects of unionization. Nor did the company's statements correlate unionization with a loss of job security. The statements were devoid of any implications that the company would take adverse actions against employees if they selected the union. The company also explained that the tension mentioned in its letter referred to its earlier filing of objections to the election at Fiorello's and to the union's filing of unfair labor practice charges against that restaurant. Such charges and countercharges could reasonably be expected to occur at Cafe Tartuffo as well.

The company requested that the union's exceptions to the election and the unfair labor practice charges filed by the union should be dismissed, and that the NLRB should certify the results of the representational election.

QUESTIONS

1. Evaluate the union's contentions that the company letter went far beyond the permissible employer statements allowed by Section 8(c) of LMRA.

2. Evaluate the company's contentions that its letter was legitimate and permissible within Section 8(c) of LMRA.

3. Some companies hire management attorneys or consultants to conduct their campaigns prior to a union representational election. Why is the final decision in this type of case (irrespective of which side prevails) an extremely "close call" of important precedent implications?

5. DISCRIMINATION CHARGES DURING A UNION ORGANIZING CAMPAIGN

Company: Northwest Propane Company, Inc., Farmington, Michigan

Union: International Brotherhood of Teamsters, Chauffeurs, Warehousemen and Helpers of America, Local 614

BACKGROUND

During a union organizing campaign at the Northwest Propane Company of Farmington, Michigan, a series of events occurred which brought unfair labor practice charges filed by the Teamsters union against the company. Each of these incidents will be described separately, although they did not necessarily occur sequentially as presented in this case.

The Discharge of Employee Don Meyers[1]

Northwest Propane Company sells propane gas and related products at Farmington, Michigan. Its business is seasonal, and its peak season occurs between November and March. During the slack season, the company usually reduces it work force.

Company offices and the main plant are situated along a main highway known as Northwestern Highway. The office building is approached by a large driveway which leads from the highway and passes along the front of the office. Offices of the company president and other executives are in the front of the office building, directly overlooking the driveway and also the highway.

Around May 12, 1971, Rollie Johnson, one of the company's employees, phoned an organizer of the union. The organizer advised Johnson that he would go to the company's premises the following day to handbill and to solicit authorization card signatures.

---

[1] The names of all individuals have been disguised.

At around 4 P.M. the next day, the organizer went to the company's premises and stayed there for about an hour and 40 minutes. During the time that he was handbilling, he wore a bright blue jacket on the back of which was written the word *Teamsters* in gold letters. He stationed himself at the driveway entrance leading into the company's property. While he was there the company president, Ken Schader, drove into the property, parked his car on the driveway, looked in the organizer's direction, and then went into the main office building. Sometime later, Schader and office manager Anton Gibson repeatedly looked out the window of the office building to observe the union organizer.

While the organizer was handbilling the employees, employee Rollie Johnson, employee Jack Tobin, and a third employee, Don Meyers, left the company premises in Meyers's Mustang car. After driving south on Northwestern Highway, they reversed direction and crossed the highway stopping on a crossover area approximately 150 feet from the company office. Johnson, who initially had contacted the organizer, waved his hand and called to the organizer; Johnson was seated on the passenger side of the front seat of the car. Tobin, who was seated on the right-hand passenger seat in the back of the car, also called and waved to the organizer. At this moment, both Tobin and Meyers observed President Schader standing in his office window.

After the union organizer had left the company premises, he met with a group of employees at a local restaurant. All the employees present signed authorization cards. These employees included Tobin, Johnson, and Meyers.

The following afternoon, company President Ken Schader terminated Meyers. Schader told Meyers he had been terminated because business had slowed down and the employer could not use Meyers's services. Meyers was employed as a truck driver and he had a weak, defective left hand which made it difficult for him to load and unload gas cylinders. Schader reminded Meyers that he had been told previously in April that his employment would not be continued during the upcoming slack season.

The Discharge of Employee Jack Tobin

Employee Jack Tobin heated his home with propane gas and also owned a rental property heated by propane gas. Tobin purchased the gas for his two properties from Northwest Propane Company.

In early May, Tobin received a call from the owner of the property adjacent to his rental property. The owner asked Tobin to remove three propane gas cylinders which were lying near the rear of Tobin's rental property. These cylinders had been ordered by Tobin for use at his rental propery. However, the rental property was vacant, and the cylinders had not been hooked up but were lying unattended on the ground for several months. That same day Tobin loaded the cylinders in his car and brought them to his residence.

On the Monday after Tobin took the three propane gas cylinders home, he told office manager Gibson that he had the cylinders at his home. Subsequently, pursuant to instructions by Gibson, Tobin brought two of the cylinders back to the company storage area, but the third cylinder remained at his home.

A few days later, because Tobin had not received his own bulk delivery of propane gas from the company, Tobin told the office manager that if he did not receive his bulk delivery, he would probably have to hook up the remaining cylinder to maintain heat and hot water in his home. Gibson replied that he could do so. Subsequently, Tobin hooked up the remaining cylinder to the heating system in his home.

On May 25, President Schader discharged Tobin for "stealing" this gas cylinder.

The Discharge of Employee Joyce Dees

In late May the office manager, Anton Gibson, told the bookkeeper and another employee, "If the union gets in, the employer will close the business!" The bookkeeper, Joyce Dees, was one of the union's supporters. On June 7, she went to President Schader and complained that during the preceding several weeks, office manager Gibson had followed her whenever she went to the rest room or got a drink of water. In response to Schader's inquiry, Dees stated that the office manager had been following her because she was talking to her fellow employees about the union.

Later the same day, Dees was informed by Schader and Gibson that she was being discharged effective immediately. They told her that she was discharged because she had various work deficiencies, including failure to finish her bookkeeping work on time, rudeness to customers, and general disruption of the office by talking to other employees about the union on company time.

The union filed unfair labor practice charges on behalf of each of these employees and also a general complaint against the company alleging an overall pattern of antiunion activity.

POSITION OF THE UNION

In the case of employee Don Meyers, the union claimed that Meyers had been illegally discharged in violation of Section 8(a) (3) of the LMRA because of his union activities. The union claimed that

Meyers was discharged because he was observed as the owner and driver of a car whose passengers waved to the union organizer, and because Meyers had signed a union authorization card. The union claimed that this discharge action was part of the company's total pattern of activities designed to interfere with and discriminate against the union organizing campaign. The union requested that Meyers be reinstated and be given full back pay for employment that he had missed.

In the case of employee Jack Tobin, the union argued that Tobin similarly was discharged because of his union activities, thus violating Section 8(a) (3). The union claimed that Tobin did not steal any propane gas cylinders. Tobin had been a good employee for four years, and his discharge did not occur until after the company had learned that Tobin was involved in the union campaign and a request for a representational election had been filed. Concerning the alleged stealing of the gas cylinder, the union claimed that this was strictly a fabricated charge and pointed out that Tobin actually had received permission from the office manager to hook up the one cylinder to his heating system in his home. The union requested that Tobin be reinstated with full back pay for any period of employment missed.

In the case of employee Joyce Dees, the union again claimed that the company had violated Section 8(a) (3) by discharging Dees for her union sympathies and activities, not the alleged work deficiencies which company management had stated. Dees had been a satisfactory employee for over five years. The union argued that she could have been discharged at any time previously in the five years for work deficiencies. The union also pointed out that office manager Gibson had told Dees that her talking about the union with fellow employees on company time was part of the company's reasons for taking disciplinary action against her. The union requested that Dees be reinstated to the position of bookkeeper, and that she be granted full pay for wages missed during the time of her termination.

The union also filed a general complaint which claimed that the company had violated Section 8(a) (1) of the Act by continued surveillance of its employees' union activities and by threatening employees with closing of the business if a union was successful in the organizing drive. The discharge actions against the three employees cited previously were part of a concerted total management effort to defeat the union. The union requested that the company be ordered to cease and desist from discouraging union membership and, in any other ways, from interfering with the process of having a fair representation election held at the company premises.

POSITION OF THE COMPANY

The company denied that it had embarked on a systematic effort to spy on employees involved in union activity. The company claimed that its actions taken against the three employees in this case were reasonable and fair under the circumstances and only coincidental with the union organizing campaign.

In the case of employee Don Meyers, the company pointed out that he had been told that his employment would not be continued during the slack season. Meyers was not physically capable of performing as much work or of performing his work as satisfactorily as other employees because of his defective left hand. The fact that Meyers was observed riding in a car with two other employees who waved to a union organizer was not related to the termination of Meyers. The company claimed that Meyers's termination was strictly due to economic reasons, plus the fact that Meyers was not physically capable of carrying out the required job duties.

In the case of employee Jack Tobin, the company claimed that this discharge action was strictly for the attempted theft of the gas cylinder involved in the case. The company claimed that it was clearly against company policy for any employee to have unauthorized private possession of company-owned gas cylinders for private use. There was a communications misunderstanding between Tobin and the office manager concerning the hooking up of the cylinder to his private premises. All of the three cylinders in question should have been returned to the company premises, since they were not being utilized at Tobin's rental property where they had been delivered. Tobin knew that he had no right to hook up the cylinder at his home, but he did so anyway. Consequently, claimed the company, Tobin was discharged for his actions which the company considered to be as "stealing the cylinder," and the discharge was not due to his union activities.

Concerning employee Joyce Dees, the company again claimed that she was discharged for work deficiencies, and not for union activities. Dees had been wasting considerable time talking to employees about the union on company time; she knew she was not permitted to do this. Her discharge was the culmination of various types of poor job performance which had existed over a long period of time. The fact that her discharge came partly as a result of her talking to other employees about the union was because this was "the straw which broke the camel's back." The company further claimed that its statement to Dees regarding closing the business was meant not as a threat, but rather it was a reflection of the fact that increased operating costs associated with a union in its situation might cause the company to go out of business.

The company claimed that it had not violated the LMRA by its various actions and that all of the unfair labor practice charges against it should be dismissed.

QUESTIONS

1. Evaluate the union charges of unfair labor practices concerning each of the three employees. What remedies, if any, should be effected?
2. What is meant by the union's charge of the company's "total pattern of activities" designed to interfere with and discriminate against the union organizing campaign?
3. How can the NLRB determine whether the incidents were isolated or part of a systematic management effort in violation of the law? Discuss.
4. Why must the burden of proof in this case rest upon company management to demonstrate that its actions were for reasons that clearly did not have an antiunion origin?

6. THE PREELECTION POLL CONTEST

Company: Glamorise Foundations, Inc., Williamsport, Pennsylvania

Union: International Ladies' Garment Workers Union, AFL-CIO

BACKGROUND

A representational election was to be held among employees at the Williamsport plant of Glamorise Foundations, Inc. The election was scheduled to be held during the last week of July 1971. On June 30, 1971, about a month before the scheduled election, company management sent a notice to the employees announcing a contest. This contest was one in which employees were invited to guess the number of "no" votes which would be cast in the forthcoming union representational election. Supervisory personnel helped distribute flyers captioned in large letters as follows to employees: "IT IS IMPORTANT TO VOTE. HERE'S A CONTEST TO INTEREST YOU TO VOTE ON ELECTION." Among other things, the flyer also stated, "We all know that the employees will reject the International Ladies' Garment Workers Union. But who can give us the score?" The winning entry was to be identified by a numbered receipt which the employee was to retain, and employees were told that it was not necessary for them to sign their names. The employees were given until the close of the following day to deposit their entries in a box placed near the plant's time clocks. After the end of the next day, the box was sealed, and it was not to be opened until after the election results were known. A $50 U.S. savings bond and a $25 bond were to be given to the two employees who came closest to guessing the total of "no" votes cast in the election.

Upon announcement of this contest, the union immediately protested the contest as being illegally interfering with and trying to influence the outcome of the election.

94

Subsequently, the company decided not to open the sealed box in which the contest entries were placed because a union representative stated at the conclusion of the union representation voting in late July that he was filing objections to the election outcome because of the company-sponsored contest. Management decided to keep the contest entries sealed pending a ruling by the NLRB. The union did lose the election and immediately filed unfair labor practice charges against the company relating to the preelection contest.

POSITION OF THE UNION

The union filed exceptions to the outcome of the election under Section 9(c) of the LMRA, claiming that the company contest was illegal interference in violation of Section 8(a) (1) of the Act. The union claimed that the company contest essentially was a poll of employee sentiment concerning the outcome of the election. This type of poll, in the union's opinion, was a type of straw ballot which was aimed at influencing employees in their decision concerning union representation. Further, the union claimed that the poll was designed to help the company obtain information concerning union sentiments, since employees would talk about the various votes that would be taken, and a general discussion of estimates was sure to come to the attention of the company. The union argued that the poll was a very significant factor in the results of the election, and it requested that the results of the election be set aside and that a new election be held free of any illegal employer interference.

POSITION OF THE COMPANY

The company contended that the contest which it sponsored was not a private poll of employee sentiment. The company claimed that it was merely a type of raffle intended to stimulate interest in the election, and therefore the election should be permitted to stand on its merits. No employee was coerced to participate in the poll, and safeguards were included to guard the identity of any employee until after the actual representational election was held. There was no intent on the part of the company to interfere illegally with the free choice of the employees concerning the matter of union representation. The company claimed that the union was simply using this issue as a means to obtain another election. The company requested that the unfair labor practice charges be dismissed, and that the election results be certified.

QUESTIONS

1. Was the company poll a type of straw ballot aimed at influencing employees in their decision concerning union representation? Why, or why not?

2. Evaluate the union charge that such a poll might help the company obtain information concerning union sentiments, even though the poll itself was secret and results would not be available until after the election.

3. Evaluate the company's argument that the poll was merely a type of raffle, and that the union was simply using the issue as a device to obtain another election.

4. Is there a difference in the legal right of a union to try to measure employee sentiments concerning union representation prior to an election as compared to management's right in this regard? Discuss.

5. If the Board should rule that the company preelection poll was illegal interference, was the interference of sufficient magnitude to justify a new election? Why, or why not?

7. RESTRICTIVE USE OF THE PLANT'S PUBLIC ADDRESS SYSTEM

Company: The Heath Company, a wholly owned subsidiary of Schlumberger Technology Corporation, St. Joseph, Michigan

Union: United Steelworkers of America, AFL-CIO

BACKGROUND

A union representation election was scheduled for October 27, 1970, to be held in the Heath Company plant. The proposed bargaining unit consisted of about 700 production and maintenance employees. A few weeks before the election, the company personnel director prepared a list of about 25 to 35 supervisors and nonbargaining unit employees. An administrator in the personnel department subsequently contacted these individuals for the purpose of tape recording antiunion speeches for broadcast by the company over its public-address system. About a dozen of those individuals contacted agreed to make such speeches for the company. No management representative was present during the 12 separate taping sessions. Although the antiunion talks were monitored before being broadcast by company management, there was no attempt by management to write or otherwise influence the content of the speeches.

Six of the 12 taped speeches were played over the company's plant public-address system on October 22 and 23. They consisted of noncoercive but otherwise favorable testimonials on the company's behalf and against unionization.

All but one of the speechmakers were supervisors within the meaning of Section 2(11) of the LMRA. The exception was Maria Hoover,[1] a nonbargaining unit employee.

After listening during work time to the broadcast of the antiunion speeches over the public-address system in the plant, several employees asked an official of the personnel department whether they

---

[1] The name has been disguised.

could use the system to reply to those testimonials. They were denied access to the system on the ground that only management was entitled to use it. In any event, they were told, other means were available for contacting prounion employees. The employees who asked to use the public-address system were given permission to use the cafeteria during lunch to present the union's case to their fellow employees.

On October 27 the representation election was held. Of the 692 eligible voters in a unit of all production and maintenance workers in the plant, 293 cast valid ballots for, and 355 cast valid ballots against, the union. There were five challenged ballots, and two were void.

Subsequently the union filed unfair labor practice charges, contending that the company had illegally interfered in the election process.

POSITION OF THE UNION

The union contended that the actions of the company constituted interference in violation of Section 8(a) (1) of LMRA. Specifically, the union held that it should not have been denied access to the public-address system to reply to the six antiunion testimonials given over the system by procompany employees. These testimonials, given only several days prior to the election, were, in the union's opinion, very influential in the outcome of the election, which was very close.

The union claimed that the use of the public-address system by the company to present "antiunion propaganda" during work hours to all employees was an unfair advantage. The public-address system should have been made equally available to the union, but the company prohibited such access in violation of the union's rights.

The union also objected to the company's actions in soliciting supervisors and nonbargaining unit employees to deliver the speeches. The union particularly claimed that the company had coerced a nonsupervisory employee, Maria Hoover, to deliver an antiunion speech. This, too, claimed the union, violated Section 8(a) (1) of the Act. For these reasons, the union argued that the results of the representation election should be set aside, that a new representation election should be held, and that the company should be ordered to stop its illegal interference during the period prior to the next election.

POSITION OF THE COMPANY

The company held that it did not engage in illegal preelection conduct in soliciting its supervisors to tape record and broadcast statements over the public-address system. These statements, by the union's admission, were not coercive and did not include any threats or promises of benefit to workers dependent upon the outcome of the union representation election.

The company claimed that it did not exert pressure on Maria Hoover to make the statement, which she agreed to do. Further, her statement was only about a minute in duration, and it could hardly have had any major impact on the outcome of the representation election.

But, primarily, the company claimed that the union had no inherent right to utilize the company's public-address system on an equal basis to reply to the six statements which the union considered to be antiunion. Although it was not required to do so, the company did permit union supporters to use the cafeteria during lunch time to present their views. This afforded reasonable opportunity to union supporters to explain their positions to employees.

The company requested that the unfair labor practice charges be dismissed, and that the results of the representation election be upheld.

QUESTIONS

1. Should the union have been given equal access to the company public-address system to reply to the antiunion statements made by the company supervisory personnel? Why, or why not?
2. Evaluate the union's arguments that the alleged antiunion statements by supervisors were "very influential in the outcome of the election" and constituted an "unfair advantage" to the company side.
3. Was the company guilty of an unfair labor practice in soliciting supervisors and nonbargaining unit employees to deliver the so-called antiunion speeches? Why, or why not?
4. Was the company obligated to permit union supporters to use the cafeteria during the lunchtime to present their prounion views? Did this provide a reasonable balance for the speeches made over the company public-address system by the supervisory and nonbargaining unit personnel?
5. If the NLRB rules that unfair labor practice charges should be upheld, were the violations of sufficient magnitude to justify a new election? Discuss.

8. THE DISCHARGE OF THE NEWLY HIRED EMPLOYEE

Company: L. J. Folkins Company, a Standard Oil Company Distributor, Spokane, Washington

Union: International Brotherhood of Teamsters, Chauffeurs, Warehousemen and Helpers of America

BACKGROUND

The company distributes petroleum products in Spokane, Washington, under contract with Standard Oil of California. On Sunday, February 11, 1973, Al Benton,[1] a delivery route driver who had just quit his job with the company, told his friend Bob Bruckner that there might be a job for the latter if he appeared at the employer's facility the following morning. Bruckner did so, and he was hired.

On the morning of February 12, Bruckner began riding with one of the company's other drivers, Bill Evers. However, shortly after, Evers's truck broke down, and the company manager, Gene Calhoun, told Bruckner to ride with another driver, Alvin Commons. Bruckner spent the balance of the day with this driver, who mentioned a meeting to be held at the union hall that evening.

That evening, Bruckner and three others went to the union hall. The union obtained signed authorization cards from Bruckner and two others. The following day, two union representatives visited company manager Calhoun in his office. They requested recognition of the union as bargaining agent for a unit consisting of five truck drivers employed by the company. They furnished Calhoun with copies of three authorization cards that the union had obtained from among the five truck drivers employed by the company. Company manager Calhoun later asked each employee whose signature appeared on a card if his signature was genuine. Each said it was.

---

[1] The names of all individuals have been disguised.

Bob Bruckner was riding with another driver on February 13. At about noon, Calhoun met Bruckner and told him that he "could see no opening." He explained that it appeared, from information received that morning, that he had just lost a package lubrication contract with the city of Spokane. Further, the "energy crisis" and an attendant limitation of production availability would cause reduced business for the company. Additionally, the truck that had broken down the day before would be "down" for a considerable period. Bruckner was terminated effective at 5:00 P.M.

Subsequently, the union filed unfair labor practice charges against the company claiming that Bob Bruckner had been discharged for signing a union authorization card. The company's action allegedly was in violation of Sections 8(a) (3) and 8(a) (1) of the LMRA.[2]

POSITION OF THE COMPANY

The company argued that its reasons for terminating Bob Bruckner on February 13, 1973, were motivated solely by economic reasons, not because of Bruckner's union status. According to the company, Bruckner was hired as a temporary, not a permanent employee replacement.

Company manager Calhoun claimed that he had agreed to give the newly hired employee a job in anticipation of a warehouse audit to be conducted by Standard Oil of California on February 14. However, a combination of circumstances came to the company's attention on February 12, which necessitated the termination of Bruckner's employment. The company was informed by Standard Oil that the warehouse audit was postponed. Therefore, Bruckner's services in the warehouse would not be needed. The company also learned that day of the loss of a package lubrication contract with the city of Spokane, which was a loss of some 8 percent of the company's anticipated business. The breakdown of one of its trucks made it economically impossible to keep Bruckner on the payroll in any capacity. The overall uncertainty of the energy crisis at this juncture contributed to management's decision to terminate Bruckner, a newly hired employee with only two days of service with the company.

The company argued that the unfair labor practice charges against it should be dismissed, since its motives in this matter were economically justified.

---

[2] Note: The union did not file charges at this time concerning the question of whether the company should be required to recognize the union for purposes of collective bargaining. A representational election subsequent to this incident was later conducted by NLRB.

POSITION OF THE UNION

The union argued that the company had violated Section 8(a) (3), and therefore also Section 8(a) (1) of the Act, by discharging Bob Bruckner. The union claimed that Bruckner had been hired for a permanent position, not as a temporary employee as claimed by the company. Regardless, Bruckner's discharge occurred on the same day that the union demanded recognition and the employer had learned that Bruckner had signed a union card. Since the union had received signed authorization cards from three employees in a proposed five-employee unit, the discharge of one card signer would destroy the union's majority. Bruckner, as the most recently hired employee, was chosen by the company for discharge.

The union argued that the company's reasons alleging that Bruckner was hired on a temporary basis were not persuasive. Bruckner was hired immediately after another driver had quit. Bruckner never worked in the warehouse, but spent all his time accompanying other drivers.

Further, the union claimed that the loss of the city package lubrication contract amounted to a loss of perhaps 1 percent of the employer's business, not the 8 percent indicated by the employer. Regardless, the company knew on February 12, and perhaps earlier, that the loss of this contract was likely.

With respect to the unavailability of the broken-down truck for several days, the union said that a standby truck was ready for use. The postponement of a warehouse audit was irrelevant to the hiring or retention of a truck driver, and the company knew of the "energy crisis" weeks before the new employee was hired.

For all of these reasons, the union claimed that Bob Bruckner really had been discharged because of signing a union authorization card. This discharge was in clear violation of the Act. The union asked that Bruckner be restored to his position with full back pay for the time off that he was illegally discharged.

QUESTIONS

1. Were the company's arguments of economic justification for terminating the new employee persuasive?
2. Why is the timing of the discharge of the new employee of critical significance in determining the company's motives and actions? Discuss.
3. Are temporary employees protected by the provisions of the LMRA? Why, or why not?
4. Although the union apparently did not contest the action, was the company's query of each employee concerning the signatures on the union's organization cards in violation of the LMRA? Why, or why not?

9. DISCHARGE FOR LYING, OR A PRETEXT FOR TERMINATING A UNION ORGANIZER?

Company: Industrial Label Corporation, Omaha, Nebraska
Union: Local No. 520, Graphic Arts Union

BACKGROUND

Martin Dalton[1] worked as a press operator on the company's day shift. The company operated 8 presses; 18 employees worked on the day shift, and 6 employees at night. Dalton was sometimes required to complete press runs on jobs which a night-shift operator had started. On June 19, 1980, a night-shift operator, Alice Higgins, had left a job for Dalton to run. Dalton ran the job, but it was discovered that a significant error had been made, and the run had to be repeated. On the same day, Dalton saw Higgins when she reported for the night shift. She told Dalton that she heard that the morning job had to be rerun. She then asked Dalton if he had obtained supervisory approval to run the job. He responded that he had done so. On the following day, June 20, Dalton was called to President Robert Fishman's office and was asked in the presence of Vice-President Carl Neilson and an office secretary whether he had obtained supervisory approval for the previous day's press run. Dalton acknowledged to Fishman that he had not received supervisory approval. Fishman then asked Dalton whether he had told Higgins that he had received approval. Dalton then admitted that he had lied to Higgins, explaining his action as being prompted by Neilson's earlier caution to avoid arguing with night-shift employees. Fishman then discharged Dalton, stating that his dishonesty violated a company policy and that Dalton had been warned earlier that if he lied again he would be discharged.

---

[1] The names of all individuals have been disguised.

Shortly thereafter, the union filed unfair labor practice charges on behalf of Martin Dalton against the company. The union claimed that Dalton's discharge primarily was motivated by Dalton's union organizing efforts, and his discharge thus violated Sections 8(a) (3) and 8(a) (1) of the Labor Management Relations Act.

POSITION OF THE UNION

The union pointed out that in March 1980, Martin Dalton had openly undertaken a one-person organizing campaign for the union among company employees. Dalton distributed union literature, carried a notebook bearing the union's logo, left the notebook in plain view at his work station, and placed union decals prominently on his automobile. In May 1980, the union formally notified company management that an organizing campaign was underway.

Martin Dalton testified that during his morning break on June 18, 1980, he telephoned the union's president, Otis Strong, from company Vice-President Carl Neilson's office to report on the status of the campaign. Dalton told Strong that based on the number of signed authorization cards, the union would win an election. However, Carl Neilson had come to the doorway of the office, and he overheard Dalton's part of this conversation. Upon being observed by Dalton, Neilson shook his head and walked away. Later that day, Neilson told Dalton to keep the "damn union crap" for his own personal time.

Concerning the incident which the company claimed precipitated his discharge, Martin Dalton testified that his so-called lying to Alice Higgins was in response to a direct order by the company Vice-President, Carl Neilson. Dalton noted that he worked as a day-shift press operator, and Higgins operated the same press during the night shift. In February 1980, they had a very heated argument regarding the cleanliness of their shared work area. Shortly thereafter, Carl Neilson told Dalton to "take any steps necessary" to avoid arguments with Higgins. Dalton did not deny that he told Higgins on June 19, 1980, that he had obtained supervisory approval to run the job in question. But he said that he was just trying to avoid an argument with Higgins as he had been told to do.

The union contended that the real reason why the company discharged Martin Dalton was because of Dalton's union activities. Company management was aware of Dalton's conspicuous union activities and discovered on June 19 that Dalton thought the union could win an election. Dalton was discharged the very next day after the company learned of the apparently successful union campaign.

In the union's view, the company chose to magnify an insignificant event into one of major proportions in order to justify discharge. The so-called lying incident was not the actual reason for the discharge of Dalton. The company was not harmed by Dalton's lie to Higgins. But by claiming that Dalton's lie was in violation of the company's dishonesty policy and of a previous warning, the company seized upon this opportunity to discharge Dalton. This exaggeration of a minor event cast serious doubt as to the company's asserted motivations for the discharge.

In summary, the union claimed that the company had seized upon Dalton's lie to Higgins as a pretext for terminating the chief union organizer among its employees, and thereby violated Sections 8(a) (3) and 8(a) (1) of LMRA.

The union requested that the company be ordered to reinstate Martin Dalton with full back pay and restoration of all benefits, and that the company be ordered to cease and desist in its discriminatory actions and interference with the union organizing efforts.

POSITION OF THE COMPANY

The company maintained that it had discharged Martin Dalton for lying to a fellow employee about a work-related matter, and that this was the third such incident involving dishonesty on Dalton's part.

The company first introduced its employee policy manual—which Dalton acknowledged having received—which specifically included a statement to the effect that "dishonesty" in company matters would be considered an automatic ground for dismissal.

Company President Robert Fishman testified that he had had two prior confrontations with Dalton involving dishonest statements. In July 1976, Dalton was accused of lying about the nature of certain work instructions previously given to him by a supervisor. Since the company could not definitely determine who was lying, Fishman only warned Dalton that he would be disciplined if the company later determined that he had lied.

In December 1979, Dalton suffered a back injury and was hospitalized. The attending physician recommended that Dalton rest for 8 to 10 weeks before returning to work. Fishman requested that Dalton seek a second opinion from his own personal physician. Dalton consulted a local clinic physician, who confirmed the original diagnosis. Dalton then reported this information to Fishman but presented it as the opinion of his own doctor. Fishman, however, spoke to Dalton's personal physician and determined that Dalton was lying. He confronted Dalton with this knowledge. After some discussion, Fishman told Dalton that he would be terminated if he ever lied about a company matter again.

The lying incident by Dalton on June 19, 1980, was in the company's view, sufficient ground in itself for terminating Dalton. But when he terminated Dalton on June 20, Fishman reminded Dalton that he had been warned twice before about lying, and he was being discharged for his cumulative acts of dishonesty which represented direct violations of company policy.

The company maintained that it had the right to discharge Dalton for his repeated dishonesty which could no longer be tolerated, and that this discharge action had nothing to do with Dalton's union organizing activities. The company urged that the unfair labor practice charges filed by the union should be dismissed in their entirety.

QUESTIONS

1. Was the company's discharge action taken upon Martin Dalton justified, or was it a pretext to terminate a union organizer in violation of LMRA? Discuss.

2. Was Martin Dalton's past record relevant to conclude that his cumulative pattern of "dishonesty" justified his termination? Discuss.

3. Why is it difficult for the NLRB to determine the employer's true motive in a situation of this sort?

4. Compare the issues in this case with those in Case 13, "Suspension for Absenteeism, or Retaliation for Union Activities and Giving Testimony?"

10. THE UNION'S DEMAND FOR RECOGNITION AND BARGAINING RIGHTS

Company: First Lakewood Associates, Chicago, Illinois

Union: Janitors Union, Local 1

BACKGROUND

The employer owned and managed an apartment building and townhouse complex where it employed a number of janitorial workers. On December 5, 1975, the union held an organizing meeting with these workers and obtained signed authorization cards from 6 of the employees in a proposed unit of 11 employees. One other employee in the unit was already a member of the union. On December 8, 1975, Orval Schimmel,[1] a union organizer, advised Thomas Hall, the employer's property manager, that the union represented a majority of the employer's janitorial employees and requested recognition and bargaining rights. Hall responded that he had nothing to do with union matters, and that the appropriate person with whom to speak was vice president Carl Alton.

On December 8, 1975, after the union had first requested recognition, maintenance supervisor Larry Melton telephoned employee George Thompson at his home and asked if any union people had contacted him. Thompson replied that none had. The next morning Melton entered the maintenance office where the janitorial employees reported for work and asked employee Alice Coleman, "What has the union done to you?" Coleman did not reply. Melton then entered his own office and called in employee Theo Ewing. Melton told Ewing that he knew that the employees had brought in an organizer and wanted to organize a union. He then asked Ewing if he attended the meeting and if he knew who sent for the organizer.

---

[1] The names of all individuals have been disguised.

When Ewing denied attending the meeting and any knowledge about who sent for the organizer, Melton repeated the questions and told Ewing not to sign anything or talk to any organizer and to keep him informed of any such activities.

On the evening of December 9, 1975, Melton again telephoned George Thompson and asked whether he had spoken to any union people. Thompson admitted that he had, but refused to offer any further information. Melton continued to question him about why he was doing this and who attended the meeting. After several unsuccessful attempts to elicit additional information, Melton said to Thompson, "You are either on my side of the fence or your side of the fence. . . . You always had it good. I have given you . . . you got a nice job, you got an apartment. . . . This is your last chance." Thompson still refused to answer.

That same evening, December 9, Melton telephoned Gloria Greer, another employee, and asked why she had not told him about the union meeting. Greer denied knowledge of the meeting. Melton then telephoned Ewing and then asked who brought in the organizer. He repeatedly attempted to elicit this information, but Ewing said he did not know. Melton ended the conversation by telling Ewing to keep his ears and eyes open and to let him know if he heard anything. He also told him not to sign anything.

On December 10, 1975, Melton called Al Holt, an employee, into his office and asked, "So you want to join the union, huh?" Holt responded, "Who told you that?" Melton said, "The union man." Holt then left, and Melton called in Cecil Snow and asked him if he had joined the union. Snow responded that it was none of his business. Melton told him that he just wanted him to know that there were no hard feelings, and that he would probably do the same thing if he were in Snow's position.

On December 24, 1975, supervisor Larry Melton was terminated by the company, and he was replaced by Leo Nord. At about this same time, the company announced that it was improving its sickness and health benefits program for employees, including a new benefit to cover maternity medical expenses for employees and/or their spouses.

On January 30, 1976, the morning of the representational election, supervisor Leo Nord told employee Cecil Snow that if the union won the election, the employer would take the rent-free apartments away from the janitors' helpers, and charge the head janitors for the second bedroom in their apartments.

On January 30, 1976, the union lost the representation election 6 to 4. The union filed numerous unfair labor practices charges, claiming that these violations had dissipated the union's majority status as established by the authorization cards. These violations, in the union's view, were so serious and widespread that they made a fair rerun election unlikely. The union requested that the company be ordered to recognize the union and bargain with the union on the basis of the union majority previously established by the signed authorization cards, which it had secured in early December 1975.

POSITION OF THE UNION

The union filed unfair labor practice charges against the company, claiming that the company had violated Section 8(a) (1) of the LMRA by:

    (a) repeatedly interrogating employees concerning their union activities;
    (b) threatening employees with deprivation of benefits if the union should be selected to represent them;
    (c) threatening an employee for refusing to reveal the identities of employees who attended a union meeting;
    (d) informing an employee that it knew (or heard) that the employee had joined the union;
    (e) promising to pay and paying employees for certain medical benefits to discourage them from supporting the union.

The union urged that the company should be found in violation of the Act accordingly and ordered to cease and desist in these practices. Further, because the company's violations were so severe and pervasive, a valid union majority status had been dissipated, and it would be impossible to have a fair rerun election in the climate created by the company's actions. The union requested that the company should be ordered by the NLRB to recognize the union's majority status as of December 8, 1975, and to bargain with the union as the authorized representative of a bargaining unit of janitorial employees.

POSITION OF THE COMPANY

The company presented a number of contentions in urging that the union's unfair labor practice charges be dismissed.

First of all, company management claimed that it was unaware of the telephone calls and other questioning of employees conducted by former supervisor Larry Melton. Regardless, most of Melton's statements and questions to employees were not coercive, but they were legitimate inquiries necessary to determine whether the union had the majority status which it claimed. Melton never specifically threatened employee George Thompson on December 9; his statement to Thompson was very vague and inconclusive in nature.

Concerning the granting of improved sickness and health benefits in late December 1975, the company contended that these improved benefits were part of the company's annual review of its benefit program. The company announced the benefit change to coincide with the Christmas season, and this had nothing to do with the union representational campaign.

The company pointed out that supervisor Larry Melton was terminated by the company on December 24, 1975, and the election was not held until January 30, 1976. Thus Melton's influence on the election, if any, had "totally evaporated" and was no longer a factor. The statement of new supervisor Leo Nord to employee Cecil Snow on that day did not constitute a threat, but it was a legitimate prediction and Nord's own personal opinion concerning what unionization logically would bring to the company. This was "free speech" protected by Section 8(c) of the Act.

Finally the company claimed that even if the Board held that the company had violated the Act in any way, such violations were minor and did not influence the outcome of the representational election, which the union lost. The union's claim to a majority status in December 1975, based on signed authorization cards, was never accepted by the company or verified by the NLRB. The union was promulgating unfair labor practice charges against the company in an effort to gain representational rights after losing an NLRB election. The election was a true determination of the majority of the employees' feelings, and the Board should allow the results of the election to stand.

QUESTIONS

1. Evaluate the various claims made by the union and counterclaims made by the company regarding the unfair labor practice charges. Which of the arguments are most persuasive?

2. Was the statement of supervisor Nord to employee Snow on the date of the representational election a threat or a legitimate prediction and personal opinion protected by the free speech provisions of the Act?

3. Was the company obligated to accept the union's majority status claim based on authorization cards submitted by the union?

4. If the company is found to have violated the Act, what would be the appropriate remedy, a bargaining order or a new election?

11. WAS THE FRANCHISE BARBECUE RESTAURANT IN INTERSTATE COMMERCE UNDER THE ACT?

Company: Love's Barbecue Restaurant, Hayward, California, and Love's Enterprises, Inc.

Union: Hotel, Motel, and Restaurant Employees and Bartenders Union, Local 50

BACKGROUND

Love's Enterprises operated and franchised a number of restaurants on the west coast. In December 1973, Love's Enterprises took over the direct operation of a Hayward, California, restaurant from a prior franchise operator. Earlier in 1973, a memorandum agreement had been signed between the Hayward restaurant franchise operator and Culinary Workers and Bartenders Union, Local 823, of the Hotel and Restaurant Employees and Bartenders International Union, AFL-CIO. Under the terms of this agreement, the restaurant agreed to recognize Local 823 as the sole collective bargaining representative for a bargaining unit to consist of "all employees at the Hayward restaurant engaged in the preparation, handling, and serving of food and/or beverages, excluding office clerical employees, guards, and supervisors as defined in the Act." The agreement also provided that: "The Employer agrees to accept, adopt, and observe all of the wages, hours, and other terms and conditions of employment contained in the Collective Bargaining Agreement between the Union and the East Bay Restaurant Association, Inc., California Licensed Beverage Association, Inc., or its successors" as well as "the Restaurant and Tavern Health Fund Trust Agreement, the Southern Alameda County Restaurant and Tavern Pension Trust Agreement, the health and pension plans established thereunder, and all amendments to said Trust Agreements and plans." When Love's Enterprises took over the Hayward restaurant in December 1973, the Hayward restaurant continued to adhere to the memorandum agreement with the union.

110

In 1975, by virtue of a merger of three unions, Local 50 of the Hotel, Motel, and Restaurant Employees and Bartenders Union succeeded Local 823 and became the Hayward employees' collective bargaining representative.

On September 26, 1977, Love's Enterprises closed its Hayward restaurant and terminated all of the employees who had been working there. On October 20, Lester Coleman[1] opened the Hayward restaurant for business under a franchise agreement, equipment lease, and real property sublease with Love's Enterprises. Coleman operated the restaurant as Love's had done using the same equipment for the same customer market at the same location under the name, "Love's Barbecue Restaurant." Coleman, however, did not hire any of the employees who previously had been employed by Love's at Hayward. Nor did he recognize the union or adhere to the memorandum agreement. Instead, Coleman began nonunion operations with an entirely new complement of approximately 30 employees. On October 21 the union commenced picketing at the Hayward restaurant to protest the restaurant's failure to reemploy any of the former employees and its failure to recognize the union as the collective bargaining representative.

Subsequently, the union filed unfair labor practice charges against Love's (Hayward) Barbecue Restaurant and its parent, Love's Enterprises, Inc., claiming that the company had violated Sections 8(a) (1), 8(a) (3), and 8(a) (5) of the LMRA.

POSITION OF THE UNION

The union first of all claimed that when Lester Coleman reopened on a franchise basis Love's (Hayward) Barbecue Restaurant on October 20, 1977, this in fact was a successor employer to the restaurant which had been operated directly by Love's Enterprises, Inc. All of the factors which the NLRB has determined for finding successorship were present here except for the fact that former employees of the restaurant were not retained. The Board has also ruled, however, that successorship exists in such circumstances if the new owner fails to hire a predecessor's employees because of their affiliation or possible affiliation with a union.[2] In the union's view, Lester Cole-

---

[1] The names of all individuals have been disguised.

[2] According to a number of NLRB precedent decisions, an employer who purchases or otherwise acquires the operations of another may be obligated to recognize and bargain with the union which represented the employees before the business was transferred. In general, these bargaining obligations exist—and the purchaser is termed a *successor employer*—where there is a substantial continuity in the employing enterprise despite the sale

(continued on next page)

man refused to hire the former employees of Love's Hayward restaurant for discriminatory reasons.

The union presented evidence to show that after entering into the franchise agreement with Love's Enterprises, Lester Coleman reserved two rooms at the Vagabond Motel, located several miles away from the Hayward restaurant, to be used for interviewing job applicants. He placed advertisements in the *Oakland Tribune* and the *Hayward Daily Review* which stated that a "new restaurant" was hiring and that applications should be made in person at the Vagabond Motel. The name of the restaurant did not appear in the advertisements. Coleman conducted interviews at the motel for two and a half days starting on October 12, and he subsequently hired 30 individuals through this process who had never worked at Love's Hayward restaurant previously. In the union's view, this entire hiring procedure was carefully calculated to virtually ensure that former Hayward union employees would not know about the job interviews.

To further support its claim that in hiring an all-new employee work force Coleman was motivated by discriminatory intentions against former union employees, the union cited a number of specific instances:

a. When former union employees began picketing at the restaurant, Coleman had an assistant manager take pictures of every union picket. The union claimed that this was illegal surveillance.

b. Several of these persons did fill out application forms for jobs. Coleman told one of them, former waitress Mary Peters, "If you put down your picket sign, we might rehire you at your old job. But this restaurant will be nonunion." Two others, George Pranschke and Carlos Kuvacka, applied for cook positions which they formerly held. Coleman told both of them that he might be able to offer them jobs "at some future date" but only as a busboy or as a dishwasher. The union claimed that this was designed to discourage Pranschke, Kuvacka, and other former union employees from seeking positions at their former job

---

and transfer of the business. Whether the purchaser is a successor employer is dependent on several factors, including the number of employees taken over by the purchasing employer, the similarity in operations and product of the two employers, the manner in which the purchaser integrates the purchased operations into its other operations, and the character of the bargaining relationship and agreement between the union and the original employer. See the following precedent cases: *NLRB v. Burns International Security Service,* 406 U.S. 272 (1972), and *Potter's Drug Enterprises, Inc. d/b/a Potter's Chalet Drug and Potter's Westpark Drug,* 233 NLRB No. 15 (1977).

levels which they had held or achieved through prior union seniority.

c. Coleman was heard on one occasion to remark to several union pickets, "I had a choice to make, and I chose to operate non-union."

In summary, the Union claimed that by (1) expressing his intention not to have the union in his restaurant, (2) unlawfully photographing union pickets, (3) conducting his initial job interviews under conditions which virtually ensured that most former union Hayward employees would not know of the interviews, and (4) avoiding hiring former Hayward employees because of their affiliation with the union, Coleman and his company had violated Section 8(a) (3) of the Act by refusing to hire the former Hayward employees of Love's. Further, these employees had been represented by the union in an appropriate unit. If it were not for this unlawful conduct, the union's status as the exclusive collective bargaining representative would have survived Coleman's takeover of the Love's (Hayward) restaurant. This, together with Coleman's continued operation of the restaurant at the same location and in substantially the same manner as before, made the restaurant under Coleman a legal successor with respect to the company's bargaining obligation to the union. Thus, the union claimed that Coleman and Love's (Hayward) restaurant had violated Sections 8(a) (5) and 8(a) (1) of the Act by disavowing the company's bargaining obligation to the union.

The union requested that all former Hayward employees be reinstated to their former jobs and be made whole for all lost pay and benefits with full previous seniority rights. Further, the union requested that the company should be ordered to recognize the union as the employees' bargaining representative and to bargain with the union as it would have if the union's lawful status had been acknowledged on October 20, 1977.

POSITION OF THE COMPANY

Lester Coleman, in denying that he and the company had engaged in unfair labor practices, offered a number of explanations accordingly.

First of all, he claimed that when he franchised the Hayward restaurant, he felt he could not operate it profitably unless he had a new complement of employees. Since he was under no legal obligation to hire the former Hayward personnel employed by Love's Enterprises, he decided to interview all new people whom he could hire at an acceptable wage level and whom he could train the way he wished. In fact, Coleman had been informed by several managers of Love's Enterprises that the Hayward restaurant had been closed down in September 1977 for economic reasons, including the high wage rates being paid to the union employees.

When the former union employees began picketing the restaurant, he ordered their pictures taken in case there was trouble and disruptive behavior which might require calling the police.

Coleman stated that he had been reluctant to hire former Hayward employees, such as Pranschke and Kuvacka, into their old jobs because the kitchen when he took over the restaurant was dirty and in disorder, which reflected the old employees' poor job attitudes.

Coleman could not recollect making the statements which the union alleged he made to Mary Peters and several other union pickets. Even if he had made these type statements, they were "isolated" in nature, and they had occurred after he had hired an entirely new complement of employees. Because his work force was entirely new and these new employees had not expressed a preference for or voted for a union to represent them, Coleman claimed that he had no legal obligation to bargain with the previous union. That union only represented employees who had been dismissed by the previous operation of the restaurant, that is, Love's Enterprises, Inc.

Regardless, counsel for the company claimed that the entire set of unfair labor practice charges should be declared moot, because Love's Barbecue Restaurant in Hayward, California, was not engaged in interstate commerce at the time the charges were filed. The NLRB's standard to claim jurisdiction over a retail enterprise is gross annual sales of over $500,000.[3] In the previous year of operations under Love's Enterprises, the Hayward restaurant did have gross sales in excess of $500,000. But in the first year of operation under Coleman's franchise arrangement, gross sales at the Hayward restaurant were projected to be under the $500,000 level. Coleman testified that he attributed this drop in revenue in part due to the union's picketing which had interfered with his business to some degree.

In summary, the company denied committing unfair labor practices. But even if the NLRB should find on behalf of the union position, the NLRB had no jurisdiction over a restaurant which in the applicable period was not engaged in interstate commerce under the NLRB's standards for interstate determination.

---

[3] This is required under Sections 2(6) and 2(7) of LMRA. See footnote 4 on pages 7 and 8 in the Introduction to the LMRA for a list of NLRB jurisdictional standards.

QUESTIONS

1. At the time of the unfair labor practice charges, was the restaurant in interstate commerce within the meaning of the LMRA? Why, or why not?

   On the assumption that the NLRB would claim jurisdiction in this case:

2. Was Lester Coleman obligated under the Act to hire all, some, or none of the former unionized Hayward employees? Why is the answer to this question crucial in regard to determination of the employer's motivations (i.e., discriminatory or nondiscriminatory intent)?

3. Evaluate the union's contentions and proposed remedies.

4. Evaluate Coleman and the restaurant's explanations in urging the Board to dismiss the unfair labor practice charges.

5. Compare the issue of "successorship" in this case with that involved in Case 14, "Was the Picketing to Protect Jobs, or for Recognition by a 'Successor' Employer?"

12. DISCHARGE FOR FAILURE TO PAY UNION DUES

Company: R. H. Macy & Co., Inc., Bronx, New York

Union: Local 3, International Brotherhood of Electrical Workers

Individual: Alan Gomez[1]

BACKGROUND

Since 1978 until his discharge on January 8, 1981, Alan Gomez had been employed by Macy's as an electrician. In that capacity, Gomez was covered by a collective bargaining agreement containing a union security clause. This clause required that, as a condition of employment, all bargaining unit employees become and remain members of the union after 30 days of employment. As the contract did not contain a dues-checkoff provision, unit employees submitted their dues directly to the union. From April 1978 to September 1979, Gomez paid his dues on a quarterly basis. However, because of personal financial difficulties, Gomez did not remit any dues for the last quarter of 1979, and until December 17, 1980, he had remitted no dues for any quarter period in 1980.

In late December 1980, Gomez feared that he might be discharged pursuant to the terms of the union security agreement if he did not correct his union dues delinquency. On December 17, 1980, Gomez forwarded a check to the union for $252.80 covering dues owed for the four quarters of 1980; he believed that this amount was all he owed the union. However, Gomez had not paid dues for the last quarter of 1979, and he was therefore still in arrears for that quarter.

On December 22, 1980, the union's executive board met to discuss the dues status of various members, including that of Gomez. A form letter dated December 30, 1980, was thereafter mailed out to

---

[1] The names of all individuals have been disguised.

Gomez advising him that he had been listed as a "ceased" member,[2] and that if he wished to remain a member he would have to pay the sum of $66.70 which represented dues owed for the last quarter of 1979, plus a reinstatement fee of $30. According to the letter, such payments would assure him "good standing in the union until December 31, 1980." Gomez did not receive that letter until several days after the December 30 date. Upon receipt of the letter, Gomez (believing that his dues had been brought up to date by his December 17 check) phoned the union office. After questioning the contents of the union's letter, Gomez was told that if he paid the amount stated in the letter, he would no longer be a "ceased" member but would be reinstated.

However, prior to this on December 22, 1980, George Hulser, a Macy's manager, had informed Macy's Vice President for Labor Relations Bernice Wambles that Union Business Representative Tony Mataya had requested that Gomez be discharged for failing to pay union dues for a long period of time. Wambles advised Hulser that such a request must be in writing. Thereafter, a letter dated December 26, 1980, and signed by Mataya was mailed to Wambles stating that according to the union's records Gomez was not a member in good standing having failed to pay his dues since September, 1979; the union requested that Gomez be discharged from his position as of the date of this letter. Wambles did not receive this letter until January 5, 1981.

Upon receipt of the union's letter, Wambles reviewed the collective bargaining agreement to insure that the union's request for Gomez' discharge was proper. After doing so, she notified Macy's Personnel Manager Alice Kelso of Gomez' apparent dues delinquency and instructed that in accordance with the union-security agreement Gomez should be discharged. On January 8, 1981, Kelso summoned Gomez into her office, and informed him that at the union's request, he was being terminated for failing to pay dues as required under the union contract. Although Gomez protested that a mistake had been made, he was advised by Kelso that he would have to take the matter up with the union. Gomez responded that the union was out to get him because of an earlier discrimination suit he had filed against the union concerning job assignments.

Immediately after leaving Kelso's office, Gomez went directly to the union's office where he tendered a check postdated for the

---

[2] A member was classified as "ceased" when his dues were in arrears for six months or more. A "lapsed" member was one whose dues were in arrears for only three months. Although a lapsed member was still considered a union member, a ceased member was not.

following day, January 9, 1981, in the amount of $225 covering the amount requested by the union in the December 30 letter plus an advance payment of dues for two additional quarters. Gomez then returned to Kelso's office later that afternoon in an effort to get reinstated, but he was denied reinstatement because of his failure to produce a receipt indicating his union dues had been paid.

Subsequently, Alan Gomez filed charges with the NLRB against the company alleging a discriminatory discharge in violation of Sections 8(a) (3) and 8(a) (1) of the Labor Management Relations Act. Gomez filed similar charges against the union alleging violations of Sections 8(b) (1) (A) and 8(b) (2) of the Act.

While these charges were still being litigated, Gomez was reinstated to his former position in late May 1981.

POSITION OF ALAN GOMEZ

Although Alan Gomez acknowledged that he had fallen behind some 15 months in his dues payments to the union, his failure to make any payments during that period did not result from a willful and deliberate attempt on his part to avoid his financial obligations to the union. Rather, his failure to keep up with his payments resulted from his personal financial difficulties and by the union's own inattention to the matter. On his own initiative, Gomez had mailed a check to the union, before any request for his discharge had been made, in an amount which he in good faith, but erroneously, believed was sufficient to cover all of his dues obligations. Gomez claimed that his failure to include his dues for the last quarter of 1979 in his December 17, 1980, check did not result from an intentional act, but from a lack of knowledge as to the extent of his dues delinquency which primarily was the fault of the union.

Alan Gomez claimed that by failing to inform him specifically of his 1979 dues obligations and by failing to give him an opportunity to clear up his dues account prior to seeking his discharge, the union had discriminated against him in violation of Sections 8(b) (1) (A) and 8(b) (2) of the LMRA. In part, Gomez felt that the union was retaliating against him for his having filed an employment discrimination suit against the union a year or so previous, a suit which he subsequently dropped. And since the company had unlawfully discharged him based upon the request of the union, the company too, had violated Sections 8(a) (3) and 8(a) (1) of the Act. Alan Gomez requested that his discharge of January 8, 1981, should be rescinded, and that he should be made whole by the union and/or the company for the period that he was terminated until his reinstatement.

POSITION OF THE COMPANY

The company claimed that it simply acted on the request of the union to terminate Alan Gomez for his failure to pay dues as required by the collective bargaining agreement. The company had no reasonable basis whatsoever to believe that the union's request was either improper or unlawful. The union's dues problem with Alan Gomez was an internal union matter. If there was anything unlawful about what happened, it was the union's total responsibility, not the company's. The company requested that the unfair labor practice charges filed against the company by Alan Gomez should be dismissed.

POSITION OF THE UNION

The union argued that it had the right both under its collective bargaining agreement with the company and under Section 8(b) (2) of the LMRA to request the company to terminate Alan Gomez for his failure to pay all of his delinquent union dues. Although Gomez did make an effort to pay most of his delinquent dues at the end of 1980, he still owed dues for the last quarter of 1979 when the union made its request to the company to have Gomez terminated. Gomez had been a "free rider" for a long period of time, and the union could not overlook his dues delinquency any longer. The union requested that the unfair labor practice charges filed against the union by Alan Gomez should be dismissed.

QUESTIONS

1. Evaluate the company's position that it simply acted upon the union's request to discharge Alan Gomez for his failure to pay union dues. Does a valid union shop clause in a negotiated labor agreement absolve the company of any responsibility in this matter?
2. Evaluate the union's position that it had the right to request Alan Gomez' discharge both under the labor contract and within the provisions of LMRA, even though Gomez did pay most of the dues he owed.
3. Was Alan Gomez discriminated against in violation of the Act? If so, by the company, the union, or both?
4. Regardless of the NLRB's findings concerning the discrimination charges, why is a case such as this "embarrassing" to both the company and the union?

13. SUSPENSION FOR ABSENTEEISM, OR RETALIATION FOR UNION ACTIVITIES AND GIVING TESTIMONY?

Company: Best Products Company, Sacramento, California

Union: Local 588, Retail Clerks International Association

BACKGROUND

Best Products Company, a Virginia corporation, was a nationwide showroom merchandiser with two locations in the Sacramento area. In the summer of 1975, authorization cards for local 588 Retail Clerks International Association were distributed to employees of both Sacramento, California showrooms. Subsequently, the union filed a petition for elections at both locations in September 1975. Employee Sally Hong[1] participated in the solicitation of cards and in the election campaigns on behalf of the union. On November 21, 1975, elections were held at both Sacramento showrooms. The union lost both elections. On December 1 of that year, the union filed post-election objections. In March 1976, hearings on those objections were held at a regional office of the NLRB. Sally Hong was present and testified at those hearings. On June 10, 1976, the NLRB's hearing officer issued a report sustaining certain objections, recommending that the November 21st elections be set aside and ordering subsequent elections for each showroom. In October of 1976, the Board adopted the hearing officer's report. However, the union subsequently withdrew its request for second elections, and the elections were never held.

During the fall of 1976, Sally Hong was frequently absent from work. During an approximate three month period, she missed 13 full days and 4 partial days of work. These absences were primarily due to illness, and they occurred during the company's peak work pe-

---

[1] The names of all individuals have been disguised.

riod. The months of October, November, and December are the industry's busiest time of year due to the holiday season. Approximately 50 percent of Best's annual business occurs during those three months.

On January 10, 1977, Showroom Manager Estelle Laclede called Sally Hong into her office and read to Hong the following statement:

SUBJECT: EXCESSIVE ABSENTEEISM

COMMENTS: For the past 3 months your absenteeism has been exceptionally high again this year as it was the previous year during the same time period. This imposes a severe burden upon your department and the showroom in general. We hereby are directing you to take a two month leave of absence to hopefully restore you to good health.

Leave to commence 1-10-77

Leave to terminate 3-10-77

Two days later, a statement was read to other employees of the Best showroom stating that Sally Hong had taken a leave of absence for health reasons.

Subsequently, Sally Hong and the union filed unfair labor practice charges against the company. They claimed that her two month suspension was in retaliation for her union activities and for her giving testimony at an NLRB hearing. Such retaliation was in violation of Sections 8(a) (3), 8(a) (4), and 8(a) (1) of LMRA.

POSITION OF THE UNION

The union claimed that the real motive for the company's suspending Sally Hong was that she had been a union activist who was openly involved in the union's representational campaign. Sally Hong had testified and participated in an NLRB hearing which resulted in the company's being found guilty of unfair labor practices during the union's representational campaign. Among the conclusions of a Board hearing officer was that the company had shown a "general antiunion animus" and had engaged in unfair labor practices including asking employees to remove union buttons while in the showroom area, questioning employees regarding union activities, and discriminatorily enforcing a no-solicitation rule.

Sally Hong's testimony was significant in this Board hearing, which resulted in an NLRB order setting aside the results of the elections (which the company had won).

In the union's view, the company's past record coupled with the timing of the disciplinary action taken upon Sally Hong supported the conclusion that the suspension was primarily motivated by retaliation for Hong's union activities, and not for absenteeism. The union requested that the company be ordered to remove the suspension action, to make her whole for lost earnings, and to cease and desist in discriminatory unfair labor practices.

POSITION OF THE COMPANY

The company first presented evidence to show that Sally Hong had been frequently absent from work during the fall of 1975 for which she had been given a written warning for "excessive absenteeism." The company next showed that Hong's rate of absenteeism was the highest for any employee during the fall 1976 period. Company evidence further was introduced which showed that disciplinary action was common in cases such as Hong's. The previous year, another employee was terminated after absences of 15 days. Other employees were routinely given warnings or suspensions when their absenteeism reached 10 days or so. Hong had not been treated differently than other employees who had unsatisfactory attendance records.

The company argued strongly that Sally Hong's two month suspension was intended as a "leave of absence" for her to recuperate from any illness and to have her health restored. The company did not single her out for disparate, discriminatory treatment. Hong's absenteeism record during fall of 1976 was intolerable, and the company could not afford to have any employee continue such an attendance pattern without taking efforts to correct it.

The company maintained that the union's unfair labor practice charges were frivolous. The company had suspended Sally Hong for a terrible and unacceptable absenteeism record; this action was within its management judgment and for sound business reasons. The union's unfair labor practice charges should be dismissed.

QUESTIONS

1. Why is it difficult for the NLRB to establish an employer's true motivation in a case of this type?
2. Should the employer's previous record of unfair labor practices during the union representational campaign be considered as a directly relevant factor in regard to its actions toward Sally Hong? Why, or why not?
3. Was the two months' suspension of Sally Hong for absenteeism a legitimate management/business decision, or discrimination against Hong for union activism and testifying in an NLRB hearing? Discuss.
4. Compare the issues in this case with Case 9, "Discharge for Lying, or a Pretext for Terminating a Union Organizer?"

14. WAS THE PICKETING TO PROTECT JOBS, OR FOR RECOGNITION BY A "SUCCESSOR" EMPLOYER?

Company: Don Davis Pontiac, Tonawanda, New York

Union: United Automobile, Aerospace and Agricultural Implement Workers of America, and Its Amalgamated Local 55 (to be referred to as UAW)

BACKGROUND

The company operated an automobile dealership located on Bailey Avenue in Buffalo, New York, until June 11, 1976. At this location, some 20 service employees were represented by the UAW. The company's collective bargaining agreement with the UAW expired on March 20, 1976, but was renewed on a day-to-day basis during negotiations for a new contract thereafter until May 19, 1976. On that day, the company's final contractual offer was rejected by the union negotiators, and the UAW commenced picketing the Bailey Avenue location with signs bearing the legends: "UAW ON STRIKE FOR JUSTICE" and "UAW ON STRIKE FOR EQUITY." A strike followed at midnight, May 19, 1976.

Because of declining business conditions for some months—at least since November 7, 1975—the company had been considering the sale of the Bailey Avenue dealership and the acquisition of another which was acceptable to the Pontiac Motor Division of General Motors Corporation. In April 1976 the company was advised by Pontiac that the Al Ives Pontiac dealership in Tonawanda, New York, would probably be available, and that the company would be considered as a candidate for the purchase of that dealership. Subsequent negotiations between the managements of the Davis and Ives dealerships were substantially completed on May 20, 1976. On the day prior thereto, May 19, 1976, the company notified the UAW by letter that "we are contemplating a decision to terminate our Bailey Avenue shop operations for economic reasons."

As part of the purchase agreement with Ives, and as a condition

123

precedent imposed at the insistence of Ives, the company was required to retain all of the Ives employees, including the unit represented by Auto Mechanics Lodge 1053 of District 76, International Association of Machinists and Aerospace Workers (IAM), AFL-CIO, and to assume the IAM contract in its entirety. Likewise, the company agreed to purchase the Ives inventory, its equipment, fixed assets, and goodwill, along with assuming all of the Ives's liabilities. The IAM had been certified as the exclusive bargaining representative of all service employees at the Ives place of business on October 14, 1975, and a collective bargaining agreement, effective February 4, 1976, continuing until February 4, 1979, was outstanding. Some 16 service employees were in the IAM bargaining unit at this time.

In response to the company's letter of May 19, the UAW advised that there was no purpose in meeting to discuss the situation, as "the closing or termination of your shop operations is solely your decision to make;" but the UAW nevertheless reserved the right to negotiate the effects of that decision.

On June 3, 1976, the company notified the UAW that it had decided to terminate the business effective June 11, 1976, but invited the UAW "to meet and discuss with you the effects of our decision." On June 14, the purchase from Ives was finalized. On the following day, June 15, 1976, the company commenced operations at the Tonawanda location, which was situated about 15 miles from the Bailey Avenue location. Also, the company and the IAM executed an agreement on June 15, 1976, carrying into effect the recognition of the existing labor agreement between Ives and IAM.

The next day, June 16, 1976, pursuant to prior telephone conversations, the company's vice president and its attorney went to the offices of UAW and met with representatives of the Local and International. The UAW was notified that operations had been terminated at the Bailey Avenue location, that the company had acquired the Ives operations on Niagara Falls Boulevard in Tonawanda; and that an agreement had been signed with IAM pursuant to the company's obligation to assume under the buy-sell agreement with Ives. A discussion was held regarding the nature of the closing of Bailey Avenue operations and whether the UAW was going to picket the Niagara Falls Boulevard operation. The UAW requested the company to hire UAW members on a preferential basis. The company attorney said that they would be considered on a nondiscriminatory basis without preferential treatment.

UAW picketing with the same legends on the signs continued at the Bailey Avenue location until June 26, although the company had closed its operations at the end of the day on June 11. On June 21, 1976, the UAW commenced picketing the Tonawanda site, again with the same legends on the signs. On June 28, by letter, the UAW made an offer to return to work at the Tonawanda facility.

The letter of June 28 stated in part:

> The Union is terminating the strike and all striking employees are ready and willing to return to work unconditionally on Tuesday morning at 8:00 A.M., June 29, 1976.

No picketing took place on June 29; but in response to the company's denial of the union offer, picketing was resumed on June 30 with picket signs carrying the legend: LOCAL 55 PROTESTS THE REFUSAL OF DAVIS PONTIAC, INC., TO REEMPLOY ITS MEMBERS.

Picketing continued until July 19 when the regional office of the NLRB requested a U.S. District Court to issue a preliminary injunction against the UAW's picketing at the Tonawanda premises.

This injunction was in response to company charges of unfair labor practices filed against the UAW, as well as the UAW's unfair labor practice charges against the company.

THE UNFAIR LABOR PRACTICE CHARGES

On June 30, 1976, the company filed unfair labor practice charges against the union, which specified in part:

> Since on or about June 21, 1976, and continuously thereafter, it, a labor organization, by its officers, agents, and representatives, has picketed Al Ives Pontiac (now Don Davis Pontiac, Inc.) at its premises at 2277 Niagara Falls Boulevard, Town of Tonawanda, New York, with an object of forcing or requiring Don Davis Pontiac, Inc., to recognize or bargain with United Automobile, Aerospace and Agricultural Implement Workers of America, and its Amalgamated Local 55, as the representative of his employees notwithstanding that District No. 76, International Association of Machinists and Aerospace Workers, AFL-CIO, has been certified on October 14, 1975, and a question concerning representation may not appropriately be raised under Section 9(c) of the Act.

The company requested that the UAW be ordered to cease and desist in its picketing and in its efforts to force the company to recognize and negotiate with the UAW.

On July 6, 1976, the UAW filed a petition for certification and unfair labor practice charges against the company. The charges against the company were actually signed by the union business agent on June 28, 1976, but not filed until the date noted above. The union claimed that the company had violated Sections 8(a) (1), 8(a) (2), 8(a) (3), and 8(a) (5) of the LMRA. Specifically, the UAW claimed:

(a) Since on or about May 19, 1976, the employer by its officers, agents, and representatives has dominated and assisted the formation among its employees of a labor organization known as Auto Mechanics Lodge 1053, AFL-CIO, and, at all times since that date, has interfered with the operation and administration of the charging party.

(b) Since on or about June 29, 1976, the employer, by its officers, agents, and representatives has terminated the employment of all of the members of the bargaining unit represented by the charging party by refusing the unconditional offer of each such employee to return to work and by unlawfully recognizing another labor organization to represent employees in the appropriate bargaining unit represented by the charging party because of the membership and activities of said employees on behalf of the charging party.

(c) Since on or about May 1, 1976, and at all times thereafter, the employer by its officers, agents, and representatives has refused to bargain collectively with the charging party, a labor organization chosen by a majority of its employees in an appropriate unit for the purpose of collective bargaining in regard to rates of pay, wages, and other conditions of employment.

The UAW requested the NLRB to certify the UAW as the appropriate bargaining unit representative, to order the company to cease and desist in recognizing a unit of IAM employees, to bargain with the UAW, to reinstate all UAW employees to their former positions, and to make them whole for any lost pay and benefits.

POSITION OF THE COMPANY

The company argued that the sole purpose of the UAW picketing at its Tonawanda facility was to force the company to recognize and bargain with the UAW, when the company as a successor employer agreed to recognize an existing bargaining unit and labor agreement with the IAM. The union's picketing was in direct violation of Section 8(b) (7) (A) of the Act which states:

(b) It shall be an unfair labor practice for a labor organization or its agents—

(7) to picket or cause to be picketed, or threaten to picket or cause to be picketed, any employer where an object thereof is forcing or requiring an employer to recognize or bargain with a labor organization as the representative of his employees, or forcing or requiring the employees of an employer to accept or select such labor organization as their collective bargaining representative, unless such labor organization is currently certified as the representative of such employees:

(A) where the employer has lawfully recognized in accordance with this Act any other labor organization and a question concerning representation may not appropriately be raised.

The company pointed out that it is settled labor law that a successor employer may be obligated to recognize and bargain with a duly certified representative of a predecessor owner's employees.[1] The UAW collective bargaining agreement with the company, which expired March 20, 1976, contained a successor clause which provided for the sale of the business, notice to UAW, and potential assumption by a purchaser of the bargaining agreement. The buy-sell agreement of May 20, 1976, between Don Davis Pontiac and Al Ives Pontiac, Inc., contained an express clause as follows: "Buyer shall, on the date of closing, assume all obligations of Seller, as of that date, under Seller's contract, dated February 4, 1976, with the Auto Mechanics Lodge Local 1053, International Association of Machinists and Aerospace Workers."

Don Davis Pontiac, when it acquired Ives, became in fact and law a successor to Ives. This was not a mere relocation but was, in fact, a successorship. The company took over the Ives operation; it sold the same kind of automobiles; new franchise agreements were executed; the Ives inventory parts and equipment were acquired and used by the company; and all employees (except officers) of the Bailey Avenue former operations were terminated as of the close of business on June 11, 1976.

The company requested that the unfair labor practice charges filed against it by the UAW should be dismissed; that the UAW should be found in violation of Section 8(b) (7) (A) of the Act; and the UAW should be permanently ordered to cease and desist in its picketing of company facilities.

POSITION OF THE UNION

The UAW argued that it was the company, not the union, which had violated the Act. The union's picketing of the company's facilities at Tonawanda was legitimate and protected activity, since the union was engaged in efforts to protect the job rights of its members.

In testimony, the union business representative for Local 55, UAW, pointed out that even after the company notified the UAW that it had terminated the Bailey Avenue operations, he caused the pickets to be moved to Tonawanda; and that he was still concerned with negotiating a contract for the company's employees who formerly worked at the Bailey Avenue site.

---

[1] See *NLRB v. Burns International Security Services*, 406 U.S. 272, 89 LRRM 2225, 1972.

Counsel for the UAW claimed as follows: "The employer, it is our contention, had a bargaining agent; it was us. When they relocated, they still had a bargaining agent, and therefore could not recognize the other bargaining agent for the employees on Niagara Falls Boulevard. Our picketing was engaged in because (a) the employer failed to negotiate with us regarding the relocation, which he had an obligation to do; and (b) he relocated and recognized another bargaining agent in violation of our members' rights. So in essence, we became unfair labor picketors because at this time what the employer did was wrong and illegal; they recognized another union at a time that valid questions concerning representation existed."

In support of its arguments, the union claimed that Don Davis Pontiac was not really a successor employer to Al Ives Pontiac. The company had used the purchase device simply to "relocate its operations." This was evidenced by the fact that the company transferred considerable equipment from its Bailey Avenue location to the Tonawanda location and the officers and management of the firm did not change. Therefore, the union did not violate Section 8(b) (7) (A) of the Act by picketing at Tonawanda, since the UAW had a legitimate and legally protected right to try to preserve jobs which rightfully belonged to the Bailey Avenue employees. The only means available to the union to achieve this result was through picketing Davis at Tonawanda. Since the object of the UAW's picketing after June 16 was job preservation, the picketing at Tonawanda therefore did not violate Section 8(b) (7) (A), and the company's unfair labor practice charges against the union should be dismissed.

The union urged that its unfair labor practice charges against the company should be upheld by the NLRB, and that the company should be ordered by the Board to bargain with the UAW and to reinstate and make whole all UAW employees as appropriate.

QUESTIONS

1. What is meant by a "successor" employer in labor relations? What criteria are appropriate in order for the Board to determine whether an employer is a successor employer, or simply a former company which has relocated its prior operations?

2. Were the actions of the UAW primarily to protect jobs, or to force the company to recognize the UAW at the new location?

3. Did the company properly follow bargaining procedures with the union, or did it fail to bargain in good faith when it made its decision to purchase the new dealership?

4. What should be the appropriate disposition and remedies, if any, for the various charges and countercharges of unfair labor practices filed by the company and the union?

15. THE UNION'S THREAT TO DISCIPLINE ITS MEMBERS DURING AN ORGANIZING CAMPAIGN

Company: S & M Grocers, Inc., Silver Spring, Beltsville, and Hyattsville, Maryland

Union: Amalgamated Meat Cutters and Allied Workers of North America, Local 593, affiliated with the Amalgamated Meat Cutters and Butcher Workmen of North America

BACKGROUND

The company operated three supermarket-type grocery stores in three separate locations. In March 1976 the union began an organizational drive at these three supermarkets. On May 12, 1976, the union held an organizing meeting with the employees. At this meeting, a number of employees stated that some of the union's members who worked for the company were not participating in the organizational effort.

Many of the company employees also held part-time or full-time jobs in other stores, which already were under contract with the union. They were union members pursuant to a union security clause in collective bargaining agreements with their other employers.

On June 21, 1976, the vice president of the union, on behalf of the union's Executive Board, wrote a letter to those union members who were employees of S & M Grocers. In relevant part, this letter stated as follows:

> All members are hereby requested to assist and cooperate with the organizing committee of this union.
>
> Any member of this union that does not support, when so requested, or actively opposes the organizing activities of this union, will be called before the Executive Board and shall suffer such disciplinary action as the Board deems necessary including but not limited to expulsion from this union.

A number of S & M employees complained to company management about this letter from the union. Jointly with the company, they subsequently filed unfair labor practice charges against the union claiming that the union had violated Section 8(b) (1) (A) of the LMRA by threatening disciplinary action upon certain employees in violation of their rights guaranteed by Section 7 of the Act.

POSITION OF THE COMPANY AND ITS COMPLAINANT EMPLOYEES

The principal arguments presented by the company and certain employees generally focused upon the contention that the union had violated Section 8(b) (1) (A) of the Act by threatening to discipline members who did not support or participate in or who actively opposed the organizing drive at the company's stores.

Although the proviso to Section 8(b) (1) (A) preserves a union's "right . . . to prescribe its own rules with respect to the acquisition or retention of membership therein," it is well established that this proviso does not permit union actions which undermine an overriding public interest, or which conflict with Section 7 rights guaranteed under the Act. Thus, while a union ordinarily has the right to discipline members for failing to obey internal rules aimed at solidarity, employees at the same time have a long-established statutory right to be free of coercion in the process of choosing a collective bargaining representative. During union organizing campaigns, employees are guaranteed rights to have full freedom to exchange views and ideas on the subject of union representation with other employees as well as having the right to make their own decision on whether to vote for or against the union.

It would be quite understandable and reasonable for an employee to choose union representation at one employer and decide to reject it at another—because of differing circumstances in the employment relationships the employee had with his or her respective employers. Further, some employees become union members primarily because of union security agreements already in place as a condition of their employment. At a different employer, they might choose to reject union membership if they had the option to exercise their free choice.

In this situation, the union sought to prevent full discussion by employees because it threatened that any criticism of or opposition to the union would subject employees who already were union members to discipline or expulsion from the union.

And while the employee might be free to vote against the union in an election, that freedom was substantially inhibited by the effects of the union's coercion of employee members' preelection activities. Therefore, the union's threatened disciplinary action constituted improper and unjustified restraint or coercion of employees in the selection of their collective bargaining representative.

The union should be held in violation of the Act, and be ordered to cease and desist and to refrain from its unfair labor practices accordingly.

POSITION OF THE UNION

The union claimed that its letter of June 21, 1976, to employees of S & M Grocers who already were union members because of being employed by other employers, did not violate the LMRA. The union argued that union discipline does not violate the Act unless the disciplinary action either reaches an employee's employment status or infringes on certain other rights under the Act. The union's letter of June 21 was in furtherance of its legitimate desire for solidarity in its drive to organize the company's employees. While the letter may have sought to restrict certain members' exercise of free speech during an organizational drive, the purpose was to require them to act only in a manner consistent with their membership status in the union. As members, they participated in the election of officers and in the other internal affairs of the union which led to the decision to organize particular employees. They could resign the union at any time if the union set out on a course they did not agree with.[1] Having resigned, they would be totally free to campaign against the union. Thus, there was no coercion in such a setting, as maintained by the company and the complainants. However, as long as they remained members, the union had a right to expect their support, including actual participation in the union's organizational efforts. Moreover, although the members were subject to the discipline if they did not support the union's campaign and did not in the alternative resign, they were still free to make their own determination as how to vote at S & M Grocers on the issue of union representation. Thus, the union's effort at member discipline was a valid enforcement of a legitimate internal regulation that did not contravene an overriding policy of labor law.

The union pointed out that the Board and the courts have long held that labor organizations have the right to promulgate reasonable rules and regulations and to discipline members in order to carry out their duty and responsibility to organize and represent employees. The union urged that the unfair labor practice charges should be dismissed.

[1] The union constitution permitted this. Under union security clauses in effect, resigned members would still be obligated to meet their financial obligations (i.e., dues or a dues equivalent) to the union as a condition of employment.

QUESTIONS

1. Evaluate the arguments presented in support of the unfair labor practice charges. Which of these arguments is most compelling?
2. Was the union's letter primarily aimed at "union solidarity" or to coerce certain employee members improperly?
3. Evaluate the union's contention that there was no coercion, since the members involved could resign the union if they wished.
4. Why is the issue in this case important from a broad public labor policy point of view?

16. THE OBJECTIONABLE UNION STATEMENT DURING A REPRESENTATIONAL CAMPAIGN

Company: Miller's Pre-Pared Potato Company, Inc., Blue Island, Illinois

Union: International Brotherhood of General Workers

BACKGROUND

This case involved an objection raised by the company concerning certain statements in a letter sent by the union to company employees just four days prior to a union representational election. On that election, the union won representation rights for bargaining unit employees by a vote of 21-17. The company filed objections to the election under Section 9(c) of the LMRA requesting that the election results be set aside.

The company's objections primarily focused upon a letter sent by the union to its employees four days before the election. That letter stated in relevant part:

> The Union will negotiate for better pay and benefits. The members of this Union get salaries between $3.90 and $200 an hour.

POSITION OF THE COMPANY

At the time of the election in late 1978, newly hired unskilled laborers were paid $2.85 per hour by the company. While the lower wage figure mentioned in the union letter was apparently accurate, the company asserted the higher figure was totally misleading. Because the company did not learn of the statement of the union to the employees until after the election, the company was unable to respond to the union's misleading claims.

The company contended that the union statement implied that the union had negotiated wages in the range cited for employees in

133

bargaining units represented by the union. In fact, the union office simply had acted as a talent agency in arranging a number of performance dates for certain persons who were entertainers at salaries which exceeded $200 per hour. But the union could not prove that those entertainers were its members. Similarly, while some members of the union who were also entertainers received salaries in excess of $200 per hour, the union had not negotiated such wages for those individuals. These union members typically negotiated their own fees with individuals, groups, and others who employed them. Thus, the union had substantially misrepresented its success in negotiating high wages for employees.

The company presented evidence that prior to the election, two or three employees had asked the union business agent about the union's statement in the letter. The business agent admitted that the $200 per hour salary applied only to a number of "entertainer members" of the union. However, apparently only these several employees received this clarification; other employees were not so informed and thus were conceivably misled.

The company contended that this "material misrepresentation" could have swung the balance in the close election. Under its election standards, the NLRB has held that material misrepresentation is grounds for setting aside election results. The company urged that the election results be voided, and a new election held.

POSITION OF THE UNION

The union claimed that it did not interfere with the representation election, when four days before the election it sent a letter to certain employees stating that its members get salaries of "between $3.90 and $200 an hour." This statement was neither literally untrue nor within the range where it was likely to mislead employees.

The union pointed out that the claim in the letter was technically accurate. The union represented employees in a number of bargaining units involving differing crafts and skills. Some union members were actually entertainers who earned over $200 an hour at times. Misrepresentation could arise only through drawing an inference that the union meant to claim that it had negotiated the union members' entertainers' salaries, but circumstances did not warrant such an inference. The fact that the statement was vaguely worded and subject to different interpretations could not establish such misrepresentation as to require setting aside the election. Additionally, the fact that some employees may have inquired about the higher wage figure in the statement should not mandate the conclusion that the statement had a tendency to mislead.

The union claimed that the company was merely using this objection as a means to avoid the results of the election. The union argued that the election be certified, and that the company be ordered to recognize the union as its employees' bargaining unit representative and to bargain with the union accordingly.

QUESTIONS

1. Evaluate the union's letter sent to the employees. Was this "material misrepresentation" as claimed by the company?
2. Since a number of employees inquired about the union letter, does this indicate that the union letter was confusing and/or misleading?
3. Why would the union send a letter of this nature to employees if its purpose was not to influence employee opinion?
4. Even if the union's letter was improper, was it serious enough to cause the NLRB to order a new election?

17. A COMMENDATION FOR EXCELLENCE, OR AN UNFAIR LABOR PRACTICE?

Employer: United States Postal Service, Cleveland, Ohio

Union: Branch No. 40, National Association of Letter Carriers

BACKGROUND

Midpark Branch is one of numerous branch facilities of the United States Postal Service serving the greater Cleveland, Ohio, metropolitan area. In July 1979, acting upon the recommendation of Midpark Branch Manager John Canterra,[1] the Cleveland Postal Service office decided to issue a Certificate of Excellence to the staff of 10 postal clerks employed at the Midpark Branch facility. On July 12, 1979, the 10 postal clerks and the 64 letter carriers were gathered together for the presentation ceremony. Supervisory personnel read copies of the certificate to the assembled group and gave each of the 10 postal clerks a copy. A copy was also placed in each clerk's personnel file. The certificate, signed by Midpark Branch Manager Canterra and Cleveland Postmaster Leslie Spiegel, stated as follows:

> This Certificate of Excellence is presented to the Clerical Staff at Midpark Branch of the Cleveland Ohio Postal Service for Outstanding Achievements during the Fiscal Year of 1979 in the categories listed below:
>
> 1. Outstanding Public Relations
> 2. Outstanding Productivity
> 3. Very Satisfactory Audit
> 4. Minimum Time Lost Due to Sick Leave Usage (Of 20,800 scheduled clerk hours, only 189 Sick Hours or 9 percent were used.)
> 5. No Lost Time Due to Injury on Duty (I.O.D.)
> 6. No Registered Complaints or Grievances
> 7. No Registered E.E.O. Complaints
>
> I would like to commend each employee in this group for his

---

[1] The names of all individuals have been disguised.

productivity, devotion to duty, dependability, and professionalism. All of you have demonstrated that the key to a successful operation is teamwork: congratulations!

After a number of meetings between the parties about this matter, the union in January 1980, filed unfair labor practice charges against the employer. The union claimed that the Postal Service management had interfered with employee rights guaranteed under Section 7 of LMRA and in violation of Sections 8(a) (3) and 8(a) (1) of the Act.

Several weeks later in February 1980, the employer issued and posted the following notice—signed by Cleveland Postmaster Leslie Spiegel—on several bulletin boards at the Midpark Branch facility:

> NOTICE TO EMPLOYEES: Branch 40, National Association of Letter Carriers, AFL-CIO, filed an unfair labor practice charge with the National Labor Relations Board on January 8, 1980, which alleges that the Postal Service is attempting to induce the Letter Carriers from not filing grievances by giving nonmonetary awards to members of another craft, who do not file grievances. This allegation has to do with a July 12, 1979, Certificate of Excellence presented to the clerical staff at Midpark Branch of the Cleveland Post Office. In our view it would be indeed ironic that what we first considered as an innocent and simple form of employee recognition for employees' cost consciousness and productivity would ultimately result in potential litigation for the Postal Service. We did not intend the Certificate to be considered as an inducement to our employees to relinquish their rights to file or process grievances. Moreover, I wish to take this opportunity to reiterate the Postal Service's policy that all our employees be free to file and process grievances without interference, restraint, or coercion. To the best of my knowledge no employee at Midpark Branch has ever been discriminated against because of his grievance filing activity and no one will be discriminated against in the future either. We believe that the language of the Certificate is protected by the First Amendment and Section 8(c) of the National Labor Relations Act and sincerely hope that this clarifies the matter for all concerned.

POSITION OF THE UNION

The union pointed out that the Certificates of Excellence were given only to the clerical employees at the Midpark Branch who were members of a different independent and separate employee organization. These certificates were based in part upon the fact that the clerical employees had not filed any grievances. Such certificates thus rewarded and encouraged the clerical employees not to file grievances and also attempted by direct inference to induce the letter carrier employees to refrain from filing grievances and to avoid utilizing the union's grievance machinery under its labor contract with the employer. By issuing the award and by placing it in the employees' personnel files, the employer was thus discriminating against those employees who chose or who in the future might choose to exercise their Section 7 rights to file grievances, thereby discouraging union activity in violation of Sections 8(a) (1) and 8(a) (3) of the Act.

The union requested that the employer be found in violation of the Act as stated above, and that the employer be ordered to (a) disavow the Certificates of Excellence it had issued, (b) cease and desist from issuing any similar awards in the future, and (c) post a notice to this effect accordingly.

POSITION OF THE EMPLOYER

The Post Office management contended that the unfair labor practice charges filed by the union were trivial in nature and designed to harrass the employer in its efforts to recognize good employee performance and to promote positive and constructive employer/employee relations. In this regard, the employer argued that the issuance of the Certificates of Excellence was protected communication under Section 8(c) of LMRA—the so-called free speech provisions—since the certificates contained no "threat of reprisal or force or promise of benefit."

Concerning the unfair labor practice charges, the employer contended that there was no evidence whatsoever that the employer had discriminated or would in the future discriminate against any employee for filing a grievance. Thus, the 8(a) (3) allegations were totally without foundation and should be dismissed. And even if the Certificate of Excellence contained some wording which by broad (although incorrect) inference might have been construed as a technical violation of Section 8(a) (1) of the Act, the fact that the employer issued and posted an explanatory notice in February 1980 was "ameliorative action" which should have been sufficient to eliminate any finding of an unfair labor practice and remedial order from the NLRB. The employer urged that all of the unfair labor practice charges should be dismissed.

QUESTIONS

1. Evaluate the union's contentions that the Certificates of Excellence were an inducement to employees not to file grievances and/or exercise their Section 7 rights under LMRA.
2. Evaluate the employer's contentions that the Certificates of Excellence

did not violate the Act, and that the union's charges were trivial and harrassment tactics.

3. Did the employer's explanatory notice of February 1980 absolve the employer of any technical violation of LMRA? Why, or why not?
4. Why should any notice or letter of commendation—such as the one in this case—be carefully worded so as to avoid possible unfair labor practice charges (and also possible charges of discrimination under the Civil Rights Act)?

18. THE HOSPITAL'S WITHDRAWAL OF RECOGNITION AND REFUSAL TO BARGAIN WITH A NURSES' UNION

Employer: Windham Community Memorial Hospital, Windham, Connecticut

Union: Registered Nurses Unit 62, Connecticut Nurses Association

BACKGROUND

On August 7, 1975, nonsupervisory nurses employed at the Windham Community Hospital voted in a union representational election. On the date of the election, the hospital employed 65 nonsupervisory nurses. A two-thirds majority of those voting selected the Connecticut Association as their collective bargaining representative. The actual vote was 38-19 in favor of the union, with 8 employeys not voting.

The union was certified by the NLRB on August 15, 1975, and negotiations commenced on November 6, 1975. After several negotiating sessions, major issues remained unresolved and the union voted to engage in an economic strike. After giving the hospital and the Federal Mediation and Counciliation Service (FMCS) due notice as required by Section 8(g) of the LMRA, the union commenced its strike on April 21, 1976. Negotiations continued for a time, but were suspended on June 9, 1976.

On August 23, 1976, Marjorie Mueller,[1] a union agent, called Richard Stone, the hospital's attorney and a member of the negotiating team, and told him that the union would like to resume bargaining. The substance of this conversation was later disputed. Stone claimed that he was told that resumption of negotiations was preconditioned on reinstatement of 23 employees and on the union's "getting something to show for the strike."

Mueller claimed that she merely indicated the union's willingness

---

[1] The names of all individuals have been disguised.

to make certain concessions, such as reducing the number of employees to be immediately rehired from 42 to 23 and altering wage demands.

Stone immediately contacted the hospital's administrator, Fred Richter, and communicated the union's desire to resume negotiations. At that time, Richter told Stone that the hospital would no longer negotiate with the union, because he felt that the union no longer had the support of a majority of the hospital's nurses. Later that day, the union was notified that the hospital had refused to resume bargaining and had withdrawn recognition from the union.

Statistically, it was established that at the time of the walkout, 72 nurses were employed in the bargaining unit.[2] Of these, 57 employees initially engaged in the strike, while 15 employees did not strike but continued working. Nine striking employees returned to work, and another six employees resigned the union and returned to work by August 23, 1976. The hospital also had hired 42 replacement employees by August 23, 1976.

Both the quality and quantity of picketing had gradually diminished over the months. Such activities had been officially terminated by the union on August 8, 1976.

POSITION OF THE UNION

The union contended that the hospital's withdrawal of recognition and refusal to bargain with the union were unlawful for several reasons.

First of all, the union pointed out that it is settled labor law that except under unusual circumstances, a union's representative status is presumed to continue during the first year following certification, so that the collective bargaining relationship has the opportunity to become established. Withdrawal of union recognition by management during this period is an unfair labor practice and violates the Act. Following the expiration of the certification year, the presumption of union recognition remains in effect unless an employer can show conclusively either that (1) on the date recognition was withdrawn, the union in fact did not have majority support; or (2) by presenting sufficient evidence to show that a refusal to bargain was based on a serious good faith doubt of the union's majority. In this case situation, neither of the above had occurred.

The union contended that the hospital had failed to establish that as of August 23, 1976, the union was in fact no longer supported by a

---

[2] Apparently, a total of seven additional nursing employees had been hired beween August 7, 1975, and April 21, 1976.

majority of the hospital's employees. The union pointed out that of the 57 original strikers, only 9 employees returned to work and only 6 other employees resigned the union and returned to work before August 23, 1976; this left a total of 42 strikers who obviously supported the union. For purposes of determining majority status of the union, all of these remaining 42 strikers retained their legal rights under the Act as employees and must be considered members of the bargaining unit in support of the union.[3]

Concerning the 15 nonstrikers and the 9 strikers who did not resign the union but who returned to work before August 23, 1976, the union maintained that many of them still strongly wanted the union to represent them. Among these employees were nurses who felt that they could not afford economically to go out or stay out on a strike and/or who felt that a strike by nurses was inappropriate to their profession. The union claimed that of these 24 employees, it could be approximated that two thirds (or 16) of them supported the union in the same 2-to-1 ratio by which the employees originally voted for the union.

This meant that on August 23, 1976, there was a total of 58 employees in favor of the union: 42 strikers plus 16 of the 24 nonstrikers and returnees. Thus, even if it were assumed that the 42 replacement employees did not support the union, a majority of employees still did so; that is, 58 of the 114 employees in the applicable employee bargaining unit should be counted as being for the union.

---

[3] The union relied on NLRB policy, labor case law, and court decisions in making these assertions. In general, employees who strike for a lawful object fall into two classes—economic strikers and unfair labor practice strikers. Both classes continue as employees, but unfair labor practice strikers have greater rights of reinstatement to their jobs.

If the object of a strike is to obtain from the employer some economic concession such as higher wages, shorter hours, or better working conditions, the striking employees are called economic strikers. They retain their status as employees and cannot be discharged, but they can be replaced by their employer. If the employer has hired bona fide permanent replacements who are filling the jobs of the economic strikers when the strikers apply unconditionally to go back to work, the strikers are not entitled to reinstatement at that time. However, if the strikers do not obtain regular and substantially equivalent employment, they are entitled to be recalled to jobs for which they are qualified when openings in such jobs occur if they, or their bargaining representative, have made an unconditional request for their reinstatement.

Employees who strike to protest an unfair labor practice committed by their employer are called unfair labor practice strikers. Such strikers can be neither discharged nor permanently replaced. When the strike ends, unfair labor practice strikers, absent serious misconduct on their part, are entitled to have their jobs back even if employees hired to do their work have to be discharged.

If the Board finds that economic strikers or unfair labor practice strikers who have made an unconditional request for reinstatement have been unlawfully denied reinstatement by their employer, the Board may award such strikers backpay starting at the time they should have been reinstated.

The union contended that its reduction of picketing activity during the summer months of 1976 was attributable to the combination of several different factors: summer vacations, family responsibilities engendered by school vacations, and the strikers' feelings that additional picketing was no longer necessary because the continuation of the strike itself was sufficient to notify the hospital that the union was still pressing its claims.

Thus, the union argued that on August 23, 1976, it was still the legally constituted representative of the nursing unit employees. Since the hospital unlawfully withdrew its recognition of the union and refused to bargain with the union as required by Section 8(d) of the Act, the hospital had caused the nurses' economic strike to become an unfair labor practice strike. The real motive of the hospital was its determination to destroy the union. The union was willing to negotiate concerning reinstatement of certain strikers, but the hospital refused to bargain whatsoever.

The union urged that hospital be found to have violated Sections 8(a) (5) and 8(a) (1) of the Act. As remedies, the hospital should be ordered to (a) cease and desist from unfair labor practices; (b) recognize and bargain, on request, with Windham Community Memorial Hospital, Registered Nurses Unit 62, Connecticut Nurses Association (the union); and (c) reinstate with back pay, or otherwise to make whole, all striking employees.

POSITION OF THE HOSPITAL

The hospital claimed that it had not violated the Act because it was justified in concluding that the union no longer had a majority status among the nursing employees on August 23, 1976.

First of all, the hospital claimed that the union itself had abandoned the strike in August 1976. The diminution in enthusiasm for picketing indicated loss of support for the union by the employees.

Secondly, the hospital contended that its failure to return to the bargaining table in response to the union's August 23 initiative did not constitute a "refusal to bargain" within the meaning of Section 8(a) (5) of the Act. The union's offer was preconditioned with a demand by the union to reinstate 23 strikers. Neither the Act nor NLRB policy required the hospital to accept such an offer as a condition for bargaining.

But most importantly, the hospital argued that the union had lost its majority status. By the union's own statement, only 23 of the 42 strikers wanted their jobs back on August 23, 1976; the other 19 strikers who did not ask for their jobs back should not be counted as being part of any applicable bargaining unit. Thus, the union no longer had a majority status, since the conceivable bargaining unit consisted of only 95 employees, not 114 employees as claimed by the union. Of these 95 employees, the 42 replacement employees and the 15 nonstrikers should clearly be presumed to be against the union, plus the 6 striking employees who resigned the union and who returned to work.

The hospital thus asserted that it had good faith doubt about the union's majority status in August 1976, and its objective data supported its decision to withdraw recognition of the union accordingly. The hospital urged that the unfair labor practice charges should be dismissed in their entirety.

Alternatively, the hospital argued that if the Board should conclude that the company erred in not bargaining with the union in August 1976, that the appropriate remedy should be a new NLRB representation election to determine whether the union had a majority status. The hospital contended that nothing in the record indicated prolongation or aggravation of the strike by the withdrawal of recognition from the union, that would justify the union's extraordinary claim that strikers should be reinstated and/or made whole for lost pay and benefits.

QUESTIONS

1. Evaluate the union's statistical contention that it still represented a majority of employees at the time of this case.
2. Evaluate the hospital's statistical contention that the union no longer represented a majority of employees.
3. Was the union's statement to the hospital on August 23, 1976, a precondition for bargaining, or merely a bargaining position which was negotiable?
4. If the hospital is found to have violated the Act, is the appropriate remedy a reinstatement and making whole of employees, or a new representational election to determine the union's representational status?

19. WAS THE EMPLOYEE'S WALKOUT PROTECTED CONCERTED ACTIVITY?

Company:	Ontario Knife Company, Franklinville, New York
Individual Employee:	Mary Costello[1]

BACKGROUND

Ontario Knife Company was a knife manufacturer, which at the time of this case employed about 300 persons on a day and night shift basis. The plant was nonunion.

Mary Costello was first hired in 1976 as a riveter; she was assigned to the second shift (3:30 P.M. to midnight) where she worked with two other employees, Veronica Thorp and Julie Moore. Their basic work was to rivet wood or plastic handles to knives. For several years, they had encountered major difficulties and problems in the riveting of handles to machetes, one of the company's major products. These difficulties adversely affected their additional incentive pay. Also, the work was dirtier than on other knives; in the six months preceding the incident in this case the machete blades had been dipped in oil to retard rusting.

Mary Costello, Veronica Thorp, and Julie Moore frequently brought complaints about the situation to their leadman George Wilson, the night foreman Carl Saunders, and the plant manager Marvin Schwartz. In response to these complaints, management took a number of steps to adjust the incentive pay problem. Further, employees who performed the riveting work were placed on rotating schedules with respect to machete production. However, the three night shift employees continued to complain, and in mid-1978 their major grievance was that the burden of machete work was unfairly distributed between the day and the night shifts.

---

[1] The names of all individuals have been disguised.

In June 1978, the complaints of the night shift employees became particularly vocal because no first shift operator had worked on machetes on June 20 when Costello did, on June 21 when Moore did, or on June 22 when Thorp was scheduled to do so. This imbalance was explained by Schwartz as due to the fact that Ontario was behind schedule in its machete deliveries. Blades, handles, and special rivets often did not arrive until the afternoon; therefore, the night shift was obligated to start the work to get the production out. The day shift foreman normally made out the night shift production schedule.

On arriving for work on Thursday, June 22, Mary Costello looked at the day foreman's desk for the night shift instructions and found that machetes were on the list. It was Veronica Thorp's turn to do that work that night, with Costello's turn to come the next night if machetes should again be scheduled. On the previous day Costello had complained to George Wilson about the unequal distribution of the machete work between day and night shifts. While she and Veronica Thorp were complaining to each other on the afternoon of June 22, Wilson came through their department. Costello asked him what he had found out in the office about her complaint of the previous day. Wilson said nothing, but he then reported to the night foreman, Carl Saunders, that "Costello and Thorp are upstairs griping again about the machines and doing the machetes." Saunders and Wilson then went upstairs, brought Costello and Thorp into another room, and asked them what the problem was. Costello answered that Wilson was supposed to find out from someone why the night shift employees were doing machetes when the day crews had not done any. Saunders responded that Wilson had no reason to go to the front office, since he (Saunders) was the boss and it was his place to decide the schedules. After more discussion, the two employees said that the next time it was their turn to work on machetes, they were going to refuse. Saunders responded that the employees were bound to do whatever work was described on the day foreman's list, and that if they didn't like the type of work so described, they should get out and the employer would find other people. Looking directly at Costello, Saunders said, "If there is a thing on there (the day foreman's list) that says you have to kiss my ass, that is what you are going to do!" Costello retorted, "I don't need this garbage!" She walked to her machine, shut it down, packed her belongings, left the job, and punched out, crying as she left.

Saunders and Wilson then went to the office in order to report the incident to Marvin Schwartz. Not finding him there, Saunders contacted Ivan Kilgore, the personnel manager. The next day Costello telephoned Kilgore, told him her story, and asked if she was to come to work that evening. Kilgore replied that he didn't know and asked why she had walked off the job. Costello answered that she was upset by the unfair work assignments; that she felt Saunders was not concerned about the employees' complaints; and his offensive, insulting remark had caused her to become angry. She offered to get a doctor's slip to verify her nervous condition. Kilgore advised against this and said he would have to discuss the matter with Schwartz. On Monday, June 26, Kilgore called Costello to tell her that she was being terminated for "walking off the job."

Shortly thereafter, acting with the assistance of legal counsel, Mary Costello filed unfair labor practice charges against the company claiming that her discharge had violated the Labor Management Relations Act as amended.

POSITION OF THE EMPLOYEE

Counsel for Mary Costello argued that Ontario's discharge and refusal to reinstate Mary Costello violated Section 8(a) (1) of the Act which makes it an unfair labor practice "to interfere with, restrain, or coerce employees in the exercise of the rights guaranteed in Section 7." That section gives employees the right "to engage in . . . concerted activities for the purpose of collective bargaining or other mutual aid or protection." Employees Mary Costello and Veronica Thorp, in registering their complaints with management over the discrimination against the second shift in the recent assignments of machete work, were engaged in a "concerted activity" for the purpose of "mutual aid or protection."

Citing a precedent NLRB decision,[2] it was a well-established Board policy that a concerted walkout of employees in a nonunion situation to protest job conditions could be activity protected by the LMRA. This is particularly supported where employees have no other recourse open to them; where there has been no prior work stoppage involving the employees' refusal to perform work; where the employees have not made specific demands on an employer; and where a decision to walk out is for a single day and not designed to be continued in future plans of the employees.[3]

Mary Costello and Veronica Thorp had been acting together—along with Julie Moore—in protesting working conditions at the Ontario Company. The precipitating incident of June 22 found both Costello and Thorp jointly registering their complaints to management. The night foreman was not really listening to their complaints, and after direct, offensive provocation by this foreman, Mary Costello refused to perform any work that evening. Even though she

---

[2] *NLRB* v. *Washington Aluminum Company,* 370US9, 50—50LRRM2235 (1962).

[3] *NLRB* v. *Polytech Incorporated,* 195NLRB No. 126 (1971).

was not joined in her refusal to work by Veronica Thorp, Mary Costello was acting on behalf of and in concert with her co-employees. Since the employees did not have a labor union to represent them, this was precisely the type of protected and concerted activity within the meaning of Section 7 of the LMRA.

Counsel for Mary Costello argued that the company should be found guilty of violating Section 8(a) (1) of the Act, and that Mary Costello should be reinstated and made whole for all lost earnings accordingly.

POSITION OF THE COMPANY

The company strongly contended that Mary Costello was terminated for walking off the job on the evening of June 22, 1978. This action by Ms. Costello was in direct defiance of legitimate management authority. She chose to leave the company plant on her own volition, and she was not accompanied by anyone else in this unauthorized behavior. Even her fellow complainant, Veronica Thorp, did not join Mary Costello in her temperamental refusal to perform her job that evening. Costello's walkout could not be condoned by management; if not dealt with severely, such insubordination could lead to a wholesale breakdown of discipline among company employees. Management justly terminated Costello's employment for her gross misconduct.

As to the unfair labor practice charges, the company characterized these charges as being a desperate effort by Mary Costello to be reinstated to her job. In the company's view, Costello walked off the job by herself, and no one joined her in doing so. This behavior by Costello alone could hardly be identified as "mutual" or "concerted" activity.

The company urged that the unfair labor practice charges filed by Costello should be dismissed.

QUESTIONS

1. Discuss the meaning of the terms, "concerted activities" and "mutual aid or protection" within Section 7 of LMRA. Why are these terms difficult to define in nonunion work situations?
2. Was Mary Costello's walkout under the case circumstances entitled to protection within the meaning of Section 7 of the Act? Why, or why not?
3. Does it make any difference that Mary Costello left the plant by herself and was not joined in her walkout by any other employees?
4. Why does company management view Costello's behavior as being a defiance of management authority with the potential for a wholesale breakdown of employee discipline?

20. A REFUSAL TO BARGAIN CONCERNING SELECTION OF AN INSURANCE CARRIER

Company: Connecticut Light and Power Company

Union: System Council U-24, International Brotherhood of Electrical Workers, (IBEW), AFL-CIO, comprised of Locals 420, 753, 1045, 1175, 1226, 1317, and 1817

BACKGROUND

Connecticut Light and Power Company is a public utility engaged in the production, distribution, and sale of electricity and gas. System Council U-24, International Brotherhood of Electrical Workers, AFL-CIO, and its Locals 420, 753, 1045, 1175, 1226, 1317, and 1817, together serve as the exclusive representative for all the company's employees within the relevant bargaining unit. For many years, the company and union have had a collective bargaining relationship.

The company had long provided its employees with a noncontributory, company-paid medical-surgical insurance plan. Since 1967 the carrier of this insurance plan, which included major medical coverage, had been the Aetna Life Insurance Company (Aetna). Prior to 1967 the company had contracted with Blue Cross-Connecticut Medical Service (Blue Cross) for the basic medical-surgical insurance, and with the Hartford Accident and Indemnity Company for major medical insurance.

In 1969 the union informed the company of its dissatisfaction with Aetna's administration of the insurance plan. As a result, the company negotiated and secured various changes from Aetna. Nevertheless, during the 1971 collective bargaining negotiations, the union again expressed its dissatisfaction with Aetna and sought to include in those negotiations the reinstatement of Blue Cross as the carrier for the employee insurance plan. The company did bargain during the 1971 negotiations with respect to coverage, benefits, and administration of the plan. But the company steadfastly refused to bargain about the selection of the carrier, maintaining that the company had the right unilaterally to choose the carrier.

On May 14, 1971, the union filed unfair labor practice charges with the NLRB alleging a refusal by the company to bargain in violation of Sections 8(a) (1) and 8(a) (5) of the Act. The union claimed that the selection of an insurance carrier under the circumstances was a mandatory subject for bargaining within the meaning of Section 8(d) of the Act.

POSITION OF THE UNION

The union argued that Section 8(a) (5) and Section 8(d) of the LMRA require an employer to bargain with a union concerning "wages, hours, and other terms and conditions of employment." It is well established that included within that language are such "non-wage" benefits as the group health insurance here involved.

The NLRB has held repeatedly that the term *wages* must be construed to include certain employee benefits, like pension and insurance benefits, which may accrue to employees out of their employment relationship. These benefits become an integral part of the entire wage structure.

In this case, the company refused to bargain with the union concerning which insurance company should be the carrier for the employees' medical-surgical insurance plan. This was despite the fact that the union had raised objections and expressed general dissatisfaction with the Aetna Company's administration of that insurance plan. It is impossible to separate the insurance benefits available to employees from the insurance carrier which administers an insurance plan. Certainly, the choice of the insurance carrier has a major impact on the nature of the benefits made available to the employees in the bargaining unit. Therefore, the company should be obligated to bargain over the question of the insurance carrier, just as it is obligated to bargain with the union concerning the insurance benefits themselves.

The union requested that the Board find the company in violation of the Act, and that the company should be ordered to (*a*) cease and desist from refusing to bargain collectively as to the selection of an insurance carrier, (*b*) bargain in good faith on that subject upon request of the union, and (*c*) take necessary other affirmative actions to comply with this requirement.

POSITION OF THE COMPANY

The company pointed out that in its 1971 negotiations with the union, there had been no specific allegations made by the union concerning any desired changes in coverage, levels, or administration of the plan. All the union had alleged was general "dissatisfaction" with Aetna as the insurance carrier. Previously, the company had responded to several specific complaints with good faith negotiation, and the company was able to obtain several modifications from Aetna in its plan.

In the company's view, this was all that it was obligated to do under the mandatory bargaining requirements of the Act. The company pointed to several previous rulings of the NLRB and federal courts, which have held as follows:

> Since practically every managerial decision has some impact on wages, hours, or other conditions of employment, the determination of which decisions are mandatory bargaining subjects must depend upon whether a given subject has a *significant or material relationship* to wages, hours, or other conditions of employment.[1]

The company agreed that the benefits, coverage, and administration of its insurance plan were proper bargaining subjects. However, since the company had negotiated about those matters, it was free to choose any carrier that would satisfy the company's agreement with the union.

In summary, the company claimed that it had at no time refused to negotiate with the union concerning any subject that "vitally affected the terms and conditions of employment." The company, therefore, requested that the unfair labor practice charges should be dismissed.

QUESTIONS

1. Evaluate the union's argument that it was not possible to separate the insurance benefits available to employees from the insurance carrier which administers an insurance plan.

2. Evaluate the company's arguments that it was not obligated to bargain concerning the specific insurance carrier.

3. What criteria should the NLRB and courts use in determining whether a given bargaining subject has a significant or material relationship to wages, hours, or other conditions of employment?

4. Even if the company should choose to bargain concerning the selection of an insurance carrier, would the company still have the right to select an insurance carrier to which the union might still object? Discuss.

---

[1] *Westinghouse Electric Corp.* v. *NLRB* 66LRRM 2634.

21. WAS THE COMPANY'S BENEFIT OFFER AN UNFAIR LABOR PRACTICE?

Company: Mountaineer Excavating Company, Inc., Big Stone Gap, Virginia

Union: United Mine Workers (UMW), District 28

BACKGROUND

The company commenced its coal mining operations in July 1977. On July 6, 1977, the company and the union entered into a collective bargaining agreement in which the company recognized the union as the representative of its employees and agreed to be bound by the terms of the National Bituminous Coal Agreement of 1974, effective December 6, 1974, to December 6, 1977. However, the company itself did not become a member of the Bituminous Coal Operators Association (BCOA).

On July 28, 1977, the international union acting on behalf of District 28, notified the company of the union's intention to terminate the agreement and indicated it was prepared to meet and confer with company representatives for the purpose of negotiating a new agreement and to engage in good-faith collective bargaining. On September 26, 1977, the company wrote the international union indicating that it also desired to terminate the contract and requested that a representative of District 28 contact it when it was ready to begin negotiations on a new agreement. There were no further communications between the parties until December 1, 1977.

On December 1, 1977, Bert Colby,[1] the company president, wrote Roger Mateo, president of District 28, noting the earlier communications and commenting that the company had not heard from anyone in the union regarding the company's request to begin bargaining. Colby further noted that from the newspapers, it appeared that there

---

[1] The names of all individuals have been disguised.

would be a strike after December 6 because of the failure of the union and BCOA to reach an agreement covering the BCOA members, but that the company was not a member of BCOA. In his letter, Colby asserted that the company was not obligated to sign any agreement entered into with BCOA, and that it was willing to negotiate with the union for a new agreement between it and the union. Colby went on to state:

> If there is a strike called December 6, we understand that the health care insurance benefits under the present contract will be cut off for our miners and their families due to lack of funds. If this happens it is our intention to provide our men with a new life and health care insurance policy. We also want to negotiate a better pension plan for our men.
>
> We will be happy to answer any questions you may have about our proposed insurance and pension benefits we would like to give our men and their families. We will be happy to negotiate with you on these and other proposals at your earliest convenience.

During the evening of December 1, a previously scheduled dinner meeting of management and the employees was held. Most of the employees attended the meeting. During the course of the meeting, copies of Bert Colby's speech were distributed to the employees. Following his speech, Norris Anderhub, the company's business manager and secretary, presented the proposed health and pension plan referred to by Bert Colby in his speech. According to the printed version of the speech, Colby told the employees:

> And the worst part of it all, according to UMW officials, it looks like your hospital care may not be any good after the strike begins. From what I can read and hear, the union is saying that your health and welfare fund is almost bankrupt and they may not pay any benefits at all during the strike. If the miners walk out December 6, medical benefits will be cut off immediately.
>
> They say that pension payments could be cut from the first week in January.
>
> As you know, since the health and welfare and pension funds are financed and paid for by coal companies royalty payments, if there is no coal being produced, there will be no royalties paid into the funds during the strike. A long strike will completely bankrupt every UMW health and welfare and pension fund for future benefits.
>
> For those miners who do not work during the strike, the $100 weekly sickness and accident benefit could be lost to them. Under the law, the coal operators are not required to continue paying the insurance premiums for the $100 weekly sickness and accident benefit.
>
> We intend to keep paying this premium for every man who continues to work for us during the strike.
>
> What about your hospital and doctor bills for yourself and your

154

family? What are you going to do about it? Unless you have enough money saved to pay these bills, they may not give you any services at the clinics except for cash.

We have thought a lot about this serious problem for you and your family. We have contacted several insurance companies that provide good health care benefits for employees and their families.

We have come up with what we consider to be one of the best health care insurance programs. The beauty of this plan is that the hospital benefits are *guaranteed* to you and your family when you need them during the strike.

If your hospital and medical benefits are cut off next Wednesday, we intend tõ cover all of our men who continue working under this new hospital insurance plan for Mountaineer.

What will it cost you? Absolutely nothing.

On December 5, 1977, Bert Colby met with the employees at the work site. Since the contract was due to expire the next day and the UMW had called a strike for December 6, he asked the employees for a show of hands as to who would not work the next day. None of the employees raised their hands, so Colby then told them their jobs would be available. During this same meeting, employee Wally Banks handed Colby a petition signed by 10 of the 13 employees that they wished to withdraw from the UMW. Banks told Colby that he had begun circulating this petition several weeks prior to December 1, 1977. Colby was unaware of this petition prior to his receiving it.

On December 6, 1977, the UMW commenced a nationwide strike against the BCOA, which was ultimately settled on March 27, 1978, when the UMW ratified a new contract. On December 6, the company put into effect its new hospitalization and pension plans. Approximately two weeks later, Colby granted his employees a week's vacation during the Christmas period.

On January 3, 1978, District 28 of the UMW filed unfair labor practice charges alleging that since on or about December 6, 1977, the company had interfered with, restrained, and coerced its employees in violation of Section 8(a) (1) of the Act. Further, by unilaterally granting employees sickness, accident, and vacation benefits without negotiating these matters with the union, the company had violated Section 8(a) (5) of the Act.

Subsequently, on January 31, 1978, Drew Milliken, president of UMW District 28, wrote the company to report the unfair labor practice charges and stated that the UMW was and had been ready and willing to engage in good-faith negotiations, and offered to begin negotiations with the company. There were no further communications between the company and representatives of the UMW until March 1978, when the regional office of the Board met with the company and union representatives concerning the unfair labor practice charges.

POSITION OF THE UNION

The union claimed that the company had illegally and unilaterally approached its employees and had offered them substantial benefits without notice to or bargaining with the union at a time when the union was the bargaining representative of the employees and the union's collective bargaining agreement with the company was still in effect. Such conduct was nothing more than an attempt to bargain individually with the employees in order to discourage the employees from participating in the impending strike and to cause the union to lose its majority status.

According to the union, if the company really had been desirous of entering into negotiations with the UMW, it needed only to direct timely communications to the union requesting dates for negotiating sessions or making specific proposals to the union. The company was obligated to do either or both, but it did neither. Rather, the company played a waiting game until the bargaining at the national level reached a crisis stage, and then sent the December 1 letter to the union requesting negotiations. On that very same evening, the company met with employees, predicted dire economic circumstances, and offered them substantial economic benefits designed to induce them to abandon the union and bargain directly with the company. The union claimed that the company obviously timed the December 1 letter so as to preclude any possibility of the union consulting with the employees, or any real or meaningful consideration by the union of the company's plan to institute certain benefits as of December 6. On December 5, the company again unilaterally offered its employees substantial economic benefits when it inquired of the employees as to whether any of them were going to strike the next day and advised them that their jobs would be available. Having precluded any meaningful response by the union by virtue of the timing of its action, the company then took the final step on December 6 by unilaterally putting into effect both the hospitalization plan and the pension plan.

The union urged that the company be found in violation of Sections 8(a) (1) and 8(a) (5) of the LMRA, that the company be ordered to cease and desist in its unfair labor practices, and that the company be further ordered to recognize and bargain in good faith with the union concerning the terms and conditions of a new collective bargaining agreement.

POSITION OF THE COMPANY

The company contended that it did not violate the Act in any way.

First of all, the company claimed that it had fulfilled its legal obligations to bargain with the union by its offers to meet with the union, which were made on September 26, 1977, and December 1, 1977. The union did not respond to either of the company's offers to negotiate. Section 8(d) of the Act imposes a "mutual obligation" upon both parties to meet and confer at reasonable times in regard to entering into a new collective bargaining agreement. It was the union, not the company, which failed in its obligation to bargain with the company. The union's offer of January 31, 1978, to begin negotiations with the company was untimely, since the previous contract had expired and the union already had filed unfair labor practice charges against the company.

Second, the company contended that after December 6, 1977, the company was free to implement whatever changes it wished to do so since the contractual agreement with the union had expired. The company was not a party to the BCOA negotiations, and the company was not obligated to be bound to the terms of any BCOA agreement negotiated after December 6, 1977. Since the contract had expired, and since the union had failed to respond to the company's initiatives for contract negotiations, the company was free to change the employee benefits in any way the company wanted.

Finally, the company contended that the union had lost its majority status among the employees. On their own initiative, 10 of 13 employees had signed a petition given to company management on December 5, 1977, indicating they wished to withdraw from the UMW. Thus, when the contract expired on the following day, the UMW no longer had a majority representative status among company employees, and it would have been improper for the company to recognize and negotiate with the UMW, even if the UMW had been willing to negotiate at that time.

The company claimed that the union had filed the unfair labor practice charges in an effort to offset the union's own failures to bargain in good faith, and as a pretext to regain bargaining representative status which the union had lost. The company urged that the unfair labor practice charges should be dismissed.

QUESTIONS

1. Evaluate both the company and the union arguments in regard to the unfair labor practice charges.
2. Discuss the company's position that it was the union, not the company,

which had failed to meet the "mutual obligations" requirements of Section 8(d) of LMRA.

3. Did the fact that the previous contract had expired give the company the right to institute the new benefit and vacation programs? Why, or why not?

4. Is the company required to accept provisions of the new BCOA agreement since the company previously had been subject to that agreement?

22. MUST THE UNION NOTIFY THE STATE DEPARTMENT OF HUMAN RESOURCES?

Company: Wilhow Corporation operating Town & Country Supermarkets, Baxter Springs, Kansas

Union: Retail Store Employees, Local 322

BACKGROUND

Wilhow Corporation owned and operated Town & Country Supermarkets as a Kansas corporation engaged in retail sale and distribution of groceries and related products at various facilities, including one in Baxter Springs, Kansas. The company's annual gross volume of business in the state of Kansas in 1977 exceeded $500,000, and it purchased directly from points outside the state of Kansas goods, products, and materials valued in excess of $10,000 for use in its Kansas facilities. Retail Store Employees, Local 322 represented certain employees in an appropriate bargaining unit.

The company and union had negotiated several prior collective bargaining agreements, the most recent of which was to expire on August 3, 1977. On May 4, 1977, the union sent a notice to the company indicating that it sought to negotiate modifications and changes in the collective bargaining agreement. Notice on an appropriate form was simultaneously sent to the FMCS. However, no notice of any type was sent to any agency of the state of Kansas concerning this matter.

Following the May notice, representatives of the union and the company met on five occasions to negotiate a new collective bargaining agreement. The parties were unable to reach final agreement, and on August 12, 1977, the union struck the company.

Shortly thereafter, the company filed unfair labor practice charges against the union charging that the union had violated Section 8(b) (3) of the LMRA because it had failed to give notice to an appropriate state mediation agency as required by Section 8(d) (3) of the Act.

After receipt of these charges, the union on August 24, 1977, did

158

notify the Kansas Department of Human Resources concerning the labor dispute and strike. But the union claimed that this was not a state agency to which a Section 8(d) (3) notice was required under the Act.

POSITION OF THE COMPANY

The company claimed that the Kansas Department of Human Resources was a state mediation agency within the meaning of Section 8(d) (3) of the Act. By failing to give it notice before engaging in a strike, the union committed an unfair labor practice within the meaning of Section 8(b) (3) of the Act.

It was factually stipulated that in 1976 the Kansas state legislature reorganized the government and created cabinet departments. Certain functions formerly performed by a State Labor Commissioner were transferred by statute to the Department of Human Resources. The statute that was material to the issue involved here read as follows:

> K.S.A. 44-817. Mediators; appointments; functions; compensation. The secretary of human resources shall have the power to appoint any competent, impartial, disinterested person to act as mediator in any labor dispute either upon his own initiative or upon the request of one of the parties to the dispute. It shall be the function of such mediator to bring the parties together voluntarily under such favorable auspices as will tend to effectuate settlement of the dispute, but neither the mediator nor the secretary of human resources shall have the power of compulsion in mediation proceedings. The secretary of human resources shall provide necessary expenses for such mediators as may be appointed under reasonable compensation not exceeding fifty dollars ($50) per day for each such mediator, and prescribe reasonable rules of procedures for such mediators.

Milton Pasquale,[1] an employee of the Department of Human Resources, testified that he had been with this agency since 1970. During this period, the agency had not been involved in any mediation matters, either formally or informally.

However, as further testified to by Pasquale, the state agency did have personnel available to perform mediation services, had the funds to do so, and routinely proffered its services to parties who were involved in contract negotiations. Pasquale said that the agency made 11 such offers in 1977.[2] He indicated that if the parties had

---

[1] The name has been disguised.

[2] Pasquale explained that his state agency received periodic screenout lists from the FMCS on which the FMCS indicated which employers were too small to justify its intervention. From this, the state agency made its determination to proffer its services.

requested mediation assistance, his agency would have been available to assist accordingly.

The company contended, therefore, that the Kansas Department of Human Resources was a state mediation agency to which notice was required to be sent within the meaning of Section 8(d) (3) of the Act.

Therefore by striking on August 12, 1977, without having given the state agency notice as required by Section 8(d) (3), the union had engaged in an unfair labor practice within the meaning of Section 8(b) (3).

The company requested that the union be issued a cease and desist order dissolving the strike and requiring the union to fulfill its statutory requirements for bargaining in good faith as mandated by the Act.

POSITION OF THE UNION

The union contended the Kansas Department of Human Resources by its own admission had not, for at least seven years, exercised any authority to mediate disputes, did not view its function as including mediation of contract negotiations, and had no funds directly earmarked for mediation. Accordingly, this agency should be found not to meet the statutory definition of Section 8(d) (3). Thus, the union's failure to give notice to an effectively nonexistent state agency was not an unfair labor practice on the part of the union.

In any event, the union claimed that the alleged violation of Section 8(d) (3) by the union was a mere technicality of little importance. The union did give the required statutory notice to the FMCS, and the union and the company had bargained for several months before the union initiated a strike on August 12, 1977.

Further, the company's charges were beyond remedy, since the union did on August 24, 1977, notify the Kansas Department of Human Resources concerning the labor dispute, even though the union believed it was unnecessary as a matter of complying with the Act.

The union claimed that the company was trying to undermine the union's lawful right to strike through the filing of trivial unfair labor practice charges. The union argued that these charges should be dismissed or alternatively, the charges should be declared moot given all the circumstances of the case.

QUESTIONS

1. Was the Kansas state agency, which had not mediated any labor disputes in seven years previously, a state mediation agency within the meaning of Section 8(d) (3) of LMRA? Why, or why not?
2. Is this a trivial, technical issue as claimed by the union? Discuss.
3. If the union was found to have violated Section 8(b) (3) of the Act in this case, what could be the potential consequences to the union and its membership for having struck the company?
4. Since the union eventually did notify the Kansas state agency—even though the union believed it was unnecessary—does this alter and/or mitigate the findings/remedies open to the NLRB?

23. REFUSAL TO BARGAIN OVER A "REPRESENTATION FEE" IN A "RIGHT-TO-WORK" STATE

Company: International Paper Company, Natchez, Mississippi

Union: Local No. 681, International Union of the United Association of Journeymen and Apprentices of the Plumbing and Pipefitting Industry of the United States and Canada

BACKGROUND

At the time of this case in 1977, pipefitters at company plants in Springhill, Louisiana, Panama City, Florida, Natchez, Mississippi, and Camden, Arkansas, belonged to union locals in these four states. Costs of union administration were borne by the locals; costs of negotiating a contract traditionally had been split between the locals and the international union.

In 1974, the union (including Local 681 in Natchez, Mississippi) had added a yearly assessment of 2 percent of wages to the existing union dues of $8.25 per month. Many pipefitters at the Natchez, Misissippi plant quit the union rather than pay the assessment. In 1977, Local 681's membership in Natchez declined from 38 to 1, the last member being the shop steward who by virtue of his position was not required to pay dues. But as required by the Labor Management Relations Act, Local 681 and the union remained obligated to represent the Natchez employees even though none of them paid dues.

The other locals in the other states did not have similar problems. Two locals retained all of their members, and only 2 of 29 pipefitters represented by the third local refused to pay dues.

When the union opened contract negotiations with the company in May 1977, it proposed clauses levying "representation fees" on nonmember pipefitters. The union's final draft of the clauses was:

> The cost and expenses of representing all members of the bargaining unit, without regard to union affiliation or lack of same, must be borne by all bargaining unit employees.

> Those unit employees who voluntarily choose not to become union members shall be required to contribute a pro rata share of the costs and expenses incurred by the union that are directly related to enforcing and servicing the collective bargaining agreement. The representation fee will apply only when a collective bargaining agreement is in effect. Furthermore, in no case will the fee exceed the dues and assessments required of union members.
>
> Failure of any *permanent* employee to make payment of the representation fee each month and to maintain the payments during employment for dismissal after 10 days written notice to the employee and the company.
>
> The amount of the representation fee will be based upon an independent audit to determine those services performed by the union directly related to the collective bargaining process.

The union and the company reached agreement on all other contract provisions. But on September 28, 1977, the company rejected the representation fee clauses on the ground that they violated the right-to-work laws of Arkansas, Florida, Mississippi, and Louisiana,—states in which the company operated plants. On October 17, the union wrote to the company to insist on the clauses, and to announce that picketing would commence at Natchez on October 31. The company then filed unfair labor practice charges against the union claiming that the union had violated Section 8(b) (3) of LMRA by its insistence on bargaining for these representational fees in right-to-work states.

POSITION OF THE COMPANY

The company acknowledged that in non-right-to-work states, representational fees of the type proposed by the union were probably permissible under Section 8(a) (3) of the Act. However, the company claimed that under Section 14(b) of LMRA,[1] states were authorized to prohibit union shops and other arrangements which required employees to pay dues or fees to a union as a condition of their employment. The state of Mississippi passed its right-to-work statute in 1947; in pertinent part, it reads:

> No employer shall require any person, as a condition of employment or continuation of employment, to pay any dues, fees, or other charges of any kind to any labor union or labor organization.

---

[1] Section 14(b), the so-called right-to-work provision, reads as follows: "Nothing in this subchapter shall be construed as authorizing the execution or application of agreements requiring membership in a labor organization as a condition of employment in any State or Territory in which such execution or application is prohibited by State or Territorial Law."

The right-to-work statutes in Georgia, Louisiana, and Arkansas contain similar provisions. For the union to insist that the company must bargain over and agree to a contractual provision which would violate such state right-to-work statutes was, in the company's view, a clear violation of Section 8(b) (3) as clarified under Section 8(d) of LMRA requiring good-faith bargaining. The company requested that the union should be ordered to cease and desist in all of its efforts to negotiate and attain a representational fee contractual provision.

POSITION OF THE UNION

The union claimed that its proposed representational fees were necessary, appropriate, and legally permissible under the Labor Management Relations Act in order to carry out its required representational functions.

In regard to the situation at Natchez, the union pointed out that Local 681 continued to represent employees at the Natchez mill long after it ceased to have any dues-paying members at that location. Between May 1976 and June 1978, the union's business agent traveled to Natchez once a week to handle grievance, insurance, pension, vacation, and other matters and to attend safety meetings. The union prosecuted 19 grievances, negotiated a new contract after frequent bargaining sessions resulting in wage increases and other added benefits for the Natchez employees, and hired an attorney to represent Local 681 in a Title VII civil rights action. In the fiscal year ending June 30, 1977, Local 681 expended approximately $10,700 in order to represent the employees at the Natchez mill.

The union attempted to remedy this erosion of its financial resources by proposing the "representation fee" clause to the company during contract negotiations in May 1977. The clause would have collected from each nonunion employee "a pro rata share of the costs and expenses incurred by the union that are directly related to enforcing and servicing the collective bargaining agreement," with a provision for "an independent audit to determine those services performed by the union directly related to the collective bargaining process." The initial representation fee required of the 38 employees at the Natchez mill would have been $5 a week, allowing the union to collect approximately $9,900 a year, or somewhat less than the $10,700 expended by Local 681 in representing those employees. The clause specifically stated that in no event would the representation fee exceed the dues and assessments required of union members. Had the Natchez employees remained in the union and paid all their dues and assessments under the preexisting dues structure, the union would have collected a total of $14,200—which would have provided approximately $3,500 in additional income that it could have used for institutional expenses.

As to the legal issues involved, the union claimed that the core question to be determined was whether the Mississippi law banning payment of "charges of any kind" constituted a prohibition of "membership" that was within the scope of Section 14(b) of LMRA.

In the union view, the fee-for-service (or representational fee) charge provision that it was attempting to attain was not within the meaning of the term "membership in a labor organization" as specified by Section 14(b). Section 14(b) was aimed only at allowing states to prohibit union shop or agency shop labor contracts which are based upon membership dues. But the Mississippi law went far beyond these limits. Since the Mississippi law was in conflict with and outside the scope of the LMRA, the union was within its legal rights under the LMRA to bargain and to take actions to secure a representational fee which otherwise was permissible under Sections 8(a) (3) and 8(d) of the Act.

The union argued that the differences between membership dues and representation fees were more than a matter of dollars alone. Representation fees are payments for services rendered; membership dues support an institution. All the union was trying to achieve was a pro rata share for representation expenses incurred by the union in order for the union to carry out its legally mandated duty to represent all employees in a bargaining unit.

Common sense and fundamental fairness should support the concept that a labor organization can attempt to collect expenses it incurs on behalf of nonmembers (called free-riders) that the union by law must represent. Even in a right-to-work state, nonunion employees in a bargaining unit benefit directly from union efforts on their behalf. Letting unions recoup these costs of representation does not constitute coerced "membership" within the meaning of Section 14(b) of LMRA.

For all of these reasons, the union claimed that it was well within its rights to bargain to impasse and to take other actions in its effort to secure a representational fee provision. The union requested that the Section 8(b) (3) unfair labor practice charges filed by the company should be dismissed.

QUESTIONS

1. Evaluate the union's arguments concerning the need for representational fees to cover the union's expenses to represent nonmembers in

the bargaining unit. Why is this problem at the core of any union's efforts to attain a union shop in those states where union shops are not prohibited by state law?

2. Why did the company file unfair labor practice charges against the union rather than bargaining over the representational fee issue? Discuss.

3. Why was this case an important one in the continuing controversy of union representation and security rights in so-called right-to-work states?

4. Discuss the pros and cons of Section 14(b) of LMRA both from the standpoint of this case as well as labor relations in general. Why will Section 14(b) likely continue to be an ongoing controversial issue?

24. THE UNION'S REFUSAL TO PROCESS A GRIEVANCE TO ARBITRATION

Company: Leshner Corporation, Hamilton, Ohio

Union: Local Union 148T, Amalgamated Clothing and Textile Workers

BACKGROUND

On April 18, 1979, employee Ruth Kesten[1] was involved in two separate physical altercations during worktime—one with employee Arlene Walker, the other with employee Elaine Davis. All three employees were fired pursuant to an employer rule against fighting. Thereafter the union on behalf of Kesten and Walker filed grievances protesting their "unjust" discharges. (Elaine Davis attained employment elsewhere and she did not choose to have the union file a grievance on her behalf.)

At a first-step grievance meeting, plant manager Jess Jones stated that the company was willing to reinstate Ruth Kesten but not Arlene Walker. The company's position was based on its belief that Kesten had not been the aggressor in either fight and merely had defended herself. Union representatives, especially Carol Monday, the union's financial secretary, responded to this company "offer" stating that if it was company policy to discharge all employees involved in a fight or none, then both grievants should be reinstated or neither. At a second grievance meeting, Jess Jones again stated that the company would reinstate Kesten but not Walker whom Jones termed a "troublemaker." Union representatives again insisted that both grievants or neither be reinstated. Because Walker could not attend the second-step meeting, a third meeting was held so that she could give her version of the events. During that meeting, Tom Wozik, the union's business representative, requested again

---
[1] The names of all individuals have been disguised.

that both Kesten and Walker be reinstated. Carol Monday added that the company should reinstate both grievants if it were going to reinstate one. Jess Jones, plant manager, replied that he earlier would have brought Kesten back, but now he would "have to take it up to corporate management." Subsequently the union was notified in writing that both grievances were denied. The union did not process either grievance to arbitration.

Shortly thereafter, Ruth Kesten filed unfair labor practice charges against the union claiming that the union had violated Section 8(b) (1) (A) of the Labor Management Relations Act by failing to properly represent her.

TESTIMONY OF THE COMPANY

Although the company was not charged in this matter, plant manager Jess Jones testified that at all times the company's "offer" to reinstate Kesten was conditioned upon the union's acceptance of the company's refusal to reinstate Walker. At no time did any company representative offer to reinstate Kesten without adding that the company would not reinstate Walker. Jones further testified that the company was willing to reinstate Kesten and continue processing Walker's grievance to arbitration. But he also testified, "When they said both or none, we said if we couldn't take just Kesten back, we would take none." The company claimed that it did not need the union's approval before it could unilaterally reinstate Kesten without reinstating Walker. But since the union rejected the company's "offer," it was up to the union to decide whether or not to process either or both of the grievances to arbitration on behalf of Kesten and Walker. The union unilaterally decided not to do so.

POSITION OF RUTH KESTEN

Ruth Kesten claimed that the union had failed to properly represent her in violation of the union's statutory obligation to do so under Section 8(b) (1) (A) of LMRA. Since the union refused to accept the company's offer to reinstate her to her job but not Arlene Walker, Ruth Kesten was denied her job by a discriminatory decision of her union. Further, after having rejected the company's offer, the union decided not to process either her or Walker's grievances to arbitration. This union decision, too, closed off whatever chance Ruth Kesten might have had to get her job back through the arbitration process. In total, Ruth Kesten claimed that the union had discriminated against her and had violated its obligation under LMRA to represent her fairly. Ms. Kesten requested that the union be required to make her whole in an equitable amount for lost earnings she had incurred as a result of her loss of employment and the union's failure to represent her fairly in this matter.

POSITION OF THE UNION

The union cited a previous NLRB and court decision in claiming that it had not violated Section 8(b) (1) (A) of LMRA. According to this prior decision, a union breaches its statutory duty of fair representation when its conduct toward a member of the collective bargaining unit is arbitrary, discriminatory, or in bad faith.[2] The union argued that there was no evidence or contention that the union's actions regarding Ruth Kesten's grievance were the result of bad faith or hostility toward Kesten. Nor was there any evidence of disparate treatment. The union leaders in processing the grievances had tried diligently to have both Kesten and Walker be reinstated. Further, in processing the grievances the union actively advocated its position, but the company adamantly refused to reinstate both grievants.

A number of union officers testified that at a regular union meeting, the grievances of Kesten and Walker were discussed. This discussion included the pros and cons of the likelihood of winning either or both grievances in arbitration. After the discussion, the union membership present voted by a large majority not to process either case to arbitration. Based upon this vote, the union leaders decided to drop the grievances. This, too, demonstrated that the union did not act arbitrarily, unreasonably, or in any way which was discriminatory to Ruth Kesten. The fact that Ruth Kesten did not agree with the union's decision does not indicate that the union failed to represent her in a manner required by the LMRA. The union urged that Kesten's unfair labor practice charges should be dismissed.

QUESTIONS

1. Why does a case such as this place the union in an extremely difficult position both legally and politically?
2. Was the company's offer a "squeeze play" on the union designed to place the union in an untenable position? Discuss.

---

[2] Truck Drivers, Helpers, Taxicab Drivers, Garage Employees, and Airport Employees Local Union No. 335, affiliated with International Brotherhood of Teamsters, Warehousemen, and Helpers of America (Monarch Institutional Foods), 229 NLRB 1319, 95 LRRM 1232 (1977), affd. 597 F.2d 388, 101 LRRM 3142 (4th Clr. 1979).

3. Did the union fail to properly represent employee Ruth Kesten? If so, what type of remedy should the NLRB order, since employment at the company no longer is open to Ms. Kesten?

4. Evaluate the union's contentions that it did not act in an arbitrary, discriminatory or unreasonable manner in this case.

5. It is widely recognized that labor union leaders often process some grievance cases to arbitration primarily to avoid unfair labor practice (i.e., failure to properly represent) charges such as occurred in this case. Why is this (a) understandable, and yet (b) not necessarily desirable? Discuss.

25. THE EMPLOYER'S REFUSAL TO PROCESS A GRIEVANCE TO ARBITRATION

Employer: St. Joseph Hospital Corporation, Flint, Michigan

Union: Local 2635, State, County, and Municipal Employees and Council 25, State, County, and Municipal Employees, AFL–CIO.

BACKGROUND

Since 1973, the St. Joseph's Hospital Corporation had collective bargaining agreements for certain service, housekeeping, and other employees with Local 2635 and Council 25 of the American Federation of State, County, and Municipal Employees, AFL–CIO. In early May 1978, Council 25 was engaged in efforts to organize some of the hospital's technical employees. In an attempt to aid Council 25 in its organizational drive, Marie Kraft,[1] president of Local 2635, sought out the assistance and participation of other unions in a "demonstration" to be conducted on the hospital's premises. In conjunction with other union leaders, Marie Kraft had published under her name an article in the May 10 edition of the Flint UAW News–Local 599 newspaper "Headlight Edition". In addition to seeking the support of UAW members in the upcoming demonstration, the article was highly critical of hospital management. Kraft wrote in the article that "the hospital administration has continually lied to, harassed, and even threatened to jail the union representatives at St. Joseph's Hospital."

On May 13, the hospital's director of personnel and labor relations, Elliott Sternberg, obtained a copy of this newspaper article. After consulting with the hospital president and its legal counsel, Sternberg sent Kraft a mailgram advising her that the demonstration scheduled for May 23 was unlawful under Section 8(g) of the Labor Management Relations Act. Further, Sternberg indicated that Kraft's

---

[1] The names of all individuals have been disguised.

appeal for a mass demonstration was "an irresponsible act," and that the hospital would "take appropriate action" to ensure that quality patient care would continue to be provided. On May 20, a local newspaper, the Flint Journal, published an article on the upcoming demonstration which identified Marie Kraft as being a leader in the demonstration.

On May 23, the hospital was picketed by union members as well as by several other labor organizations at various hospital entrances and on the hospital parking lot. Among those engaged in the picketing on behalf of Local 2635 were Kraft and employees Dan Slovic and Theresa Kolb. Both Slovic and Kolb, like Kraft, were union officials. The hospital shortly thereafter filed unfair labor practice charges against both Local 2635 and Council 25 of the union claiming that the union had violated Section 8(g) of LMRA.

On May 25, 1978, a union representational election was held. A majority of employees in a proposed technical employees bargaining unit voted against having Council 25 represent them.

On May 26, the day after the election, Elliott Sternberg advised Kraft, Slovic, and Kolb that he was considering taking disciplinary action against them. He told them that when he returned from his vacation and had reviewed the facts and consulted legal counsel, he would inform them what disciplinary action, if any, would be taken. Upon his return from vacation on June 5, Sternberg reviewed the matter with the hospital's attorney and president. They decided to discipline only Marie Kraft, because they were not sure whether Slovic or Kolb had helped organize or had been leaders in the picketing.

At a meeting held on June 7, 1978, Sternberg handed Kraft a letter advising her that she was being suspended for two weeks for having been a leader and organizer in an illegal picketing demonstration and for having violated a hospital rule which prohibited employees from making "vicious, false, or malicious statements about employees of the hospital." However, because of Kraft's good work record, she was not required to serve out the two-week suspension but a record of the disciplinary action was placed in her personnel file. Kraft requested that the hospital remove from her file the record of the action taken against her, but the hospital declined to do so. She then filed a grievance pursuant to the grievance-arbitration procedure in the parties' collective bargaining agreement. At the same time, Kraft and the union also filed a charge with the NLRB on June 27 alleging her suspension as being in violation in Section 8(a) (3) and 8(a)(1) of the Act.

By a letter dated July 5, the hospital advised Kraft and the union that by filing a charge with the NLRB, Kraft had elected to pursue "a legal or statutory remedy." Accordingly, under Article V, Section 5, of the collective bargaining agreement, she was barred from further processing her grievance, and the hospital considered the grievance matter closed. Article V, Section 5, in part provided that, "The sole remedy available to any employee for any alleged breach of this agreement shall be pursuant to the grievance procedure, provided, however, that nothing herein shall prevent an employee from electing to pursue a legal or statutory remedy providing such election will bar any further or subsequent proceedings for relief under the grievance procedure."

Subsequently, the union filed amended charges against the hospital claiming that by refusing to process Marie Kraft's grievance, the hospital was discriminating against Kraft in violation of Sections 8(a) (4) and 8(a) (1) and refusing to bargain in violation of Sections 8(a) (5) and 9(a) (1) of the Act.

POSITION OF THE EMPLOYER

The hospital claimed, first of all, that the union's picketing of hospital premises was in direct violation of Section 8(g) of LMRA as amended, which requires that a union in a health care institution must give a written notice to the hospital and the Federal Mediation and Conciliation Service at least ten days prior to "engaging in any . . . picketing . . . at any health care institution." The hospital requested that the union be ordered to cease and desist in any such unlawful activities in the future.

Concerning its disciplinary suspension action upon Marie Kraft, the hospital claimed that it was well within its rights to discipline Ms. Kraft for her unlawful conduct and for her false and malicious statements in a published article. These statements were in direct violation of a published hospital rule. The hospital's rule prohibiting employees from making false statements about other hospital employees had been in effect for many years, and it had nothing to do with interfering with legitimate union activities and efforts.

The two week disciplinary suspension was not excessive by comparison to Ms. Kraft's gross misconduct.

Finally, the hospital argued that it was not obligated to process Marie Kraft's grievance protesting her suspension, because Article V, Section 5 of the hospital's labor agreement with the union specifically barred an employee from pursuing both a grievance and a statutory legal remedy simultaneously. The union had negotiated this provision in good faith with the hospital; therefore the hospital was well within its rights to refuse to process Ms. Kraft's grievance when she filed unfair labor practice charges at the same time with the NLRB. The hospital urged that all of the unfair labor practice charges filed against it should be dismissed.

POSITION OF THE UNION

In regard to the Section 8(g) charge filed against the union by the hospital, the union claimed that the union's "demonstration" or "picketing" of the hospital on May 23, 1978, was only informational in nature and of the type specifically permitted under Section 8(b) (7) (c) of LMRA. The union and its supporters were merely informing other employees about the representational election to be held, and there was no attempt to disrupt deliveries or services. Therefore, the hospital's unfair labor practice charge was without merit and should be dismissed.

The union made various contentions concerning the numerous unfair labor practice charges it had filed against the hospital. First of all, the union claimed that the hospital's rule concerning so-called false statements was in itself a violation of Section 8(a) (1) of the Act. The union pointed out that the rule even prohibited employees from inadvertently making false statements; the NLRB long has held that such statements are protected within the context of concerted activity. Further, the hospital rule was so broad as to prohibit employees from making any such statements even during an employee's nonworking time and while off company property. The union urged that the hospital be ordered to cease and desist in promulgating and enforcing such an unlawful rule.

The union claimed that the hospital's two-week disciplinary action upon Marie Kraft was in direct retaliation for her having engaged in lawful, protected activity on behalf of her union. The union requested that the hospital be found in violation of Section 8(a) (3) for this discrimination against her, be ordered to remove the two-week disciplinary suspension from Marie Kraft's file, and be ordered to cease and desist from any such unlawful actions in the future.

Finally, the union contended that by refusing to process Marie Kraft's grievance, the hospital was directly retaliating against Ms. Kraft because she and her union had filed unfair labor practice charges against the hospital. This was a direct violation of Section 8(a) (4) of LMRA. Further, the hospital was also in violation of Section 8(a) (5) of the Act, since the hospital was refusing to carry out its required obligations under the negotiated labor agreement. In the union's view, Article V, Section 5 did not preclude an employee from pursuing both a legal as well as a contractual remedy for the company's numerous discriminatory and unlawful actions taken against her. The union requested that the hospital be ordered to process

Marie Kraft's grievance under the required steps of the contractual grievance procedure, and be further ordered to cease and desist from refusing to carry out its obligations to bargain in good faith and live up to the terms of its negotiated agreement with the union.

QUESTIONS FOR DISCUSSION

1. Was the union "demonstration" or "picketing" in violation of Section 8(g) of the Act, or was it permissible under Section 8(b) (7) (c)? Discuss.
2. Was the hospital rule concerning "making false statements" a violation of Section 8(a) (1) of LMRA? Why, or why not?
3. Evaluate the contentions pro and con made by the union and the hospital concerning the other unfair labor practice charges filed by the union.
4. Was the hospital within its contractual rights to refuse to process Marie Kraft's grievance? Why, or why not?

26. WAS THE SUPERSENIORITY CLAUSE AN UNFAIR LABOR PRACTICE?

Company: Preston Trucking Company, Toledo, Ohio

Union: Teamsters International Union, and Teamsters Local 20

BACKGROUND

This case involved unfair labor practice charges filed by an individual employee against both the company and the union. Specifically, the issue focused upon whether the company and union had violated LMRA by negotiating a superseniority clause, which gave preference to union shop stewards that went beyond layoff and recall privileges.

Preston Trucking Company was an interstate shipper, and it was one of approximately 9,800 companies engaged in multiemployer bargaining with the Teamsters International and its various local unions, including Local 20. The company and Local 20 were parties to a contract effective April 1, 1976, to March 31, 1979, called the National Master Freight Agreement and Central States Area Over-the-Road Local Cartage Supplemental Agreement.

As part of this agreement, a new superseniority provision for shop stewards had been negotiated. This superseniority clause provided, in pertinent part,

> Stewards shall be granted superseniority for all purposes, including layoff, rehire, bidding, and job preference, if requested by the local union within sixty (60) days after the effective date of this Agreement; but only one (1) steward shall have superseniority for such purposes.

Under this clause, the shop steward, Albert Ross,[1] was assigned a route that he bid on in April 1977. Another employee, Willie Chang,

---

[1] The names of all individuals have been disguised.

would have secured that route assignment if Local 20 had not requested superseniority for Ross. The route selected by Ross returned him to Toledo three times each week, whereas his previous schedule had returned him to Toledo only once each week.

Under the collective bargaining agreement, seniority was the sole consideration in those areas enumerated in the superseniority clause, along with "desire" and "preference," for assignment by the employer of vacation periods.

Subsequently, employee Willie Chang filed unfair labor practice charges against the company, the International union, and the local union claiming that the superseniority clause violated Sections 8(a) (1) and 8(b) (1) (A), respectively. Further, by implementing the superseniority clause on behalf of shop steward Albert Ross, the company and the local union had violated Sections 8(a) (3) and 8(b) (2) of the Act, respectively.

POSITION OF THE EMPLOYEE

In arguments presented on behalf of employee Willie Chang, counsel for the employee claimed that the superseniority clause in the applicable labor agreement went far beyond what was necessary for a union shop steward to carry out his representational responsibilities.

Maintaining a contractual clause that grants superseniority to stewards for "all purposes" unlawfully encouraged union adherence. The union did not justify the need for maintaining such a broad superseniority clause.

Counsel for the employee acknowledged that it was settled labor law that superseniority for union stewards which was limited to layoff and recall rights was legal.[2] But any superseniority privileges for union stewards beyond layoff and recall must be justified by representational necessity.

In this case, shop steward Ross had adequately performed his union duties while scheduled on his previous route. In Willie Chang's view, Ross had exercised his superseniority bidding rights under the disputed clause in order to secure a more preferred route; it was not because of union-mandated requirements.

In summary, counsel for employee Chang argued that the superseniority clause and its application in the company conveyed to employees that special contractual benefits were open only to union stewards. This type of treatment was discriminatory to employees

---

[2] In this regard, counsel referenced the *Dairylea* case, 219 NLRB 658, 89 LRRM 1737 (1975).

who were not interested in union activities or in serving as shop stewards. Counsel urged that all of the unfair labor practice charges should be sustained, that the contractual clause and its application in this company should be voided, and that a cease and desist order should be issued accordingly.

POSITION OF THE COMPANY AND THE UNION

First of all, the International union, although supporting Local 20's contentions, claimed it was not properly a party to this matter because the International union was not a signatory to the contract between the company and Local 20. Further, the disputed clause specifically made superseniority a local union option.

The company acknowledged that it was a party to signing the agreement with Teamsters union Local 20. The company had to permit shop steward Ross to exercise job bidding rights over employee Chang as provided for in the superseniority clause in the agreement. The company claimed that the superseniority clause was essentially an internal union matter. The company had agreed to the clause and its application because of union demands. The company felt that the unfair labor practice charges against the company should be dismissed, since the superseniority clause was strictly a union matter which the company did not control.

Local 20 of the union defended the superseniority clause for "all purposes" as not being overly broad, since the collective bargaining agreement afforded no benefits based on seniority other than those mentioned in the disputed clause. As regards the express benefits of "bidding and job preference," the union claimed that they were one and the same, since all of the employees are drivers, and the only "preferences" involved route assignments that were bid for. Enforcing the clause with respect to job bidding was justified because the route chosen by shop steward Ross best enabled him to perform his duties by being present to process grievances and attend to necessary business at the union hall. The union claimed that Ross could have chosen an assignment permitting his return to Toledo five times each week instead of three, but did not since it would leave insufficient time for him to transact union business after allowing for commuting and sleeping time. The union also pointed out that the route which Ross selected (and which Chang also desired) did not result in increased earnings for Ross as compared to his previous route.

In summary, the union contended that the superseniority clause and its application at the company were lawful, since the objective was the furthering of the effective administration of the bargaining agreement at the local level by permitting the continued presence of the shop steward on the job. The union urged that the unfair labor practice charges should be dismissed.

QUESTIONS

1. Was the superseniority clause "overbroad" as contended by employee Willie Chang?
2. Could the International union properly claim that it was not a party to this matter, since the superseniority clause was in effect a local union option?
3. Evaluate the contentions made by the union to justify the superseniority clause and its application at the company.
4. Why does a case such as this place the company in an awkward position?

27. THE CONSUMER BOYCOTT SIGNS ON THE COMPANY PARKING LOT

Company: Firestone Tire & Rubber Company, Pottstown, Pennsylvania

Union: United Rubber Workers (URW), Local 336

BACKGROUND

At the time of this case in 1978, the company's production and maintenance workers were represented by a local of the United Rubber Workers Union, and they were engaged in an economic strike against the company as a result of their inability to reach agreement on a new contract. As part of this strike activity, a lawful consumer boycott had been organized by the United Rubber Workers Union against Firestone products. In order to publicize this boycott, bumper stickers and posters had been prepared, and they were displayed among other places at the picket line patrolling the company's main entrance.

Carla King,[1] a union shop steward, was employed by the company at this time and was represented by URW Local 336, a unit of technical employees. Local 336 was a sister local to the URW local which represented the production and maintenance employees. The technical employees continued to work during the strike of the production and maintenance unit employees, and King continued to cross the picket line and perform her assigned duties. However, King also was a participant in the union's consumer boycott activities off the company premises, and she had marched in a parade with a boycott sign shortly after the start of the strike. In order to further show her support of the boycott, King affixed to her car several prominent signs stating "Support URW" and "Don't Buy Firestone Products." Thereafter, King and her family continued to use this car

---

[1] The name has been disguised.

as they had done previously, for example, to go shopping and as transportation to and from the plant. After arriving at the plant, King would normally leave her car in a lot containing approximately 800 spaces. This lot was used primarily by employees; however, other persons parked there as well, and there were a number of spaces designated as visitor spaces. After King had placed the signs on her car, she attempted to continue to park her vehicle where she previously had parked. But on July 15, 1978, and thereafter, company supervisors informed her that as a condition for her continued use of the lot, King would have to remove these signs. She refused, and as a result she was told to remove her vehicle from the parking lot and was issued a written reprimand for her "disloyal conduct." On behalf of King, the union subsequently filed unfair labor practice charges against the company.

POSITION OF THE UNION

The union claimed that by denying King the right to use the company parking lot because of the signs affixed to her car, the company had violated Sections 8(a) (3) and 8(a) (1) of the LMRA.

The union claimed that except for the fact that the parking lot was located on the company's premises, King was clearly engaged in protected concerted activities. The union cited a number of previous NLRB and court decisions which held that actions taken in sympathy with other striking employees fall within the protection of Section 7 of the Act. Such actions may even include the advocacy of a boycott of the employer's product, as long as the boycott is tied to a labor dispute and does not disparage the employer's product.[2]

The consumer boycott signs displayed by King on her car were related to the strike of the production and maintenance unit employees, particularly in view of the fact that similar signs were located among the picketing production and maintenance workers positioned at the main entrance to the company plant. Further, these signs did not in any way disparage or criticize Firestone products. Most importantly, the signs in no way interfered with production or otherwise disrupted company operations.

In summary, the union argued that by denying Carla King the use of the company parking lot because of the boycott signs affixed to her car, and by reprimanding her, the company had discriminated against her in regard to a "term or condition of employment"—an 8(a) (3) violation—and had interfered in and coerced her in the

---

[2] The union here cited several previous NLRB cases in which this principle was enunciated by the Board.

182

"exercise of rights guaranteed in Section 7" of the Act—an 8(a) (1)
violation. The union requested that the NLRB issue a cease and
desist order upon the company.

POSITION OF THE COMPANY

The company argued that its actions toward King were legitimately a part of its property rights and its normal managerial rights
to maintain decorum and order. Employees do not have any legal or
statutory rights to affix prounion, anticompany posters on an employer's property. King brought her automobile on the company
parking lot with offensive, anticompany posters. Uncontrolled, this
could lead to arguments and possible fights between union ad-
herents and individuals such as visitors, customers, and nonunion
personnel who were not sympathetic to the union strike and consumer boycott.

In summary, the company claimed that its actions toward King
were not discriminatory or coercive against her in violation of her
protected rights under the Act. The company only exercised its usual
and customary property and managerial rights, which were legally
protected. The unfair labor practice charges should be dismissed.

QUESTIONS

1. Compare the issues at dispute in this case with the issues in Case 28,
   "The Offensive Sweatshirts." What similarities and differences are
   apparent?
2. Which is superior under law: a company's property rights, or protected
   employee rights under the LMRA? Discuss.
3. Does it make any difference that this case involved a single employee
   rather than numerous employees? Discuss.
4. Would it have made any difference if Carla King had been a member of
   the production and maintenance workers local union of URW? Of an
   entirely different union, for example, the Teamsters? Discuss.

28. THE OFFENSIVE SWEATSHIRTS

Company: Southwestern Bell Telephone Company, St. Louis, Missouri

Union: Communications Workers of America, AFL–CIO

BACKGROUND

Southwestern Bell Telephone Company has its headquarters offices located in St. Louis, Missouri. Since 1947 the union has represented employees at various facilities in a five-state area, including three St. Louis area exchange facilities involved in this case, known as Mission, Parkview, and Bridgetown exchanges.

On June 22, 1971, the company and union commenced negotiations for a contract to replace that which was to expire on July 17. On June 23, eighteen employees at the Mission exchange appeared at work wearing sweatshirts with the slogan, "Ma Bell Is a Cheap Mother." Later that day two employees at the Parkview exchange wore shirts bearing the same slogan. On July 21, after the company and union had signed a collective bargaining contract and a seven-day strike had ended, three employees at Bridgetown wore the "cheap mother" shirts.

On each of these three occasions, company managers told the employees who wore the shirts that they would have to leave the company premises if they did not remove the shirts or cover up the "cheap mother" inscription. All 23 employees at the three facilities exercised the option of leaving work. None of them was paid for the time which they took off work, and all of them returned the day after they left, no longer displaying the "cheap mother" slogan.

The union filed unfair labor practice charges with the NLRB, contending that the company's actions had violated Sections 8(a) (3) and 8(a) (1) of the LMRA.

POSITION OF THE UNION

The union argued that the slogan on the sweatshirts worn by the employees was only a "skilled, artful, and humorous form of highlighting the differences between the company and union in the negotiations then pending." The slogan should be considered as part of privileged free speech by union employees. The 23 employees wore the sweatshirts to support the union's position in contract negotiations with the employer. The slogans displayed on the sweatshirts were not so offensive, obscene, or obnoxious as to justify the company's requirement that the employees remove or cover them or else leave the premises. On their jobs, these employees did not come into contact with the general public. Nor did the wearing of these sweatshirts in any way interfere with the work performance of any employees.

The union contended that by its actions, the company had illegally interfered with these employees' protected union activities in violation of both Sections 8(a) (3) and 8(a) (1) of the Act. The union requested that the company be directed to cease and desist such actions, and that the 23 employees involved in this case be made whole for the loss of pay they suffered while being forced to be off work by the company.

POSITION OF THE COMPANY

The company argued that the phrase in question on the sweatshirts was capable of more than a single interpretation—one innocent and the other obscene. Several union witnesses had even admitted that the slogan on the shirt could convey an offensive connotation, and that they heard the word mother used in an obscene context in this situation. Four management officials testified that they considered the slogan on the sweatshirts as vulgar and profane, as directed at them and the company, and designed to taunt them and provoke incidents. In view of the controversial nature of the language used and its "admitted suspectibility to profane construction," the company felt that it could legitimately ban the use of the provocative slogan as a reasonable precaution against discord and bitterness between employees and management, as well as to assure decorum and discipline in the plant.

The company contended that its actions in this situation were not in any way reflective of antiunion sentiments or interference with the union employees' rights of free expression. The company pointed out that it had maintained a satisfactory relationship with the union for almost 25 years. During this time, the company had recognized the employees' rights as union members and had not discriminated against employees for their union activities. In the case at hand, however, the company's order to these employees to refrain from displaying offensive slogans during working hours or else leave company premises was a reasonable and protected management prerogative. None of the employees was discharged or disciplined, except to the extent that they were docked for wages lost for the hours they elected to absent themselves. The employees could, and without company objection did, use other insignia to publicize their bargaining demands.

The company requested that the unfair labor practice charges should be dismissed.

QUESTIONS

1. Since the employees did not come into contact with the general public and since their sweatshirts did not directly interfere in work operations, did the company have the right to issue the ultimatum to the employees?
2. What are the limits of protected free speech in union-management relations under the LMRA?
3. Evaluate the union's argument that the slogan was a humorous and skilled slogan as compared to the company's argument of a possible obscene interpretation. By what standards can such value judgments be ruled upon by the NLRB?
4. Was the company's action interference in protected bargaining unit activities, or an attempt by the company to maintain employee discipline?

29. A "THREAT" TO PICKET, OR "COOPERATION" WITH A NEUTRAL EMPLOYER?

Company: Johns-Manville Products Corporation, Waukegan, Illinois

Union: Truck Drivers, Oil Drivers, Filling Station and Platform Workers, Local 705, of the International Brotherhood of Teamsters

BACKGROUND

Employees of the Trumbull Asphalt Company, an asphalt supplier in Waukegan, Illinois, are represented by Teamsters Local 743. This local was engaged in a strike for a labor contract from June 1972, until the time of the hearing of this case in late February 1973. A Johns-Manville Company plant in Waukegan produces roofing materials; in its business at this plant, Johns-Manville purchases materials from Trumbull which in 1972 exceeded $1.2 million. In December 1972 when the alleged unfair labor practice occurred, Johns-Manville was receiving three to four truckloads of Trumbull materials per day.

On December 14, 1972, Tony Presko,[1] Local 705's business representative, accompanied by two other union officials, met with Johns-Manville's regional purchasing manager and employee relations manager, respectively William Driscoll and Arthur Carr. During the course of the meeting, Presko told them that he had received instructions from Jerry Holmes, Local 705's secretary-treasurer, to handle the problem that had arisen. Presko told the Johns-Manville representatives that Local 743 was a local of "inside" workers who were on strike at Trumbull. The sister local, Local 705, had members working for Heaffey Motors, which normally hauled Trumbull's materials to Johns-Manville's plant. Local 705's members were honoring Local 743's picket line. Business reresentative Presko further stated that Trumbull was hauling its material into Johns-Manville's

---

[1] The names of all individuals have been disguised.

plant by using drivers and vehicles which it had brought in from its plant in Texas. Presko stated that in view of the action of Local 705's members in honoring Local 743's picket line, Local 705 had been asked to help Local 743 get the strike resolved. Presko said that he was going to be contacting several customers of Trumbull in the hope that they would stop accepting material for delivery. He further said that Local 705's representatives were there for the purpose of seeing if Johns-Manville would stop accepting deliveries from Trumbull. The union representative then declared that if the deliveries continued, Local 705 might have to "throw up a picket line at Johns-Manville's main gate," in which case "nothing would get in or out of the plant." Driscoll and Carr neither acceded to nor refused the union's request.

Johns-Manville shut down its roofing operation (the operation which uses Trumbull products) for preventive maintenance between December 16, 1972, and January 3, 1973, during which period no shipments were scheduled to be received from any source. In the meanwhile, on December 19, 1972, Johns-Manville filed unfair labor practice charges against Local 705, protesting the union's alleged threat to picket its plant as a violation of the secondary boycott provisions of the LMRA.

Local 705 received the charge on December 21, 1972. On December 29, 1972, the union sent a telegram to the company and the NLRB stating that the purpose of the telegram was to "remove the misunderstanding that the union had threatened to picket the Johns-Manville plant." Also mentioned in the telegram was a statement that the union had no intention of picketing the plant in the event it continued to use the services of Trumbull, because the sole purpose of contacting the company was "to ask for its cooperation."

Johns-Manville was never picketed by the union, and its business proceeded at all times in a normal manner. Trumbull shipments were resumed a few days after the roofing operations started up again in early January 1973.

POSITION OF THE COMPANY

The company argued that the statements of union business representative Tony Presko to company managers William Driscoll and Arthur Carr on December 14, 1972, constituted a "threat" in violation of Section 8(b) (4) (i) (ii) (B) of the Act. In the company's view, Presko was acting under instructions from an officer of Local 705. The intent of Local 705's threat to picket the Johns-Manville plant was to force the company as a neutral employer to cease doing business with another employer with which Local 705's sister local had a primary dispute. The union's threat of picketing posed a threat of quick and substantial economic damage to the company, which was a neutral employer in this dispute. The union's telegram withdrawing this threat was sent only after the company had filed unfair labor practice charges against the union. During most of the period after the union's threat, picketing would have been of limited use because of the company's maintenance shutdown. Nevertheless, the union's threat to picket the company's premises represented a substantial possibility of serious interference, since about 100 or more trucks would pass daily into the Waukegan facility when the plant resumed operating in January 1973.

The company requested that the union be found in violation of the above secondary boycott provisions of the Act, and that the union be ordered to cease and desist from this and similar threats and activities.

POSITION OF THE UNION

The union claimed, first of all, that the remarks of union business representative Tony Presko were not meant to be a "threat" as construed by the company. Presko had been instructed by his superior, Jerry Holmes, the secretary-treasurer of Local 705, to meet with Johns-Manville officials to ask for their "cooperation." The union merely had sought the "cooperation" of Johns-Manville in this matter, which the company could either extend or withhold.

Regardless, Presko's alleged "threat" was a single remark which was of minimal consequences. Upon receiving a copy of the company's complaint to the NLRB, Local 705 sent a telegram to the company and the Board, which retracted any alleged "threat" to picket the Johns-Manville plant and denied any attempt of the union to interfere with the company's dealings with the Trumbull Company. This telegram, which clarified the union's lawful intent, should have rendered the unfair labor practice charges against it as moot.

Finally, the union pointed out that no picketing whatsoever was conducted by the union. For the NLRB to issue a cease and desist order would merely forbid the union to engage in conduct already forbidden by the Act, and which the union had repudiated by its telegram of December 29, 1972. The union requested that the unfair labor practice charges should be dismissed.

QUESTIONS

1. Were the statements of the business representative a "threat" to picket or merely a request for "cooperation" with a neutral employer? Why is

it difficult to determine the intent of a conversation of the nature described in this case?

2. Since the union sent a telegram to the company and the NLRB withdrawing any intention of picketing, did this render the unfair labor practice charges against the union moot?

3. Why would the company press unfair labor practice charges against the union, even though the union had withdrawn whatever "threat" might have been given to the company earlier?

4. Evaluate the union's argument that if the NLRB would issue a cease and desist order, this would merely reiterate what already was specifically prohibited in the Act and which the union formally had repudiated.

30. SECONDARY BOYCOTTING, OR FREE SPEECH AND ACTS OF CONSCIENCE?

Company: New York Telephone Company, New York, New York

Union: International Brotherhood of Electrical Workers (IBEW), Local 3, AFL–CIO

BACKGROUND

New York Telephone Company (Telco) has for many years subcontracted to independent contractors the jobs of installing telephone wire and cables and fastening certain iron work and terminals in buildings under construction or major alteration. In early 1971, Telco contracted with L. K. Comstock and Company (Comstock), Lord Electric Company (Lord), and J. Livingston and Company (Livingston) to do such work on a number of Manhattan job sites. The employees of these contractors were represented by IBEW, Local 3. Under the usual procedure the material used by the contractor was delivered to the job site by Telco employees, who unloaded it from the trucks. The Local 3 members then would transfer the material to the point of use, and install it.

In July of 1971, Telco employees, represented by the Communications Workers of America (CWA), went out on strike. Consequently, Telco management personnel were assigned the delivery jobs outlined above. Until August 31, 1971, these deliveries were generally accepted by the contractors' employees and installed, but a few instances occurred where several union members refused to accept or place the materials.

On August 31, a luncheon meeting took place between George Carr,[1] IBEW union business manager, Walter Weinhold, a Telco legal representative, Paul Schaeffer, Comstock's telephone superin-

---

[1] The names of all individuals have been disguised.

tendent, and Harry Tolman, Lord's general superintendent who also was a vice president of Local 3. The instances of nonacceptance of Telco deliveries were discussed. Carr would not say whether union members had been instructed not to accept such deliveries, or whether he felt that such actions were individual acts of conscience on the part of Local 3 members. The meeting did not resolve the dispute.

However, in an effort to avoid such problems, Telco management subsequently decided to contract with several independent truckers to deliver the materials to the job sites. A number of such deliveries were accepted by Local 3 employees. However, on September 7, a telephone conversation took place between Carr and Weinhold. Weinhold was told that Tolman and Schaeffer had met with Carr, who informed them that the new delivery arrangement "might also lead to difficulties." Carr would not state that union members had been instructed to refuse deliveries; he only emphasized that this was a "distinct possibility."

On September 9, Local 3 held its regular monthly membership meeting. In the course of his business report, Carr discussed the Telco situation and told the membership that it was his view that "when Telco management or independent truckers delivered materials to job sites, they were acting as strikebreakers." He further stated that, "If we were to be true to trade union principles, there would be no basis for our men working under these circumstances." Carr emphasized, however, that this was "his personal view," and that others would "have to make up their own minds." Carr also made these views known in a number of individual discussions with Local 3 members after the meeting in various locations.

On September 10, a meeting took place between Weinhold and Carr. Weinhold told Carr that Telco was taking a serious view of any refusals to accept deliveries, and might either bring court action or eliminate the subcontracting system entirely, leaving the installation work to be done by Telco employees. Carr replied that he "was sorry," but "we have taken a trade union stand that we could not be in a position of aiding or abetting strikebreakers." He considered the material deliveries to be "strikebreaking."

At about the same time, a number of interruptions began to occur on Manhattan projects. On September 9, employees of Comstock on a job at 94th and Park Avenue and employees of Lord at a job on Madison Avenue refused to install wire and cable. On September 10, a Livingston foreman, a member of Local 3, refused to do a job at One Liberty Plaza involving deliveries by management personnel. On the same day, Livingston employees at 1409 Broadway refused to accept deliveries from "strikebreakers." On September 17, Livingston electricians at 919 Third Avenue refused to install material delivered by an independent trucker.

On September 21, 1971, Telco filed unfair labor practice charges against the union claiming violations of Section 8(b) (4) (i) (ii) (B) of the LMRA. Pursuant to Section 10(1) of the Act, the NLRB's regional director sought a temporary restraining order against the union's work interruptions. Such an order was issued by the District Court for the Southern District of New York on October 20, 1971.

POSITION OF THE COMPANY

In its arguments in support of the unfair labor practice charges,[2] the company claimed that the union's actions were violations of the following Section 8(b) (4) secondary boycott provisions of LMRA which make it an unfair labor practice for a union:

> (i) to engage in, or to induce or encourage any individual employed by any person engaged in a commerce or in an industry affecting commerce to engage in, a strike or a refusal in the course of his employment to use, manufacture, process, transport, or otherwise handle or work on any goods, articles, materials, or commodities or to perform any services; or (ii) to threaten, coerce, or restrain any person engaged in commerce or in an industry affecting commerce, where in either case an object thereof is—

> * * * * *

> (B) forcing or requiring any person to cease using, selling, handling, transporting, or otherwise dealing in the products of any other producer, processor, or manufacturer, or to cease doing business with any other person.

The company pointed out that the various meetings and statements of IBEW union business representative George Carr were all directed toward causing a work stoppage or a refusal to perform work by IBEW union members. Carr was the business manager of the union, solely responsible for results in the field. He had stated at an official union meeting to his membership that his interpretation of trade union principles required a refusal by union members to handle Telco deliveries. Soon following, there were a number of such refusals. While it may have been theoretically possible for a union member to view Carr's statements as solely personal, and not the

---

[2] The company also subsequently petitioned through the NLRB that the District Court be asked to issue a permanent injunction against the union's activities.

official position of Local 3 of the union, it is far more likely that Carr's statements were taken to be either an order or strong encouragement or inducement by Local 3 members to refuse to accept or install Telco deliveries while the CWA union was on strike against Telco. Regardless, it is clear in at least four instances that Local 3 members employed by neutral contractors refused to accept or install materials delivered by Telco management personnel or by independent truckers. These were hardly acts of individual conscience, but rather a concerted effort on the part of the union.

The company asked that the union be found in direct violation of the above provisions of the Act, and that the union be ordered to permanently cease and desist in such activities.

POSITION OF THE UNION

The union contended primarily that Carr's statements at the September 9 union meeting represented only his own personal views and that union members were explicitly told that they had to make up their own minds concerning what they individually would do. Thus, no "inducement or encouragement" prohibited under Section 8(b) (4) could have taken place. The refusals by a number of union members to accept delivery or install materials from those whom the union considered to be "strikebreakers" were individual acts of conscience. Such individual acts are not prohibited in the Act.

Regardless, the union argued that even if Carr's statements were assumed to be "inducement or encouragement," a number of factors precluded the finding of Section 8(b) (4) violations. First the union contended that the statements fell within the scope of Section 8(c) of the Act which provides:

> The expressing of any views, argument, or opinion, or the dissemination thereof, whether in written, printed, graphic, or visual form, shall not constitute or be evidence of an unfair labor practice under any of the provisions of this Act, if such expression contains no threat of reprisal or force or promise of benefit.

According to the union, this section means that only inducements or encouragements which involve a threat of reprisal or force or promise of benefit would be prohibited by Section 8(b) (4). Since these factors were absent in Carr's statements, there was no violation under the Act.

The union made the following additional arguments in support of its position.

1. In view of the fact that the refusals by Local 3 members to accept deliveries were few in absolute number and did not totally

halt work on any project, no 8(b) (4) (i) or (ii) (B) cessation of business object was shown.

2. Since the purpose of the secondary boycott provisions is to protect neutral employers from entanglement in labor disputes not their own, no 8(b) (4) violation could be found in this case where Telco, not the contractors, was the charging party

3. A part of Section 8 (b) (4) (D) contains the following provision:

> *Provided*, that nothing contained in this subsection (b) shall be construed to make unlawful a refusal by any person to enter upon the premises of any employer (other than his own employer), if the employees of such employer are engaged in a strike ratified or approved by a representative of such employees whom such employer is required to recognize under this Act.

In the union view—under the circumstances of this case situation—the term *refusal to enter* could well be interpreted to mean "refusal to work" or "refusal to handle" by members of Local 3, and thus would be activity protected by the Act.

In summary, the union's main contention was that Carr's statements to union members were personal opinions, not "inducement" or "encouragement" prohibited by Section 8(b) (4), and that the refusals to accept deliveries were acts of individual conscience on the part of union members. But even if the NLRB would hold that Carr's statements were "inducement" or "encouragement," the various other provisions of the Act cited above would support the position that the union had not committed unfair labor practices in this matter. The charges against the union should be dismissed.

QUESTIONS

1. Were the statements of the union business manager personal opinions, or were they inducement and encouragement prohibited under Section 8(b) (4) of the Act?

2. Were the refusals of the union members to accept deliveries or install materials individual acts of conscience, or secondary boycotting? Why is this difficult to ascertain?

3. Evaluate the union's argument that Carr's statements were protected under the free speech provisions of Section 8(c) of the Act. Is there any contradiction between the provisions of Section 8(c) and Section 8(b) (4) in regard to permissible statements of management or union representatives?

4. Evaluate each of the arguments of the union that various provisions of the Act permitted the statements made by the union representative and the acts of the union workers in this matter.

5. Why would the company request a permanent injunction against the union and not sue for economic damages under the Act?

31. THE CHALLENGE TO THE ARBITRATOR'S AWARD

Company: Illinois Bell Telephone Company, Centralia, Illinois

Union: International Brotherhood of Electrical Workers (IBEW), Local 339, AFL–CIO

BACKGROUND

The facts of the case were not in dispute. Elisha Morgan[1] had been employed by the company as a janitor since October 1964. Between 1967 and 1970, he was examined on three separate occasions by management officials with respect to stolen property, but it was never established that Morgan took the property in question and accordingly he was never disciplined.

On December 22, 1973, Morgan worked overtime between the hours of 3 A.M. and 5 A.M. cleaning a garage located across from a district office building of the company. Although he was not assigned to work in the district office that morning, he entered the building at approximately 4 A.M. in order to retrieve a daiquiri glass which he had given to another employee the previous night. In the course of looking for the glass, Morgan unsuccessfully attempted to pull open the desk drawer of his supervisor, Barney Trottman. He subsequently discovered the glass on the desk of the employee to whom he had offered the drink and began to exit the building.

The district office building alarm system, installed in late 1973 after a number of thefts had been reported, sounded in a local police station at the time Morgan was in the building. When Morgan exited, a waiting policeman informed him that the alarm had gone off. The officer told him that he was to wait until district supervisor Helen Carter arrived. Upon Carter's arrival, she informed Morgan that a few things had been missing from the building. While two

---

[1] The names of all individuals have been disguised.

policemen searched the building, Morgan and Carter retraced Morgan's route inside. When the search was completed, Carter permitted Morgan to finish his work in the garage. Carter subsequently asked Morgan to turn over his key to the district office building and told him that she would talk to him later about "the situation." Morgan responded that he would be on vacation the following week but told Carter how he could be reached.

On December 24, Morgan described the incident to his union steward, Alvin Gray, and told him that Carter wanted to talk to him about it. The steward then informed Morgan of his "rights," among which he related was entitlement to the presence of a union representative when he met with representatives of the company in regard to the incident.

On January 2, 1974, Morgan's supervisor, Barney Trottman, asked him to speak with the company's chief security representative, Steven Flasker. Morgan refused to speak with Flasker without a union representative also being present. Trottman demanded Morgan's cooperation and ordered him to speak to Flasker. Morgan was told that it was company practice for employees to be alone when they spoke to security personnel. When Morgan again refused, Trottman collected his keys and ID card and told him he was suspended until such time as he would speak to security department personnel.

By letter dated February 26, 1974, the company warned Morgan that unless he cooperated with the investigation he would be discharged. The letter, in part, said as follows:

> On or about 4:30 A.M., Saturday, December 22, 1973, you were in our building at 100 E. McCord Street, Centralia, Illinois. You were under no call or authorization from the Company to be anywhere in that building at the time in question.
>
> It is important to the Company to be fully satisfied as to your total activity while in that building without authorization. For that reason you have been requested to discuss this matter with a representative of our Security Department in accordance with Company practice. You have a duty to cooperate in our investigation of this matter. Nevertheless, you have refused to meet alone with the Company's Security representative who requested to interview you. As you were told, our Security Department does not allow third parties to be present when an employee is interviewed.
>
> Because of the questionable circumstances of your presence and your continued refusal to cooperate in the investigation, you leave the Company with no alternative but to base their decision in this matter on all the facts at hand.
>
> Therefore, since you have had ample time to consider your refusal, unless you comply with the Company's instructions by Friday, March 8, 1974, we will move to dismiss you.

On March 11, 1974, supervisor Trottman told Morgan that he had been suspended because he "refused to meet with the company without a union representative." He warned him that if he did not return to work by March 13 and speak to the security department, he would be discharged. Because he did not comply with Trottman's directive, Morgan was terminated on that date.

Local 399, International Brotherhood of Electrical Workers, AFL–CIO, grieved his discharge which eventually went to arbitration. In the arbitration proceeding, the company contended that, given the absence of a specific contract provision, Morgan had no right under the collective bargaining agreement to union representation in a purely investigatory interview. The union, which had also filed unfair labor practice charges with the NLRB on behalf of Elisha Morgan, contended in the arbitration hearing that in cases such as this the NLRB had interpreted Section 7 of the LMRA so as to afford a right to employees to have union representation in an investigatory hearing.

On October 15, 1974, while this case was pending with the NLRB, the arbitrator issued an "Opinion and Award" in which he found that Morgan "was discharged for just cause." Accordingly, he denied the grievance. During the course of his decision, the arbitrator expressly refused to consider or decide upon the LMRA statutory issue presented by the union. Instead, he concluded that, "What is relevant to a resolution of this grievance is the meaning and intent of applicable contract terms." In this regard, the arbitrator found that the only time the contract expressly permitted or required the presence of a union representative was after a grievance had been formally referred to the company by the union. He found no language in the contract which would obligate the company to permit a union representative to be present at an investigatory interview. Nor did he find any evidence of a company past practice of allowing such representation. On the contrary, he found that it had been company practice to refuse employee requests for union representation prior to formal submission of grievances.

In his decision, the arbitrator referred to several arbitration awards finding that an employee is entitled to be accompanied by a union representative when an interrogation is related to prospective discipline, or when the employee has reasonable grounds to expect to be disciplined. The arbitrator concluded, however, that based upon the record presented, (1) Morgan's interrogation was not related to prospective discipline, and (2) Morgan had no reasonable grounds to expect to be disciplined.

The arbitrator's award became a major aspect of the union's unfair labor practice charges against the company, which alleged that the company had violated Section 8(a) (1) of the Act in interfering with Elisha Morgan's Section 7 rights.

POSITION OF THE UNION

The union claimed that Elisha Morgan should have been allowed to have union representation with him if he was to be interrogated by the company's security department, since he had "reasonable grounds" to believe that disciplinary action might be taken against him. The facts of the case included the following particulars:

1. Morgan had previously been accused by the company of stealing tools and equipment.
2. His entry into the district office building on December 22 was completely unauthorized.
3. He acknowledged having unsuccessfully tried to open the desk drawer of his supervisor.
4. He was the only employee on the premises when the alarm sounded.
5. He was immediately detained by a police officer.
6. Supervisor Carter told him that some things were missing, took him back into the building, and asked him to retrace his steps.
7. Subsequently Carter asked Morgan to turn over his key to the district office building and be available for further questioning about the situation.

All factors pointed toward Morgan being a theft suspect. In the union's view, to conclude in the face of this evidence that Morgan did not have reasonable grounds to fear disciplinary action would simply be to ignore the facts.

The union argued that the arbitrator's decision under the grievance procedure in the labor contract between the parties was not binding upon the NLRB in administering the LMRA. The union claimed that Section 7 of the Act guarantees individual employees the right to engage in "concerted activities" for "mutual aid or protection." In this case, Elisha Morgan was denied this right by the company, which refused to allow him to have a union representative with him during a proposed interrogation by its security department. The union argued that (a) the arbitrator's decision in this matter should be disregarded by the NLRB, (b) the company should be found in violation of Section 7 and Section 8(a) (1) of the Act, and (c) Elisha Morgan should be reinstated to his position and made whole for all lost wages and benefits.

POSITION OF THE COMPANY

The company claimed that it had not violated any provisions of the LMRA. Elisha Morgan was discharged for insubordination for refusing to be interrogated by the company's security personnel. Such interrogation was standard company practice in situations of this type. The purpose of the proposed interview was not to discipline Morgan but to get at the facts of the case. Since Morgan refused to submit to an interrogation without a union representative being present—contrary to company policy and practice—the company was forced to discharge Morgan for insubordination.

The company pointed out that its position was upheld by the arbitrator who heard the case under the grievance-arbitration procedure. Nothing in the labor agreement required the company to permit a union representative to be present when its security department interviewed individuals concerning security matters.

In the company's view, the union simply was trying to salvage Elisha Morgan's job by filing unwarranted unfair labor practice charges after failing to accomplish its objective through the grievance-arbitration process. The NLRB should not overturn an arbitrator's award unless there is substantial evidence to the contrary that the arbitration award was unjust.

The company requested that the unfair labor practice charges should be dismissed.

QUESTIONS

1. Why would the company refuse to permit an employee to have his union representative present for an interview as part of the security department's investigation? Is such a policy sound? Discuss.
2. Evaluate the arbitrator's refusal to consider or decide upon the LMRA issue presented by the union. Why do arbitrators normally refuse to rule on legal matters presented as part of arbitration disputes?
3. Although the NLRB and the courts generally prefer to support private arbitration of union-management disputes, are they bound to defer to an arbitrator's award in a case such as this? Why, or why not?
4. Evaluate the company argument that the union simply was trying to salvage the employee's job by filing unfair labor practice charges against the company after having lost in the arbitration decision.

32. DID THE UNION FAIL TO PROPERLY REPRESENT A MINORITY EMPLOYEE?

Company: King Soopers, Inc., Denver, Colorado
Union: Retail Clerks Union, Local 7
Employee: Tony Cortez,* acting as an individual

BACKGROUND

The company operated a chain of grocery stores in the Denver, Colorado, area. On July 3, 1972, Tony Cortez, a young man of Hispanic American descent, began working on the night shift at one of these stores as an all-purpose clerk. In late April 1974, Arthur Gribbins, a co-worker, was promoted to night crew foreman, a position that Cortez felt should have been given him. A similar decision not to upgrade Cortez occurred in August. He protested these promotional bypasses to management in both instances, claiming that he was passed over because he was Hispanic American. The situation was never resolved to his satisfaction, and around mid-September he filed a complaint with the Colorado Civil Rights Commission (CCRC). On September 18, he also formally complained to the Equal Employment Opportunity Commission (EEOC).

On September 17, 1974, Cortez's wife informed Shirley Steinman, the service department manager who was Cortez's supervisor, that her husband was ill and would not be at work that evening. The following day, pursuant to the service department manager's request, Cortez obtained a medical certificate stating that he would not be able to work for three days. On September 19, Mrs. Cortez presented this certificate to Carl Danforth, the store manager. An altercation over whether Mrs. Cortez should be the one to report her husband's illness ensued, and the manager asked Mrs. Cortez to leave. Subsequently, Tony Cortez and his wife reported this incident

---

* The names of all individuals have been disguised.

to Dan Kennedy, business representative for Local 7 of the Retail Clerks Union. Cortez expressed concern that there would be trouble when he reported for work the next evening. Kennedy promised to talk the next day to the store manager, Danforth.

When Cortez reported for work the following evening, the store manager Danforth summoned him and asked him in words to this effect, "What's this with you? Who do you think is discriminating against you? Who in the hell do you think you are that you should be treated specially?" Cortez replied that he would not talk unless his union representative was present. Consequently, Danforth refused to permit Cortez to work that day. Cortez reported for work during the next two days, but each time he refused to talk without his union representative. Therefore, the manager refused to let him work.

On September 23, Cortez went to the union office and presented a written statement of his grievance. This statement protested the employer's refusal to permit him to work September 20, 21, and 22, and alleged that the employer's failure to promote him "was discriminatory." However, Kennedy, the union representative, replied that the grievance "could not be put that way; it had to be in accordance with company procedures."

On September 24, at a step one grievance meeting, Cortez advised Danforth that he had filed charges with the EEOC and CCRC. Danforth accused Cortez of "going over his head," and he then told Cortez that he was "suspended indefinitely" until he "dropped the charges." Cortez turned to Kennedy, the union representative, and said that the manager's decision violated the no-discrimination clause of the collective bargaining contract. Kennedy replied that Cortez also had "gone over his head, too," and that the matter was "out of his hands." After the meeting, Cortez and his wife complained to Mary Dilling, the union's secretary-treasurer, about Kennedy's answer and conduct. Dilling, the secretary-treasurer, promised to talk with Kennedy about the matter.

At the next grievance meeting on October 14, Albert Eley, the company's employment supervisor, advised Cortez that the company had decided "not to give him anything back under the grievance procedure," and that he could either start over again at the same store or be transferred to another store. Cortez protested that he would lose his seniority and asked his union representative, Kennedy, "to do something about it." However, Kennedy replied that he agreed with the company position because Cortez would not have been working anyway due to a strike by another labor organization that temporarily had closed the store where he worked. Cortez replied that he was going to file unfair labor practice charges with the NLRB against both the company and the union. He asked Kennedy to take his grievance to arbitration, but Kennedy replied that he would not. After the meeting, Cortez and his wife again complained to the union's secretary-treasurer, Dilling.

About a week later, Cortez asked the secretary-treasurer if the union was going to take his grievance to arbitration. Dilling told Cortez that she did not want to talk with him because Cortez "had filed charges with the NLRB."

POSITION OF TONY CORTEZ

Tony Cortez filed unfair labor practice charges against both the company and the union in this matter.

Cortez claimed that the company had discharged him, a Hispanic American employee, for filing charges with the CCRC and with the EEOC. Cortez claimed that he had filed these charges because the company had discriminated against him in failing to promote him as he felt was deserved. He was trying to make the company live up to the no-discrimination clause included in the collective bargaining agreement. Since the company had refused to consider his complaint as a union employee and subsequently discharged him because he refused to capitulate to an unfair economic threat, Cortez claimed that the company had violated Section 8(a) (1) of the LMRA.

Concerning the union, Cortez claimed that the union had violated Section 8(b) (1) (A) by failing to properly represent him in his dispute with the company. Cortez argued that the union had refused to fully and fairly process his grievance because (1) he had filed unfair labor practice charges against the company and union, and (2) he had attempted to enforce the no-discrimination clause of the collective bargaining contract by filing charges with the state fair employment practices agency and the EEOC. Cortez pointd to the fact that at the first step of the grievance procedure, union representative Kennedy had agreed with the company that Cortez should be suspended indefinitely until he dropped his charges with the Colorado agency and EEOC. Cortez claimed that Kennedy had demonstrated continued hostility toward his pursuit of the discrimination aspects of his grievance. When he asked Dilling, the union's secretary-treasurer, if his grievance would be taken to arbitration, she refused to talk to him because he had filed charges with the NLRB.

For all of these reasons, Cortez argued that the union had failed to properly represent him. This "restraint and coercion" exercised against him by the union was in clear violation of Section 8 (b) (1) (A) of the Act.

Cortez requested that both the company and union be found guilty of unfair labor practices; that he be restored to his job position;

and that he should be made whole by either the company, the union, or both, for all lost wages and benefits resulting from his suspension and discharge.

POSITION OF THE COMPANY AND THE UNION

The company claimed that it had suspended and later discharged Tony Cortez for what it considered to be conduct detrimental to the best interests of the firm. The company claimed that after its actions against Cortez were carried out, the union did not process Cortez's grievance to arbitration, since the union leadership, too, felt that Cortez had been discharged for just cause. It would have been improper for the company to deal with Cortez as an individual directly, since Cortez was part of the bargaining unit and the company was obligated to follow provisions of the established grievance procedure.

Even granting the possibility that Cortez was discriminated against as a minority (i.e., Hispanic American) person, the company argued that Cortez's proper statutory remedy was to follow procedures under Title VII of the Civil Rights Act of 1964. The company argued that it had not violated Section 8(a) (1) of LMRA, and that Cortez was just using these charges as a way of trying to salvage his job. The company claimed that the unfair labor practice charges against the company were without merit and should be dismissed.

The union position was analogous to that of the company. The union claimed that it had properly represented Cortez in this matter. The union felt that Cortez's grievance was not worthy of processing any further under the grievance procedure. Not every grievance filed by a member of a bargaining unit is meritorious. In this case, the union concurred with the company's decision to discharge Cortez, and therefore the union did not process his grievance to arbitration. The LMRA does not require the union to take an employee's grievance to arbitration, just because a union member thinks it should be done. If Cortez felt he was being discriminated against by the union as well as by the company, his proper course for seeking relief was through provisions of Title VII of the Civil Rights Act of 1964. The union claimed that it had properly represented Cortez, and the union requested that the unfair labor practice charges against the union be dismissed.

APPENDIX

Subsequent to the hearings of this case by an ALJ and before the case was appealed to the full NLRB, a District Director of the EEOC ruled that there was "no reasonable cause to believe that Respondents (i.e., the company and union) had violated Title VII of the Civil Rights Act of 1964," based on charges filed by Tony Cortez.

QUESTIONS

1. Evaluate the claim of employee Cortez that the company had violated Section 8(a) (1) of the LMRA because the company had failed to consider his complaint that he was trying to make the company live up to the no-discrimination clause in the collective bargaining agreement.

2. Evaluate the company's claim that it would have been improper for the company to deal with Cortez as an individual, since Cortez was part of the bargaining unit and the company had to follow the established grievance procedure.

3. Did the union fail to properly represent Cortez in his dispute with the company? Must a union process a grievance to arbitration if a union member requests it in order to carry out its duties under the LMRA? Discuss.

4. Evaluate the argument of the company and the union that Cortez's proper remedy, if any, was through the Civil Rights Act.

5. To what degree, if any, should the ruling of the EEOC noted in the Appendix of the case influence any decision which the NLRB might render?

33. WHO SHOULD INSTALL THE CONCRETE PLANKS?

Company: Spancrete Northeast, Inc., Ulster, New York

Union: International Association of Bridge, Structural and Ornamental Iron Workers, Local 417, AFL–CIO (to be referred to as the Ironworkers union)

Laborers International Union of North America, Locals 17 and 190, AFL–CIO (to be referred to as the Laborers union)

BACKGROUND

In early 1975 the Spancrete Company contracted with the Eberhardt Construction Company to manufacture and install precast, pre-stressed hollow core planks, known by the trade name Spancrete, at the town office building in Ulster, New York. Spancrete's president, Amos Hagen,[1] described the work of installing the planks as follows:

> Rigging and placing would commonly be defined as the work that's related to the physical and actual rigging or set up of the crane, the actual and physical work related to the rigging or securing of a choker of a lifting device or a belt to the item that's to be picked up by the crane. Placing would refer to the guiding and hand handling and signaling to direct that piece to its final location on the stuctural frame of the building and removal of said chockers or sling from the member permitting the crane boon then to swing back to its beginning position over the load. . . . Upon completion of the rigging and placing, the material would be aligned. That means it's aligned into its final half-inch of position by pry bars or some other method of moving it slightly; leveling it, so that it's level with the member that's adjacent to it; the grouting; the cutting of any structural chases; and further the caulking of the underside joints to enhance the ultimate appearance, the application of latex concrete underlayment to properly smooth the top surface.[2]

---

[1] The names of all individuals have been disguised.

[2] This final phase of the erection process—namely, the aligning of the precast, pre-stressed concrete products—always was performed by employees represented by the Laborers union, and it was not here in dispute.

On February 14, 1975, before 8 A.M., Spancrete shipped five truckloads of its Spancrete product to the Ulster job site and ordered a crane from the Kingston Crane Service Company to provide the power equipment necessary for rigging and placing the planks. At about the same time, Spancrete dispatched to the construction site an erection crew consisting of three of its permanent employees, all represented by Laborers Local 190, and two local area employees, both represented by Laborers Local 17. At about 8 A.M. Spancrete's erection superintendent, Andy Ibsen, observed Ironworkers union business agent, Harry Burgess, at the job site with two pickets carrying signs which read,

> This contractor does not employ members of the Ironworkers Local 417 on this job. We wish to inform employees and the public that we do not ask anyone to refuse to cross our picket line, refuse to perform work, or refuse to patronize any service or product.

At this point, the crane operator and the oiler refused to work because of the picketing. A few minutes later, Burgess told Amos Hagen that the Ironworkers union was demanding the work of rigging and placing the planks and threatened to permanently picket the site if the Ironworkers did not get the work of rigging and placing the planks. Hagen did not agree to Burgess's demands, and the Ironworkers continued to picket the job site.

The company filed unfair labor practice charges against the Ironworkers union claiming a violation of Section 8(b) (4) (D) of the LMRA. Under Section 10(k) of the Act, the NLRB requested the federal district court to issue an injunction against the picketing by the Ironworkers union. The court issued this injunction in early March of 1975.

POSITION OF THE UNION

The Ironworkers union claimed that the work in contention belonged to the Ironworkers, and that the Ironworkers union was justified in its actions which were necessary to preserve its contractual rights.

First of all, the union pointed out that the Ironworkers union and the Eberhardt Company were signatories to a labor agreement wherein jurisdiction over the "fabrication, production, erection, and construction of precast, prestressed, and poststressed concrete structures" specifically was assigned to the Ironworkers. Therefore, the union was within its rights to picket the Eberhardt construction site in order to force Eberhardt to live up to this agreement.

Second, the Ironworkers union pointed to a 1972 decision of the NLRB in which the Board awarded a similar Spancrete construction job in New York City to the Ironworkers union.[3] The 1972 case was basically identical to this situation and supported the Ironworkers' claim to the disputed work.

Third, the union in the person of Burgess testified that other area contractors, with the exception of Spancrete, used Ironworkers to perform work similar to the work here in dispute, and that masons or laborers were normally hired to perform the final portion of the installation process—namely, the aligning, leveling, grouting, etc. In support of its position, the Ironworkers union introduced into evidence letters from area contractors to the effect that they assigned installation of this type of work to Ironworkers. Documentary evidence showed several area projects where Ironworkers were employed to perform similar functions, as well as several Joint Board awards from other areas in the United States awarding the type of work in dispute to the Ironworkers union.[4]

Finally, the Ironworkers union pointed out that the Ironworkers conducted a three-year apprenticeship program which included on-the-job and classroom instructions covering all phases of the disputed work. In the Ironworkers' view, members of the Laborers union did not receive comparable training in the rigging and placing phase of the installation of prestressed concrete planks. Thus, to promote the interests of efficiency, economy, and safety, this work should be awarded to the Ironworkers.

In summary, the Ironworkers union argued that its picketing action was necessary to protect work rights which historically, contractually, and properly belonged to the Ironworkers. The unfair labor practice charges should be dismissed, and the work in question should be awarded by the NLRB to the Ironworkers union.

POSITION OF THE COMPANY

The company pointed out, first of all, that Laborers Locals 190 and 435 had been certified by the Board as collective bargaining representatives of Spancrete's employees at its South Bethlehem and

---

[3] Local 40, International Association of Bridge, Structural and Ornamental Iron Workers, AFL–CIO (Spancrete Northeast, Inc.), 197 NLRB 822 (1972).

[4] This refers to the Impartial Jurisdictional Disputes Board of the AFL–CIO. All labor organizations affiliated with the Building and Construction Trades Department of the AFL–CIO and various employer associations who employ their members have signed a stipulation to be bound by decisions of the Impartial Jurisdictional Disputes Board. In essence, when there is a dispute or potential jurisdictional dispute following an assignment of work, either the contractor(s) or labor union(s) involved may refer the issue to the Impartial Jurisdictional Disputes Board for a decision. There is a rather detailed procedure for both filing complaints and appealing rulings of the Board. See *Procedural Rules and Regulations of the Impartial Jurisdictional Disputes Board and Appeals Procedures,* a pamphlet published by the AFL–CIO Building and Construction Trades Department (June 1973).

Rochester facilities respectively. Neither certification, however, made specific reference to the crews which Spancrete used to perform erection work such as the one here in dispute.

Since it commenced doing business in 1963, however, Spancrete had executed a national agreement with the International Laborers Union of North America, AFL–CIO, which specifically covered "all field construction . . . and all work performed by the Employer. . . ." Additionally, that agreement provided that the covered work jurisdiction was specified in Article III, Section 1(b) of the International Laborers union's constitution which, in turn, encompassed the work outlined in the International Laborers union's "Manual of Jurisdiction." That manual included within the Laborers' jurisdiction the following work:

> Where pre-stressed or pre-cast concrete slabs, walls, or sections are used, all loading, unloading, stockpiling, hooking, setting, and barring into place of such slabs, walls, or sections. All mixing, handling, conveying, placing, and spreading of grout for any purpose.

Spancrete had also executed separate agreements with various Laborers' locals representing employees at each of its facilities. These agreements covered the manufacture and installation of Spancrete's concrete products. In accordance with the above, the Spancrete Company pointed out that it had been its practice to assign the installation of its products to an erection crew typically consisting of three permanently based Spancrete employees represented by the Laborers union and two employees hired locally for the particular job. The local employees would be represented by the Laborers local with jursdiction over the particular geographical area in which the job was located. This practice was consistent with the specific provisions of the national agreement mentioned above, and Spancrete was satisfied with this arrangement. In the instant case, as noted previously, the crew's permanent employees were represented by Laborers Local 190, while the two employees hired locally were represented by Laborers Local 17. The only exception to this practice occurred in the New York City situation cited by the Ironworkers union. In that case, the NLRB had awarded the disputed work to the Ironworkers, since Ironworkers historically had performed this type of work in New York City.

Spancrete did not dispute the evidence produced by the Ironworkers union. However, the company claimed that since it commenced doing business in 1963, 95 percent of the 20 million square feet of Spancrete which it had produced had been installed by crews of Laborers under the arrangement described above. Of that total, about 1,065,000 square feet were installed in Ulster County (the town of Ulster is located in Ulster County) and the three neighboring counties of Greene, Duchess, and Orange. Thus, although there was evidence of area and industry practice to support the Ironworkers claim, it was also clear that in the areas where Spancrete operated, it had been its general practice to assign the disputed work to employees represented by Laborers. This was true in all areas except New York City as mentioned previously.

The company claimed that it employed permanent installation crews of Laborers who were required to go through work orientation and safety sessions, as well as a six-month on-the-job training period in order to perform rigging and placing work efficiently and safely. For the Laborers hired locally to supplement the permanent crew, Spancrete tried whenever possible to hire local Laborers whom it had employed before. When, by necessity, inexperienced local men were hired, they were tutored about Spancrete's safety rules and assigned to perform the less dangerous facets of the installation work.

Finally, as to factors of efficiency and economy, Hagen testified that the degrees of work coordination and scheduling, as well as the speed of erection, would be augmented if the disputed work were awarded to Laborers. It was advantageous to Spancrete to use a permanent crew of specialized workmen who were accustomed to handling its products and familiar with the best tools and procedures to achieve the desired results. In contrast, Hagen stated that Ironworkers were less familiar with Spancrete's products, and that an award in favor of them would result in a less effective and more costly operation. In this respect, the company claimed that Ironworkers would utilize more manpower to perform the same amount of work.

For all of the above reasons, the company claimed that it had the right to assign the disputed work to workers represented by the Laborers union. The company requested that the NLRB find the Ironworkers in violation of Section 8(b) (4) (d) of the Act which prohibits a union from:

> . . . forcing or requiring any employer to assign particular work to employees in a particular labor organization or in a particular trade, craft, or class rather than to employees in another labor organization or in another trade, craft, or class, unless such employer is failing to conform to an order or certification of the Board determining the bargaining representative for employees performing such work.

The company asked the Board to *(a)* direct the Ironworkers union to cease and desist in its unfair labor practices, *(b)* award the disputed work to the Laborers union, and *(c)* issue a broad work award on behalf of the Laborers union to be applicable throughout the area in which the Spancrete company operated so as to prevent similar jurisdictional disputes.

QUESTIONS

1. Evaluate the arguments of the Ironworkers union in claiming jurisdiction of the disputed work.
2. Evaluate the arguments of the company in claiming that it had the right to assign the disputed work to the employees belonging to the Laborers union.
3. Why would the company prefer to have the Laborers union rather than the Ironworkers union be awarded the disputed work by the NLRB?
4. If the NLRB should uphold the company position concerning the work jurisdiction, was the company's remedial request appropriate? Discuss.

Case Problems in Union–Management Relations

CASES FROM GRIEVANCE ARBITRATION

Conflict Resolution, Grievance Procedures, and Arbitration

Selected Bibliography

Index to Cases for Part Two

THE CASES

CONFLICT RESOLUTION, GRIEVANCE PROCEDURES, AND ARBITRATION*

The potential for conflict exists within every organization. This is true of the family unit, business organizations, social groups, or government agencies. Conflicts may range from minor differences of opinion to open hostility resulting in physical violence. Yet, humane democratic institutions attempt to resolve intraorganizational and interpersonal conflicts in an orderly manner. While conflict can be destructive, and it often is, it need not be so. Differences of opinion when openly confronted and fully aired can and often do lead to new understandings and subsequent improved relationships on the part of those involved.

The avoidance of conflict is important; its resolution is critical to personal, group, and organizational viability. Conflict creates within both individuals and organizations tensions and diversions which hinder or prevent the attainment of goals. Furthermore, striving to attain goals in itself creates tension and conflict. It is imperative that these conflicts be resolved in such a manner that striving to attain the goals of the organization will not be thwarted. Hopefully, conflict will produce new understanding and harmony, which will propel the organization toward its goals at an increased pace.

While an organization is concerned with the attainment of its goals and objectives, individuals within the organization are also concerned about the attainment of their own goals and objectives.

---

* This section provides a brief introductory overview of major considerations and issues inherent in the grievance-arbitration process. It does not include, however, a discussion of the sizable body of law on labor arbitration which has developed on this subject. This topic usually is covered fully in major texts with which these cases are normally used. A selected bibliography is included at the end of this section.

214

Hence, the potential for conflict between an organization and the individuals within it arises. For example, an organization's need for productivity may come into conflict with an individual's need for security in advancing years. As a consequence, differences may develop over the relative importance of productivity and length of service in determining layoffs.

Not all individuals within an organization share the same objectives. For example, young employees may attach less importance to length of service in determining promotions than older employees. Interpersonal and intergroup conflict within organizations arises from such differences.

Ours is a democratic society which places a high value upon justice and upon the protection of individual rights. The democratic ideal has stimulated the concept of participation in organizations. Values attached to protection of human rights have stimulated the development of various mechanisms which aim to promote the administration of laws, policies, rules, and procedures in a humane and equitable manner, giving full consideration to human dignity and welfare.[1]

APPROACHES TO RESOLUTION OF CONFLICT

Concern for human rights in our society has resulted in the development of various means whereby injured parties may appeal decisions made by those exercising power over them. In fact, almost every type of organization has developed one or more appeal procedures.

Most government agencies have developed appeal procedures which enable employees to seek redress from acts of agency administrators. Labor unions have developed internal procedures for the protection of members from harassment within their own ranks. For example, the International Union of United Automobile, Aerospace and Agricultural Implement Workers of America has expended unusual effort to provide its members a fair opportunity for defense against union decisions concerning them, and has provided well-defined and speedy avenues of recourse in the event of unjust acts by officers and administrators. Religious institutions have developed appeal procedures which provide members with avenues of recourse against the clergy. For example, the Roman Catholic Church has

---

[1] For an excellent discussion of this aspect of arbitration, see Walter E. Baer, *Discipline and Discharge under the Labor Agreement* (New York: American Management Association, 1972), pp. 25–43.

developed elaborate procedures which members may employ to seek redress.

Business organizations also have developed appeal procedures. They exist in both union and nonunion companies. Many nonunion organizations have developed formalized problem solving or grievance procedures which guarantee employees the right to appeal decisions made concerning them by their supervisors. In most instances, recourse may be sought all the way up through the organization to the president. Many nonunion employers are even providing opportunities for "juries" of employees to render final decisions in complaints which have gone through a number of steps without resolution.

Formalized appeal procedures seem to become more necessary as organizations become larger and more institutionalized. Further, the more demanding and more urgent the goals and objectives of the organization, and the more that they press upon individuals in the organization, the less freedom an individual is able to exercise. The hierarchical and authoritarian nature of some organizations tends to produce dependency of the subordinate on the superior. Dependency, in turn, tends to create frustration in the individual seeking freedom of self-expression on the job. Inability to exercise freedom of self-expression, in turn, tends to block the individual in a search for satisfaction through work.

Thus, grievance procedures provide an opportunity for individuals to exercise greater control over their environment and may expand the opportunities for them to achieve their life goals through work. But probably most significantly, such procedures give individuals a chance to contest those decisions or actions of management which employees feel unfair and which violate their rights and the obligations of the employer.

GRIEVANCE PROCEDURES

Appeal opportunities are generally formalized in unionized organizations in grievance procedures which are included in the collective agreement. These formalized procedures vary considerably from organization to organization. Typically, however, they provide that, at the first step, the employee takes the grievance to either the immediate supervisor or the union steward.[2] The super-

---

[2] A distinction customarily is drawn in labor relations between a *complaint* and a *grievance*. A complaint refers to any feeling of injury or injustice, real or imagined, expressed or unexpressed. A grievance is a complaint which has been formally presented to the supervisor, union steward, or some other union official under the provisions of a grievance procedure, alleging a violation of the labor agreement.

216

visor, the steward, and the employee discuss the issue and hopefully arrive at an amicable settlement. Most grievances are settled on an informal basis at this first step. If the parties are unable to agree, either because the supervisor disagrees with the request of the employee or because the supervisor lacks authority to make a decision, the grievance is appealed to the second step of the grievance procedure. Typically, the grievance committee of the union and the plant superintendent or office manager attempt to reach a settlement. However, grievances which are not settled at the first step of the grievance procedure may not be settled at the second step either; they are then usually appealed to the third step of the grievance procedure. At this level, the handling of the grievance is quite formalized; the parties involved may include members of top management of the company and members of the international office of the union. An estimated 97 percent of all collective agreements provide that if the parties are unable to arrive at a decision at the third (or fourth) step of the grievance procedure, either party may petition for arbitration of the dispute by a third party.

The following is a quite typical grievance procedure which shows the various steps to be followed in processing a grievance to ultimate resolution.[3]

ARTICLE XIX—GRIEVANCE PROCEDURE

Section 19.1 Should differences arise between the Company and the Union, or between the Company and employees of the Company, or should trouble of any kind arise in the plant, such differences shall be handled through the Grievance Procedure as set forth elsewhere in this Agreement.

Section 19.2 Except as set forth below, no grievance or differences shall be processed under the Grievance Procedure set forth herein unless presented by the employee, or the Union, to the Company in the First Step within three (3) days from the time the aggrieved acquires knowledge of such grievance.

Section 19.3 No grievance involving discharge, suspension or discipline shall be processed unless presented in writing to the Company within seven (7) working days from the date of which the Union receives notice of such discharge, suspension or discipline.

Section 19.4 No other grievance and/or claims involving back pay shall be effective retroactively beyond thirty (30) days prior to the filing of the grievance and/or the claim. This shall not apply to claims for

[3] From 1983–86 Agreement between FDL Foods, Inc., Dubuque, Iowa, and Local 758, International Union of Operating Engineers, AFL–CIO, pp. 20–22.

back pay involving general wage increases or regular allowances, such as clothing changing time.

Section 19.5 Grievances shall be processed as follows:

STEP ONE: The employee with or without the Union Steward, may present the grievance to the Foreman. The Foreman shall reply within twenty-four (24) hours.

STEP TWO: In case the employee, or the Union, is dissatisfied with the decision of the foreman in the First Step, the Union representative, with or without the aggrieved employee, may present the grievance to the Department Supervisor, or any representative appointed by the Company within forty-eight (48) hours. The grievance presented by the Union in Step Two shall be in writing, and the Company shall reply in writing within forty-eight (48) hours after the Company receives such written grievance. The answer will be given to the Steward.

STEP THREE: In case the employee, or the Union is dissatisfied with the decision in the Second Step, the Union must notify the Company within seventy-two (72) hours after receipt of the Second Step response, in writing, of their desire to move the grievance to Step Three. Third Step grievance meetings will be held on the first Wednesday of each month if there are any grievances pending. This date and time may be changed by mutual agreement between the Union and the Company. The Grievance Committee of the Union, composed of not more than three (3) Union Representatives, together with the Local Union Business Agent and Recording Secretary or their representatives, shall meet with the Department Supervisors and other representatives appointed by the Company for the purpose of discussing the grievance involved. In grievances involving particularly complex or controversial problems, the Union shall be allowed to have an employee from the department of the aggrieved employee serve on the grievance committee as an additional member of the group. The grievance in Step Three shall also be in writing and the Company shall reply in writing within seventy-two (72) hours after the hearing. The answer will be given to the Union Business Agent or his representative.

STEP FOUR: In case the Union is dissatisfied with the decision in the Third Step, the Union must notify the Company within five (5) days after receipt of the Third Step response, in writing, of their desire to move the grievance to Step Four. The grievance will be presented to the Plant Manager and one other person designated by the Company and the Local Union President and one other local Union representative and/or the International Union Representative, or their designated deputies, for discussion and settlement.

STEP FIVE: If no satisfactory settlement is reached in Step Four within five (5) days, then either party may request arbitration. Within five (5) days after such request is made, the Company and the Union may request the Federal Mediation and Conciliation Service to submit a list of seven (7) names, and the Union and the Company shall select one to arbitrate the grievance. The arbitrator shall render his decision as soon as possible after the hearing is concluded, but no later than thirty (30) days after the closing of the hearing, unless time is extended by mutual agreement. Both parties may call witnesses and present written and oral evidence to support their respective positions. The decision of the Arbitrator shall be final and binding upon all parties. The Arbitrator shall have no right to modify, amend, or add to the terms of this Agreement, or to require of the Company, of the Union, or of the employee, any act which is not required by law or by this agreement to be performed.

The time limits stated in the grievance procedure exclude Saturday, Sunday and holidays. Forfeiture of a grievance due to the time limits reverts back to the last position in the grievance procedure either Company or Union. Forfeiture is considered a settlement on a no precedent basis.

Section 19.6 The fees of the Arbitrator, as well as all other costs incidental to the arbitration, shall be borne equally by both parties.

Although grievance procedures are used for numerous reasons, the following are among the most important purposes which grievance procedures provide. First, they serve to locate problems which exist in the relationship between the union and the company, and also to locate problems which exist within both organizations. Second, they tend to open the channels of communication between employees and management. They are especially helpful in stimulating communication upward from employees to management, often to the discomfiture of the managers! Third, the grievance procedure is the instrument which enables the parties to initiate action, to interpret provisions of the collective agreement, and to apply the contract to new and changing aspects of daily relations between the employees and management. Finally, it serves as valuable source of data at contract negotiation periods.

ARBITRATION

Arbitration constitutes the final step in most grievance procedures for settling disputes. It begins where the other procedures leave off, since the parties are presumed to have explored alternatives of settlement and compromise before resorting to an arbitrator. When the parties turn to arbitration, they voluntarily agree to refer their dispute to an impartial third person. The arbitrator's determination will be made on the basis of the evidence and arguments presented by the disputants, who agree in advance to accept the decision of the arbitrator as final and binding.

In the United States, grievance-arbitration is essentially a voluntary system. Federal labor law does not require the parties to include an arbitration clause in their collective agreement. However, the NLRB and the federal courts normally will defer to private arbitration those disputes which occur during the life of a labor agreement, provided that there is no dispute involving a legal statute. Thus, grievance-arbitration is considered as a voluntary process in the United States, since an arbitration clause is the result of negotiations between management and a labor union.[4]

Arbitration is usually viewed as a judicial process. However, the parties do influence this process by the internal policies which each has adopted with respect to it. For example, either the company or the union may follow a policy of carefully screening disputes which are referred to arbitration. Their objectives may be to present to arbitration only those cases which have merit and which the appealing party believes it has a good chance of winning. On the other hand, one or both parties may operate on a percentage basis. If they adopt this approach to arbitration, they may elect to appeal doubtful cases on the theory that arbitrators will tend to compromise. According to this reasoning, they expect to win certain points that they might otherwise have conceded. Of course, this approach to arbitration can be short-sighted; the theory that arbitrators will split decisions is generally not valid, since most arbitrators try to judge each case on the specific issues involved in the case. Thus, while the arbitration process is essentially a judicial one, in certain respects it is an extension of collective bargaining.

Arbitration has become an important means for the resolution of conflict. First, it has prevented open conflict, which tends to be very costly in terms of income lost to workers and profits lost to companies. Second, arbitration creates a better climate for the resolution of conflict. The parties resolve, as a matter of principle, to settle their disputes amicably. It can promote a spirit of cooperation which tends to pervade the entire grievance-handling process. Third, the parties know in advance that if they do not settle a dispute between themselves, it will ultimately be settled by a third party. While this may, in a few instances, prevent the parties from behaving in a mature and responsible manner, as a general rule arbitration has helped to develop mature dispute settlements. Finally, no-strike and no-lock-

---

[4] Arbitration of a grievance as the final step of a grievance procedure is referred to as "rights arbitration," meaning arbitration of rights already established within a collective bargaining agreement. If an arbitrator is asked to render a decision which specifies contractual language, that is, which in effect establishes new terms of a contract, this is referred to as "interest arbitration."

out provisions in a collective agreement are possible only if an alternative means for ultimate settlement exists. If a union gives up the right to strike and if a company gives up the right to lock out employees over a grievance during the life of the agreement, both must be assured that some other method for settlement of disputes is available.

Many years ago, Harry Shulman, former dean of the Yale School of Law and a distinguished labor arbitrator, summarized the role of arbitration and of the arbitrator in a classic statement as follows:

> The arbitration is an integral part of the system of self- government. And the system is designed to aid management in its quest for efficiency, to assist union leadership in its participation in the enterprise, and to secure justice for the employees. It is a means of making collective bargaining work and thus preserving private enterprise in a free government.

> * * * * *

> The important question is not whether the parties agree with the award but rather whether they accept it, not resentfully, but cordially and willingly. Again, it is not to be expected that each decision will be accepted within the same degree of cordiality. But general acceptance and satisfaction is an attainable ideal. Its attainment depends upon the parties' seriousness of purpose to make their system of self-government work, and their confidence in the arbitrator. That confidence will ensue if the arbitrator's work inspires the feeling that he has integrity, independence, and courage so that he is not susceptible to pressure, blandishment, or threat of economic loss; that he is intelligent enough to comprehend the parties' contentions and empathetic enough to understand their significance to them; that he is not easily hoodwinked by bluff or histrionics; that he makes earnest effort to inform himself fully and does not go off half-cocked; and that his final judgment is the product of deliberation and reason so applied on the basis of the standards and the authority which they entrusted to him.[5]

LIMITS AND OBJECTIONS TO ARBITRATION

Voluntary arbitration is a valuable device for settling disputes during the life of a contract, when the arbitrator's function is primarily that of interpreting the language or intent of the parties. Both management and unions generally reject arbitration as a method for determining the language of the contract. The contract is "law," since it represents critical areas of managerial and union decision

---

[5] Harry Shulman, "Reason, Contract, and Law in Labor Relations," *Harvard Law Review*, vol. 68, 1955, p. 999.

making. Matters in dispute often are considered by the parties to involve issues of principle, rights, or prerogatives. Neither management nor unions wish to permit an outside third party to resolve such important issues. Not only do they fear losing control over their destinies, but they also fear that a provision of an agreement determined by arbitration could never be changed. This is in contrast to their belief that if an arbitrator's ruling on a clause of an existing contract indicates to a party that the clause is unsatisfactory, that party can hope to change or eliminate that clause in the next contract negotiation.[6]

Arbitration is most useful when the parties resort to its use sparingly and only as a last resort. Constructive conflict can lead to new insights and understandings by the parties. Agreements reached after serious negotiation also tend to be more acceptable than those imposed from outside. Serious negotiation further helps to develop maturity and responsibility. If the parties turn to an arbitrator as a means to escape a serious confrontation or to save face, they reduce their potential for developing their collective bargaining skills and the maturity essential for a satisfactory relationship. In fact, arbitrators often make comments about unsatisfactory grievance handling such as the following: "This case should never have gotten to arbitration," or "The parties should have been able to resolve this case themselves."

ARBITRATION PROCEDURES

Arbitration clauses in collective agreements usually are individually tailored to meet the specific needs of each union-management relationship. The American Arbitration Association some years ago developed a broad standard arbitration clause, which provided a very basic framework for those parties who were willing to utilize and rely upon the AAA's services.

> Any dispute, claim or grievance arising out of or relating to the interpretation or the application of this agreement shall be submitted to arbitration under the Voluntary Labor Arbitration Rules of the American Arbitration Association. The parties further agree to accept the arbitrator's award as final and binding upon them.[7]

However, the overwhelming majority of collective agreements are much more detailed and specific than the preceding type of general

---

[6] See Frank Elkouri and Edna Asper Elkouri, *How Arbitration Works*, 3d ed. (Washington, D. C.: Bureau of National Affairs, Inc., 1973), pp. 44–67.

[7] American Arbitration Association, *Labor Arbitration, Procedures and Techniques* (New York, 1960), p. 7.

clause. For example, the following arbitration provisions limit both the issues subject to arbitration and the authority of the arbitrator.[8]

Step 4. In the event any employee's grievance is not settled to the satisfaction of the Union in the previous steps, the Union shall, within the time herein set out, request the appointment of an arbitrator. The selection of the arbitrator shall be carried out by the parties in accordance with the rules of the American Arbitration Association or the Federal Mediation and Conciliation Service. The parties will jointly stipulate the question to the arbitrator, or if they are unable to agree to a stipulation, each party shall submit to the other its written statement of the question at least five days in advance of hearing thereof, and both statements shall be submitted to the arbitrator.

The arbitrator shall have authority to decide only matters involving grievances which were processed and handled in accordance with the Grievance Procedure and which involve a dispute as to the meaning of terms found in this Agreement, or as to the existence of facts which affect the manner in which the terms found in this Agreement are applied. He shall have no authority to rule on any of the matters excluded from the Grievance Procedure or from arbitration by this Agreement and shall have no authority to add to, subtract from, or modify any of the terms of this Agreement, nor to establish any conditions not contained in this Agreement.

All expenses and fees of the arbitrator shall be shared equally by the Employer and the Union. Expenses of witnesses and other expenses incurred by the parties shall be paid by the party incurring such expenses.

Any decision made in conformance with this arbitration procedure shall be accepted by both the Employer and the Union and shall be final and binding on both parties and shall be complied with within five working days after the decision is rendered.

The Grievance Procedure and arbitration provided for herein shall constitute the sole and exclusive remedies to be utilized for the determination, decision, adjustment, or settlement of any and all grievances as herein defined.

The American Arbitration Association has developed a standard set of rules and procedures which govern any arbitration which it administers.[9] If American Arbitration Association rules are not utilized by the parties, the arbitration section of the collective agreement usually will contain a statement of policy indicating that certain disputes shall be arbitrated and will outline other rules governing the

[8] Agreement between Whirlpool Corporation (Fort Smith Division) and International Union of Allied Industrial Workers, Local 370, AFL–CIO, September 1974, pp. 40–42.

[9] See pamphlet, *Voluntary Labor Arbitration Rules of the American Arbitration Association,* (New York: 1979), American Arbitration Association.

conduct of arbitration proceedings. Issues which must be met in the arbitration clause or by agreement by the parties include:

1. What is arbitrable? The clause quoted above provides that any dispute arising out of or relating to the interpretation or application of the agreement may be submitted to arbitration. On the other hand, the parties sometimes wish to exclude certain matters from arbitration, such as wage rates or determination of production or quality standards. Presumably, the parties prefer to decide what course of action they will take, including the possibility of strike or lockout, if they fail to reach an agreement at the last step of the grievance procedure at the time when the deadlock occurs.

2. How is the arbitrator appointed, including what procedures shall be followed if the parties are unable to agree upon an arbitrator? Shall the parties appoint a permanent arbitrator to hear all disputes, or should an ad hoc arbitrator be appointed for each dispute? Most arbitrators are certified and obtained through either the Federal Mediation and Conciliation Service or the American Arbitration Association.

3. What are the rules and procedures governing the conduct of an arbitration? This includes methods for initiating an arbitration, time and place of hearings, swearing of witnesses, representation by legal counsel, recording of the proceedings, filings of briefs, rules of evidence, time within which an award will be made, and to whom it shall be delivered. Most of these issues will be determined by the parties themselves, but sometimes the arbitrator will be asked to rule on such procedural matters.

4. Who bears the cost of an arbitration? Typically, but not always, the parties will agree to share equally in these costs.

Disputes are brought to arbitration by one of two routes, either by a "submission" from the parties or by a "demand for arbitration" filed by either party. A submission agreement is a statement signed by both parties indicating the specific nature of the issue under contention and the specific relief which the injured party is seeking. A demand for arbitration is a formal request made by either of the two parties to the other for arbitration of an issue in dispute.

Among the major types of evidence and testimony presented and considered by arbitrators are:

1. The language of provisions of the Agreement.
2. The intent of the parties in negotiating Agreement provisions.
3. Past practice or precedents in handling similar or parallel matters.
4. Practices at other plants in the same industry or in other industries.

5. Equity or fairness in certain matters, "just cause" in disciplinary cases.
6. Arbitration rulings and precedents established by other arbitrators.
7. Industrial relations practices accepted as desirable or undesirable.

The American Arbitration Association has identified 10 common errors committed by parties in arbitration.[10]

1. Using arbitration and arbitration costs as a harassing technique.
2. Overemphasis of the grievance by the union or exaggeration of an employee's fault by management.
3. Reliance on a minimum of facts and a maximum of arguments.
4. Concealing essential facts; distorting the truth.
5. Holding back books, records, and other supporting documents.
6. Tying up proceedings with legal technicalities.
7. Introducing witnesses who have not been properly instructed on demeanor and on the place of their testimony in the entire case.
8. Withholding full cooperation from the arbitrator.
9. Disregarding the ordinary rules of courtesy and decorum.
10. Becoming involved in arguments with the other side. The time to try to convince the other party is before arbitration, during grievance processing. At the arbitration hearing, all efforts should be concentrated on convincing the arbitrator.

The parties to a dispute seek an award from the arbitrator. The purpose of the award is to arrive at a final and conclusive decision with respect to the controversy. The arbitrator must not exceed the authority given him or her under the terms of the collective agreement. Most agreements, for example, state in some way that the arbitrator may not add to, detract from, or otherwise modify any part of the collective agreement. Even where this is not specifically stated in a collective agreement, this restriction is generally implied in the submission of a dispute to the arbitrator. The award of the arbitrator is to be accepted by both parties, and it will be upheld in the courts unless the arbitrator exceeds the authority granted him or her by the parties, fraud or some other breach of ethics is proved, or the result is contrary to law (e.g., an arbitrator enforces an illegal union security provision).

---

[10] American Arbitration Association, *Labor Arbitration, Procedures and Techniques* (New York, 1960), pp. 20–21.

Expedited Arbitration. Expedited arbitration is a fairly recent and in some situations still an experimental approach designed to simplify and speed up the arbitration process. A typical arbitration may require several months or more to complete and cost each side thousands of dollars, when costs of personnel, lost time, and attorneys' and the arbitrator's fees and expenses are calculated. In 1983, according to FMCS data, an arbitrator's fees and expenses alone averaged about $1,300 per case. In 1971, 10 of the country's largest steel companies and the United Steelworkers Union agreed to a three-year experiment which they named "expedited arbitration" or "mini-arb." The experiment was successful, and they subsequently incorporated this procedure into their collective agreements. Numerous companies and unions are currently utilizing this procedure.

Expedited arbitration system is not a substitute for regular arbitration. It is usually employed to settle certain types of disputes at some agreed-upon step of the grievance procedure after the parties have not settled at a previous step, and then only after a joint labor-management committee agrees to the abbreviated procedure.

This arbitration technique is marked by informality. The hearing is usually conducted in the office or shop, sometimes at the workplace rather than in a hotel room or other neutral site. The arbitrator may interview witnesses on the spot. The more legalistic rules of evidence often employed in arbitration proceedings are considerably relaxed. The arbitrator normally renders his or her decision within 24 to 48 hours of the hearing. Sometimes the arbitrator renders it the same day, on occasion within minutes after the conclusion of the hearing. This is called a bench decision.

The procedure is more applicable to some cases than others. It has been most useful in settling minor disciplinary cases, although it has also been employed to decide nondisciplinary issues, including compensation and employee rights questions. It is less useful in resolving issues involving interpretation of the meaning of a major contractual clause or questions of principle. Some disputes involve issues so fundamental to the parties that one or both may refuse to submit them to an expedited arbitration. For example, questions involving the meaning of management or union "rights" provisions in the contract, subcontracting, or production standards are more appropriately resolved by means of a more thorough arbitration procedure.[11]

---

[11] For a brief, but balanced, view of this topic, see Lawrence Stessin, "Expedited Arbitration: Less Grief over Grievances," *Harvard Business Review*, no. 1 (1977): 128–34. Also see pamphlet, *Expedited Labor Arbitration Rules of the American Arbitration Association* (New York: American Arbitration Association, 1979).

Although expedited arbitration normally is associated with settlement of rather minor grievances, some companies and unions are utilizing the concept for discharge and other selected cases where the parties wish to speed the arbitration process to a swift conclusion. Here the parties may well have a very thorough and formal arbitration hearing of the case matter, but the selection of the arbitrator, the scheduling of the hearing, and the rendering of the arbitrator's decision are all accomplished within a specified and relatively fast period of time. The following "Expedited Procedure" is representative of this type of approach.[12]

Section 4(a). If a grievance involving the discharge of an employee shall have been submitted but not adjusted under Step 3, the following Expedited Procedure shall apply unless the Employer and the Union mutually agree to waive any of these provisions:

1. If the Union wishes to proceed to arbitration, it must give written notice to the Employer of its demand for arbitration within five (5) days after its receipt of the Employer's written reply following the Step 3 meeting.

2. The Employer will promptly notify the appropriate arbitrator selected as set forth below and schedule a hearing which is to take place within the five-day period following the Employer's receipt of the Union's demand for arbitration.

3. The arbitrator shall render a written decision within ten (10) days following the close of the hearing, and within sixty (60) days following the close of the hearing, the arbitrator will render a written opinion explaining the reasons for the decision.

In conjunction with any Expedited Arbitration hereunder, either party may, at its option, submit a pre-hearing brief. And, either party may, at its option, request a court reporter for the hearing at its own cost, unless both parties request a transcript in which case the cost of the court reporter will be shared equally.

The decision of the arbitrator shall be final and conclusive on both the Employer and the Union. The arbitrator shall have no power to add to, detract from, or alter this agreement in any way. Pending final decision by the arbitrator, there shall be no action taken by either party to the controversy. Any expense incidental to and arising out of the arbitrations shall be borne equally by the Employer and the Union except as otherwise provided in this Article.

(b). Expedited Arbitration Panel—Within thirty (30) days following the effective date of this Agreement, and annually thereafter, the Employer and the Union shall select a panel of five (5) arbitrators

---

[12] From 1981–84 Agreement between Anheuser-Busch, Inc., of St. Louis, Missouri, and Bottlers Local Union No. 1187, affiliated with the International Brotherhood of Teamsters, Chauffeurs, Warehousemen, and Helpers of North America.

designated to decide Expedited Arbitration cases under this Article. The panel of five (5) arbitrators shall be selected as follows: The Federal Mediation and Conciliation Service will be asked to provide five (5) lists of arbitrators with each list containing names of seven (7) names from the Midwest area comprised of the states of Michigan, Illinois, Indiana, Iowa, Arkansas, Kansas, Nebraska, and Missouri. One arbitrator will be chosen from each FMCS list by the procedure of alternating strikes—the party having the first strike on the first list will be determined by a coin flip and thereafter the party having the first strike on the remaining lists will alternate. The five (5) arbitrators thus chosen will constitute the Expedited Panel for proceedings under this Article.

(c). Selection of an Arbitrator from the Expedited Panel—The arbitrator for an Expedited Arbitration shall be selected from the Expedited Panel as follows: The five (5) arbitrators on the Expedited Panel shall be listed in alphabetical order and cases will be referred to the arbitrators in that sequence until a new Expedited Panel is chosen (for example, the first expedited arbitration will be referred to arbitrator No. 1, the second will be referred to arbitrator No. 2, the fifth will be referred to arbitrator No. 5, the sixth will be referred to arbitrator No. 1, the seventh will be referred to arbitrator No. 2, the tenth will be referred to arbitrator No. 5, and so on). However, in the event the arbitrator designated by this procedure is unable to schedule a hearing within the five-day time period provided for above, the case will be referred to the next arbitrator in sequence and so on until an arbitrator is designated who can schedule the hearing within the appropriate time period, and any arbitrator thus bypassed will not be designated again until his name comes up in the regular sequence. Provided further that in the event none of the arbitrators on the Expedited Panel is able to schedule a hearing within the five-day time period described above, then that case will be referred to the arbitrator on the Expedited Panel who is able to schedule the earliest possible hearing, and again the sequence of selection of arbitrators for subsequent cases will start with the next arbitrator on the list and any bypassed arbitrator will not be designated again until his name comes up on the regular sequence.

It would appear that expedited arbitration in one form or another will become more commonplace in future years. Expedited arbitration that serves the mutual interests of the parties thus represents another form of conflict resolution that can foster a more constructive atmosphere in union-management relationships.

THE CASES

The cases included in this section all resulted from actual disputes which were processed through grievance procedures in their respective collective bargaining agreements, remained unsettled, and were subsequently submitted to arbitration. The cases provide, in a condensed form, the essential information available to the arbitrator. By studying the issues in these cases, one has the opportunity of experiencing actual arbitration situations and of arriving at one's own decisions with respect to the disputes.

SELECTED BIBLIOGRAPHY

Baer, Walter E./*Discipline and Discharge under the Labor Agreement*. New York: American Management Association, 1972.

Beal, Edwin, and James Begin. *The Practice of Collective Bargaining*. 6th ed. Homewood, Ill.: Richard D. Irwin, 1982.

Briggs, S. S., and J. C. Anderson. "An Empirical Investigation of Arbitrator Acceptability." *Industrial Relations*, 19, (Spring 1980), pp. 163–174.

Britton, R. L. "Judicial Review and Enforcement of the Arbitration Award," *Trial*, 16 (March 1980), pp. 22–25.

Bureau of National Affairs. *Labor Arbitration Reports*.

Code of Professional Responsibility for Arbitrators of Labor-Management Disputes. Published jointly by the National Academy of Arbitrators, American Arbitration Association, and the Federal Mediation and Conciliation Service, November 1974.

Commerce Clearing House. *Labor Arbitration Awards*.

Coulson, Robert. *Labor Arbitration—What You Need to Know*. 2d ed. New York: American Arbitration Association, 1979.

Dennis, Barbara D., and Gerald G. Summers, eds. *Labor Arbitration at the Quarter-Century Mark*. Proceedings of the Twenty-Fifth Annual Meeting of the National Academy of Arbitrators. Washington, D. C.: Bureau of National Affairs, 1973.

Edwards, Harry T. "Labor Arbitration at the Crossroads: The 'Common Law of the Shop' versus External Law." *Arbitration Journal*, June 1977, pp. 65–95.

Elkin, Randyl D., and Thomas L. Hewitt. *Successful Arbitration—An Experiential Approach*. Reston, Va.: Reston Publishing, 1980.

Elkouri, Frank, and Edna A. Elkouri. *How Arbitration Works*. 3d ed. Washington, D. C.: Bureau of National Affairs, 1973.

Elkouri, Frank. "Informal Observations on Labor Arbitration Today," *Arbitration Journal*, 35, (September 1980). pp. 41–45.

Fairweather, Owen. Practice and Procedure in Labor Arbitration. Washington, D. C.: Bureau of National Affairs, 1973.

Feller, David E. "A General Theory of the Collective Bargaining Agreement." *California Law Review*. 61, No. 3 (May 1973).

Finston, Howard V., and James L. Porter. *Selected Cases in Labor Relations— An Experiential Approach*. Reston, Virginia: Reston Publishing, 1983.

Fossum, John A. *Labor Relations: Development, Structure, Process*. 3d. ed. Plano, Tex.: Business Publications, 1985.

Fowler, Aubrey R., Jr., "Responsibilities in Arbitration: A Tripartite View," *Personnel Administrator*, November 1984, pp. 83–90.

Fulmer, William E. *Problems in Labor Relations: Text and Cases.* Homewood, Ill.: Richard D. Irwin, 1980.

Hilgert, Raymond L. "An Arbitrator Looks at Grievance Arbitration." *Personnel Journal*, October 1978, pp. 556–59.

Hilgert, Raymond L. "Handling Employee Complaints and Grievances." *Louisiana Business Survey*, January 1980, pp. 10–11.

Hill, Marvin, Jr., and Anthony V. Sinicropi. *Evidence in Arbitration.* Washington, D. C. Bureau of National Affairs, Inc., 1980.

Horton, Raymond D. "Arbitration, Arbitrators, and the Public Interest." *Industrial and Labor Relations Review*, July 1975, pp. 497–507.

Imundo, Louis V. *The Arbitration Game.* Cincinnati: South-Western Publishing, 1982.

Kochan, Thomas A. *Collective Bargaining and Industrial Relations.* Homewood, Ill.: Richard D. Irwin, 1980.

Marmo, Michael: "Arbitrating Sex Harassment Cases," *Arbitration Journal*, 35, (March, 1980), pp. 35–40.

McDermott, Thomas J., and Thomas H. Newhams. "Discharge-Reinstatement: What Happens Thereafter." *Industrial and Labor Relations Review.* 24, No. 4 (July 1971).

McPherson, Donald S., with Conrad John Gates and Kevin N. Rogers. *Resolving Grievances: A Practical Approach.* Reston, Virginia: Reston Publishing, 1983.

Pops, Gerald M., *Emergence of the Public Sector Arbitrator.* Lexington, Mass.: D. C. Heath, 1976.

Prasow, Paul, and Edward Peters. *Arbitration and Collective Bargaining—Conflict Resolution in Labor Relations.* 2d ed. New York: McGraw-Hill, 1983.

Ratner, M. G. "Observations on Some Current Issues in Labor Arbitration," *Labor Law Journal*, 32, (February 1981), pp. 114–118.

Rehmus, C. M. "Binding Arbitration in the Public Sector," *Monthly Labor Review*, 98, (April 1975), pp. 53–56.

Robinson, James W.; Wayne L. Dernoncourt; and Ralph H. Effler. *The Grievance Procedure and Arbitration: Text and Cases.* Washington, D. C.: University Press of America, 1978.

Scheinman, Martin F. *Evidence and Proof in Arbitration.* Ithaca, NY: New York State School of Industrial and Labor Relations, 1977.

Serrin, William. *The Company and the Union.* New York: Vintage Books, 1974.

Siegal, Boaz. *Proving Your Arbitration Case.* Washington, D. C.: Bureau of National Affairs, Inc. 1979.

Trotta, Maurice S. *Arbitration of Labor-Management Disputes.* New York: American Management Association, 1974.

Trotta, Maurice S. *Handling Grievances: A Guide for Management and Labor.* Washington, D. C.: Bureau of National Affairs, 1976.

Index to Cases for Part Two

Case Number and Title	Management Rights	Union Rights and Activities	Seniority and Employee Rights	Discipline and Discharge	Work Assignments and Job Bidding	Work Performance	Technological Change/Past Practices	Wages and Benefits	Employee Health, Safety, and Security	Discrimination
34. The Chronically Depressed Absentee	X		X	X		X		X	X	
35. Caught in the Act?	X			X						
36. Stolen Kisses	X			X		X				X
37. Impaired Performance	X			X	X	X			X	
38. One "Wife" Too Many	X			X				X		
39. Infringement of Bargaining Unit Work	X	X	X		X			X		
40. The Speedy Finisher				X	X	X				
41. A Request for Parental Leave			X					X	X	
42. Riding the Tiger	X			X				X	X	
43. No More Coffee or Bottled Water	X	X	X			X	X			
44. The Bypassed Senior Clerk	X	X	X		X		X	X		

#	Case	1	2	3	4	5	6	7
45.	Too Much Telephone Time?	X	X	X	X			
46.	The Disabled Blower Motor	X	X			X		
47.	The Subcontracted Heaters	X	X	X				
48.	The Car Pool and the Overtime Refusal	X	X	X	X			
49.	The Disputed Holiday Pay		X	X		X	X	
50.	The Rescheduled Lunch Period	X	X	X	X	X		
51.	A "Horns of a Dilemma" Situation	X	X	X	X			
52.	The Right to Work on a Birthday Holiday	X		X	X	X	X	
53.	Sunday Is the Sabbath Day	X	X	X				X
54.	My Time Is Not the Company's Time	X	X	X	X			
55.	Which Duty Calls?	X	X	X				
56.	Terminated at 59 Days	X	X	X	X			X

Index to Cases for Part Two (concluded)

Case Number and Title	Management Rights	Union Rights and Activities	Seniority and Employee Rights	Discipline and Discharge	Work Assignments and Job Bidding	Work Performance	Technological Change/ Past Practices	Wages and Benefits	Employee Health, Safety, and Security	Discrimination
57. No Date, No Job?			X			X				X
58. To Promote, or Hire from the Outside?	X	X	X		X	X				
59. Who Must Pay for the Safety Shoes?	X		X				X	X	X	
60. Who's Telling the Truth?	X			X						
61. A Disciplinary Warning to the Union President	X	X		X						
62. The Sleepy Inspector	X			X		X			X	
63. A Weighty Problem	X		X		X					X

Case	1	2	3	4	5	6	7
64. The Jurisdictional Dispute		X			X	X	X
65. The Wastebaler and the Custodian	X			X		X	X
66. The Refused Assignment		X	X	X	X	X	X
67. Emergency Leave Pay		X	X				
68. The Disputed Test	X			X	X	X	
69. The Forbidden Nuptials			X			X	
70. The Frustrated Bus Drivers	X	X	X	X	X		X
71. No Bread in the Store				X	X	X	
72. One Last Chance				X		X	
73. The Payroll Error		X				X	
74. The Unrecorded Purchase			X	X	X	X	

34. THE CHRONICALLY DEPRESSED ABSENTEE

Company: Husky Oil Company, Salt Lake City, Utah

Union: Oil, Chemical, and Atomic Workers International Union, Local 2-578

BACKGROUND

Walter Jackson[1] began working at the North Salt Lake Refinery as a chemical operator trainee on June 23, 1961, and was terminated on August 13, 1974, for excessive chronic absenteeism.

Jackson's sick leave record from 1968 to August 13, 1974, was as follows.[2]

Year	Days of Sick Leave
1968	10
1969	20
1970	6
1971	17
1972	16
1973	29
1974 (to August 13)	20

The management of Husky noted Jackson's sequence of frequent short-term absences late in 1969. His supervisor, William Fielding, discussed his attendance problem with him first on April 5, 1972. Management again noted Jackson's excessive absenteeism in January 1974. Fielding sent him three written warnings between January and May 1974.

---

[1] The names of all individuals have been disguised.

[2] Husky Oil Company purchased the North Salt Lake Refinery in 1968. None of Jackson's records were available from the previous owner.

234

Relevant portions of these letters follow:

Letter of January 7, 1974:

Dear Walter:

I am very concerned about your physical condition in regard to your ability to perform your job. This concern results from the fact that you have taken more sick leave than any other employee in the refinery, with the exception of three men. These three men were on sick leave for specific ailments or injuries, whereas you have been off on sick leave as a result of minor ailments.

I am requesting that you take a physical examination at the company's expense to determine whether or not you are physically able to perform your job. The company has the right to require you to submit to a physical examination according to Article 25.02 of the Agreement. If the results of this examination reveal that you are incapable of performing the various tasks that are part of your job, then we will take appropriate action. Article 5.16 of the Agreement states that if an employee becomes incapable of performing the duties of his regular classification through illness or accident, such employee may be transferred to a classification which he is capable of performing. The company has discussed this situation with the Workman's Committee, and they are in complete agreement with our actions.

Letter of March 15, 1974:

Dear Walter:

I have recently reviewed your personnel records and I'm very disturbed by your sick leave record with Husky Oil Company during the past three years. In an effort to determine whether or not your physical condition was the cause of this extensive amount of sick leave, the company requested that you take a physical examination at the company's expense . . . This examination clearly indicates that your physical condition is not a reason for your poor attendance record during the past three years. We have checked the sick leave records at the North Salt Lake Refinery, and the average sick leave taken per man for each of three years is significantly below the number of days of sick leave that you have taken.

You were hired as a full-time employee and you are expected to work as such since we pay you on that basis. Your attendance record to date with the company is little more than that of a part-time employee.

The company has discussed this matter with you on several occasions. This letter is to warn you that your absenteeism will no longer be tolerated. Unless your attendance record improves very significantly, we will replace you.

Letter of May 10, 1974:

Dear Walter:

I am writing to confirm our discussion that took place on May 9, 1974, concerning your recent absenteeism. The company is very concerned about your attendance during the past few years as was pointed out in my letter to you dated March 15, 1974. You have taken 11 days of sick leave since my letter dated March 15 was sent to you. The company is aware that the sick leave taken during this period was for a legitimate purpose; however, the company is very concerned about the fact that your attendance has not improved in this last two months.

You stated at this meeting on May 9 that your attendance would improve. I informed you at this time that if your attendance did not improve, then the company would terminate your employment. The company is very hopeful that you will improve your attendance record and that no further action on the part of the company will be necessary in this matter.

If I can be of any further help or you have any other matters that you need to discuss with me concerning this situation, please contact me at your convenience.

Jackson's work record, aside from his absenteeism, was very good. He advanced from a trainee position to that of chemical operator and finally to alkylation operator. This latter position was highly skilled and the second highest job classification in plant operations, requiring several years of training to perform competently. The Husky management found Jackson's performance on the job very satisfactory.

Jackson underwent the physical examination required by the company on January 18, 1974. He was found to be in good physical health and fully capable of performing the work of an alkylation operator.

The report on his physical condition was made without a full medical history. Jackson exercised his right to refuse to answer three questions on the Report of Medical Examination pertaining to (1) personal history; (2) whether he had been hospitalized or a patient in a clinic, hospital, or sanitarium for observation, operation, or treatment during the past 10 years; and, (3) family medical history. He steadfastly refused to discuss the reasons for his absence with his supervisor, other than to cite medical reasons.

Jackson was again absent on August 10 and 11, 1974. After he finished the night shift on August 12–13, Fielding informed him that he was being released from his employment as of that date because of excessive absenteeism.

On August 23, 1974, Jackson and the union filed a grievance in which he denied excessive use of sick leave. The union claimed that Jackson had been discharged without just cause, and that he should be reinstated without any loss in pay or benefits.

Shortly after filing the grievance, Jackson and his union steward told company management that Jackson had a chronic condition of recurring mental depression which accounted for his frequent absences of short duration. The company refused to reinstate Jackson.

POSITION OF THE UNION

The union supported its contention that Jackson was discharged without cause with the following arguments:

1. Jackson had not indulged in excessive absenteeism. The sick leave time taken by him in a period of about six years totaled a "little over three months." For a person with his type of illness, three months out of six years is not excessive.

2. Jackson had not abused his sick leave. He was absent for legitimate illnesses and was officially excused for such absences by the company. The company had not disputed that these absences were excused and authorized under the Agreement.

3. The employee had not applied for long-term leave under Articles 15.04 and 15.05[3] because he was utilizing his sick leave benefits as provided in Article 15.02 and which provided full pay while ill, rather than one-half pay under the long-term disability plan. In only one year, 1973, did he exceed his 25 days sick leave allowance. Jackson was entitled to use his full sick leave entitlement before applying for long-term disability benefits.

4. Jackson had been given a clean bill of health by company physicians on January 18, 1974. Jackson was understandably reluctant to discuss his mental illness with management and company physicians. Mental depression carries with it a social stigma; though unwarranted, it is very real to those who suffer from it. It would be especially difficult for someone subject to this illness to discuss it with others.

5. Even though the company had incomplete knowledge of Jackson's condition, it failed to exhaust all available procedures and facilities before moving to discharge him. He was entitled to exhaust all his sick leave and long-term disability benefits before becoming subject to discharge.

6. Although Jackson was reluctant to discuss his problem with

---

[3] See Appendix to this case for relevant contract provisions.

238

the company, he was being honest, certainly as honest as he could be, considering the problem he had. On his own, he went to both doctors and the hospital to try to correct his problem. He even used part of his vacation for this purpose. He was not malingering, but rather making an honest attempt to resolve his difficulties as best he knew how.

7. The company's contention that Jackson's frequent short-term absences created problems and ill-will among other operators because they had to work overtime to fill in for him was without foundation. Workers expect to help out both the absent employee and the company by filling in. This procedure had evolved over several years of experimentation by both the company and the operators.

8. Jackson's absences did not create a safety hazard as the company insisted. Any operator who became fatigued could be replaced by calling in another operator who was on his day off.

9. Jackson's excused absences should not be counted in assessing excessive absenteeism. Absences which are authorized and excused cannot count in determining absentee percentages. Jackson's absences were both authorized and excused by the company.

10. Jackson, during the six months he had been off his job, had successfully undergone therapy. He no longer needed drugs for his illness; in fact, he had not used them for four months. Jackson was mentally and physically fully capable of returning to work as an alkylation operator for the company, and he was entitled to reinstatement accordingly.

POSITION OF THE COMPANY

The company contended that Walter Jackson was discharged for cause based on excessive absenteeism, and the union grievance should be denied for the following reasons:

1. The company terminated the employment of Jackson because of his extreme lack of dependability which resulted from his frequent absences from work. The essential facts concerning his employment and absenteeism were not in dispute.

2. Jackson's frequent short-term absences reduced the value of his services "to a nullity," and as a result, the company had no choice in fairness to other employees but to terminate his employment. Such termination was necessary, even though the cause of the absences was a series of illness.

3. Jackson was fully and formally warned of the possibility of discharge if the absences on sick leave continued. He was counseled in April 1972, and formally warned three times by letter during the

period January–May 1974. Jackson was fully aware through these warnings of the consequence of continued excessive short-term absences.

4. The physical examination of January 18, 1974, indicated no basis for Jackson's short-term absences and indicated that he was physically capable of performing his work.

5. Jackson's absences made it impossible for the company to depend upon him. Implicit in the contract of any full-time employee is his obligation to attend work with reasonable regularity. When he does not so attend, the contract is broken and the company no longer has a duty to maintain his employment.

6. Although Jackson's record showed a high level of sick leave during the past six years, his record became intolerable during the past two years with 29 sick days in 1973 and 20 in 1974 prior to his termination. Of these absences, 43 occurred on the first or last day of his work period which provided him with "long weekends" at the beginning or end of his work period. Moreover, most of the absences were a single day in duration, presenting to the company the most difficult scheduling and manning problems.

7. Jackson had the highest number of absences of any employee in the plant.

8. When Jackson was absent, employees on the two adjacent shifts each worked an extra four hours to cover for him. The company not only had to pay four hours overtime to each substitute employee but also pay Jackson his straight-time sick pay.

9. Jackson's absences created a serious safety hazard. The alkylation operator was a skilled position, also considered to be one of the most hazardous in the refinery. To require other employees to work repeated overtime created a special hazard because of the fatigue factor.

10. Jackson's repeated absences created considerable inconvenience, and even hardship, to other operators. As a consequence, morale suffered and the company received many complaints.

11. It was evident from his record that his attendance habits would not improve. The recurrent short-term absences had been going on for several years and even continued after three warnings and his promise to correct the situation.

12. Jackson's "cavalier attitude" toward his employment was illustrated by the fact that after repeated warnings, and knowing that his job was in jeopardy because of absences, he requested an extra day of absence from work at the end of June 1974 to get a "head start" on his one-month vacation. Further, upon his return July 29, he reported for the wrong shift, causing great inconvenience to other employees.

240

13. The company had the right to discharge an employee for excessive absenteeism even though that employee had not exhausted his sick leave allotment. Sick pay is not cumulative; employees do not receive payment or other credit for unused days. An employee cannot claim a vested interest in sick leave where his frequent absences of short duration disrupt the business of the company. Sick pay, unlike vacation pay, is not vested in the employee. It is a cushion to be used when needed, but it is not intended to set standards for attendance.

14. The union's contention that Jackson would be eligible and should have been carried on long-term disability leave was groundless under Articles 15.04 and 15.05. These sections deal with long-term leave and therefore are clearly inapplicable to Jackson's case, for he had been absent for short durations for minor ailments.

15. The company's action with respect to Jackson was made in good faith, upon fair examination and careful consideration of the situation. Even the union did not allege that the company had acted arbitrarily, capriciously or unfairly.

APPENDIX

Relevant Provisions of the Contract

Article 9.01. A grievance may be filed for the purpose of adjusting complaints, disputes, claims, or unfair treatment, or alleged discharge without cause involving the terms of this Agreement or the interpretation thereof.

Article 15.01. An employee required to be absent from work because of nonoccupational injury to himself or nonoccupational illness of himself will be allowed sick leave with pay as follows: . . .

After ten (10) years work—up to five (5) weeks leave with pay.

Article 15.02. Any person claiming sick pay must have notified his immediate Supervisor as follows: If sickness occurs while the employee is at work, he shall report to his immediate Supervisor and secure permission to stop work. If sickness or disability occurs at home or while the employee is off duty, his Supervisor must be notified as soon as possible, giving the details concerning his sickness or disability. The company must be notified at least three (3) hours beforehand of when the employee will return to work . . . The purpose of this clause is to provide the company with adequate notice of an employee's inability to work so that a replacement may be located if required.

Article 15.03. If an employee is ill or disabled and away from work, a doctor's certificate verifying the illness may be required for payment of sick leave or disability payments under this Agreement. . . . Sick leave shall not be cumulative from year to year. False statements or misrepresentations will be deemed a form of dishonesty.

Article 15.04. An employee with one (1) year of work for the company, who is a member of the Group Insurance Plan and absent from work because of nonoccupational illness of himself or nonoccupational injury to himself, will receive one half (½) his regular rate of pay (Long-Term Disability), minus other income benefits from the company, after he has exhausted all his full sick pay and vacation entitlement.

Article 15.05. An employee will receive this one-half (½) pay, referred to above, as long as he is disabled from performing his regular job but not exceeding six (6) months from the date disability begins.

Article 22.01. Except as expressly limited by this Agreement, the management and direction of the company is the prerogative of the company. This includes but is not limited to, the right to hire and assign employees, apply discipline, demote or discharge employees for cause, and determine the size of the working force.

QUESTIONS

1. Why is this case a difficult one from the standpoint of both the union and the company involved?
2. Evaluate each of the arguments of the union as countered by the arguments of the company. Which arguments are most crucial to the positions of each party?
3. Was employee Walter Jackson obligated to answer all of the questions placed to him concerning the reasons for his absenteeism?
4. To what lengths must a company go to accommodate an employee who has physical or mental problems such as the employee in this case? Discuss.
5. If an employee discharged for absenteeism is reinstated by the arbitrator, how excessive must any future absenteeism become on the part of the reinstated employee before the company may reinstate disciplinary action?

35. CAUGHT IN THE ACT?

Company: Kast Metals Corporation, Keokuk, Iowa
Union: International Molders, Local 333

BACKGROUND

John Doerr[1] had been an employee of the company for about seven years at the time of the incident in question. He had been a satisfactory employee throughout his employment, and he was serving as a utility man in the cleaning department at the time of his discharge.

About 10:45 P.M. on February 25, 1975, George Burns, a security guard at the company, noticed someone in the plant parking lot "bobbing up and down" four or five times. Burns proceeded to the fifth row of the lot where he had seen the movement, and discovered Doerr squatting near the right rear wheel of a car. Burns asked Doerr if the car was his, and he felt that Doerr responded affirmatively. However, upon examination of the window sticker, Burns determined that the car belonged to another employee of the plant. Upon further examination of the area, Burns found a styrofoam coffee cup sitting just in front of the right rear wheel. The cup was half to three-quarters full of what appeared to be wine. Burns carried it back into the plant where he gave it to Thomas Hardin, Doerr's supervisor. Hardin examined the cup and concluded it contained wine and strong liquor which were "reddish" in color. Upon questioning about his presence in the lot, Doerr told Hardin that he was taking a break.

Burns related to Hardin that he had seen Doerr "bobbing up and down" beside the car, that Doerr had said the car was his, and that

---

[1] The names of all individuals have been disguised.

he had found the cup of wine near where Doerr had been crouching. Burns also told Hardin that Doerr had not mentioned his being on break at any time in the lot.

A decision was made by company management about 12:30 A.M. on February 26, 1975, to discharge Doerr, and he was so informed. The company based its action on Doerr's violation of Discharge Rules—Group II (see Appendix to this case), which prohibited possession or consumption of alcoholic beverages in the plant.

Doerr then filed a grievance on February 27, 1975, charging that the company did not have just cause for his dismissal as there was insufficient evidence of his violation of Discharge Rule—Group II.

POSITION OF THE UNION

The union maintained that there was insufficient evidence to warrant Doerr's discharge for violation of the "no alcohol" rule. No one saw Doerr in actual, physical possession of liquid of any kind, either alcoholic or otherwise. All witnesses agreed that Doerr did not appear to be under the influence of alcohol, nor could they smell it on his breath. Neither was there any bottle or flask on Doerr or near the car by which he was discovered, although there was no major effort undertaken to locate such an item. No analysis was ever conducted to determine the actual contents of the cup.

At the arbitration hearing, Doerr denied telling Burns that it was his car. He stated that at the time he spoke to Burns, he had been on his way to the adjacent parking lot to move his truck nearer to the plant in order to leave more quickly at the end of the shift. He said that he had stopped beside the car in order to remove some slag from his shoe. He also testified that after having been taken to the office, he had offered to take a breath analysis test.

Since the company had failed to bear the burden of proof to show conclusively that Doerr either had consumed alcohol or had it in his possession, the discharge action was improper. The union asked that Doerr be returned to his job with full restoration of lost pay, benefits, and seniority rights.

POSITION OF THE COMPANY

The company argued that there was sufficient evidence of Doerr's activities to warrant the conclusion that he had alcohol in his possession for purposes of consuming it; therefore his dismissal was justified.

At the hearing, Burns testified that Doerr had not told him he was on his break when discovered near the car, and Burns related the other events and dialogue in the parking lot. Hardin stated that neither he nor any other witness could detect alcohol on Doerr's breath, but that Doerr was discharged on the basis of "the suspicions created by the circumstances as related by Burns' oral report." The company maintained that those circumstances and their implications were sufficient to constitute "just cause" for dismissal of Doerr for violation of Discharge Rules—Group II, and the company was within its rights as outlined in the contract under Article III. The company requested that its discharge action should be sustained.

APPENDIX

Relevant Provisions of the Agreement

ARTICLE III—FUNCTIONS OF MANAGEMENT

Nothing in this Agreement shall limit the Company in the exercise of its functions of management under which it shall have, among other things, the right to hire new employees and to direct the working force, to discipline, suspend, or discharge for a just cause, transfer, or lay off employees because of lack of work; require employees to observe company rules and regulations not inconsistent with the provisions of this Agreement, to decide the number and locations of its plants and the products to be manufactured, the methods and schedules of production, including means and process of manufacturing, all matters relating to finance, sales, and pricing of the product, provided that the Company will not use these functions of management for the purpose of discrimination. It is agreed that the enumeration of these functions of management shall not be deemed to exclude other functions not enumerated.

DISCHARGE RULES—GROUP II

Any of the following will be sufficient grounds for immediate discharge:

* * * * *

Possession or consumption of alcoholic beverages within the plant or reporting for work under the influence of intoxicants in any degree whatsoever.

QUESTIONS

1. To what degree is circumstantial evidence sufficient or insufficient in this case to support the position of the company?

2. Was the explanation of the employee about the circumstances of this case believable, or was the employee's explanation primarily self-serving?

3. Many arbitrators in discharge cases require a company to show that the "preponderance of evidence" is sufficient to warrant upholding discharge action. Did the company demonstrate conclusive evidence to justify discharge action? A lesser penalty?

36. STOLEN KISSES

Company: Williams Brothers Markets, Santa Maria, California

Union: Retail Clerks Union, Local 899

At 11:00 A.M., October 5, 1974, Henry Hampton,[1] vice president of Williams Brothers Markets, discharged Joyce Stephens and George Folsom for "unbecoming conduct." In a letter of discharge addressed to them jointly, Mr. Hampton stated:

> We believe that two adult married people are morally wrong when they kiss (on many occasions) at their place of employment. We believe that this is not socially acceptable and therefore is unbecoming conduct.

The company claimed that the employees' activities were in violation of Section A of Article III of the collective bargaining agreement which reads:

> The Employer shall have the right to discharge an employee for good cause, such as dishonesty, insubordination, incompetency, intoxication, unbecoming conduct, failure to perform work as required, and excessive absenteeism.

Joyce Stephens immediately filed a grievance in which she asked for reinstatement to her former position, payment for lost wages, and restoration of all rights and benefits.

BACKGROUND

Joyce Stephens was a checker at Store 3 in Arroyo Grande, California, a position she had held since February 1974. At this same time George Folsom was employed as a produce manager in the same

---

[1] The names of all individuals have been disguised.

market. On September 17, 1974, Folsom confided to Arnold Singleton, produce merchandiser, that he was in love with Stephens. Singleton told him that the company could not tolerate "two married people playing around on the job." He also advised Folsom to terminate the relationship. Singleton immediately reported his "confidential" conversation to store manager Daniel Vandenberg, who indicated that he had already been aware that Folsom had a "greater than average attraction to Stephens."

On September 23, Willis Goode, an auditor for the company, was at the store investigating a money shortage problem. He noted that both Stephens and Folsom had gone into the produce processing room, and that Folsom acted "very excited." Goode followed them into the room where he observed them kissing.

Goode, Vandenberg, and Hampton agreed that if any disciplinary action was to be taken, they should catch Stephens and Folsom in the act of kissing. They set up a "blind" in the produce processing room, and on October 5 confronted them in the act of embracing and kissing. It was at this point that Hampton discharged them "on the spot."

POSITION OF THE UNION

The union contended that Stephens had been observed kissing on only two occasions, neither of which were while she was on duty. No customer or employee had observed the kissing or embracing; nor had any customer or employee complained. On the two days in question, Stephens had not "clocked in." In other words, she had not started work. It was customary for her to arrive about 15 to 20 minutes early to check the produce department for recent price changes and to check for new price changes and specials throughout the store. It was her practice to check the price lists and then go into the produce processing room to have a cup of coffee before starting work.

The union also contended that Stephens did not encourage Folsom's "amorous antics." She admitted that he was kissing her when they were discovered. She claimed, however, that she was not returning the kiss, and that in fact, she was attempting to discourage his advances. She said that they were good friends, they had a number of acquaintances in common, that they had a mutual approach to problems, and that on their breaks they spent time discussing matters of mutual interest.

The union also pointed out that Stephens was a good employee. Her performance appraisals described her as a "good checker," "better than average," and "competent." She had never received any warnings or complaints, either written or verbal, regarding her work. While both Singleton and Vandenberg had warned Folsom about having an "amorous relationship" with another employee, no such warnings had ever been given Stephens.

The union added that the company had never adopted any standards defining unbecoming conduct. It was not until October 5 after this incident that a policy had been decided upon. The company had acted arbitrarily in discharging the employee without warning and without prior notice of what constitutes unbecoming conduct.

The union requested that Joyce Stephens be returned with no loss of seniority to her position as checker, and that she be made whole for all loss of pay and benefits while she was off work due to her improper discharge.

POSITION OF THE COMPANY

The company contended that the conduct of Stephens and Folsom was detrimental to the conduct of business. In the company's view, the public is sensitive to the behavior of employees in retail organizations. Customers who disapprove of amorous behavior between married adults will trade elsewhere if the company condoned such behavior on the part of its employees.

The company also argued that it is commonly accepted that an employer cannot tolerate married employees kissing and embracing others than their spouses at their place of employment. It is not necessary to spell out this type of behavior as specifically constituting unbecoming conduct.

The agreement specifically gives the company the right to discharge employees for unbecoming conduct. The company exercised this right appropriately in this matter, and the grievance should be dismissed.

QUESTIONS

1. Was the behavior of the female employee in relationship to the produce manager "unbecoming conduct?" Was it conduct of sufficient gravity to justify discharge in this case? Discuss.
2. Did management under the agreement have the right to determine standards for defining "unbecoming conduct?" Why, or why not?
3. Should conduct of employees in a retail supermarket be of a higher standard than in a factory situation where employees do not come into regular contact with the public?
4. If the arbitrator should return employee Joyce Stephens to her position, would the company be obligated also to return the produce manager back to his position? Why, or why not?

37. IMPAIRED PERFORMANCE

Company: Public Service Electric and Gas Company, Burlington, New Jersey

Union: Public Utility Construction and Gas Appliance Workers, Local 274

Having satisfied the job requirement of typing 50 words per minute and meeting the other application prerequisites, Nancy Bell[1] was hired as a general clerk, second class, by the company on December 22, 1969. She began work in the Burlington district office, and on December 1971 she was promoted to general clerk, first class, a job which principally required strong typing skills. She was regarded as an excellent worker; periodic management appraisal reviews noted her good typing ability, quickness to learn, and rated her as an above average to excellent performer.

On December 6, 1972, Nancy Bell suffered serious head injuries in a three-car accident. She remained comatose for two weeks, and then began to slowly recover from a spastic left hemiplegia. In mid-January, 1973, she began receiving occupational therapy at Thomas Jefferson Hospital and was eventually released from the hospital on January 28, 1973. Following her hospitalization, Bell remained under close medical supervision until August 29, 1973. She was then discharged from full care, and she returned to her job on September 4, 1973, with her doctor's approval that she was physically capable of such work.

Bell still had difficulty walking, as her left-side coordination was weak. Following an examination on September 26, her physician at Thomas Jefferson Hospital reported that "she still has evidence of a

---

[1] The names of all individuals have been disguised.

very mild organic brain syndrome with periods of emotional liability." However, he, too, concluded that she was capable of returning to work.

From the beginning, Bell's work did not match her former level of
performance, either in quality or quantity. Her typing output was
slow and often contained many errors. Initially management chose
to overlook her poor performance, attributing it to her long absence
and physical problems. However, on January 31, 1974, she was
advised that her work performance had been very poor, and that if
she did not improve within three months, she would face "more
severe disciplinary actions." Bell's typing, nevertheless, remained
below the minimum requirement of 50 words per minute, and she
continued to perform her other tasks at an unsatisfactory level. On
February 25, 1974, her supervisor again reviewed her poor performance with Bell, and informed her that if her work did not improve to
a level satisfactory to the company by April 30, 1974, the company
would consider her discharge.

Recognizing her difficulty, Nancy Bell enrolled in an evening
typing course at a local high school in an attempt to improve her
speed and accuracy. She reported that she had increased her productivity from 37 words per minute with five errors to 55 words per
minute with no errors by the end of May. Management, however,
did not notice any significant improvement in her performance on
the job. Subsequently, in June 1974 management reassigned her to
the dispatch office as a general clerk, second class, although she
continued to be paid as a general clerk, first class. In this position,
Bell was primarily responsible for receiving emergency telephone
calls, logging information, and preparing service orders, a job to
which most persons adapted within a few days. Nevertheless, Bell's
work over the next few months continued to be rated "unsatisfactory" by her supervisor, principally because of her slowness, and in
early October 1974 she was transferred back to the district office.

Again, her work did not show any improvement, and on October
24, 1974, the division superintendent requested that the company
physician examine her to determine if she was "capable of improving
her work output to acceptable levels." She was examined by Charles
Wallace, M.D., on November 14, 1974. He concluded that Bell had
suffered a "cerebral contusion with posttraumatic cerebral edema
and partial left hemiparesis." He went on to conclude in his report:

> In my opinion, this young woman has reached a point of recovery
> which will not progress any more. I also feel that her recovery has
> been nothing short of remarkable considering the severity of her

accident. She has lost some mental facility because of the prolonged coma secondary to the cerebral edema and brain damage. It is my feeling that this facility will never be regained. Without specific psychological testing, it is impossible to precisely pinpoint her main areas of deficiency. However, one gets the impression that her ability to think automatically and relate one thing to another is somewhat impaired. She must study everything, make a decision, and then go ahead. Apparently, when she does this, she performs adequately, but obviously this process is quite slow. It is my medical opinion that she can do the type of job she is now assigned to, but management must accept the fact that her work will be slow and her output less than that of someone who has not had a severe brain injury.

Several weeks after receiving Dr. Wallace's report the company decided to terminate Bell. She was placed on a six-month disability leave beginning December 10, 1974, and was then terminated.

The union filed a grievance on Bell's behalf alleging that the company lacked "just cause" (see Appendix to this case for Article II of the agreement) for its discharge of Bell and seeking her reinstatement to active service with the firm.

UNION POSITION

The union contended that the company had not done all within its power to determine whether Nancy Bell's work could be further improved. The union maintained that she was fully capable of performing at an acceptable level, based upon Bell's assertion that she could perform "adequately." She argued that she was, at the time of arbitration, capable of performing at a level close to what she was doing before the accident, and she felt she would continue to improve. For these and for humanitarian considerations, the union requested full reinstatement of Bell to her former or to an equivalent position.

COMPANY POSITION

The company maintained that it had given Nancy Bell ample opportunity to achieve an "acceptable" level of productivity. Management maintained that it regretted her inability to perform adequately, and pointed out that it had allowed her an extensive period of readaptation to her work routine. However, it contended that Bell had demonstrated that she was unable to achieve acceptable levels of performance, and management was well within its rights to discontinue her from its service. The discharge action should be sustained.

APPENDIX

Relevant Provisions of the Agreement

ARTICLE II—UNION-EMPLOYER RELATIONSHIP

It is specifically agreed that the management of the plant and the direction of the working forces shall be vested exclusively in the Employer. This right shall include but not be limited to, the right to hire and discharge (for just cause), the right to suspend from duty (for just cause), and the right to transfer personnel from one position to another (for just cause), provided, however, that the foregoing shall not impair any of the rights of the Union or the employees granted by other provisions of the Agreement.

QUESTIONS

1. Did the company give the employee reasonable time and opportunity to achieve an acceptable level of performance following her accident? Discuss.
2. Is a company obligated to assist an employee in a rehabilitation program following a serious physical and mental injury?
3. Evaluate the union's argument that humanitarian considerations should be considered in asking for reinstatement of employee Nancy Bell.
4. Why is a case of this sort difficult for all parties involved, including the arbitrator who is asked to decide the issue?

38. ONE "WIFE" TOO MANY

Company: Pennsylvania Power Company, Philadelphia, Pennsylvania

Union: Utility Workers Union of America, Local 140

On February 26, 1975, Lawrence J. Groves,[1] manager of personnel relations of the Pennsylvania Power Company, received an anonymous telephone call from a woman who claimed to be "a friend of Mrs. Lieber." The caller stated that one of the company's employees had a woman falsely registered at the Northside Youngstown Hospital as his wife. Groves telephoned the hospital which, after some investigation, reported that a Laura Robertson was, in fact, registered there as Mrs. John Lieber.

After a thorough investigation of the case, Groves sent Lieber the following letter:

> On Monday, March 10, 1975, you were suspended until further notice. Effective Tuesday, March 18, 1975, your employment with Pennsylvania Power Company has been terminated.
>
> This action is taken as a result of claims you submitted for hospitalization and doctor services for a person other than an eligible family member.
>
> All benefits are canceled including your Group Life Insurance Plan and Hospitalization and Surgical-Medical Insurance Plan. Your anniversary date is March 17, 1959, which entitles you to 3 weeks or 15 working days' vacation. Payment for this accrued vacation will be included in your final paycheck.

On March 20, Lieber's personal attorney wrote a joint letter to the company and to the president of Local 140, making the following observations:

---

[1] The names of all individuals have been disguised.

254

We represent Mr. John Lieber who on March 18, 1975, was given notification of his discharge as an employee of Pennsylvania Power Company.

Under all the facts of this case, the discharge of Lieber was unwarranted and unjust, and accordingly, we have been authorized by Lieber to give you notice of his objection thereto.

Please consider this letter as the filing of a complaint to discharge as required under the provisions of Article 5, Paragraph (C), of the agreement dated November 6, 1974, between Pennsylvania Power Company and Utility Workers Union of America, Local 140. (See Appendix to this case.)

The company and the union agreed to submit the case to arbitration. They stipulated that the issue was:

Did the Company violate the agreement on or about March 18, 1975, when they discharged the grievant, John Lieber, for a claim submitted for hospitalization and doctor services for a person other than an eligible family member?

BACKGROUND

When Lawrence Groves, the manager of personnel relations, first called John Lieber into his office on February 28,1975, Lieber refused to answer questions about the woman registered at the hospital as his wife. The following day, Lieber returned to Groves' office and said, "She is my wife." Groves told Lieber that he knew that the woman was not his wife. Lieber then asked Groves not to notify the Prudential Insurance Company until he had an opportunity to talk with his attorney. Groves agreed to this.

The company then undertook a complete review of its records. It discovered that between 1971 and 1974 (exclusive of the current 1975 incident responsible for Lieber's discharge), Prudential had paid out over $3,600 in claims for a woman purporting to be Nora Lieber, the wife of John Lieber. The company paid the entire cost of premiums for hospitalization and medical insurance.

During the investigation, Lieber stated that he was long separated from his wife and "there's no divorce possible." He had been living with Laura Robertson since 1970. When she became ill, her doctor diagnosed her illness as ulcerated colitis. The prescribed medication did little good. She received further treatment, including X rays and additional medicine. By this time she had lost her job as a nurse. When her physician had her hospitalized, Lieber told her "to use my wife's name to get an appointment there." He said, "I felt Prudential would cover it." She returned home after one week, but the condition returned about nine months later. She returned to the hospital as Mrs. Lieber. About six months later she was returned to the hospital for further treatment, and she entered a fourth time on August 28, 1974, for an operation; she was discharged on September 9, 1974. Her fifth and final hospitalization occurred on February 19, 1975; she was still in the hospital on March 18 when Lieber was dismissed.

Lieber was hired in 1959. At the time of discharge he was a Lineman "A," a position he had held for the previous nine years. He had made good progress on his job. The quality and quantity of his work was good. He had been cited once for excessive absenteeism and once for insubordination during his 16 years of employment.

POSITION OF THE UNION

The union argued first that the "punishment does not fit the crime." Lieber was in the process of making restitution of money to Prudential. The $3,600 in claims paid by Prudential during the period 1971–74 was small compared with the $2,088,000 which had been paid by the company to Prudential during the same period. The union agreed that Lieber's actions were dishonest, and that he should repay the $3,600. On the other hand, this sum was trivial in comparison to the size of the premiums paid, and the size of both the insurer and the company.

The union further argued that Lieber was being discharged for the entire amount of which the company had been defrauded indirectly, rather than for $1,305.50 in hospital charges incurred in 1975. The previous charges should not be considered because the company did not know of them at the time of discharge.

The union also contended that Lieber had not intended to defraud either his employer or Prudential. He had never sought medical benefits for both Laura Robertson and his legal wife. He had claimed only one person, Laura Robertson, as a dependent. She was, in his view, his "wife."

The union also pointed out that lifestyles have changed during the past quarter century. Many men and women have maintained a loving relationship without going through the formality of a wedding ceremony. In fact, Lieber had demonstrated that his relationship with Laura Robertson was a stable and loving one, enduring over many years both in sickness and in health.

Finally, the union contended that Lieber did not intend to defraud the company. His actions, although not to be condoned, were understandable, considering the circumstances. He acted impulsively to protect a person whom he loved and whom he perceived to be desperately ill. Furthermore, he did not feel that he had done anything wrong with respect to Pennsylvania Power Company, since he had made claims against the Prudential Insurance Company.

The union requested that John Lieber be reinstated with full back pay and that all rights and privileges be restored to him.

POSITION OF THE COMPANY

The company stated that the discharge was based on the "fraudulent use of the hospitalization plan using a claimant other than what is described in the union contract:—that is, a wife and children.

The company argued that Lieber's intent was to defraud the company and the insurer. Even in 1971 when he first registered Laura Robertson as his wife, his salary was over $12,000 per year. In addition, he owned a bar-restaurant and had sizable savings with which he could have paid her medical and hospitalization expenses. Furthermore, his fraudulent behavior continued over a period of years, negating any possible claim that he had acted impulsively.

Lieber's behavior was directed toward defrauding the company, since the company paid the premiums and premiums are based upon the claim experience of the company.

The company argued that it was justified in arriving at its decision to terminate John Lieber, and the grievance of the union in this matter should be denied.

APPENDIX

Relevant Provisions of the Contract

Article V. (C) When an employee is summarily discharged, an officer of the Local Union shall be notified as soon as practicable. Any employee who feels that he has been unjustly discharged, shall file a complaint in writing with the company and the union within three (3) normal work days of twenty-four (24) hours each after discharge. Unless the complaint is filed within such time, it shall be deemed waived. It is recognized by both the company and the union that such a complaint should be settled at the earliest possible time and should take precedence over complaints or grievances of a different nature and that settlement should be reached within five (5) days if possible.

If a settlement cannot be reached in that time, the Committee appointed by the Executive Board of the union and the representatives of the company shall continue to meet on days to be mutually agreed upon until the matter is disposed of, and if it is found that such employee has been unjustly discharged, he shall be reinstated with all rights and privileges enjoyed before said discharge and shall be compensated for all normal time lost at his regular rate of pay.

If settlement cannot be reached by the procedure set forth above, the matter shall be submitted to arbitration as set forth in Article 4.

QUESTIONS

1. Was the action of employee Groves in this matter fraudulent, or was it an impulsive action based upon an emotional involvement? Discuss.

2. Does the fact that the employee had 16 years of service and a good employment record mitigate against sustaining a discharge action? Why, or why not?

3. Should the fact that the employee was making restitution be considered by the arbitrator as a significant factor in support of the union position?

4. Evaluate the union argument concerning the comparison in claims paid by the insurance agent as compared to the company premium payments to that insurance agency. Why would the union introduce an argument of this type?

5. With lifestyles and societal mores changing, should companies become more flexible in their benefit plans to accommodate situations of this type? Discuss.

39. INFRINGEMENT OF BARGAINING UNIT WORK

Company: Lammerts Furniture Company, St. Louis, Missouri

Union: Furniture Warehousemen, Teamsters Local 688

On Saturday, August 9, 1975, Ronald Cunningham[1] and Joseph Foley, the manager and assistant manager, respectively, of Lammerts' St. Louis Hills store, spent the day moving and rearranging stock in the store. The St. Louis Hills store was scheduled to be closed and vacated by October 1, 1975, and Cunningham and Foley were shifting the store's inventory in order to display and sell as much stock as possible by the closing date. Their work primarily involved moving furniture from the smaller second floor to the larger display areas on the first floor and basement levels, and rearranging various major displays on the lower levels to accommodate the additional furniture moved from the second floor.

On Monday, August 11, 1975, Henry Walton, a receiving clerk at the St. Louis Hills store and a member of Teamsters Local 688, reported to work at the store. Upon noticing the changes which had been made over the weekend in the arrangement of displays and stock, Walton telephoned David Roberts, the union shop steward, who worked at Lammerts' Clayton store. Walton explained the changes effected at the St. Louis Hills store, and noted that all of the moving had been performed by nonunion employees over the weekend. Roberts visited the St. Louis Hills store on Tuesday, August 12, where Walton showed him the empty second floor and pointed out various display alterations on the lower levels. Walton estimated that about 20 recliners and 10 dinette sets had been moved from the second floor to the lower two levels and noted that numerous other

---

[1] The names of all individuals have been disguised.

items had been rearranged throughout the store. Roberts estimated that to carry out the changes alleged by Walton would have required at least eight hours work by two employees.

Because no union personnel had been involved in the movement of the furniture on Saturday, August 9, Walton and Roberts felt that the warehousemen's contractual rights had been violated, and filed the following complaint on August 13, 1975, alleging:

> Violation of Article XIII and any other Articles that may apply. Sales people and employees other than bargaining unit employees have been performing bargaining unit work.
>
> Settlement requested: Eight hours pay to the affected employees on layoff for every day work was performed. Time and one half for Saturday work; fringes to be paid accordingly.

On August 18 the company sent the following reply to the union:

> Grievance denied. On this grievance and others of a similar nature, the company has always maintained that it has the right to move furniture for display purposes, regardless of distance, once it has been placed on the display floor by a warehouseman.

> John Mann, Vice President
> J. P. Payne, General Manager, Operations

The company cited Article II, Management Rights, and Article XIII, Work Assignments, to substantiate its position.[2]

The parties failed to resolve their dispute in the grievance procedure and finally submitted the following issue to the arbitrator for resolution:

> Did the Company violate the Agreement when it had nonbargaining unit personnel move furniture in its St. Louis Hills store on August 9, 1975?

POSITION OF THE UNION

In the arbitration proceedings, the union first presented the testimony of David Roberts. Roberts stated that he had been with the company for 14 years and had been the shop steward for one year. He then related the incident of Walton's call on August 11, 1975, and his visit to the St. Louis Hills store the following day. He testified that he had not been at the St. Louis Hills store within two weeks prior to August 12, and thus was relying on Walton's statements concerning the rearrangement of displays and merchandise.

---

[2] See Appendix at end of case.

Roberts stated that warehousemen typically brought furniture onto the floor of the stores where the managers decided on arrangement of the pieces. The arrangement was then typically performed by salesmen with or without the assistance of warehousemen. Roberts testified that such adjusting usually involved moving an item from one display area to another or rearranging displays to show pieces more effectively. Normally, however, movement or alteration of a total display area was performed by warehousemen. He stated that, to his knowledge, union personnel had always moved furniture from one floor of a store to another floor. He said the union had never objected to the occasional rearranging of display pieces for decorating or sales purposes, but that in the instant case the union was objecting to the large-scale movement of furniture by nonbargaining unit personnel, a task properly reserved to union personnel.

Stephen Murdock, business representative for Local 688, then testified concerning two previous similar incidents which involved use of nonunion personnel to move furniture. Both occurred within the previous 12 months. One such incident occurred at the company's South County store where Murdock received numerous complaints from union members. Murdock stated that in a closed union meeting concerning the problem, the warehousemen voted to "go along with the company" in order to allow management flexibility in rearranging furniture. However, he noted that the men had also voted that this was not to be considered a final and binding precedent for any future incidents.

A second similar incident occurred at the company's Clayton store where employees had filed a grievance protesting the major movement of furniture by nonbargaining unit personnel during a remodeling project. In this instance, too, the union personnel unanimously agreed to drop the grievance because the situation at the Clayton store was a temporary one.

The union acknowledged that Article XIII of the agreement provided for some flexibility in moving furniture by union and nonbargaining unit personnel. The union noted evidence of this principle of flexibility in the first part of Article XIII which allowed nonunion performance of bargaining unit work "where agreed by the union to cover special contingencies." However, the union noted that the primary effect of Article XIII is to limit company assignment of bargaining unit work, in order to protect work "regularly performed by members of the bargaining unit."

The union contended that the August 9 incident constituted a violation by the company of Article XIII "beyond a degree of reasonable flexibility" intended by that article. It alleged that bargaining unit personnel customarily moved furniture from one floor to another, and also customarily moved entire display areas within the store as appropriate. The union did not object to nonbargaining unit personnel moving furniture within a display area, or single movements of furniture involving replacements and minor rearrangements. But the union did object to the wholesale movement of furniture between floors, one floor to another, and across floors. This was definitely bargaining unit work.

Finally, the union pointed out that during periods of economic recession, this type of issue becomes more sensitive to union members. Union members had been reasonable in interpreting the agreement. Failure to press this issue in the past did not constitute the waiving of their right to do so now. In this case the union felt that "the line had to be drawn," and abuses of the intent of the agreement had to be brought to a halt.

The union asked the arbitrator to uphold the grievance which the union was limiting to this grievance alone. It also requested an award to Henry Walton of eight hours pay at the appropriate overtime rate, plus all associated fringe benefits for the work he could have performed on August 9, 1975.

POSITION OF THE COMPANY

The company presented the testimony of John Mann, vice president of Lammerts, who stated that the arrangement of display layouts was the responsibility of the individual store managers, buyers, and the president of the company. He noted that changes in layouts were made from time to time to improve sales impact. Normally, there was minimal movement between floors, but considerable shifting of pieces on the same level. Mann stated that, in his judgment, bargaining unit work consisted of receiving furniture in the warehouse, moving it into the store display areas, and removing it for sales, transfer, and loading. Historically, movement of furniture in the stores had been done by the store managers, assistant managers, buyers, the company president, and warehousemen when they were available.

Regarding the instant grievance, Mann noted that the St. Louis Hills store was scheduled to be closed October 1, 1975, and the manager moved the furniture down from the second floor in order to promote sales of the remaining stock. He stated, "This was a degree of movement; it was a bit unusual, but the difference was only one of degree."

Mann also cited the two incidents noted by Murdock in which management personnel were involved in large movements of furniture in the South County and Clayton Stores. Mann stated that the problem at the South County store arose when the store was being readied for opening. Over a period of about a month, large quantities of furniture were moved by the entire management group, sales personnel, and two warehousemen from Local 688. He said,"We moved furniture all over in order to get the store ready on time." Mann pointed out that the situation at the Clayton store was also a temporary one occurring during a major remodeling project when management and sales personnel, as well as men from Local 688, were all involved in major movements of merchandise.

He further stated that while the union protested the movement of furniture on both occasions at these stores, the issues were resolved without serious difficulty.

Philip Schneider, manager of Lammerts' South County store, also testified for the company. Noting that he had advanced from salesman to manager over a period of 21 years with the company, Schneider testified that in stores in which he had worked, warehousemen had placed furniture in the stores, but anyone involved in sales or displaying the furniture could move it within the store. He attested that for movements within the store, he would "use warehousemen when they were available." He noted, however, that nonunion personnel had previously moved furniture between store floors without union objection, although he was aware of the two incidents referred to by Murdock in which the union had objected to such activity.

In its closing arguments, the company asserted that the primary question involved in the grievance was that of interpretation of the respective rights of the company and the union as stipulated by Article XIII of the agreement. Since the parties had never arrived at a specific understanding of the provisions of Article XIII, the arbitrator must limit his interpretation to the words of that provision. The company pointed out that Article XIII only restricted management from doing bargaining unit work which was "regularly performed by members of the bargaining unit." The company interpreted regular work of warehousemen to be limited to bringing furniture into the stores and onto the floors. Union personnel would be utilized for intrastore rearranging of furniture if they were available, but the company maintained that such work was "irregular" for bargaining unit personnel and subject to the prerogative of management under the agreement.

The company asserted that the interpretation of the scope of Article XIII of the agreement was a matter which needed to be resolved through negotiation between management and the union. However, it contended that the arbitrator was not empowered to restrict management's rights under the provision.

The company maintained that it had not violated any of the agreement provisions on August 9, 1975, and requested that the grievance be denied.

APPENDIX

Relevant Provisions of the Agreement

ARTICLE II—MANAGEMENT RIGHTS

The management of the company and the direction of the working forces, including the right to plan, direct, change, and control company operations, working practices, and work tasks will be vested exclusively in the Employer, not inconsistent with other provisions of this Agreement.

ARTICLE XIII—WORK ASSIGNMENTS

Except where agreed by the Union to cover special contingencies, employees other than those in the Bargaining Unit may not perform the work regularly performed by members of the Bargaining Unit, provided that one (1) employee not of this Bargaining Unit may assist a customer in removing his or her merchandise if a warehouseman is not present, provided it is not a scheduled will-call. On all scheduled will-calls at least one (1) member of this Bargaining Unit shall be present.

QUESTIONS

1. Evaluate the union argument that the incident of August 9, 1975, was a violation by the company of the agreement "beyond a degree of reasonable flexibility."
2. Since both parties agreed that union personnel and nonbargaining unit personnel had moved furniture within the store, how can either party claim jurisdiction over the contested work? Discuss.
3. Were the previous occurrences cited by the union and management relevant to the instant case situation, or were they unrelated incidents which should not influence the arbitrator's decision?
4. Evaluate the company's argument that an arbitrator is not empowered to restrict management's rights under Article XIII of the agreement.
5. What is meant by the provision within Article XIII restricting management from doing bargaining unit work which is "regularly performed by members of the bargaining unit"? Why is this type of provision often the focal point of dispute between management and a union?

40. THE SPEEDY FINISHER

Company: Olin Corporation, East Alton, Illinois

Union: International Association of Machinists and Aerospace Workers, Victory Lodge 609

At 4:00 P.M. on November 16, 1973, Roy Walker,[1] a stock repairman in the finishing and repair department of Arms Operations, received the following disciplinary action notice from Dan Robinson, his department foreman:

> On November 16, 1973, you informed another employee that her production was too high and that she should adjust such production to a limited fixed amount of 100 pieces to be consistent with the "pegged" output of the group.
>
> Inasmuch as this violates the no-strike provision of the Labor Agreement, you are suspended from 11/16/73 to and including 11/20/73, and you are further warned any further occurrence will result in your discharge.

On the following day, Walker filed a grievance claiming that the five-day suspension levied against him violated Article 23 (see Appendix to this case) of the collective agreement.

BACKGROUND

On November 15, 1973, Mary McCarthy, a subassembler in the shaping and sanding department, was temporarily transferred because of a lack of work in her department to the finishing and repair department to work on gun stock repair. Supervisor Dan Robinson assigned her to repairing gun stocks rejected by the quality control

---

[1] The names of all individuals have been disguised.

department for a condition called open grain. This task involved rubbing the stocks with steel wool to eliminate rough and uneven spots left after final sanding. He also instructed McCarthy to set aside stocks with obvious defects, such as cracks and dents, and to work only on those which could be made right by rubbing with steel wool.[2] Mary McCarthy processed 580 units that day.

The following day, November 16, McCarthy was again assigned to the finishing and repair department to perform the same work she had done on the preceding day. At about 11 A.M., in a distressed condition, she appeared at Robinson's office located about 50 feet from her work area. She reported that one of the employees told her she "was doing too much work and that she should do only 100 pieces per day." Robinson asked her to remain in his office while he went to the work area to ascertain which employee had made the statement.

Robinson first met Henry Allen who worked next to McCarthy. Allen told Robinson that he thought that Roy Walker had said something to her. When Robinson asked Walker about speaking to McCarthy, Walker at first denied it, but then admitted saying, "You are a better worker than I am." Robinson then returned to his office and, after arranging to transfer McCarthy back to her regular department, reported the incident to Ralph Harkens, general foreman. Harkens in turn phoned Peter Dawkins, labor relations administrator. Harkens and Dawkins agreed that an investigatory hearing should be convened immediately.

At the investigatory hearing, Walker denied that he had made any remark directly to McCarthy regarding her output. He testified that he had remarked aloud, within the hearing of others, that she was a better worker than he was. Dawkins, however, claimed at the hearing that Walker had previously told him that he had told McCarthy that "she had done many racks and that she was a better worker than he was." Walker also denied that he had engaged in a slow-down, or that the stock repairmen had restricted their production.

The company decided to suspend Walker for five days based on information produced during the hearing.

Immediately following this decision, Dawkins told McCarthy that Walker had been disciplined on the basis of her statements and asked her to sign a statement for the record. She signed the following statement:

---

[2] Many of the gun stocks rejected by quality control have cracks and dents requiring the use of various hand and power tools to make needed repairs. On occasions, the repairmen are instructed to set aside defective stocks requiring substantial time to repair, and to work on the refinishing of those stocks requiring the steel wool treatment.

> On November 16, 1973, I was working as a Stock Rubber when Walker approached me and said, "What are you doing?"

Mary: "I'm rubbing stock."
Walker: "How many did you do yesterday?"
Mary: "Almost 600."
Walker: "You're a damn fool. You're just making it hard for the rest of us. I'll be goddamned if I'll do that many a day. We only do 100 a day."
Mary: "I don't care how many you do. That's my business how many I do and it's your business how many you do a day. I'll work the way I feel like it."
Walker: "Well you're a damn fool."

POSITION OF THE UNION

The union argued that the evidence did not establish that Walker made statements directly to McCarthy regarding her output. McCarthy did not testify at the investigative hearing and at no time, either at the hearing or subsequent to it, did the accused have the opportunity to confront his accuser. The accuracy of McCarthy's statements must be questioned. The union claimed that her emotional state at the time of the alleged statements by Walker reflected nothing more than "a greater-than-normal sensitivity to criticism." Nothing that Walker said, even in McCarthy's signed statement, could be construed as a threat. As a matter of fact, he did not even expressly request her to reduce her output. There was no objective basis for her strong reaction.

The union also rejected the company's contention that Walker limited his output, or that the employees in the finishing and repair department conspired to limit their output. Production records of stock repairers (a group of five to seven employees) for the period June–November 1973 showed an average daily output of 87 units. One employee, however, averaged about 140 units, another achieved 260 units one day, and Walker on two occasions produced 150 units. This data proved that employees did not limit daily output to 100 units. Regardless, the company had never indicated any dissatisfaction with employee performance prior to this incident.

Finally, the company had not shown that Walker had violated Article 35 (see Appendix to this case), the no-strike clause of the agreement, as alleged in the company disciplinary notice to Walker. Even if there was a violation in spirit, the company itself violated the clause by failing to comply with the requirement that written notice of such violation be sent to the union.

Since the company had not shown that Walker's suspension was for sufficient cause, the union requested that the disciplinary suspension be rescinded, and that Roy Walker be made whole for the five days' earnings which had been unjustly denied him.

POSITION OF THE COMPANY

The company argued that since the termination of an incentive wage plan in 1969, it had observed a "tendency by employees to peg production." Walker's statements to McCarthy constituted direct evidence that employees in the finish and repair department had arbitrarily limited production. They owed the company a fair day's work and had a duty not to discourage others from doing the same.

Mary McCarthy was highly upset by Walker's remarks to her on the morning of November 16. She did not testify in person later that day because of her emotional condition. However, she prepared and signed a written statement of her conversation with Walker. She was unavailable for direct testimony because she left the employ of the company since the incident occurred.

The company also contended that Walker did not deny that he was the person accused by McCarthy. Furthermore, McCarthy appeared at Robinson's office in a distressed state growing out of an attempt to intimidate her because she exceeded, by a very large margin, the customary output in the department.

The threats of Walker were a direct challenge to the company's rights to manage the business efficiently. Further, such threats were in violation of Article 35, in which the union pledged not to restrict work or strike. The company had ample cause to discipline Walker, and its five-day suspension action was not excessive. The grievance should be denied.

APPENDIX

Relevant Contract Clauses

ARTICLE 23—DISCIPLINE AND DISCHARGE

An employee shall not be disciplined or discharged without good and sufficient cause.

ARTICLE 35—NO STRIKE OR LOCKOUT

35.1   No strike or lockout

   a.   There shall be no lockout on the part of the Company.

   b.   The union shall not authorize any strike as defined in the Labor Management Relations Act, 1947, as amended, nor authorize any refusal by any employee to enter upon the premises of the Company and to perform work hereunder because of any strike or picket line.

35.2 Union Responsibility

a. In the event of the occurrence of any such unauthorized refusal to enter upon the premises of the Company and to perform work hereunder, the Union shall immediately upon receiving notice thereof, which will be confirmed in writing, inform the employees that such action is not authorized by the Union and deliver to the Company a letter advising that such action is not authorized by the Union and move to prevent loss to the Company and bring about an immediate cessation of such strike or refusal to enter upon the premises of the Company and to perform work hereunder.

b. All employees who participate in or are responsible for any unauthorized strike or refusal to enter upon the premises of the Company and to perform work hereunder shall be subject to disciplinary action, including discharge by the Company.

c. It is understood and agreed that the Union shall have no financial liability for the acts of its members which are not authorized by the Union.

d. It is understood and agreed that the Union's responsibilities under Section 35.2 of this Article shall not be applicable in the event the Company fails within 10 days to comply with an arbitration award, unless the Company, during the 10-day period, notifies the Union of the Company's intent to seek clarification of the award or to have the award set aside.

QUESTIONS

1. Evaluate the statement of employee Mary McCarthy concerning the conversation which she had in the plant with employee Walker. Were Walker's statements threats or attempts at intimidating McCarthy to restrict output?

2. How does one explain the production of McCarthy compared to the production record of most of the other employees? Does this suggest that employees deliberately were "pegging" production? Discuss.

3. Evaluate the company argument that Walker's statements were in violation of the no-strike clause of the agreement.

4. Must an employee who signs a written statement of charges against another employee be present at an arbitration hearing in order to be cross-examined by the person whom the employee has accused? Does this depend on the situation?

41. A REQUEST FOR PARENTAL LEAVE

Company: South Bend Community School Corporation, South Bend, Indiana

Union: National Educational Association, South Bend, Indiana

BACKGROUND

In fall 1972 it was brought to the attention of the South Bend Community School Corporation that the maternity sick leave provisions of the 1972-73 teaching contracts might be inconsistent with the requirements of the Equal Employment Opportunity Commission (EEOC). The school then entered into discussion with the South Bend chapter of the National Education Association (NEA) in order to draft a new provision. The union proposed contract language which would have provided for parental leave following pregnancies for both males and females.[1] The school corporation resisted such provisions becauase it felt that these provisions were not required by the EEOC guidelines. The union's parental leave proposals were rejected, and a new maternity sick leave directive was issued by the corporation in January 1973 which did not contain such language. Similar arguments by the union were rejected in contract negotiations for the 1973-74 and 1974-75 school year agreements.

Having signed a teaching contract for the 1974-75 school year in the spring of 1974, Carol Franklin[2] notified the school corporation on May 22, 1974, of her pregnancy and expected delivery date of June 28, 1974. She also enclosed a physician's confirmation of her pregnancy, and informed the corporation of her intention to take sick

---

[1] The arbitrator in this case refers to the NEA as a "union." The authors have employed his terminology, although some chapters of the NEA consider themselves to be professional associations rather than labor unions.

[2] The names of all individuals have been disguised.

leave for maternity purposes commencing August 26, 1974. The corporation's assistant superintendent of personnel, John Woodson, discussed the subject with a union official, but no notice of approval or rejection was ever sent to Franklin.

Following the birth of the baby on June 24, Franklin sent another note to Woodson dated July 8, 1974, confirming her earlier correspondence, informing him of the baby's birth, and again indicating her request for sick leave with pay commencing on August 26. At this time, she had accumulated 33½ days of paid sick leave and wanted to take all of this beginning August 26. She also informed the corporation that she did not wish to teach any classes during the 1974–75 school year, but intended to return to full-time teaching in August 1975. Her requests were not based on any alleged illness suffered at that time, but on a desire to take time off following her pregnancy.

In a telephone conversation in early August 1974, Woodson told Franklin that according to the Article X Sick Leave provisions of the contract (see Appendix to this case), a medical statement certifying a present illness was necessary to grant the sick leave. This was because the maternity sick leave provision of the contract, Article XIII, Section 1, did not provide for paid sick leaves in periods during which sick leave was not required because of pregnancy or recovery (e.g., summer months, Christmas holiday vacation).

Franklin did not submit any such medical certification. Nevertheless, in a letter dated August 23, 1974, Woodson approved her requested leave of absence for the 1974–75 school year, but reiterated the requirement of a physician's statement of "present illness" necessary for her to obtain paid sick leave.

Franklin contended that Section 1 of Article XIII of the contract entitled her to receive 33½ days of paid sick leave for the period beginning August 26, subsequent to the birth of her child.

The contract provided for 10 paid sick leave days plus 2 paid personal leave days each contract year beginning on August 1. Franklin claimed that she was entitled to accumulate and receive those 12 paid sick leave days, in addition to the 33½ previously accumulated sick leave days, during the 1974–75 year she was to be on leave of absence. The corporation denied that she was entitled to any of the 45½ sick leave days for which she claimed payment.

The parties stipulated that the issue to be submitted to the arbitrator should read as follows:

> Under the applicable collective bargaining contract, and applicable policies or practices, if any, was Carol Franklin entitled to sick leave for maternity purposes for any period after August 26, 1974? If so, for what period was she entitled to such sick leave?

POSITION OF THE UNION

The union maintained that Section 1 of Article XIII allowed a teacher who was absent from teaching on a maternity sick leave to receive her salary, if desired, to the extent of her normal accumulated sick leave. The union argued that this provision was intended to allow the teacher to receive paid sick leave during the period of absence due to pregnancy, regardless of whether she was ill or not. The union further argued that because there was no requirement of present illness, there was similarly no need to submit a physician's statement of such illness in order to obtain accumulated paid sick leave. The union sought from the corporation Franklin's accumulated paid sick leave beginning August 26, 1974, plus an additional 12 days based on her contract for the 1974–75 school year.

POSITION OF THE CORPORATION

The school corporation claimed that maternity sick leave was the same as any sick leave, and as such, required medical evidence of present illness if the corporation requested it. The corporation noted that, historically, postmaternity sick leave had not exceeded 24 days, and only during that part of the year when the teacher would normally be expected to be at work. The corporation also maintained that in light of the language of the contract and its surrounding negotiations, the sick leave provisions were designed to grant leave only to those who were presently ill, sick, or disabled, and to extend coverage beyond those limits would be contrary to the purpose of the provisions.

The school affirmed its willingness to rehire Franklin for the 1975–76 school year without loss of her accumulated 33½ days of sick leave, but contended that such leave should not be granted for the period beginning August 26, 1974, as sought by Franklin.

APPENDIX

Relevant Provisions of the Contract

ARTICLE X—SICK LEAVE

Sick pay is a benefit provided by the school district to permanent employees to insure against loss of income due to short-term personal illness. Sick pay is not to be used for any reason other than illness and is given only for illness-caused absence on scheduled workdays.

I. Eligibility

Although sick pay benefits accrue from the date of hire, a teacher may receive sick pay only after having completed six months of continuous service.

A teacher will not be given sick pay unless having given proper notification of illness to her supervisor. That is, prior to her scheduled work time, she must contact her supervisor to inform him that she will be unable to report for work. If the absence is longer than one day, the teacher must keep her supervisor notified of her condition on a daily basis or some other basis that is satisfactory with her supervisor.

In order to establish eligibility for sick pay for any absence due to illness, lasting five workdays or less, a teacher, at her supervisor's discretion, may be required to submit a physician's statement. For any illness which causes a teacher to miss more than five workdays, she is expected to submit to her supervisor a physician's statement of the nature and length of her illness and that she is able to return to work and to resume her normal duties without restriction.

II. Use of Sick Days

Sick days will be deducted from a teacher's reserve of sick days at the rate of one day for each day of illness.

If a teacher is a permanent employee and has more than 10 sick days accumulated at the outset of her illness and is not ready to return to work when her total number of paid sick days expires, she must go on a leave of absence at that time if eligible or be terminated.

If a teacher is a permanent employee and has 10 or less sick days accumulated at the outset of her illness and is not ready to return to work when her total number of paid sick days expires, she will be allowed up to a total of 10 days off before being required to go on a leave of absence.

ARTICLE XIII—MATERNITY LEAVE

I. Sick Leave for Maternity Purposes

Section 1. A teacher who is pregnant shall be entitled upon request to sick leave. The teacher's absence shall begin at a time mutually agreed upon between the teacher, the Assistant Superintendent of Personnel, and the teacher's physician. Said teacher shall notify the Assistant Superintendent of Personnel, in writing, at least 30 days prior to the date on which she desires to begin her sick leave and shall include in her communication a statement from her physician certifying her pregnancy.

A teacher who is pregnant may continue in active employment as late into her pregnancy as best determined after consultation with her physician, the Assistant Superintendent in charge of Personnel, and herself.

A teacher who is absent on sick leave for maternity purposes may receive salary, if she desires, for days lost to the extent of her accumulated sick leave.

Section 2. A teacher who is granted sick leave for maternity purposes shall comply with the following rules.

It shall be the responsibility of the teacher to notify the Assistant Superintendent of Personnel the date upon which she desires to return to active employment. The notification shall be made within a 30-day period, in writing, following the termination of pregnancy.

During the period of sick leave for maternity purposes, the teacher's position will be filled by a substitute teacher. Upon the receipt of notification to return, the Assistant Superintendent of Personnel and the teacher shall determine the exact date upon which she will resume her previous assignment. Prior to the resumption of her teaching duties, the teacher shall provide the Assistant Superintendent of Personnel with a statement of her good health from her physician. Failure by the teacher to notify the Assistant Superintendent of Personnel within the aforesaid 30-day period after the termination of pregnancy of her desire to resume teaching shall relieve the School Corporation of any responsibility for holding the teacher's position beyond the 30-day period.

QUESTIONS

1. What is meant by the term *sick leave* as normally utilized in union-management agreements? Does an individual have to be physically or mentally ill to be eligible for sick leave benefits?
2. Is maternity a sickness? Discuss.
3. Should an employee be entitled to accumulated sick leave benefit payments at any time when an employee would like to receive such payments? Discuss.
4. In 1978 the Pregnancy Discrimination Act was passed as an amendment to the Civil Rights Act of 1964. This law essentially mandates that pregnancy must be treated by an employer "the same" as any other sickness or disability "for all employment-related purposes." Would Article XIII of the contract in this case be legal under this Act? Why, or why not?

42. RIDING THE TIGER

Company: Randle-Eastern Ambulance Service, Inc., Miami, Florida

Union: Transport Workers Union, Local 500

BACKGROUND

James Kellerman[1] was hired by the Randle-Eastern Ambulance Service in May 1974 as an ambulance attendant. He performed his job well, receiving a commendation for service during a major disaster. Further, Kellerman had a generally good record of attendance and behavior, and he was promoted to ambulance driver within a few months.

On November 11, 1974, while driving an ambulance, Kellerman was struck by another vehicle and suffered a cracked vertebra in his back. He was then placed on compensatory sick leave by the firm to allow for his recovery. On March 13, 1975, Kellerman was examined by a physician and the following report was submitted to the firm.

> To whom it may concern:
>
> On March 13, 1975, the above patient was seen in my office for his fractured vertebra.
>
> At that time, X rays showed that there was still not enough solidity to allow him to do heavy work, such as lifting stretchers and putting any great stress on his back. However, the back was comfortable on motion. He had a good range of motion, and percussion did not produce any pain.
>
> At that time, we felt that it was safe for him to drive an ambulance but he should not be doing any lifting. We suggested that he not do any strenuous activities with his back for another four weeks. At that

---

[1] The names of all individuals have been disguised.

time, we told him he could swim but we told him he was to do no diving, no running around, no horsing around in the pool, simply to go in and float around and swim gently to exercise the back muscles.

Respectfully,
Anthony Bomarito, M.D.

Following his examination on March 13, and while still on sick leave from Randle-Eastern, Kellerman contacted Francis Anderson, the assistant information director at Gulfstream Race Track, a local horse track. Prior to his employment at Randle-Eastern, Kellerman had been a jockey working principally at Gulfstream. For several previous years, Kellerman had participated in a novelty animal race staged as part of the festivities on Florida Derby Day. This had involved his riding such animals as ostriches, brahma bulls, camels, and buffaloes. Kellerman contacted Anderson inquiring about the possibility of again participating in the 1975 race. Anderson affirmed that there was still an "empty saddle" and hired Kellerman to ride a Bengal tiger in the race. He agreed to pay Kellerman $100, with the understanding that he could withdraw from the event at any time if he considered the assignment to be dangerous.

On March 29, 1975, while still on sick leave from the ambulance firm, Kellerman finished second in the Florida Derby Day race. The tigers used in the race were domesticated, trained animals which were rather lethargic and had to be led through the race by their trainers who claimed the animals were completely harmless. (Kellerman blamed his loss on his mount's lack of competitive spirit.)

Upon learning of Kellerman's participation in the race, company officials called him into the office and charged him with a violation of Section E, Paragraph 7, of the company Operating Manual, which stated:

An employee desiring other employment while off duty from the Company is responsible for obtaining written Company permission to assure that the other employment would not be detrimental to the best interests of the Company or the employee.

The company discussed the incident with Kellerman and his union representative, then informed him that he was discharged from the firm. In dismissing him, the company based its action on the potential risk involved in such activity, and the possible detrimental effect upon Kellerman's health.

On April 10, 1975, subsequent to his discharge, Kellerman received another physical examination. A portion of the report from this examination stated:

On April 10, 1975, this patient was seen to have a full range of motion and no pain. His X rays showed that he had sufficient solidification for me to discharge him and allow him unrestricted activities. Because of his deformed vertebra, a 5 percent permanent partial disability of the body as a whole was assigned to the patient. At no time did I give this patient permission to ride a Bengal tiger.

(s) Anthony Bomarito, M.D.

Kellerman filed a grievance, which eventually was submitted to arbitration. In the arbitration proceedings, the issue agreed upon by both parties was whether Kellerman violated Section E, Paragraph 7, of the Operating Manual and thus provided the company with "cause" for discharge by his participation in an exhibition in which he allegedly rode a tiger at Gulfstream Race Track.

POSITION OF THE UNION

The union presented a series of arguments in support of its position that the company did not have "cause" to discharge Kellerman.

1.   The union challenged the company's claim of broad authority in its exercise of Article 18, the disciplinary provision, of the contract.[2]

2.   The union denied the company's assertion that management had the unlimited right to establish rules to govern employee conduct. The union acknowledged the company's right to establish operating rules, but maintained that the union reserved the right to challenge any such rule or attempted enforcement.

3.   The union contended that there were 36 pages of rules contained in the Operating Manual, and Kellerman was unaware of the restrictive provisions of Section E, Paragraph 7, and their application to his job at the race track. He could not be expected to be familiar with every implication of all of the rules.

4.   The union maintained that because of the large amount of rules contained in the Operating Manual, the company was under an obligation to explain the application of the rule concerning outside employment to its employees. There was no evidence that the company had made any effort to do so, and the union argued that Kellerman should not be held to such strict compliance as the company attempted to impose.

5.   The company had misinterpreted its own rule by construing the words "off-duty employment" too broadly. The union con-

---

[2] See Appendix at end of case for relevant contract provisions.

tended that the terms of a rule should be construed as the "proverbial reasonable man" would understand them, and that in this case a reasonable interpretation of the rule would be that it referred only to "full-time employment" and not to occasional work. The work schedule for company employees consisted of shifts of 24 hours on and 24 hours off, a system which would seemingly readily present the option to an employee for working another job. This might become a potential source of conflict if an ambulance attendant's performance or availability for extra work suffered because of fatigue due to the second job. Thus the rule had some reasonable basis, but the union asserted that it was not intended to apply to one-time or occasional jobs.

6. The union argued that the company failed to take into consideration all of the circumstances of Kellerman's activity on March 29, 1975, and erroneously characterized it as "employment." The company contended that its dismissal action was based on the potential risk involved in the race; yet the union asserted that the race was merely a staged entertainment. Kellerman was experienced and had the option of backing out at any time, and there was no foreseeable risk of injury to Kellerman, nor could the activity be seen as potentially detrimental to the company.

Based upon these arguments, the union sought reinstatement of Kellerman to his employed status with the firm with no loss of applicable pay or benefits.

POSITION OF THE COMPANY

The company's arguments supporting the propriety of the discharge rested on several points:

1. The company claimed broad discretionary authority described in the agreement and a limited right of the union to challenge that authority. It maintained that the company was only required to show that it had "cause" to penalize the employee, not that the particular penalty was appropriate.

2. The company contended that the labor agreement recognized management's unlimited right to make rules to govern employee conduct and to discipline employees for violation of such rules.

3. The Operating Manual contained rules to govern employee conduct. These rules were known by both the employee and the union. Kellerman, in spite of everything the company had done, violated Section E, Paragraph 7, by accepting employment at Gulfstream Race Track.

4. Any activity in the nature of work for another, particularly

278

when there is compensation, as in this instance, comes within a normal definition of "employment" and makes the application of Section E, Paragraph 7, appropriate. In support of this argument, the company referred to an earlier arbitration award which dealt with the issue.

The award cited by the company was *Armstrong Rubber Company v Rubber Workers* (57 LA 1267), in which the arbitrator upheld a company discharge action. The arbitrator ruled that:

> Under a contract providing for termination of employee's seniority whenever he works on another job while on leave of absence, the employer properly discharged the employee, who, while on sick leave worked for another employer on commission basis. The employer is entitled to enforce prohibition against work at another job, since prohibition serves to speed an employee's return to full-time duty. The fact that the employer stopped sending sickness and accident checks to the employee does not justify the employee's violation of agreement.

The company claimed that in view of its broad, discretionary authority in such matters as the case in question, plus the fact that the employee should have been aware of the rules, the discharge should be upheld.

APPENDIX

Relevant Provisions of the Contract

ARTICLE 3—MANAGEMENT RIGHTS

Management retains the sole and exclusive right to, and responsibility of, without being subject to the grievance or arbitration provisions herein, any and all functions and rights which it enjoyed prior to the selection of the union as bargaining agent, except to the precise extent such functions and rights are explicitly, clearly, and unequivocally taken away from management by the express terms of this Agreement.

In addition, the company being a quasi-public agency, must, without qualification, except to the precise extent such qualifications are explicitly, clearly, and unequivocally made by the express terms of this Agreement, continue to implement its policies and practices, particularly relating to safety, security, discipline, and control, as done in the past and as deemed desirable in the future.

The management of the company and the direction of its employees, including the establishment of working conditions, the hiring, promoting, demoting, transferring, subcontracting, changes in operations or mode of operations, rehiring of employees, determination of qualifications of employees, and the layoff and recall to work of employees in connection with any reduction or increase in the work force, are the exclusive and sole functions and responsibility of management to the extent that any such matters are not otherwise explicitly, clearly, and unequivocally covered or provided for in this Agreement; and provided that in the exercise of such functions, the company shall not discriminate against any employee because of his membership in, or lawful activity on behalf of the union.

ARTICLE 6—SICK LEAVE

(d) Any employee who by reason of bona fide illness as defined in Article 6 will be granted appropriate leave of absence. Only union seniority will continue to accrue during such leaves. In no event will seniority accrue for more than one (1) year. An employee accepting gainful employment while on leave of absence except as approved in writing by the company automatically terminates his employment with the company.

Time spent on medical leave of absence shall not count for any other purposes.

A medical certificate will be required upon return to duty stating the employee's ability to perform his regular duties.

During such leave of absence an employee may continue his hospitalization and life insurance at his expense subject to the insurance carrier's approval.

(e) These sick leave provisions do not apply to sickness, injury, or disability within the purview of Workmen's Compensation.

ARTICLE 7—WORKMENS COMPENSATION

Any employee who has been determined by the company's Workmen's Compensation carrier to have been injured on the job will be paid the difference between the Workmen's Compensation Insurance benefits and the employee's pay for 8 hours regular pay for each consecutive calendar day's absence occasioned by a said on-the-job injury beginning with the 8th calendar day's absence and ending with the 20th calendar day's absence, not to exceed a total of said difference as applied to 40 hours.

ARTICLE 11—GRIEVANCE AND ARBITRATION

An employee who believes that he has been unjustly dealt with or that any applicable provision of this agreement has not been properly applied or interpreted may present a grievance and/or arbitration as follows:

Arbitration

1. . . . It is expressly understood that the only matters which are subject to arbitration under this Article are grievances which were processed and handled strictly in accordance with the foregoing grievance procedure and which were made subject to the grievance and arbitration provisions of this Agreement.

3. The arbitrator shall have no power to alter, amend, change, add to, or subtract from any of the terms of this Agreement, but shall determine only whether or not there has been a violation of this Agreement in the respect alleged in the grievance, in accord with the test of coverage set out in subparagraph 1 above. The rights of Management enumerated in Article 3 are hereby incorporated by reference herein, and those rights and all other rights of management not clearly, specifically, and unequivocally limited by the clear and explicit language of a clause of this Agreement, and the provisions of the Article prohibiting strikes or work stoppage during the life of this Agreement are specifically excluded from arbitration under the provisions of this Article. The decision of the arbitrator shall be fair and equitable and be based solely upon the evidence and arguments presented to him by the respective parties in the presence of each other.

4. This Agreement constitutes a contract between the parties which shall be interpreted and applied by the parties and by the arbitrators in the same manner as any other contract under the laws of the state of Florida. The function and purpose of the arbitrator is to determine disputed interpretation of terms actually found in the Agreement, or to determine disputed facts upon which the application of the Agreement depends. The arbitrator shall therefore not have authority, nor shall he consider it his function to include, the decision of any issue not submitted or to so interpret or apply the Agreement as to change what can fairly be said to have been the intent of the parties as determined by generally accepted rules of contract construction. The arbitrator shall not give any decision which in practical or actual effect modifies, revises, detracts from, or adds to any of the terms or provisions of this Agreement. Past practice of the parties in interpreting or applying terms of the Agreement can be relevant evidence, but may not be used so as to justify, or result in, what is in effect a modification (whether by addition or detraction) of the written terms of this Agreement. The arbitrator shall not render any decision or award solely because in his opinion such decision or award is fair or equitable. The ordinary rules of evidence shall prevail in any hearing.

6. Any dispute not specifically brought under this article by the

terms of this Agreement is not subject to this article, but is to be settled exclusively by management.

7. Specifically, the standards relating to safety or security are not arbitrable, and they are not in any manner subject to evaluation, question, qualification, interpretation or judgment by the arbitrator.

ARTICLE 18—DISCIPLINE

(a) The company shall have the right to discharge or discipline any employee for "cause," as defined solely by the company. The term "cause" shall include, but not be limited to, the following: failure to perform assigned duties, failure to perform duties efficiently, failure to meet required standards of work performance, negligence in the performance of duties likely to cause personal injuries or property damage, dishonesty, insubordination, the use or being under the influence of drugs or alcoholic beverages during working hours, performance of duties in such a manner as to reflect unfavorably upon company, lack of neatness, courtesy, cleanliness, or inability to maintain proper decorum with the using public, excessive tardiness or absences, improper attitude toward the job, the company, fellow employees, customers and customer employees, improper conduct or attitude relating to government or hospital physicians, employees and representatives, failure to comply with or pass company security or safety of applicable federal, state, county, or municipal laws, rules, or regulations, violation of this Agreement or failure to comply with company rules. Any grievance or arbitration with respect to the exercise of this right to discharge or discipline shall be limited to the question of whether or not one of the above listed offenses, or other "cause," occurred and shall not include whether or not the type of discipline selected was appropriate.

(b) The right to maintain and the manner of maintaining discipline and efficiency of employees is vested exclusively in the company, provided, solely however, that no employee shall be discharged or discriminated against for exercising his rights as set forth in Section 7 of the National Labor Relations Act, as amended.

ARTICLE 21—GENERAL

(f) The company will publish an operating manual stating company policies and defining areas of responsibility of all employees. This manual will be updated from time to time and copies will be distributed to each employee. A copy will be provided to the union.

(g) Employees will abide by the company's rules and regulations as contained in the company manual or in bulletins or notices which may be posted from time to time. A copy will be provided to the union.

QUESTIONS

1. Must an employee be aware of a company operating rule before discipline may be imposed on that employee? Discuss.
2. When an employee is on a sick leave, does this mean that the employee has no right to work for pay for another employer either on a temporary or full-time basis? Discuss.
3. What standards should an arbitrator use to apply the "reasonable man" concept advocated by the union?
4. Evaluate the last sentence of Article 18(a), the disciplinary provision of the agreement. How does this provision limit the arbitrator?

43. NO MORE COFFEE OR BOTTLED WATER

Company: Ametek California Spring Company, Pico Rivera, California

Union: United Automobile, Aerospace and Agricultural Implement Workers of America, Local 509

On April 7, 1975, a directive was issued by the company plant manager informing employees that (1) coffee was no longer to be prepared during company working hours and (2) the bottled-water stations scattered throughout the plant had been replaced by water fountains as a result of a new plumbing installation. Martin Adams,[1] an employee of the company for over 20 years, immediately questioned his supervisor, John Willis, concerning the memorandum. He reminded Willis that he had been preparing a 36-cup pot of coffee in his department every working day for the previous 19 years. He noted that the practice had been initiated at the request of a foreman who was no longer with the firm, and that it only took five minutes of his time each morning unless a second pot was required later in the day. The coffee was available to anyone in the plant during their break periods, and the only limitation was that each person pay 10 cents for each cup in order to pay for supplies. Adams further noted that the company had acknowledged and supported the practice several years before by installing a water outlet in the first-aid room. This enabled Mary Miller to obtain water for the coffee when Adams was on vacation, since Adams normally obtained water from the faucet in the men's room. Willis listened to Adams' protest, but informed him that the order came from the plant manager and it had to be enforced.

The union then filed a grievance protesting the company's unilateral action in terminating the coffee-making privilege and remov-

---

The names of all individuals have been disguised.

ing six bottled-water stations in the plant. The union maintained that the company had violated past practice and Section 3 of Article XIII of the Agreement which stated:

> The Company shall not take away any privileges that are now enjoyed by the employees.

The question eventually reached the arbitration level, where the parties agreed that the issue to be resolved by the arbitrator should be:

> Did the Company violate Article XIII by removing the bottled water and refusing to allow employees to make coffee on Company time?

POSITION OF THE UNION

At the hearing, Martin Adams related the background and procedure of his daily coffee brewing, just as he had commented to Willis on the day of the directive. He particularly noted the long duration of the practice and the apparent company acquiescence in allowing it to continue and even promoting the brewing by installing the water faucet in the first-aid room. The union acknowledged that several times in the previous three or four years management had mentioned discontinuation of the practice, but that no serious effort had been made prior to April 17, 1975, actually to effectuate that policy.

The union maintained that both the coffee brewing and bottled-water stations, which had been located in the plant for approximately 10 years, were established past practices which could not be unilaterally discontinued by management. It argued that the company had acquiesced to the coffee brewing for over 19 years and had provided bottled water since the plant facility's inception. The union cited Section 3 of Article XIII of the agreement and alleged the company had violated these provisions.

The union requested the arbitrator to order the company to restore the coffee-making privilege and the bottled-water stations in the plant.

POSITION OF THE COMPANY

Alfred Perry, general manager of the plant, testified that after joining the company in his present position in 1969, he had become aware of the practice of coffee being made on company time. Perry stated that over a period of three or four years he had instructed supervisors approximately a dozen times to stop the practice, and each time he was informed that the directive had been enforced.

Management representatives further argued that the preparation and drinking of coffee on company time wasted a considerable amount of time and interfered with efficiency. Management claimed that it had the right to abolish the coffee making under Section 1 of Article II of the contract which reads:

> It is the responsibility of the management of the company to maintain discipline and efficiency in its plant.

Perry and the plant manager, Jerome Epps, also testified concerning the bottled water. They affirmed that the company had provided bottled drinking water in the plant over the years. They maintained that this was due to the fact that in the past the company had had inadequate facilities for drinking fountains. However, the remodeling completed in the spring of 1975 provided plumbing facilities so that water fountains could be installed at various points in the plant. The company argued that the need for bottled water no longer existed, and that it had acted legitimately in terminating the bottled-water system.

Finally, management contended that the installation of drinking fountains constituted an improvement in working conditions, as well as being more efficient.

The company urged that in the interests of maintaining efficiency in the plant, its position in prohibiting the preparation of coffee on company time and the installation of drinking fountains be upheld.

QUESTIONS

1. Was the coffee drinking privilege a well-established practice in the plant? Was the providing of bottled-water stations a well-established past practice? Evaluate.
2. To what degree are Section 3 of Article XIII and Section 1 of Article II of the agreement somewhat contradictory? Which of these provisions is "superior" in the circumstances of this case?
3. What standards should an arbitrator utilize to determine whether something is a well-established past practice, or whether something is within the province of management rights to handle as appropriate to efficient operation? Discuss.

44. THE BYPASSED SENIOR CLERK

Company: Marion Food Towne, Incorporated, Marion, Illinois

Union: Retail Clerks International Association, Local 896

BACKGROUND

In June 1975, Raymond White,[1] co-owner of Marion Food Towne, Charles Ridgeway, manager of the store, and Frank Costilli, assistant manager, unanimously concluded that because of increased business it was necessary to hire an additional full-time clerk at the store. At that time, seven part-time clerks were employed at the store, and the managers decided to first consider the three part-time clerks with highest seniority for the new position.

Robert Sharp, who was in his early 50s, had worked several years in a part-time position and held highest seniority among the part-time clerks. He had been passed over several times during those years by management in hiring full-time clerks because he was considered to be too slow in carrying out his duties. In spite of this, however, the managers considered him valuable for stocking in the evening when he normally worked. James Moran, 20, having been hired on April 29, 1974, was second in seniority among the part-time stock clerks. John Anthony, having been hired on June 17, 1974, also 20, was third on the seniority list. He worked on essentially the same jobs as Moran.

The managers again decided in this instance that Sharp was too slow to be promoted, although he requested the job. They then evaluated the work performance of Moran and Anthony in an attempt to determine the best man for the position. Although they considered seniority in arriving at their decision, White, Ridgeway,

---

[1] The names of all individuals have been disguised.

and Costilli were primarily concerned with hiring into the full-time position the person with the best performance record who gave promise of having most long-run value to the store.

After considering both Moran and Anthony for the promotion and consulting with White, Costilli, and other store employees, Ridgeway awarded the full-time position to Anthony, who held least seniority among the three part-time clerks. The three managers had generally agreed that Anthony was superior to Moran in handling his duties around the store. Costilli had commented that in observing both Moran and Anthony stocking shelves, Anthony was consistently quicker, neater, and more conscientious in handling his aisles. The head checker had told Ridgeway that Anthony was usually "much quicker" in coming to the checkout counter to assist in bagging, to report prices on unmarked items, and to assist customers, and that Anthony was more efficient, helpful, and friendly than Moran. Ridgeway also took into consideration several customer comments he had received in March and April of 1975 complaining of Moran's "lack of friendliness." Ridgeway had discussed those complaints with Moran, and Moran's behavior had improved somewhat following that meeting. Ridgeway concluded, however, that Anthony was more interested in his work and in the store, and that he was the best man available for the promotion. Anthony was given the full-time position in mid-June 1975.

Following Anthony's appointment, Moran filed a grievance with the union on June 23, 1975, complaining that a part-time employee of lower seniority had been hired to the full-time position without first offering the job to him. On June 25, 1975, Virgil Neickhorn, president of Local 896, sent a letter to the company, the relevant part of which stated:

> This is to advise that James Moran has filed a grievance with this office contesting the Company's action of hiring a less senior employee for a full-time job. Mr. Moran was not offered the full-time job opening.
>
> We feel this is in violation of the Agreement: Article 9—Seniority.[2]

The company and the union failed to resolve their differences in the first three steps of the grievance procedure. The two parties submitted the following issue to an arbitrator on October 9, 1975:

> Did the Company violate the Agreement when it offered a full-time clerk's position to part-time employee John Anthony rather than offering the position to James Moran, another part-time employee who had about two months seniority over Mr. Anthony?

---

[2] See Appendix to this case.

POSITION OF THE UNION

Counsel for the union interrogated store manager Ridgeway at great length during the arbitration hearing. Ridgeway related the considerations involved in promoting Anthony to the full-time position including the consultations he had had with other personnel in the store and his own observations which led him to conclude that Anthony was superior to Moran in his work and the "best man" for the full-time position. Ridgeway testified that he wanted the "best man" regardless of his seniority, and that his decision rested largely on the person's ability to do the job. He noted that in the past the company's policy of promoting the "best man" had provided the basis for promoting lower seniority part-time employees instead of Robert Sharp into full-time positions. He also stated that he regarded a full-time position as a promotion from a part-time status.

As a result of analysis of work performance, Ridgeway stated that the results had shown Anthony's work aisle was consistently in "much better shape, neater, and had less back stock" than did Moran's. Under questioning, Ridgeway also testified that he had discussed with Moran several customer complaints regarding Moran's friendliness, but had never given him any written reprimand or report to help improve his performance. The company had an "Employee Corrective Action Notice" form to be used to note for an employee any deficiencies, but Moran had never been given one of these reports. Ridgeway stated that he considered Moran to be a "satisfactory employee" but that there were significant differences between that and an "excellent" employee.

Union president Virgil Neickhorn then testified that Article 9, Section A, of the contract had remained the same throughout the past 12 years, during which he had first been a business agent for the union and, for the last 2 years, president of the local. He stated that at no time during that period had there been a similar grievance filed by any union member.

In the course of his testimony on his own behalf, Moran related that he was presently working approximately 24 hours per week and was being paid about $3.10 per hour. He stated that he "did not remember" anyone in management ever criticizing his work, nor did he recall ever being advised by Ridgeway concerning his lack of friendliness toward customers. He stated that he performed essentially the same work as Anthony. He pointed out, however, that Anthony's aisles were located closer to the checkout stations than his own, and that this probably explained why it took him longer than Anthony to respond to requests for help from the checkers.

In summary arguments, the union contended that a change from part-time to full-time employment status did not constitute a promotion but rather a straight seniority claim to additional hours of work. The union noted that under Article 9, Section A, seniority was defined as "the length of continuous employment within the bargaining unit" and that "all circumstances being reasonably equal, length of service shall be the controlling factor." The union noted that Moran had seniority over Anthony, and that the company manager admitted Moran was capable of performing the clerk's work. Moran had never been formally counseled or reprimanded, and from this it must be concluded that Moran was fully capable of performing the clerk's tasks. The union cited several arbitration decisions holding that in situations in which an employee had the ability to do a job and was a satisfactory employee, seniority should be the controlling factor in determining advancement.

The union argued that despite the fact that Article 9, Section A, did not expressly state that a senior part-time employee who was satisfactory should be offered a full-time position in preference to a lower seniority part-time worker, the provision should be interpreted in that manner. It maintained that the spirit of the agreement implicitly led to that interpretation, and that the company should have followed that guide. Ability to do the job should have been the criterion for selecting the full-time clerk. As shown by the testimony, Moran was satisfactory in his work, and the "best-man" criterion should not have entered into management's consideration. The union argued that the company's admitted general disregard for seniority in choosing a part-time employee for a full-time position was in violation of the agreement.

Counsel for the union requested that the grievance be sustained. As a remedy, counsel for the union suggested the following: (1) The grievant, James Moran, should be assigned to a 40-hour workweek schedule; (2) he should be made whole for the difference in pay that he would have received having worked a 40-hour schedule since approximately June 23, 1975, to the present time; (3) the number of additional hours that he should have been employed as a full-time employee should be credited appropriately and payments made correspondingly to the pension fund; and (4) he should have full-time seniority status effective as of June 23, 1975.

POSITION OF THE COMPANY

The company referred to the testimony provided by store manager Ridgeway during interrogation by the union counsel and cross-examination by company counsel concerning the criteria employed by the company in deciding to promote Anthony instead of Sharp and Moran. The company emphasized its long-standing policy and practice of hiring full-time employees who indicated that they possessed outstanding ability and a very good attitude. For example, in September 1974 and again in April 1975 management promoted less senior part-time men to full-time clerk positions over Sharp. In 1971 management hired a full-time clerk "off the street," bypassing all the part-time clerks who had been considered unqualified to fill the full-time position.

Frank Costilli, the assistant manager, testified that he had been employed at the store for six years, and that he had been the assistant manager for the last 18 months, though he still retained membership in Local 896. As assistant manager his job involved supervising and directing stock work by the clerks. He stated that, based on numerous observations, Anthony was consistently quicker, neater, and more efficient in his stocking work than was Moran. In fact, on average, Anthony stocked 35–40 cases per hour, while Moran stocked 20–25 cases per hour. This was true despite the fact that Moran stocked the glass aisles, traditionally easier and quicker than the cereal, coffee, and tea aisles handled by Anthony, which required stock rotation, facing out, and other special operations. Anthony was also willing to "look for other jobs when he was done with his aisle" while Moran would only "just do his aisle."

Costilli stated that he never discussed Moran's poorer performance with him because he felt that the employees might consider his observations to be "spying." He noted, too, that the Employee Corrective Action Notice form for employee evaluation had been introduced in the store in May 1975, only a month before the incident in question.

Raymond White, co-owner of the store, testified that he maintained a philosophy of management that full-time employees should be the best employees, and that such persons must be "the most conscientious people who have the store's best interests at heart and who seek a future in the business." He noted management's previous disregard of Sharp's seniority and hiring of people "off the street" as evidence of its consistent policy of hiring the "best person" for full-time positions.

White related the decision of management to employ another full-time clerk in June 1975. He testified that he normally was in the store two or three days each week, and that he took the place of one of the managers who was on vacation. During those times he was able to make comparative observations of the work of Anthony and Moran. He stated that it was his "considered opinion" that Anthony was "head and shoulders above Moran" in all aspects of work performance. When Ridgeway recommended Anthony for the full-time position, White fully concurred that he was the best man for the job, regardless of his seniority position.

In its closing arguments, the company contended that its selection from among the three highest seniority part-time employees was proof of its concern for seniority, even if it had not promoted the most senior person. The company noted that Section 9 of the agreement only required that the company "give consideration" to part-time employees in selecting full-time personnel, and that it was not required to promote the most senior part-time employee. Since the company was not prohibited by the agreement from hiring someone "off the street," the company should not be more severely constrained in considering part-time personnel than it was in hiring outsiders to full-time positions. The company maintained that the provisions of Section A of Article 9 only required the management to follow seniority in instances of layoffs and rehiring.

The company stated that it regarded the move to full-time status as a "promotion" because of health and benefit provisions and additional available hours of work. It refuted the union assertion that Anthony's new position was merely an increase in hours which should have been given to the part-time employee of highest seniority. Management also stated that the matter was not a disciplinary action requiring it to give notice to Moran of his deficiencies in order to provide him with full opportunity to improve his performance. The company maintained that having given consideration to seniority, it had the right to choose the person whom it considered best suited for the position.

Counsel for the company requested that the grievance be denied.

APPENDIX

Relevant Provisions of the Agreement

ARTICLE IX—SENIORITY

A. In layoffs and rehiring the principle of seniority shall apply. Seniority shall be defined as the length of continuous employment within the bargaining unit, with regard to an employee's experience and ability to perform the work. All circumstances being reasonably equal, length of service shall be the controlling factor. In the event a layoff, not in accordance with length of service is contemplated, the Employer shall first contact the Union and an attempt shall be made to arrive at a mutual solution. Part-time or casual employees shall not accumulate seniority over full-time employees. It is further agreed

292

that part-time employees shall be given consideration for full-time job vacancies. Seniority shall prevail among employees in each store and shall apply to part-time and full-time employees respectively. In the event of transfer it is agreed that store seniority shall prevail. Any employee so transferred shall retain his seniority previously accumulated from the store from which he was transferred for a period of one (1) year. In the matter of promotions or transfers from one type of work to the other or from one store to the other, the Employer shall have the right to exercise his final judgment after giving due regard to seniority. Agreed upon seniority lists shall be established and maintained and such records shall be available to the Union at all times.

QUESTIONS

1. Evaluate the union contention that a change from part-time to full-time employment status was not a promotion but rather a straight seniority claim to additional hours of work.
2. Even though employee Moran was not the "best man" for the full-time position, should the fact that he was a "satisfactory" employee entitle him to the full-time position because of his seniority? Discuss.
3. To what degree is the company's claim of previous practice persuasive in support of its position?
4. To what degree is the fact that the union had never grieved this particular type of situation a relevant factor?
5. Evaluate the provisions of the agreement which require the company to "give consideration" in moving employees from part-time to full-time status and to "give regard to seniority" in promotions or transfers.
6. Compare the issues in this case with those in Case 58, "To Promote, or to Hire from the Outside?"

45. TOO MUCH TELEPHONE TIME?

Company: County Sanitation Districts of Los Angeles County, Los Angeles, California

Union: Los Angeles County Employees Association, Local 660

BACKGROUND

Leo Harris[1] had been employed as a draftsman for the County Sanitation Districts of Los Angeles County since 1968. When Harris began working for the districts, employees were not represented by any type of collective bargaining organization. However, in the fall of 1972 Los Angeles County Employees Association, Local 660, initiated a drive to obtain representational rights for the employees of the districts. In February 1973 Harris was made a union shop steward for Local 660, and in May 1973 the association was recognized as exclusive bargaining agent for represented employees of the districts in a Professional Employees Representative Unit. In August 1973 a Memorandum of Understanding was executed between the districts and the association which covered various aspects of employer-employee relations.

Harris, who was working as a senior engineering assistant in the Sewer Design Section at the time of the execution of the memorandum, had no direct involvement with that instrument's negotiations or drafting. However, later that year, he was elected as one of two representatives of the professional unit to serve as a negotiator for the association at "meet and confer" sessions being held with the districts for the purpose of drafting a successor memorandum of understanding. These sessions began in March 1974 and were held during work hours. However, internal meetings of the union negotiators during these sessions were only held outside of regular work

---

[1] The names of all individuals have been disguised.

hours. Harris fully participated in all of these meetings as a union negotiator.

On May 4, 1974, while the meet and confer sessions were still uncompleted, Harris was assigned as a draftsman to a major project, Joint Outfall F. At the time of his assignment, Harris was advised of the importance of the project and the necessity that the work be completed as scheduled.

For several years, the districts had maintained a policy "prohibiting any personal telephone calls on County phones," and had published several notices to that effect. However, although all employees were aware of it, management still had difficulty enforcing the policy. Management felt that Harris was particularly guilty of violation of the policy, and he had been warned on several occasions by his supervisors regarding his excessive use of the telephones.

On May 16, 1974, assistant section head James Herd spoke to Harris, warning him that he was spending so much time on telephone calls of long duration that it was interfering with the drafting work necessary to keep Joint Outfall F on schedule. Later that same day, Herd prepared a memorandum to serve as a record of his warning to Harris. The memo stated:

> This is to make record of my counseling Leo Harris on May 16, 1974, relative to excessive use of the telephone for what appeared to be personal business during working hours.
>
> I felt that Harris was spending so much time on telephone calls of long duration that it was interfering with accomplishment of the necessary drafting of Joint Outfall F, Unit 3B Relief Section 3, on schedule, and I told him so.
>
> I counseled him that he was setting a bad example for other employees of the section in his use of the telephone on District time and that it should not continue.
>
> I instructed Harris to take as much as one minute to tell incoming callers that he is busy and he will be able to talk after hours.
>
> Through conscientious pursuit of their work, other draftsmen in the section of equal and lower salary than Harris out-produce him. The quality of his work is high, and his understanding of our work is high. The problem is application.

When the memorandum came to the attention of section head Timothy McIntyre, he called Harris into his office and informed him that the document was to be inserted into his personnel file. Harris objected and immediately filed a grievance protesting the insertion of the memo into his file.

While involved in the grievance action, Harris scheduled an appointment with union attorneys concerning presentation of his complaint. On June 3 he advised Herd that he would be leaving work one-half hour early that day in order to discuss his grievance, and he was given permission to do so by Herd. However, management reserved the right of payment for that half-hour, and later charged Harris one-half hour of compensatory time. Harris then filed a second grievance seeking compensation for those lost wages, alleging that management had violated Paragraph 3 of Article XXIV of the Memorandum of Understanding (see Appendix to this case).

The districts and union could not reach an agreement, and elected to submit the question to arbitration. Both parties agreed that there were three primary issues involved in the arbitration:

1. Was the County Sanitation Districts of Los Angeles County in violation of the Memorandum of Understanding effective September 12, 1973, when it placed a warning memorandum dated May 16, 1974, in the personnel file of Leo Harris?

2. Was the County Sanitation Districts of Los Angeles County in violation of the Memorandum of Understanding when it charged Leo Harris one-half hour of compensatory time on June 3, 1974?

3. If the answer to either or both of the foregoing inquiries is in the affirmative, what is the proper remedy?

POSITION OF THE UNION

The union claimed that the time Harris spent on the phone was an activity protected by Paragraph 3 of Article XXIV of the Memorandum of Understanding. It noted that the conversations in question occurred while negotiations were in progress and contended that Harris had a frequent need to call the Local 660 office for advice and guidance. The union also claimed that Harris had to respond to several telephone inquiries of fellow employees concerning the progress of contract negotiations. Prior to this, Harris had never been informed by management of any proscriptions in his exercise of the office of steward, including restrictions on phone calls.

Concerning Harris's second grievance, the union maintained that Harris was processing a grievance, albeit his own, but as a steward, he was entitled to do so "without loss of pay or benefits of any kind," as provided by Paragraph 3 of Article XXIV. It further maintained that Harris had satisfied the other requirements of informing his supervisor as required by Article XXIV, and he should not have been docked for the time spent in processing his grievance.

The union requested that the memorandum of May 16, 1974, be removed from Harris's file and he be made whole for the one-half hour's wage improperly denied him on June 3, 1974.

POSITION OF THE DISTRICTS

The districts maintained that the memorandum from Herd should be retained in Harris's file, since he had been warned on several previous occasions concerning his use of phones for private conversations. The districts claimed that Harris was thus on notice that he would be required to obtain the permission of a supervisor to use the phone for any purpose other than business of the districts; yet he continually failed to do so.

The districts further contended that no provision of the Memorandum of Understanding or other applicable law or agreement permitted the use of work time for the conduct of activities related to meet and confer sessions. Rather, the districts maintained that Article XXIV was the only applicable provision, and it was specifically restricted in application to stewards engaged in formal grievance actions.

In response to Harris's second grievance, the districts asserted that Article XXIV was not intended to afford stewards a right to compensation or benefits while involved in processing their own grievances. The districts requested that both grievances be denied.

APPENDIX

Relevant Provisions of the Memorandum of Understanding

ARTICLE X—NONDISCRIMINATION

The parties mutually recognize and agree fully to protect the rights of all employees covered hereby to join and participate in the activities of Local 660 and all other rights of employees provided in Government Code.

The provisions of this Memorandum of Understanding shall be applied equally to all employees covered hereby without favor or discrimination because of race, color, sex, age, national origin, political or religious opinions or affiliations.

ARTICLE XXIV—STEWARDS

It is agreed and understood by the parties of this Memorandum of Understanding that there shall not be more than eight (8) stewards for this unit.

Local 660 shall give to the Personnel Manager six (6) copies of a written list of the names of employees selected as stewards, which list shall be kept current by Local 660.

Local 660 stewards may spend a reasonable amount of time to

promptly and expeditiously investigate and process formal grievances without loss of pay or benefits of any kind. Local 660 agrees, whenever processing of formal grievances is to be transacted during working hours, only that amount of time necessary to bring about a prompt disposition of the matter will be utilized. Stewards, when leaving their work locations to process formal grievances, shall first obtain permission from their immediate supervisor and inform him of the nature of the business. Permission to leave will be granted within a reasonable time unless such absence would cause an undue interruption of work. If such permission cannot be granted when requested, the steward will be informed when time will be made available. Such time will not be more than 24 hours, excluding Saturday, Sunday, and legal holidays, after the time requested by the steward, unless otherwise mutually agreed to.

Upon entering other work locations, the steward shall inform the cognizant supervisor of the nature of his business. Permission to leave the job will be granted to the employee involved unless such absence would cause an undue interruption of work. If the employee cannot be made available, the steward will be informed when the employee will be made available. Such time will not be more than 24 hours, excluding Saturday, Sunday, and legal holidays, after the time requested by the steward, unless otherwise mutually agreed to. Denial of permission for a steward to leave his work location or for an employee to meet with the steward will automatically constitute an extension of time equal to the delay.

Local 660 agrees that a steward shall not log compensatory time or premium pay time for time spent performing any function of a steward.

Except as provided in Article VI (Work Schedules), Section 5 (Emergencies), Management will not transfer a steward to a different work location without approval of the steward or Local 660 unless there no longer is work for the steward in his classification at his work location.

ARTICLE XXXIII—PROVISIONS OF LAW

It is understood and agreed that this Memorandum of Understanding is subject to all current and future applicable laws and federal and state regulations. If any part or provision of this Memorandum of Understanding is in conflict or inconsistent with such applicable laws and regulations, or is otherwise held to be invalid or unenforceable by any tribunal of competent jurisdiction, such part or provision shall be suspended and superseded by such applicable laws or regulations, and the remainder of this Memorandum of Understanding shall not be affected thereby.

298

QUESTIONS

1. Was the time that the shop steward spent on the phone protected activity within the meaning of the Memorandum of Understanding? Why, or why not?
2. Did Article XXIV include the right of a shop steward to spend time in processing his own grievance? Discuss.
3. Would it be desirable for a company and union to negotiate specific time limits which a shop steward or union officer could spend on union business? Why or why not?

46. THE DISABLED BLOWER MOTOR

Company: Goodyear Atomic Corporation, Piketon, Ohio

Union: Oil, Chemical and Atomic Workers International Union, Local 3-689

On Monday, January 26, 1976, one of the three 50-horsepower electric motors powering high-pressure blowers developed a short circuit and required rewinding. The chief engineer estimated that 32 man-hours would be required to rewind the motor. The company sent the motor to an outside contractor, the National Coil Company, for repair. No standby motor was available while the repairs were made.

Before the motor was sent out, union steward Hugh Benfield[1] questioned the company's decision to have the work performed by an outside contractor rather than by employees of Department 711, Electrical Maintenance. He called the new contract language to the attention of the line foreman, George Lemson. He also told him that the union would file a grievance charging violation of Article XVI, Section 12,[2] if the work was not performed in Department 711.

The union's grievance was rejected by the company through all three steps of the grievance procedure. The company's reply to the union at the third step read as follows:

> This grievance challenges the Company's interpretation of new contract language, Article XVI, Section 12.
> The Union's position is that "fully utilized" as used in Section 12 means the use of overtime on all work which could be performed on plantsite that meets the criteria established in Section 12, rather than contracting out.

---

[1] The names of all individuals are disguised.

[2] See Appendix to this case.

The Company does not agree that it negotiated any such concept in regard to Section 12. No member of the Company Negotiating Team can recall any conversation between the parties which could lead to such a conclusion.

As reviewed at the hearing, the Company notes reflect the following: "Union representatives asked if the Company's opinion of offering as much work as possible to Goodyear Atomic Corporation employees is 40 hours a week." The notes further reflect that the Union representatives at one point stated, "they wanted full utilization of employees plus some overtime."

As stated in Section 12, the Company will give "full consideration to using bargaining unit employees whenever possible."

The union and the company agreed that the issue to be submitted to the arbitrator should be, "Did the company violate Article XVI, Section 12, when it contracted out the rewinding of the electric motor in question?"

NEGOTIATING BACKGROUND

The company and union negotiated a new collective agreement in May 1975. In its original proposal on April 15, the union suggested the following language for the contracting-out provision:

> The Company reserves the right to subcontract work specifically, but without limitation for new construction, installation, and structural repair thereto. They will not, however, subcontract normal maintenance normally performed by the bargaining unit.

The company countered on April 24, 1975, with the following proposal:

> The Company recognizes the desirability of full utilization of bargaining unit employees where sufficient qualified personnel are present, where time limits for job completion will permit, and where resources are available.

In response, the union resubmitted its original proposal on April 25, 1975, with a slight change in the second sentence as follows:

> They will not, however, subcontract work normally performed by the bargaining unit.

The company countered on April 27, 1975, with the following proposal:

> The Company reserves the right to subcontract, except that it will not subcontract work normally performed by the bargaining unit, for the express purpose of causing a reduction in force.

The company on the following day offered the provision which was adopted by both parties as the current Article XVI, Section 12.

While Article XVI, Section 12, is silent on the question of overtime, the parties briefly discussed overtime during their negotations on April 23, 1975:

> Henry Jenkins (company representative): "I am not adverse to overtime to get a portion of the work done rather than let it out to contractors."
>
> John Robertson (union representative): "Our objective is to maintain our work even on an overtime basis as long as no law is violated."
>
> Henry Jenkins: "Hiring more people and adding them to the payroll for short periods of time to handle peak work loads and then laying them off could be a headache to both sides."

POSITION OF THE UNION

The union contended that employees of the electrical maintenance department daily and routinely rewound motors; that no special fixture for holding the motor was needed; and that the department possessed the space, equipment, and tools for doing the work.

The union pointed out that there were 135 to 140 electricians in the department, and that none was working overtime. The union argued that these employees, while working overtime, could have completed the repairs to the motor as quickly as the outside contractor. In fact, the disabled motor remained on the shop floor for two days before the outside contractor picked it up.

The union further contended that this case involved only one motor. The work did not require a large amount of extra work extending over a long period of time.

Finally, the union pointed out that the company, on occasions in the past, had assigned work on an overtime basis to electricians in cases such as this one. The contract anticipated that employees would be called upon to work overtime from time to time, as provided in Article X, Section 3(h) (see Appendix to this case).

The union petitioned that those electricians in Department 711 who would have been assigned the rewinding of the blower motor be reimbursed for 32 hours work at the overtime rate of time and one half.

POSITION OF THE COMPANY

The company replied that none of the electricians in Department 711 was on layoff and that all were working a full 40-hour week. Under terms of the contract, this constituted the customary work-week and represented "full utilization" of all personnel.

All qualified electricians were at that time assigned priority rewinding jobs, utilizing all rewinding stands and equipment. It was not desirable to delay any of the priority work, nor was it possible to delay the repairs to the blower motor. For these reasons, the company made the decision to send the motor to an outside contractor for rewinding.

The company argued that while Article XVI, Section 12, permitted the company to utilize overtime in order to avoid contracting out work, the company was not required to do so in order to keep the work within Department 711. The company cited Article IV of the contract to support its right.

Finally, the company argued that it contracted out the work in good faith and that its actions were reasonable under all the circumstances. It urged that the grievance be denied.

APPENDIX

Relevant Provisions of the Agreement

ARTICLE XVI
Section 12 (Utilization of Work Force)

The Company recognizes a responsibility to fully utilize all its employees; and will not subcontract work without giving full consideration to using bargaining unit employees whenever possible where time limits for job completion will permit, where sufficient qualified personnel are present and where resources are available.

ARTICLE IV
(Management Rights)

The direction of the work force, the establishment of plant policies, the determination of the processes and means of manufacture, the units of personnel required to perform such processes, and other responsibilities incidental to the operation of the plant are vested in the Company. The exercise of such authority shall not conflict with the rights of the Union under the terms of this Contract.

ARTICLE X
Section 3(h) (Hours of Work)

The provisions of this Contract shall not be considered as a guarantee by the Company of a minimum number of hours per day or per week or pay in lieu thereof, nor a limitation on the maximum hours per day or per week which may be required to meet operating conditions.

QUESTIONS

1. To what degree is the negotiating background information surrounding Article XVI, Section 12, germane to the arbitration issue?
2. What is meant by the term *fully utilize* within Article XVI, Section 12? Does this provision require the company to work bargaining unit personnel on an overtime basis, rather than to subcontract?
3. Different arbitrators have utilized varying standards in applying provisions such as Article XVI, Section 12. What types of standards might be appropriate for interpreting this and similar clauses?
4. Compare the circumstances of this case with the case of "The Subcontracted Heaters" (Case 47 following).

47. THE SUBCONTRACTED HEATERS

Company: Tecumseh Products Company, Somerset Compressor Division, Somerset, Kentucky

Union: International Brotherhood of Electrical Workers, Local 2360

On November 22, 1974, 29 employees of Tecumseh Products Company filed the following grievance:

> The Company is in direct violation of Article XIX, Paragraph 138, of the current labor agreement. Adjustment desired—maintenance department employees be paid for all hours worked by outside plumbing contractors; and electrical employees be paid for all hours worked by outside electrical contractors. Plus this action be stopped immediately.

The company denied the grievance, charging that it had not been properly filed because part of the work identified in the grievance had not been contracted out until after the grievance had been filed. It also argued that even if the grievance had been properly filed, the company was within its rights to contract out the work under terms of the contract.

BACKGROUND

The Compressor Division manufactures small compressors for air conditioners, water coolers, and dehumidifiers. The company engaged two subcontractors in November 1974 to perform certain plumbing and electrical work in the plant. One of them, Brown Brothers, was engaged to install two industrial-type wash basins in the washroom (each basin is about 6 feet in diameter and can serve about 10 persons simultaneously). It also contracted to install a new rest room for truckers and a drinking fountain and waste disposal basin in the cafeteria.

The second subcontractor, Whitaker Electric Company, completed

304

the installation of large high-voltage, industrial-type electric heating units in the heating ducts servicing the office area.

The union protested that all of this work should have been performed by the maintenance department employees and should not have been subcontracted.

TIMELINESS OF THE GRIEVANCE

Position of the Company

The company argued that the union's grievance referred to work that had not been contracted out at the time the grievance was filed on November 22, 1974. The company offered in evidence a copy of purchase order SA18845, dated December 13, 1974. This purchase order completed the contract between Whitaker Electric and the company to install electric heaters. The company cited Paragraph 31 of the contract which stated in part:

> All grievances must be presented at this step within five (5) days of occurrence, otherwise it shall be deemed not to exist and shall have no merit.

Position of the Union

The union argued that various employees had observed preparations to perform certain plumbing and electrical work about the middle of November. One employee, Ronald Blanton,[1] working on the second shift, asked his foreman about the preparations. His foreman told him that the work was being subcontracted to Whitaker. At that point, the union filed a grievance. The union claimed that it would be unrealistic to expect it to undertake a complete study of the company's records and then make a legal determination of when a contract had been agreed upon before filing a grievance. The union requested that the filing date of the grievance be ruled timely, and that the grievance apply to all the plumbing and electrical work described above.

THE RIGHT TO CONTRACT OUT WORK

Position of the Union

The union contended that maintenance employees were qualified to perform the plumbing and electrical work contracted out. They

---

[1] The names of all individuals have been disguised.

had on prior occasions performed such work, and had already completed some of the work in question before the subcontractors came in and took over the jobs. They had, in fact, redone some of the work on both the electrical and plumbing contracts after the outside contractors left.

The union also maintained that if the company had originally assigned the work to the maintenance employees, they could have completed it within the company's time requirements, especially if they had been assigned the work on an overtime basis. The company could have completed both projects at less cost employing maintenance employees on an overtime basis than by contracting out the work.

The union further argued that the company violated Article XIX, Paragraph 138, which restricts Article III, Paragraphs 17 and 18 (see Appendix to this case).

The union asked that the 29 employees signing the grievance be reimbursed for all hours worked by outside contractors and that such subcontracting cease.

Position of the Company

The company argued that the work performed by the subcontractors was not "standard production work regularly performed by Bargaining Unit employees."

The company further argued that the necessary personnel were not "readily available" to complete the work "within the projected time limits" (see Appendix, Article XIX, Paragraph 138, to this case). The normal work of the maintenance employees was first and foremost to maintain the production machinery. If any time were left, it might be utilized on other projects including those of the type performed by these two subcontractors.

The company pointed out that the plumbing work was done to satisfy employee complaints that the washroom facilities were inadequate. The work had been scheduled to be performed by maintenance employees, but it did not progress fast enough because top priority was always given to the maintenance of production machinery and equipment. As the end of the budget year, December 31, approached, it became urgent to finish the job. Such installations could not be characterized as "regular" because there are not that many commodes and wash basins to be installed in a plant.

The installation of the heaters was urgent as the winter season approached. The two old gas heaters which had previously provided heat for the offices had failed. The work had to be performed after the regular office hours because of the noise in the heating ducts.

To have taken maintenance men from their regular work to finish these two projects would have resulted in down time on production lines because of failure to do necessary maintenance and repair work on production machinery.

The company further pointed out that there were no maintenance employees on layoff, and that all were working at least 40 hours per week and some were working overtime during the period the subcontractors were working.

Finally, the company contended that no provision required the company to provide any specific amount of overtime to any employees. The three employees best qualified to perform the subcontracted work all had refused or been unavailable for overtime assignment to the work in question. The first, a licensed plumber, had regularly refused overtime assignments; the second had other outside employment on Saturdays when much of the work was performed; the third regularly worked overtime in the plant repairing machines during the time they were shut down.

The company requested that in the event the arbitrator ruled the grievance was timely, the grievance should be denied as to its merits.

APPENDIX

The Bargaining Unit as defined by the NLRB, Certification of Representation is:

> All production and maintenance employees at the Employer's Somerset, Kentucky location, excluding all office clerical employees, professional employees, guards, and supervisors as defined in the Act.

Relevant Provisions of the Contract

ARTICLE I—RECOGNITION

Paragraph 1. The Company recognizes the Union as the exclusive representative for its employees as defined in Paragraph 2 below for the purpose of collective bargaining with respect to wages, hours, or other conditions of employment in the Bargaining Unit which they have been so certified by the National Labor Relations Board in accordance with the provisions of the applicable state and federal laws.

Paragraph 2. For the purpose of this Agreement, the term "employee" shall include factory employees employed at the Company's Compressor Division located in Somerset, Kentucky, excluding all salaried employees, office and clerical employees, plant protection employees, supervisory employees, foremen, assistant foremen, foreladies, professional employees, sales and engineering employees, and lab technicians.

ARTICLE III—MANAGEMENT RIGHTS
AND RESPONSIBILITIES

Paragraph 17. Except as expressly and specifically limited to or restricted by a provision of this Agreement, the Company has and shall retain the full rights of management and direction of the plant and its operations. Such rights of management include the right to plan, direct, control, increase, or decrease operations; to determine the products to be manufactured; to shift products manufactured, processes, or types of work or methods in and out of the plant; to subcontract work, except as in Paragraph 138, to change machinery, methods, and facilities, or introduce new methods, techniques, and/ or machines and products; to establish and enforce rules and regulations; to discipline and discharge employees for just causes; to assign, change, add to, or reduce the number of shifts, the schedules to be worked, and the work force; to determine who it shall hire, the number of employees it shall employ at any time, and the qualifications necessary for any jobs; to determine policies affecting the selection and training of new employees; to assign work duties, transfer employees; to set reasonable standards in accordance with its determination of the needs of the job and the operation. The Company reserves the right to move, sell, close, liquidate, or consolidate the plant in whole or in part.

It is expressly understood and agreed that all rights heretofore exercised by the Company or inherent in the Company as the owner of the business or as an incident to the management not expressly contracted away by specific provisions of this Agreement are retained solely by the Company. Any rights granted to or acquired by the employees or the Union under this Agreement or during its life shall have no application beyond the term of this Agreement or any renewal thereof.

Paragraph 18. It is agreed that the reserved management rights as set forth in this Agreement, including the foregoing paragraph, shall not be subject to arbitration or impairment by an arbitration award under this Agreement unless expressly contracted away or modified by a specific provision of this Agreement.

ARTICLE IV

Paragraph 29. For the purpose of this Agreement, the term "grievance" shall be limited to any dispute between the Company and the Union or between the Company and an employee concerning the application or violation of the provisions of this agreement.

ARTICLE VI

Paragraph 37.   The arbitrator so selected shall schedule a prompt hearing at which time he shall have the power to make determinations of fact on the questions submitted to him and apply them to the provisions of the Agreement alleged to have been violated so long as the grievance is submitted to him in accordance with the provisions, limitations, and procedures specified in this Agreement. No arbitrator shall have the jurisdiction or authority to add to, take from, nullify, or modify any of the terms of this Agreement, or to impair any of the rights reserved to Management under the terms hereof, either directly or indirectly, under the guise of interpretation; nor shall he have the power to substitute his discretion for that of Management in any manner where the Management has not contracted away its right to exercise discretion.

The arbitrator shall be bound by the facts and evidence submitted to him and may not go beyond the terms of this Agreement in rendering his decision. No such decision may include or deal with any issue or matter which is not expressly made subject to the terms of this Agreement. The decision of the arbitrator shall be in writing and shall be final and binding upon the parties when rendered upon a matter within the authority of the arbitrator.

ARTICLE XIX

Paragraph 138.   It is the Company policy that standard production work regularly performed by Bargaining Unit employees will not be contracted to a source outside of the Tecumseh Products Company, provided that the necessary manpower, equipment, and facilities are readily available and the work can be performed in an efficient, economic, and competitive manner as related to quality, quantity, cost, and performance within the projected time limits necessary to complete the work involved.

QUESTIONS

1. Was the grievance a timely grievance which was appropriately placed before the arbitrator? Why, or why not?
2. Evaluate Article XIX in comparison to Article III. Which article is superior in nature?
3. Was the plumbing work standard production work regularly performed by bargaining unit employees? Discuss.
4. Compare the circumstances of this case with the subcontracting issue involved in the "Disabled Blower Motor" case (Case 46 preceding).

48. THE CAR POOL AND THE OVERTIME REFUSAL

Company: American Can Company, New Orleans, Louisiana

Union: International Association of Machinists and Aerospace Workers, Crescent City Lodge 37

BACKGROUND

Harold Franklin[1] began working at the New Orleans plant on August 10, 1966, as a maintenance helper on the 11:30 P.M.–7:30 A.M. shift. At the time of this case in 1974, he was working as a millwright on the 3:30 P.M.–11:30 P.M. shift. He lived in Picayune, Mississippi, a small town 55 miles from New Orleans.

In March 1974, during the course of a national energy crisis precipitated by a boycott initiated by the Oil Producing Exporting Countries (OPEC), the company posted a notice which read:

> Car Pool—With the objective in mind of bringing together those persons who may, because of the present circumstances, be interested in joining or forming a car pool, we wish to offer the services of the Personnel Department.
>
> Those interested please contact the Personnel Department where a form is available. These forms will be reviewed by the Personnel Department, and persons living in similar regions of the city will be supplied with information to assist in forming a car pool.

On April 9, 1974, Franklin told his foreman, John Brodie, that he could not work four hours overtime because he was in a car pool. Franklin refused overtime assignments on six other occasions during April, May, June, and July. Each time he gave car pooling as his reason; and each time Brodie advised him that car pooling was not an acceptable reason for refusing to work overtime, although he was

---

[1] The names of all individuals have been disguised.

not required to work overtime in any of those instances. On Monday, August 12, 1974, when Franklin again refused overtime, he was given a three-day suspension.

In giving the suspension, the company cited Article 4, Section 4, Overtime Notice, from the agreement, which reads as follows:

> Local Management will give notice of daily overtime assignments as far in advance as practicable, and, to the extent customer demands are known, will give notice of weekend overtime assignments in accordance with present practices but in no event later than the end of the employee's shift on the preceding Thursday.
>
> Local Management will consider any reasonable request of an employee to be excused from overtime work, but in any event will excuse an employee from overtime on occasions where the working of overtime would cause the employee hardship or serious inconvenience.

The union filed a grievance on behalf of Harold Franklin, contending that the company violated Article 4, Section 4, of the agreement. The union requested that the company remove records pertaining to the suspension from Franklin's file and reimburse him for 24 hours pay.

POSITION OF THE UNION

The union claimed that the company's actions during the April–August (1974) period were designed to place Franklin under heavy duress. It claimed that the most recent incident of August 12 arose when foreman Brodie asked Franklin to stay overtime since millwright Paul Renaldi would not be in on the third shift because of illness. Franklin refused to work overtime because of car pooling. Brodie then asked the senior millwright, Henry Vaccaro, who reluctantly agreed to work. This incident could have been avoided, according to the union, had Brodie followed the standard procedure of offering overtime to the senior employee first. Furthermore, since the foreman knew of the overtime assignment before the end of the first shift at 3:30 P.M., and since the work could have been performed at any time during the second shift, he could have asked one of the millwrights who was working on the first shift, 7:30 A.M.–3:30 P.M., to stay over an extra four hours. Alternatively, Brodie could have called in a third shift millwright who worked the 11:30 P.M.–7:30 A.M. shift to start four hours early.

The union cited other incidents which it contended were designed to place Franklin under extreme pressure:

1. On April 30 Franklin was asked to work overtime. He refused because of car pooling. The foreman then asked George Chapin, the

senior employee, to work. Chapin, as the senior employee, should have been asked first.

2.   On May 14 the foreman wanted Franklin to work on equipment outside his normal work area. Only after he declined did the foreman ask Vaccaro, the senior millwright in that area, to work.

3.   On May 21 Franklin was asked to work overtime in case Paul Renaldi, a third shift millwright, would be unable to work. The foreman could have avoided the entire problem by telephoning Renaldi who was able to come to work and who did so.

4.   On three other occasions, June 10, June 27, and July 8, Franklin refused overtime because of car pooling. On each occasion senior employees were asked to stay over and did so upon request. No work time was lost because of his refusal to work overtime.

The union argued that Franklin began car pooling at the suggestion of the company, who looked upon it as a means for conserving natural energy resources and lessening travel costs for employees. The company encouraged Franklin to car pool. Now that he had done it, he should not be penalized by the company, which must have anticipated the potential conflict between working overtime and car pooling.

The union maintained that Franklin always worked scheduled overtime when he really was needed by the company. However, it further contended that under Article 4, Section 4, Franklin could refuse overtime work when it could cause him "hardship or serious inconvenience." Missing a ride home, especially when home is 55 miles away, would certainly cause hardship or serious inconvenience.

Finally, this clause had been in the contract only one year, and this was the first grievance that had arisen under it. Both company and union representatives have had difficulty in interpreting it. Franklin should, in any event, be given the benefit of the doubt.

POSITION OF THE COMPANY

The company countered the union's contention that employees could have been called in for overtime work from either the first or second shift on August 12. According to the company, there was only one millwright on the third shift; he had already been called in early and was working when Franklin was asked to stay over. Thus, there was no one to call in from the third shift. Similarly, employees who had worked the first shift had already worked eight hours during the day. To recall them for four hours would require that they work from 11:30 P.M. to 3:30 A.M., thereby effectively eliminating their sleep for that night. In four more hours they would have to report for their regular shift at 7:30 A.M. The company maintained that it had acted reasonably in asking Franklin to work.

The company stated that foreman Brodie asked Franklin to work overtime only after the senior millwright, Paul Vaccaro, had been asked and had declined. Vacarro finally agreed to work after Franklin adamantly refused to do so. The company followed the standard and accepted procedure in assigning overtime work in this and all previous assignments. The union had attempted to inject the issue of discrimination into a situation where none existed.

It was the company's position that it complied with Article 4, Section 4, in asking Franklin to work overtime. Foreman Brodie considered Franklin's request to be excused from working overtime by soliciting Paul Vaccaro to work. A company representative stated, "We believe very strongly that the excuse offered by Franklin, under all the circumstances present here, does not justify his being excused from overtime on the grounds that it would cause him hardship or serious inconvenience within the meaning of Article 4, Section 4."

The company expressed the belief that it had the right to expect employees to work a reasonable amount of overtime, and that employees had a corresponding obligation to do so. It further expressed the belief that employees should not be compelled to work overtime unless it was necessary. On a number of occasions prior to August 12, Franklin had been excused from overtime to accommodate his car pooling. On each of these occasions, however, he was told that since he was the junior millwright, it was very likely that he would be required to work overtime in the future and must make some arrangements to provide for this.

The company pointed out that Franklin admitted to having been told at least three times, and possibly more often prior to August 12, that car pooling would not be accepted as a reason for refusing overtime, and that he would face disciplinary action if he refused on that basis. He consulted with the union on each of these occasions. The union erroneously informed him that he did not have to work overtime. The company argued that employees who disregarded the company's instructions and relied upon the union's interpretation of the contract did so at their own risk. They could not later take refuge in the argument that they were never notified that the company considered their actions cause for discipline.

The company denied that it encouraged Franklin to car pool and thus was prohibited from disciplining him for having acted upon that suggestion. Franklin was car pooling with three other employees from Picayune prior to the memorandum issued by the company, and he was not influenced by the memorandum. In addition, the company contended that the letter neither encouraged nor discouraged car pooling. It was an offer to assist those employees who wished to car pool. The decision to car pool or not car pool was an individual one. Any employee electing to participate in a car pool had to consider the obligation to work overtime when making that decision. In Franklin's case, the company repeatedly advised him to make alternate arrangements for those rather limited occasions when he might be required to work overtime.

The company noted that many of its employees car pooled, but they also worked a reasonable amount of overtime when requested. Franklin was the only employee who had found this to be a problem. Employees may live wherever they wish, and they may make whatever travel arrangements they find most convenient. But, in exercising these choices they cannot negate the company's right to expect a reasonable amount of overtime and they cannot invoke Article 4, Section 4, to avoid their responsibility to work overtime. This article does not mean that Franklin had a right to be excused from working overtime.

The company claimed that its three-day disciplinary suspension meted upon Harold Franklin was reasonable under the circumstances and maintained that the union grievance should be dismissed.

QUESTIONS

1. Was the car pool an acceptable reason for the employee to refuse to work overtime given the circumstances of this case? Why, or why not?
2. Evaluate the meaning of the term *hardship or serious inconvenience* within Article 4, Section 4. Why would company and union representatives be likely to disagree in interpreting this provision?
3. Does a company normally have the right to expect employees to work overtime unless specifically prohibited by a labor agreement? Discuss.
4. Why would the union tell the employee that he did not have to work overtime? Should an employee be disciplined for following the instructions of the union leadership? Why, or why not?
5. Some companies have adopted flexible work scheduling which permits employees to choose their starting and ending times within certain limits. Would such arrangements mean that a company could not require an employee to work overtime?

49. THE DISPUTED HOLIDAY PAY

Company: Rheem Manufacturing Company, Fort Smith,
Arkansas

Union: United Steelworkers of America, Local 7893

BACKGROUND

David Koss[1] was an assembler in the utility department of
Rheem's heating and air-conditioning equipment manufacturing
plant located at Fort Smith, Arkansas. In accordance with the provisions of the collective agreement between the union and the company, the plant closed down Thursday and Friday, November 22–23,
1973, for the Thanksgiving holiday. Koss was scheduled to return to
work on Monday, November 26.

However, on Sunday evening, November 25, Koss became very ill
with diarrhea and nausea. His wife, that evening, telephoned the
family physician who prescribed medication and treatment. While
his condition improved, he was unable to report back to work on
Monday the 26th. Mrs. Koss attempted to contact the personnel
director early that morning to inform him of her husband's illness.
The party line was very busy, however, and she was unable to reach
the personnel office until almost 11 A.M. She was finally able to
contact Elizabeth Jackson, a nurse in the department, and inform her
that Koss would be absent from work that day because of illness. At
the same time she inquired about the effect that his absence would
have on his right to receive payment for the previous Thursday and
Friday, both of which were designated in the collective agreement as
paid holidays. Jackson informed her that his foreman might request
a "doctor's slip" to substantiate his claim for missing work on
Monday.

---

[1] The names of all individuals have been disguised.

Jackson then transferred her to Charles Bigham, assistant personnel director, to provide more precise information about the conditions for receiving holiday pay. Bigham informed her that according to Article XIII, Paragraph 2(c), of the agreement,[2] an employee was required to work both the last workday before and the first workday following a paid holiday in order to be eligible to receive the pay benefits. Thus, he informed her that Koss would have to work that day, Monday, to be eligible for the holiday pay for the previous Thursday and Friday. She informed her husband of Bigham's explanation, but he was unable to report to work until Tuesday, November 27, 1973.

Upon reporting to his job on Tuesday, Koss explained his Monday absence to his supervisor, Henry Ryan, and inquired about his holiday pay. Ryan told him that his only hope for receiving holiday pay lay in presenting a "doctor's excuse." He then sent Koss to the personnel office, where Bigham informed him that he would not receive payment for the two holidays because he did not work on the next scheduled workday following the holiday. Koss, nevertheless, following his supervisor's recommendation, submitted a physician's statement concerning his illness to the personnel department on Thursday, November 29. This note stated:

> To whom it may concern: This is to signify that David Koss was under my care from November 25 through November 26.

After receiving the physician's statement, Bigham again told Koss that he was ineligible for holiday pay due to the company's strict interpretation of Article XIII, Paragraph 2(c), of the agreement.

While discussing the loss of his holiday pay later that week with Dale Edie, another employee in Koss's division, Koss learned that Edie had received holiday pay for the Thanksgiving holidays, despite the fact that he had worked only a few hours on Monday, November 26. Edie related that he had called in sick on Monday morning and was told that he was required to work that day in order to receive holiday pay. He then reported to work. He was unable to complete the shift and went home after a few hours. Koss felt that he, too, had a case for receiving the holiday pay, and on December 5, 1973, the union filed the following grievance:

> This grievance is pertaining to Mr. Koss not receiving holiday pay for November 22 and 23, 1973.
> On November 26, 1973, D. Koss missed work due to being under doctor's care, the 26th during the next working day after the holiday in

---

[2] See Appendix to this case.

question. The settlement requested is that Mr. Koss be paid his holiday pay.

Included on the grievance form was a union allegation that the company had also violated Article XIII, Paragraph 2(g), of the agreement.[3]

The company made the following reply to the union's grievance:

> Mr. Koss did not request, nor was he granted sick leave. In order to qualify for holiday pay due to sickness, the sick leave must be approved by the Company and the holiday must fall within the 30 calendar days of the approved sick leave.

The parties were not able to resolve their differences, and the grievance was submitted to arbitration.

POSITION OF THE UNION

The union stated that David Koss was actually ill on Monday, November 26, 1973, and submitted the physician's statement as verification of such. The company did not contest this assertion.

Koss had been employed at the Rheem plant since the fall of 1970. He had a good employment record during these three years. He was a good worker, he had never been disciplined for any reason, and he had been absent for only a few days because of illness during that period.

The union contended that the company had not been consistent in requiring employees to work on the scheduled workday following a holiday in order to receive holiday pay. It cited the case of Dale Edie's receipt of holiday pay while having worked only a few hours on Monday, November 26. The union also noted a similar incident involving Loretta Smith, who had received full holiday pay even though she had been permitted to leave work early on Monday, November 26, to attend a family problem regarding relatives who had arrived in town but could not find her home. The union mentioned that situations such as the two cited indicated that the company administered its holiday pay policy inconsistently. The administration of policies such as this one should not be left to the sole discretion of management; the interests of employees should be protected and the circumstances surrounding each situation should be considered, thus ensuring a more equitable decision-making process.

The union maintained that holiday pay is an "earned benefit" to which employees are entitled. It argued that as an earned benefit the

---

[3] See Appendix to this case

318

provisions of Article XIII, Paragraph 2(g), should govern the employee's right to receive the benefit. The union contended that if an employee were actually sick and could provide a physician's statement verifying his or her illness, the employee should be considered qualified for sick leave under Article XIII, Paragraph 2(g), and be given the benefits commensurate with such leave. This was based on the contention that a physician, rather than the company, is most properly qualified to determine whether or not an employee is too ill to work. An employee who is sick should be provided the benefits specified under the sick leave provisions. Thus, under Article XIII, Paragraph 2(g), Koss would be entitled to holiday pay since a physician had verified his illness and that paragraph provides for an employee to be paid for holidays falling within the first 30 days of sick leave. The union maintained that to allow the company sole discretion to grant or withhold holiday pay without considering a physician's opinion provided it with too great an opportunity to apply the policy in a discriminatory manner.

In support of its claim that the company had not followed customary practices in handling Koss's case, the union noted that this was the first grievance of this type which it had filed. The union claimed that if management had consistently refused to grant claims such as Koss's, there would have been many more grievances since the current agreement was enacted on August 1, 1971.

In a posthearing brief, the union submitted the essence of its argument as follows:

> It does not seem ethical that we would negotiate language where illness and injury for work on a holiday would be reasons for receiving holiday pay—when the purpose and intent is that the holiday be a day of rest—and make qualifications stronger where no holiday work was required.
>
> The purpose and intent of Paragraph 2-g is very clear and broad— in fact this provision is one of the most liberal clauses for receiving holiday pay for sickness in the Steelworkers Union. At the same time if the Company so requests, they may require a technical reason from a doctor before granting holiday pay.
>
> If this section was construed to mean or be used only for long-term illness, an employee would be foolish to return to work after a one (1) day illness when he or she could remain at home under a doctor's care and receive holiday pay plus sickness and accident benefits. As we agreed in negotiations, only one person can determine whether or not one should be on a sick leave and that must be a qualified physician, not the Company

The union requested full pay for Koss for the holidays of Thursday and Friday, November 22 and 23, 1973.

POSITION OF THE COMPANY

The company justified its denial of holiday pay to Koss on several bases. In a brief submitted at the arbitration hearing, the company outlined three major points in its argument:

    1. Mr. Koss was not entitled to holiday pay because he was absent on the first scheduled workday after the Thanksgiving holiday and he was not on approved sick leave. The contract clearly defined the eligibility requirements in Article XIII, Paragraphs 2(c) and 2(g), of the labor agreement.

    2. It had never been the practice of the company to authorize holiday pay to employees who were absent on the scheduled workday before or after a holiday due to illnesses of short duration. The purpose and intent of Paragraph 2(g) under Article XIII had never been interpreted or applied to include occasional sickness of only a few days duration. In the past, employees had been approved for sick leave only in cases where an extended period of illness was anticipated and upon recommendation by a qualified physician. Since the Company received no recommendation for sick leave from a physician regarding Mr. Koss, and since he was not absent from work for an extended period of time, the company did not believe that holiday pay was justified.

    3. Mr. Koss returned to work after being absent for only one scheduled workday. The fact that Mr. Koss was sick that day is not questioned by the company. The key factor was that there was no provision in the contract that employees who were absent for a few days due to sickness in conjunction with a holiday were to be paid holiday pay.

At the hearing, Charles Koenig, director of personnel at the Rheem plant, read the above arbitration brief points and presented several further arguments. He testified that the company had consistently maintained that sick leave must be of more than one day's duration in order for Article XIII, Paragraph 2(g), of the agreement to apply. He conceded that there was no place in the agreement that "sick leave" was explicitly defined, but he argued that it implicitly referred to a period longer than just one day. In support of this argument, he presented a sick leave list dated November 23, 1973, which showed 15 employees who were on approved sick leave over the Thanksgiving holidays and who received holiday pay for such. Koenig noted that to be eligible for sick leave, the employee must apply for it and have it approved by the company. He further noted that benefits do not begin until the eighth day of illness and that employees may receive no more than $50 per week for 26 weeks. He again stated that sick leaves were considered to be longer term

320

situations and had never been construed to include single day absences.

The company next contended that it had maintained a consistent program of administering the holiday pay program since its inception. Koenig testified that to his knowledge, every employee had always been required to work at least part of the day before and day after a holiday in order to be eligible for the holiday pay. He noted that this policy explained the receipt of holiday pay by Edie and Smith, because both had worked part of the Monday following Thanksgiving. Charles Bigham, the assistant personnel director, testified that he had explained the company's application of this policy to Mrs. Koss in his conversation with her on Monday, November 26.

The company also detailed the history behind Article XIII, Paragraph 2(c). The provision had been negotiated as a very "tight" provision, with a specific requirement that employees must work on the day immediately preceding and following holidays. The purpose of this provision was to prevent excessive absenteeism around the holidays. Koenig noted that such absenteeism before and after holidays had been a serious problem at the company's plant in Kalamazoo, Michigan following its adoption of a holiday pay provision in the agreement. Koenig testified that this was the reason for the company's consistent requirement that an employee work at least part of the day before and after a holiday in order to be eligible for holiday pay. He stated that the company was not discriminating against Koss in denying him holiday benefits, but only enforcing a long-standing past administrative policy consistent with the terms of the agreement.

Koenig further testified that the company recognized only one exception to the requirements of Paragraph 2(c), namely, Paragraph 2(g), which provides for sick leave. Koss, however, had not been on sick leave. Koenig reiterated that sick leave required company approval, that a doctor's certificate was insufficient, and that one day absences had never been construed to be sick leaves. He argued finally that both the language of the agreement and past practice clearly indicated that Paragraph 2(c) was intended to be interpreted strictly, as the company had applied it in this case.

The company requested that the grievance be denied.

APPENDIX

Relevant Provisions of the Agreement

Article XIII, Paragraph 2(c). To be eligible for holiday pay, an employee must work his last scheduled workday prior to and his first scheduled workday after a holiday.

* * * * *

Article XIII, Paragraph 2(g). An employee who is granted sick leave shall be paid for holidays falling within the first thirty (30) calendar days of his approved sick leave. Such payment would be made upon the employee's return to work, provided the employee returns to work on the first scheduled day following termination of the sick leave.

QUESTIONS

1. Evaluate the union's arguments that the company had been inconsistent, and that administration of policies such as the one in this case should not be left to sole management discretion.
2. Is holiday pay an earned benefit, or is it subject to the restrictions of a labor agreement? Discuss.
3. Should a one-day sickness be considered as a sick leave within the meaning of the agreement?
4. Was the company's policy in regard to holiday pay fair and uniformly applied?
5. If the arbitrator would rule in favor of the employee, what would be the ramifications of such a decision?

50. THE RESCHEDULED LUNCH PERIOD

Company: Outagamie County, Seymour, Wisconsin
Union: Outagamie County Employees Union, Local 2046

BACKGROUND

On Friday, January 30, 1976, employees working in eight county offices of Outagamie County, Wisconsin, learned through an article in a local newspaper that their offices would remain open during the hours 12 noon to 1 P.M. starting Monday, February 2. On Monday morning, county supervisor Patrick Kelly[1] announced to these employees that starting immediately the offices would be open continuously each day, Monday through Friday, from 8:30 A.M. to 5 P.M. He also stated that some employees would take their lunch period from 12:30 to 1:30 P.M., instead of from 12 noon to 1 P.M., in order to accommodate the new schedule. The total number of hours worked each day was to remain unchanged at 7½.

The employees protested the unilateral change in their lunch schedule. After receiving no satisfaction from supervisor Kelly, they filed a grievance through their union, Outagamie County Employees Union, Local 2046, which eventually was carried to arbitration.

POSITION OF THE UNION

The union argued that the county had violated Article 1, Section 1.02, of the Agreement which stated that:

> The Employer shall adopt and publish reasonable rules which may be amended from time to time. Such rules shall be submitted to the

---

[1] The names of all individuals have been disguised.

Union for its information, thirty (30) days prior to their effective date. The Employer and the Union will cooperate in the enforcement thereof.

According to the union, the altering of employee work schedules constituted a change in a work rule. The county violated the contract by failing to submit the new rule to the employees 30 days prior to the date on which the rule became effective.

The union also contended that the new work rule was unreasonable and unnecessary. Since February 2, each of the eight affected offices had averaged only about one phone call and two business transactions per week during the noon hour. The staggered lunch hour schedules had disrupted luncheon-hour social groups, and this, too, was upsetting to the employees.

The union requested that the county be required to return to the lunch period schedule existing prior to February 2, 1976.

POSITION OF THE EMPLOYER

The county asserted that the decision as to the hours during which its offices would be open to the public was a fundamental management right, and it was not a subject upon which it was required to consult or bargain with the union. The subject was one on which management could make unilateral decisions. The county cited Article 1, Section 1.01, on management rights to support its claim. This article stated that:

> Unless otherwise provided herein, the management of the work and the direction of the working forces, including the right to hire, promote, transfer, demote or suspend, or otherwise discharge for proper cause, and the right to relieve employees from duty because of lack of work or other legitimate reasons is vested exclusively in the Employer.

The county pointed out that there was no provision in the contract which restricted its power to set the hours during which its offices would be open to the public. The contract did not specify the hours of work. It only provided for a normal work day of 7½ to 8 hours. The contract was silent as to lunch periods, and it did not contain a clause requiring the county to continue any past practices. The county cited Article VIII, Section 8.01, on the workweek to support its point.

> Permanent full-time employees shall work a normal day of 7½ to 8 hours and a normal workweek of 37½ to 40 hours (1,950–2,080 hours per year.) Overtime shall be computed on any hours worked in excess of 40 hours in any one workweek.

324

The county further contended that it had a legitimate reason to change the luncheon schedule, since its basic purpose was to provide services for the public.

The county urged that it be permitted to retain the right to change lunch schedules as necessary. The union grievance should be dismissed.

QUESTIONS

1. Was changing the luncheon schedule a reasonable exercise of management rights? Did the manner in which the schedule change was announced perhaps have any effect upon the employees' decision to file a grievance? Discuss.
2. Did the county alter a work rule? Why, or why not?
3. Evaluate the union's argument that the change in luncheon schedule was unnecessary and unreasonable.
4. Evaluate the county's claim that it had the right to change the lunch schedule without consulting the union.

51. A "HORNS-OF-A-DILEMMA" SITUATION

Company: Diem and Wing Paper Company, Cincinnati, Ohio

Union: International Brotherhood of Teamsters, Chauffeurs, Warehousemen and Helpers of America, Local 100

Managing his personal finances had always been a problem for Bob Bronson.[1] His problems while working at Diem and Wing Paper Company began with several garnishments in 1975 and culminated in the following letter from the company on July 14, 1978:

> This will confirm our meeting today during which we discussed the garnishment against your wages on behalf of Thorp Financial Services.
>
> As a result of this, and other garnishment actions, you are hereby placed on a three-day suspension, without pay, beginning July 17, 1978.
>
> If we continue to receive Orders of Garnishment, it will result in discharge from the Company.

> (s) H. W. Schuler
> Plant Manager

Bronson had been well aware that if his employer received one more garnishment, disciplinary action would be taken against him. This situation was different though. He felt that he had been entangled in a series of events which inevitably had led to this three-day suspension by the company. In frustration and anger he immediately filed the following grievance:

> This grievance is against management for an unjustified three-day suspension on a garnishing which was received on July 11, at that time having an appointment at the courthouse to go on a trusteeship,

---

[1] The names of all individuals have been disguised.

325

326

which would have stopped the garnishment. I told Bill Engle about the trusteeship appointment I had on the 11th, and he refused to let me go for 1½ hours.

(s) Robert Bronson

Bronson's grievance eventually was carried to arbitration.

BACKGROUND

Robert Bronson had been hired to work at Diem and Wing Paper Company's warehouse in 1975. Shortly thereafter, he encountered serious difficulty in managing his personal finances. He received a one-day suspension on May 24, 1976, after his wages had been subject to five orders of garnishment. His difficulties continued to mount, and from November 30, 1977, through May 24, 1978, the company received an additional seven orders of garnishment against his wages. Several other court orders issued prior to May 2, 1978, did not result in garnishments of his wages because a strike that lasted from December 6, 1977, to February 13, 1978, had reduced his wages below the garnishable level.[2]

Following receipt of a garnishment on May 2, 1978, the company sent Bronson a written notice stating that further garnishments could result in discipline up to and including discharge. The company received another garnishment on June 1, 1978. Since it was the second that the company had received within 20 days, it was returned to the court in accordance with Ohio law. Nevertheless, the company again warned him verbally that he could be disciplined up to and including discharge for additional garnishments.

On June 30, 1978, both Bronson and the company received the following Notice of Court Action to Collect Debt, dated June 28, 1978.

> If you do not pay within 15 days of the date of the mailing of this notice, we will go to court and ask that your employer be ordered to withhold money from your earnings and pay it to the court to satisfy your debt. This is called garnishment.

---

[2] Effective July 1, 1970, Title III of the Consumer Protection Act limited the amount of an employee's disposable earnings (compensation paid for personal services, less deductions required by law) subject to garnishment. The maximum part of the total disposable earnings that are subject to garnishment in any workweek may not exceed the lesser of (a) 25 percent of the disposable earnings for that week, or (b) the amount by which a worker's disposable earnings for that week exceeds 30 times the federal minimum hourly wage rate prescribed by Section 6(a) (1) of the Fair Labor Standards Act in effect at the time earnings are payable ($2.30 per hour in 1977 and $2.60 per hour in 1978).

It is to your advantage to avoid it because the placing of the extra burden on your employer can cause you to lose your job.

You can avoid garnishment by doing one of these three things within the next 15 days:

1. Pay us the amount due;
2. Complete the attached form entitled "Payment to Avoid Garnishment" and return it to us with the payment, if any, shown due on it; or
3. Apply to your local municipal or county court, or, if you are not a resident of Ohio, to the municipal or county court in whose jurisdiction your place of employment is located, for the appointment of a trustee to receive the part of your earnings that is not exempt from garnishment. You will be required to list your creditors, and the amount you will then pay to your trustee each payday will then be divided among them until the debts are paid off. This can be to your advantage because in the meantime none of those creditors can garnishee your wages.

Creditor

(s) Attorney for the Creditor

Note: Ohio Revised Code Section 2715.02 provides that the above demand shall be made after judgment is obtained, by delivering such demand to the debtor by personal service by the court or by sending it to the debtor by registered or certified letter, return receipt requested, at his usual place of residence at least 15 and not more than 45 days before the order of attachment against personal earnings or the order in aid of execution against personal earnings is sought.

In order to avoid another garnishment, Bronson sought out the court in order to establish a Municipal Court Trusteeship. He completed all necessary work on the trusteeship, except for a required appearance in court on Tuesday, July 11, to be sworn in.

When Bronson requested time off on July 11 to appear in court, his supervisor, Bill Engle, turned him down. The work load was particularly heavy that day, and several employees were already away on vacation. Engle not only refused Bronson's request but also warned him that because he had already been disciplined on one prior occasion for having walked off the job, he would be discharged if he left the job on this occasion. This was very serious since the court processed garnishments only on Tuesdays.

Bronson's situation was aggravated by an error made by the creditor's attorney who "jumped the gun" and obtained the order of garnishment from the court on July 11 which was within the 15-day grace period. Although the garnishment was unenforceable until the end of the 15 days, the company was still required to comply with

328

the court order it received on July 11, the very day Bronson was scheduled to appear before the court to establish the trusteeship which would save him from the garnishment. Release from such a court order must come from the garnisher, or the debtor must obtain a writ of prohibition as provided in Ohio statutes. It was company practice to respond promptly to court garnishment orders, which it did on July 11 by filling out the legal documents and returning them to the court.

After complying with the court order, the plant manager sent Bronson a letter advising him of the three-day suspension beginning Monday, July 17, 1978.

POSITION OF THE UNION

The union argued that Bronson had been placed in a classic "horns-of-a-dilemma" situation. He had been last counseled on June 1, 1978, concerning the many garnishments which had been filed against him. On that occasion he had been again told that if the company were to receive another garnishment order against him, he would be disciplined. His problem was doubled by the fact that he had walked off the job without permission a few weeks earlier. For this action he had been given a three-day suspension. On June 30 he received a notice of intent to garnishee from one of his creditors. He immediately set out to prevent the garnishment by applying for a trusteeship program under the terms of which he would make payments to the court which would distribute the money to creditors until all debts had been discharged. When he requested time off on July 11 to go to court to be sworn in and therefore meet the last requirement of the trusteeship, his employer refused to permit him to leave his job for that purpose. Mindful of his supervisor's admonition that he would be fired if he left his job that day without permission, he did not go to court that day.

To make matters even worse, the company received a notice from the court of a garnishment of wages that had been filed before the 15-day grace period had run out. The company immediately suspended Bronson because of the July 11 garnishment. That is why he ended up on the "horns-of-a-dilemma." If he were garnished, he faced disciplinary action by the company; if he prevented the garnishment by appearing in court, he would lose his job. The garnishment arrived earlier than allowed by law, but the company suspended him anyway. There was no way Bronson could have avoided suspension under these circumstances.

If Bronson had gone to court with the company's permission on July 11, the trusteeship could have been permitted. The union submitted a letter from the county trustee to support its position:

To whom it may concern:

Bronson applied for trusteeship in Hamilton County Municipal Court. He was to appear in court as of July 11, but was unable to get off work. He did appear July 18. For this reason, the garnishment could not be stopped.

(s) J. Goodman
Trustee Clerk

The union also submitted a letter from the county clerk attesting to Bronson's good intentions in applying for a trusteeship and to his conscientious effort to carry out the terms of the court's creditor repayment plan:

To whom it may concern:

This is to verify that Bronson applied for the Trustee to Prevent Garnishment on July 11, 1978, but was unable to get off work; therefore he was garnished.

Bronson came into the plan on July 18, 1978.

If Bronson would have entered into the plan on July 11, 1978, Thorp Finance would have been stopped from the garnishment.

If you have any questions please give us a call at 632–8895.

Bronson has paid into the plan each and every week and one of the best plan members we have.

(s) Mary Ann Waldbillig
County Clerk

The union contended that Bronson had been treated unjustly by the company and requested that it be required to compensate him for the monies lost during the three-day suspension and to remove all references to the events from his personnel files.

POSITION OF THE COMPANY

The company contended that Bronson's history of garnishments, including the excessive number of garnishments, provided proper cause for the three-day suspension. Prior to the series of garnishments in 1977 and 1978, he had received a one-day suspension for the same reason in 1976.[3] He had been counseled and warned on May 5 and June 1, 1978, including a written warning on the former occasion, that additional garnishments could result in discipline. The

---

[3] See Appendix A to this case for Bronson's suspension history.

company suspended Bronson only after it had received the ninth order of garnishment in as many months. During all those months Bronson's behavior gave no indication that he was making any progress in separating his personal financial problems from his employment. The company's action was more than reasonable; it was lenient.[4]

The company stated that it was very sympathetic to Bronson's request to be absent from work a large part of the day on July 11; however, it also had its own problems to contend with. The work load was heavy that day, and the warehouse was already short-handed because several employees were away on vacation. Furthermore, his application for a Municipal Court trusteeship was a "last-second" attempt to rectify many months of inaction. His failure to complete the terms of his trusteeship should not be charged to the company's actions.

Finally, the company was required to respond to the court's order of garnishment, even though it had been filed within the 15-day grace period allowed Bronson under Ohio law. The order could be lifted only by the court. And Bronson had not informed the company that the order was unenforceable on July 11. Operating in good faith, the company completed the necessary forms and delivered them to the court as required by law. Regardless of whether Bronson went to court on July 11, the company had to operate under the court's order.

The purpose of the company's garnishment rules was to avoid the cost and disruption incurred in processing garnishment orders. These costs were incurred when the orders were processed, regardless of whether those orders were withdrawn or subsequently voided in a court of law. The burden placed upon the company to respond to the garnishments included considerable clerical work, time spent counseling with the debtor employee and with the employee's creditors, extra payroll costs, and court appearances.

For the foregoing reasons, the company claimed that it had "proper cause" to issue a three-day disciplinary suspension upon Bronson. The company requested that the grievance be denied.

---

[4] See Appendix B to this case for relevant provisions of the contract.

APPENDIX A

Suspension History

Suspensions	Length	Reason
1976:		
May 25	1 day	Garnishment
November 4, 5, 8	3 days	Excessive absenteeism
1977:		
April 4	1 day	Excessive absenteeism
1978:		
June 22, 23, 24	3 days	Walking off job without permission
July 17, 18, 19	3 days	Garnishment

APPENDIX B

Relevant Provision of the Contract

ARTICLE 18—RIGHTS OF MANAGEMENT

The Management of the business and the direction of the working forces including the right to . . . , hire, suspend, or discharge for proper cause . . . are vested in management, provided however, that this right shall be exercised with due regard for the rights of the employees and provided further that it will not be used for the purpose of discrimination against any employee.

QUESTIONS

1. Why do most companies consider wage garnishments issued on its employees as disciplinary matters?
2. Was Bob Bronson caught on a horns-of-a-dilemma situation which was beyond his control? Why, or why not?
3. Did the company have proper cause to give Bronson a three-day disciplinary suspension? Does Bronson's previous record have any bearing upon the arbitrator's decision? Discuss.

52. THE RIGHT TO WORK ON A BIRTHDAY HOLIDAY

Company: United Salt Corporation, Houston, Texas

Union: International Chemical Workers Union, Local 680

BACKGROUND

Under the previous contracts betwen the parties, employees were paid time and one half for working on holidays. Holidays specified under the holiday article in the labor agreement were New Year's Day, Washington's Birthday, Good Friday, Memorial Day, Fourth of July, Labor Day, Thanksgiving, Christmas Eve, Christmas Day, and four hours on New Year's Eve. An employee's birthday was also designated as a holiday. Although the contract was silent, by custom employees could choose whether to work on that day or not. The company paid time and one half to employees who worked on any holiday including their birthday holiday, and regular straight time to employees who did not work on a holiday including their birthday holiday.

On September 26, 1978, the company and the union signed a new contract that revised the article on holidays. The revised contract provided that in the future employees would receive double time, rather than time and one half, for working on holidays. During contract negotiations, there was no discussion concerning whether or not the company could require employees to take off from work on their birthday holidays. The new contract was signed September 26, 1978, and became effective as of September 1, 1978.

For the past five years, John Dow,[1] a leadman in the production department, had chosen to work on his birthday, and he had received time and one-half pay for doing so. As was his custom, Dow

---

[1] The names of the individuals have been disguised.

had informed his supervisor that again he would like to work on his birthday which was October 18, 1978.

A production department work schedule was posted on October 1, 1978. This posted work schedule showed that Dow was to work on October 18, 1978. However, a subsequent memorandum was issued by the company's plant manager on October 9, 1978, as follows:

To all supervisors:

Effective immediately all Supervisors will make every effort to schedule employees off on their birthday holidays. The idea of a holiday is free time to the employee so we should do our best to see they get it. If necessary to replace the man, temporary help will be used where possible. Overtime will be used when temporary help is unavailable or unqualified.

An occasion requiring a man to work on his birthday must have prior approval by the Plant Manager.

C. B. Fox
Plant Manager

On October 11, 1978, Dow was told by his supervisor that he would not be allowed to work on his birthday. This angered Dow, since it meant he would receive only $40 instead of about $80 that he was expecting to earn that day. The company cited economic reasons for its actions and stood by its decision not to let him work on his birthday. Dow then filed a grievance stating he should have been allowed to work on his birthday as he had done in the past. His grievance eventually was carried to arbitration.

Although he had not been permitted to work on October 18, his birthday, Dow did work the following Thanksgiving, Christmas Eve, Christmas, and New Year and was paid double time for doing so.

POSITION OF THE UNION

Union president Karl Adam, who had been with the firm for 20 years, and John Dow both testified that they were present at the 1978 contract negotiations. They stated that the matter of requiring employees to take off work on their birthday holiday had not been discussed, although payment of double time for working on any holiday—including a birthday holiday—had been agreed upon. The union argued that lack of discussion on this matter during contract negotiations meant that Dow and all other employees must be permitted to continue to work on their birthday as had been the custom in the past.

334

The union contended that the choice of working on one's birthday was a well-established past practice. Therefore, management could not change this practice without negotiating on the matter. The union asserted that the company had violated the labor contract in the same manner as if it had unilaterally decided to change the agreed-upon leadman's wage rate of $5.77 per hour for 1979 without negotiating the matter with the union. The union noted that eight people in addition to Dow had birthdays between September 1, 1978, and October 9, 1978, and that at least two of them had worked on their birthday. Since the new contract already was in effect, those employees who had worked on their birthdays received double time. Thus, the company had been inconsistent in permitting some employees and not others to work on their birthday holiday. The company had unilaterally changed a condition of employment in violation of a long-standing practice under both the old and new contract. This the company should not be permitted to do.

In summary, the union contended that the company had violated the contract and past practices by denying John Dow and other employees the opportunity to work on their birthdays. The union requested that John Dow and all other employees who had wanted to work on their birthdays and who were not allowed to do so should be paid the amount they would have earned had they worked.

POSITION OF THE COMPANY

C. B. Fox, plant manager, testified that he decided in late September 1978 that due to the economic impact of paying employees double time for working on their birthdays, he would require employees not to work on their birthdays. He felt it was the general consensus of management that the average additional cost of $20 per employee per year for employees working on their birthday was too great for the company to bear. Thus, on October 9, 1978, he issued the memorandum concerning employees working on their birthday.

The company contended that its actions were justified under Article III, Management Rights, of the contract.[2] The company argued that this article allowed management the right to change for economic reasons any conditions of employment previously followed.

The company acknowledged that there was a past practice under previous contracts which permitted employees the option to work on their birthday holiday at a wage rate of time and one half their normal hourly wage. But this past practice no longer could apply,

---

[2] See Appendix to this case.

since the rate of pay for working on a holiday was changed in the new contract to double time. The company could not be required to maintain a past practice which was not applicable to the new contractual condition.

In summary, the company claimed that it had every right under the management rights clause of the contract to require John Dow and other employees to be off work on their birthday holidays. The company's motivation was economic in nature, and the company claimed that the former past practice could not apply to a changed contractual provision. The company urged that the union grievance should be denied.

APPENDIX

ARTICLE III—MANAGEMENT RIGHTS

Section 1. The management of the business and the direction of the working force, including but not limited to the right to hire, to transfer, to promote, to demote, to discipline or discharge for cause, to lay off for lack of work, and to assign employees to work shifts are rights vested exclusively in the management of the Company.

In the event any promotion, disciplinary action, transfer, suspension, or discharge is considered discriminatory or unjust, the matter will be handled in accordance with the grievance and arbitration procedure provided for in the agreement.

Section 2. The right to plan, direct, and control plant operations; the right to introduce new or improved production methods or facilities; the right to determine the amount of supervision necessary; the right to combine or split up departments as deemed necessary; the right to determine schedules of production and to establish standards of quality; and the right to increase or decrease production or employment are vested exclusively in the Company.

Section 3. Nothing contained herein shall be intended or shall be considered as a waiver of any of the usual inherent and fundamental rights of management. Any of the rights, power, or authorities the Company had prior to the signing of this agreement are retained by the Company, except to the extent that they are specifically abridged, delegated, or modified by this agreement.

QUESTIONS

1. Which should take priority in deciding an issue of this sort, the management rights provision in the contract or the previous plant practice? Discuss.

2. Evaluate the company argument that the previous plant practice no longer was applicable due to the change in the contract regarding holiday pay.

3. Does the fact that during negotiations the parties did not discuss the question of whether or not employees could be required to take off work on their birthday holiday have a major bearing on the arbitrator's decision? Why or why not?

53. SUNDAY IS THE SABBATH DAY

Company: General Foods Corporation, Food Products Division, Woodburn, Oregon

Union: Teamster Food Processors, Drivers, Warehousemen and Helpers, Local 670

BACKGROUND

The Food Products Division of General Foods Corporation in Woodburn, Oregon, purchases and processes fruit and vegetable crops grown in the Willamette Valley. The food processing occurs annually during the spring to fall harvest cycle. It is necessary to process the harvested crops as rapidly as possible because they are extremely perishable.

At the time of this case (1978), 1,200 people were employed in the production department, which operated three shifts all seven days of the week except for one shift on Sunday. The production line closed down for eight hours on Sunday in order that the sanitation department could thoroughly clean the work area.

The sanitation department employed about 75 people who worked seven days a week continuously cleaning the plant. The sanitation department sanitized the work area not only to meet government health standards but also to meet the company's standards for cleanliness quality control. The company had never experienced a case of food contamination and believed that such an incident would have a disastrous effect upon its reputation with all segments of the community, especially consumers.

Karen Lauer[1] was initially hired on April 2, 1978, as a production

---

[1] The names of all individuals have been disguised.

employee. On June 21, 1978, she bid for and received a position in the sanitation department. But during that week she informed the sanitation department supervisor, George Bergland, that she could not work on Sundays because it was against her Old Orthodox religion. Bergland explained that working on Sundays was a long-standing requirement of sanitation employees, and that it was essential that she work on that day. Bergland also pointed out that this requirement was explicitly included in the job description which had been posted on the bulletin board and which the personnel manager had explained to her when she requested the transfer. Nevertheless, Lauer steadfastly refused to work on Sundays. Therefore, on June 26, 1978, Bergland had her transferred back to the production department where she could be scheduled off on Sundays.

Lauer worked for several weeks in the production department. She then informed Bergland that she would work on Sundays if she would be transferred back to the sanitation department. On July 13, 1978, the company again transferred her to the sanitation department.

Once in the sanitation department, she did not work on Sundays. She offered a variety of excuses, such as a family reunion, illness, and lack of transportation. Supervisor Bergland gave her a verbal warning about being absent after she had been absent from work on the last Sunday in July. Her Sunday absences continued in August, and Bergland warned her after each incident. When her supervisor confronted her in mid-August on the subject, she admitted that she had been absent because of her religious obligation to observe Sunday as the Sabbath day.

On August 24, 1978, Lauer was again transferred back to the production department where she could be scheduled off on Sundays. This transfer meant she took a slight reduction in pay. Under the seniority system, she could have bid for a higher paying job within the production department when a vacancy occurred. Although job vacancies were posted, Lauer chose not to utilize this route to a better paying job. Rather, on August 28, 1978, Lauer filed a grievance claiming that she had been a victim of religious discrimination. The grievance eventually was carried to arbitration. The union and the company submitted the following statement of the issue to the arbitrator:

Whether the Company violated Article XII, Section 1(a), of the labor Agreement and Karen Lauer's rights under Title VII of the Civil Rights Act when she was transferred from the Sanitation Department to the Production Department.

POSITION OF THE UNION

The union stated that both the collective agreement and the Civil Rights Act[2] required that the company could not discriminate against an employee because of religious beliefs and practices. Further, both arbitrators and the Equal Employment Opportunity Commission (EEOC) have ruled consistently that employers must make affirmative efforts at reasonable accommodation for an employee's religious beliefs when an employee's religious needs conflict with job requirements. In this instance, the company made no real effort to do so. Lauer was merely transferred back to the production department where she was placed in work less desirable to her and where she suffered a reduction in pay rate.

Karen Lauer testified that she could not work on Sundays because she was of the Old Orthodox faith which required its members to observe Sunday as the Sabbath. When the company transferred her back to the production department where she could be scheduled off on Sundays, she was assigned to perform work which was routine and dull, and at a lower pay rate than sanitation workers. Unlike the company, Lauer did not look upon this transfer as an accommodation to her. Rather, she felt that she had become a victim of religious discrimination.

The union claimed that the company had already accommodated to an annual turnover rate of about 300 percent in the sanitation department of 75 persons. The absence of one additional person on Sundays could not have any effect upon the effectiveness of the crew. No one in the sanitation department had complained about Lauer being absent on Sundays, since the employees knew and understood that Karen Lauer's religion required her to observe Sunday as a Sabbath day.

According to the union, the company also had violated the contract because it unilaterally changed the work rules and had promulgated a new rule requiring everyone on the sanitation crew to work on Sunday. This rule was made without prior consultation with the union, and the union had never agreed to such a rule during contract negotiations.

The union argued that the company had discriminated against Lauer because of her religion. While insisting that Lauer work on Sundays, the company for many years had accommodated other employees in the sanitation department who were absent on Sundays to attend the funerals of members of their immediate family, to

---

[2] See Appendix A and Appendix B to this case.

be married, were hospitalized, were jailed, or were absent for other reasons. The company's past practices of approving Sunday absences proved that Lauer's presence was not necessary for the efficient conduct of sanitation department business on Sundays. Accommodation to Lauer's religious practices should and must be made within the sanitation department, as required by the agreement and also by the Civil Rights Act.

The union requested that the company be required to return Lauer to her job in the sanitation department and to accommodate to her religious practices. The union also requested that Lauer be made whole for the loss of pay and other benefits and privileges she lost because of her transfer back to the production department.

POSITION OF THE COMPANY

The company argued that it was impossible to accommodate Lauer's religious beliefs to the extent that she be excused from work on Sundays and keep her in the sanitation department. The sanitation department crew must work seven days a week but especially on Sundays, because production shut down that day. Production was closed on Sunday because most produce growers did not harvest on that day except in emergencies. The company attributed extreme importance to sanitation which was necessary to ensure the health of the public. The company also considered its national reputation for cleanliness quality control to be a major competitive advantage over other food processors.

The company pointed out that production workers put in extremely long hours during the harvesting season. It was not possible to count on them to volunteer to work seven consecutive days by serving as substitutes for absent sanitation employees, especially when they often worked part of a second shift during one or more days of the previous six days. Further, sanitation workers must be trained; the company needed full-time sanitation crews, not an assortment of part-time substitute volunteers.

The company admitted that turnover in the sanitation department did run very high; it was 300 percent in 1977. The department had been unstable, and training costs had been high. It would add additional costs to the company to excuse Lauer from Sunday work by having to bring in additional, untrained help in her place.

The requirement that Lauer work on Sundays was a bona fide requirement according to the company. Even federal, state, and local wage and hour laws recognized that employees in the food processing industry can be required to work seven days a week because of the special harvesting and processing demands of highly perishable fruit and vegetables. Relieving Lauer of the requirement that she work Sundays would in effect create a new policy which would lift that requirement for the entire sanitation crew. To excuse Lauer from working on Sundays would be unfair and discriminatory to everyone else in the department.

The company maintained that it had not been insensitive to Lauer's religious needs. But her demand to be relieved of the requirement that she work Sundays and hold a job in the sanitation department went beyond "reasonable accommodation." Lauer's transfer to production was an administrative transfer to reasonably accommodate her demand to be off work on Sundays. It was not a disciplinary transfer and in no way affected her good standing with the company. She could bid to better and higher paying jobs in the production department if she wished to do so.

The company insisted that it had not discriminated against Lauer because of her religion in violation of either the collective agreement or of Title VII of the Civil Rights Act. Lauer had not been treated different from other employees under similar circumstances. The company produced documents and testimony which showed that numerous employees had been transferred or terminated when they were unable to maintain regular attendance in the sanitation department. This had been the company's practice for many years.

For all of these reasons, the company asked that Karen Lauer's grievance be dismissed.

APPENDIX A

Relevant Provision of the Contract

ARTICLE XII

Section 1.   In the application of this Agreement and in accordance with applicable federal and state laws, there shall be no discrimination against employees because of race, color, religion, sex, age, or national origin.

APPENDIX B

Relevant Provisions of the Civil Rights Act of 1964, as Amended in 1972, 1975, and 1978

TITLE VII

Definitions
   Section 701.   For the purposes of this title—
   (j) The term "religion" includes all aspects of religious observance and practice, as well as belief, unless an employer demonstrates that

342

he is unable to reasonably accommodate to an employee's, or prospective employee's, religious observance or practice without undue hardship on the conduct of the employer's business.

Discrimination because of Race, Color, Religion, Sex, or National Origin
Section 703(a). It shall be an unlawful practice for an employer—

(1) To fail or refuse to hire or to discharge any individual, or otherwise to discriminate against an individual with respect to his compensation, terms, conditions, or privileges of employment, because of such individual's race, color, religion, sex, or national origin; or

(2) to limit, segregate, or classify his employees or applicants for employment in any way which would deprive or tend to deprive any individual of employment opportunities or otherwise adversely affect his status as an employee, because of such individual's race, color, religion, sex, or national origin.

(g) Notwithstanding any other provision of this title, it shall not be unlawful employment practice for an employer to fail or refuse to hire and employ any individual for any position, for employer to discharge any individual from any position or for an employment agency to fail or refuse to refer any individual for employment in any position, or for a labor organization to fail or refuse to refer any individual for employment in any position, if—

* * * * *

(2) such individual has not fulfilled or has ceased to fulfill that requirement.

(j) Nothing contained in this title shall be interpreted to require any employer, employment agency, labor organization, or joint labor-management committee subject to this title to grant preferential treatment to any individual or to any group because of the race, color, religion, sex, or national origin of such individual or group on account of an imbalance which may exist with respect to the total number of percentage of persons of any race, color, religion, sex, or national origin employed by any employer . . . in comparison with the total number of percentage of persons of such race, color, religion, sex, or national origin in any community, state, section, or other area.

QUESTIONS

1. Why is a case of this nature an awkward one for both the company and the union?
2. Was Karen Lauer a victim of religious discrimination? Why, or why not?

3. Did the company attempt to reasonably accommodate Lauer's religious beliefs, or did the company fail to do so in a reasonable manner? Discuss.

4. Does the arbitrator have power to interpret and apply the Civil Rights Act under the circumstances of this case? Why are arbitrators typically uncomfortable in a case of this nature which involves charges of violation of both the labor agreement and a federal statute?

5. Consult the EEOC's recent guidelines concerning religious discrimination and reasonable accommodation for employees' religious beliefs. Might the EEOC decide the case of Karen Lauer differently than would an arbitrator? Discuss.

54. MY TIME IS NOT THE COMPANY'S TIME

Company: Alumax Foils, Inc., St. Louis, Missouri

Union: International Association of Machinists and Aerospace Workers, District 9

BACKGROUND

On April 5, 1978, the union filed a grievance on behalf of Andrew Warlock,[1] furnace operator at Alumax Foils. The grievance document read:

> Contract violation: I was suspended from work while not under the jurisdiction of the plant (off the clock); also in the wrong manner.
> Date and time: 3:15 P.M.—4/3/78.
> How did it happen: An argument over a lie told by Brookings.
> Demand: Back pay from the time I missed on the job.

The company's industrial relations manager, Charles Janssen, sent the following reply rejecting Warlock's complaint:

> Warlock was suspended for threatening John B. Brookings with physical violence. He was in the plant without permission and was told to leave. He not only refused to leave, but threatened harm to company representatives. This threat was made in the presence of witnesses and was repeated in a meeting which included the Chief Shop Steward and several other persons. Warlock stated, "I really intended to hurt him."
> Suspension for a threat of this nature is mild disciplinary action. He has no back pay due to him.

Before this grievance could be appealed to arbitration, Warlock became involved in another situation. He failed to attend a required

---

[1] The names of all individuals have been disguised.

crew meeting on April 17, 1978, for which he was discharged. He filed a grievance on April 21 requesting reinstatement with full back pay for all time missed from work and apologies from several management representatives. Warlock attached the following statement detailing his perception of the circumstances leading to his discharge:

> On April 16 the foreman posted the notice for a crew meeting from 3:00 P.M. to 3:30 P.M. Later the same day he went around letting everybody know about the meeting. When 3:00 P.M. came, I noticed the foreman had changed the date to the 17th. If the meeting had been held on the 16th as he first posted it, I would have attended, but on the 17th I planned to be at my son's birthday party which I felt was more important than the foreman's crew meeting. (Which brings the question to mind—why did he cancel the first meeting? Did he remember he had something to do with his family; was there a personal matter he had to attend to or *what?*) My personal life has nothing to do with the company. I have a responsibility to the company for eight hours. I was relieved properly, and I informed the foreman on the 17th that I would not be able to make his meeting, and he said, "Well, I guess we'll have to make it some other time." About two hours later he came back up to me and said, "We all have to be at that meeting." I didn't attend the meeting for the reasons stated earlier. Why should the foremen be able to change their minds and change dates of so-called very important crew meetings when they have something personal to do and the employees turn around and do the same thing and the result is suspension or termination? If this is permitted, then it means that the company controls our lives 24 hours a day. As I've said in the past, I only work for Alumax; Alumax doesn't own me. I believe the real reason for my suspension was my efforts to get Brookings fired for possession of a gun on company premises, for which I have two witnesses willing to make firsthand testimony of facts. I also think the company hasn't got sufficient grounds to fire me for not attending a crew meeting. Another thing—why did Burgess fire me and send me over to personnel without a shop steward and Janssen dropped it down to a suspension after he had to call for a steward? It seems to me if an employee is to be fired, there should be no misunderstanding between two officials of the company. The steward asked Janssen why was I fired. He said he didn't have the facts yet, and still no positive action on his part to find out. There's something other than a crew meeting behind this, and it doesn't take five days to get to the bottom of this and realize what really caused the suspension.

In a reply signed by Plant Superintendent Willis Burgess, the company rejected the second grievance presented by the union on behalf of Warlock.[2]

---

[2] See Appendix to this case for relevant clauses of the contract.

> Warlock was discharged for insubordination after he refused a legitimate direction from his supervisor to stay overtime for 30 minutes, without giving a valid reason. This insubordination, following closely other exhibitions of insubordination, threats, and intemperate actions, made it impossible for the Company to continue Warlock's employment.

The union appealed both cases to arbitration. It was mutually agreed by the union and the company that the issues for arbitrator's determination could be framed as follows: Did the company have proper cause as required by the agreement when it first suspended Andrew Warlock and later discharged him? If not, what should be the proper remedies?

TESTIMONY AND EVIDENCE CONCERNING THE INCIDENTS

The April 3 Incident.   Andrew Warlock attempted to attend a grievance meeting in the office of the personnel director, Charles Janssen, early on the afternoon of April 3. The meeting involved his brother, David Warlock, who was also an employee of Alumax. When Janssen denied him admission, he waited outside the personnel office to speak with David at the close of the meeting.

According to Andrew Warlock, his brother said that the company had fired him because he had refused to work four hours of required overtime the previous day. Andrew said that he became angry when his brother told him that a second employee, Kevin Wilson, also had not worked overtime but was not being disciplined. David claimed that John Brookings, a casting department supervisor, had reported that Wilson had worked a full 12 hours on April 2. Andrew then returned to the personnel office to speak with Janssen, but was told to leave without seeing him.

Warlock then proceeded to the time clock where he unsuccessfully attempted to check Wilson's time card in order to determine whether Wilson had worked 12 hours the previous day. Warlock claimed that Wilson told him that he had not worked overtime that day.

Brookings was in the plant at about 3:15 P.M. on April 3, helping an employee locate a leak in the fuel line of a forklift truck. As he was working on the machine, Andrew Warlock strode up to him from the other end of the plant, accompanied by three employees and a friend who was not employed by Alumax. As he neared Brookings, Warlock cursed Brookings and accused him of lying about the overtime incident involving his brother and Kevin Wilson. They argued about it for a short while, and finally Brookings told him, "Get the hell out of the plant! You're suspended!" Warlock ignored this order. Brookings then reminded him that he was on company property, and gave both Warlock and his friend a direct order to leave the premises. Warlock replied that nobody could give him a direct order. He stepped outside a nearby door and drew back his fist as if to strike Brookings. Two employees restrained Warlock from hitting Brookings, whom he also tried to kick. Warlock observed Superintendent Willis Burgess walk into the plant at that point. Warlock left Brookings and talked with the superintendent about having been suspended. He admitted that he was very angry and that he had wanted to hurt Brookings. He stated that he knew that neither he nor his friend had permission to be in the plant,[3] but that he wanted to help his brother whom he felt had been given a bad deal. Burgess affirmed the supervisor's suspension and extended it to seven days.

The April 17 Incident. Brookings scheduled a mandatory overtime safety meeting for Sunday, April 16. All employees had been advised on Saturday, April 15, that this half-hour meeting would take place at the end of the shift from 3 to 3:30 P.M. Superintendent Burgess that same day asked Brookings to reschedule the meeting for the same time on Monday, April 17, in order that he might prepare additional materials for the meeting. All employees were promptly told verbally that the mandatory overtime meeting had been rescheduled to 3:00–3:30 P.M. on Monday, and a notice also was posted on the time clock.

No one, including Warlock, said anything about being unable to attend the rescheduled meeting when told about it. However, at about noon on Monday, April 17, Warlock told Brookings that he could not attend the meeting because "he had other plans." When asked about his "other plans," Warlock was very noncommittal other than to refer to "other plans." Brookings reminded him of his duty to attend the obligatory overtime meeting at premium pay. Warlock left the plant at 3 P.M. on Monday and did not attend the meeting.

These obligatory meetings were conducted about once each month, and usually concerned safety matters. In practice, the company would excuse an employee who presented a very good reason for being absent. Everyone, except Warlock, attended the April 17 meeting.

Warlock, when asked by Brookings his reason for not attending the Monday meeting (presumably to attend his son's birthday party), replied that it was "none of the company's business." He also said that he had attended safety meetings before, and felt that anything said in a half-hour meeting could be quickly relayed to him by any of the others in attendance. But it was his personal feelings

---

[3] Andrew Warlock's shift had ended at 3 P.M., and he had already clocked out.

about his duty to the company that led him to be absent. He said that he felt that his own personal business was more important than that of the company, and that he had no obligation to the job beyond eight hours. Furthermore, nothing in the contract required him to tell Brookings about his personal life. However, he agreed that the company had the right under the contract to require overtime on a mandatory basis.

Warlock later told Burgess that he felt the real reason why he was fired was because he had reported seeing Brookings carrying a gun on company property contrary to company rules against bringing firearms or other dangerous weapons into the plant. In Warlock's opinion, company management used the April 17 incident as an excuse to terminate him unjustly.

Brookings originally planned to suspend Warlock for failing to attend the April 17 meeting, but Janssen and Burgess ruled that he should be terminated.

POSITION OF THE UNION

The April 3 Suspension. The union contended that a seven-calendar-day suspension was too harsh a penalty for Warlock, who was trying to defend his brother. The union acknowledged that he should have followed the appropriate grievance procedure and that he should not have lost his temper. However, the incident should be viewed in the light of one brother trying to defend another.

The April 17 Termination. The union argued that here, too, the company's action in terminating Warlock was extremely harsh. He had simply missed one half hour of required overtime, and he had a reasonable excuse. The supervisor in this situation could have excused Warlock from attending the meeting. The union agreed that the employee should have told his supervisor the reason for missing the meeting, but discharge was far too severe for the infraction. At most, he should have received a reprimand for not attending the meeting. He did not walk off the job; he simply did not attend a meeting. The discharge should be reduced to at most a reprimand.

POSITION OF THE COMPANY

The April 3 Suspension. The company maintained that Warlock was properly suspended from April 3 to April 9, 1978, for threatening a supervisor with physical violence. The seven-calendar-day suspension was very light in view of the severity of the infraction.

The April 17 Termination. The discharge of Warlock must be considered in relationship to the previous suspension that had occurred only a few days earlier. He had been suspended from April 3 to April 9. He returned to work on April 11, and only a few days later in the incident of April 17, he refused a direct order to attend a required safety meeting. His refusal to attend a required meeting on an overtime basis without offering any reason whatsoever for not being able to attend demonstrated his unwillingness to cooperate with the company and his direct insubordination toward company authority. The company claimed that the "arrogant, uncooperative, and insubordinate conduct of Warlock justified his suspension and discharge."

APPENDIX

Relevant Clauses of the Contract

ARTICLE II—HOURS AND OVERTIME

Section 3. It is recognized that overtime work is important and, on occasion, necessary. Once the Company has determined that employees are to do certain work at a certain time and that there will be an insufficient number of employees available to perform the work during their regular schedules, employees will be selected for overtime work in accordance with assignment rules established by the Company and the Union. No employee will be allowed to work more than fifteen (15) consecutive hours, and no more than fifteen (15) hours in any one day.

ARTICLE III—MANAGEMENT

It is agreed that the management of the Company's plant and works and the direction of its working forces, including the right to hire, suspend, discipline, or discharge an employee or employees for proper cause, and the right to transfer employees, and the right to relieve employees from duty because of lack of work, or for other legitimate reasons, is vested exclusively in the Company.

QUESTIONS

1. Did the company have proper (just) cause for issuing Andrew Warlock a seven-day disciplinary suspension? Discuss.
2. Did the company have proper (just) cause for discharging Andrew Warlock? Discuss.

3. Discuss the position of the union that Warlock had a "reasonable excuse" to miss the required safety meeting. In general, does a company have a right to require employees to work a certain amount of overtime?

4. Evaluate the company position that its decision to discharge Warlock should be considered in relationship to the prior suspension action. Is such a cumulative basis for discharging Warlock appropriate in this case?

55. WHICH DUTY CALLS?

Hospital: Monroe County Hospital, Rochester, New York
Association: Civil Service Employees Association, Monroe Chapter, Local 828

BACKGROUND

As Mary Moody[1] approached her apartment on Tuesday afternoon September 19, 1978, a police car pulled up in front of her door. The officers asked her to accompany them to the juvenile detention center where her daughter, Eileen, was being held for both medical and psychological examination. Although Eileen was only 14 years of age, she had already had several encounters with the police and also had been suspended from school on several occasions because of her violent behavior toward both her teachers and fellow students.

The situation Tuesday afternoon was more serious. Earlier that day the assistant principal of Parks Junior High School had summoned police because of Eileen's threatening and potentially violent behavior toward one of the other students. She had already been suspended from school for an indefinite period and escorted to the detention center for processing and to await the arrival of her mother.

Mary Moody spent the next day at University Hospital where both she and her daughter received counseling. The counselors strongly recommended that Mary take a leave of absence from her work so that she could devote full time and attention to the care and rehabilitation of Eileen, as well as care for her four other small children for whom she was the sole support.

Mary Moody was a licensed practical nurse (LPN) who had been

---

[1] The names of all individuals have been disguised.

hired by the Monroe County Hospital on October 11, 1976. The hospital was a "chronic care" facility that housed nearly 600 patients, mostly geriatric, who were mostly long-term residents. The hospital was operated by the county and was required to conform to New York state staffing and patient services regulations. The hospital's need to maintain a full staff and to render high-quality service required it to insist upon prompt and regular attendance from employees.

The hospital deemed Moody's attendance record to be unsatisfactory and had warned her on four occasions over a period of 21 months as detailed below:

Warning	Period of Time over Which Absences and Tardiness Occurred	Date of Warning	Number of Absences	Number of Tardies
1	12/31/76–4/25/77	4/25/77	6	0
2	7/26/77–9/27/77	9/27/77	8	2
3	1/1/78–4/24/78	5/17/78	13	0
4	4/24/78–9/26/78	9/26/78	12	8

In addition, she had received counseling on one other occasion during this time for unrelated conduct and for her continuous unsatisfactory evaluations on her performance, especially for her erratic attendance. Although she did not file a grievance to protest the four warning notices, she maintained that her absences and lateness were based upon proper and legitimate causes.

On September 21, 1978, Moody telephoned the nursing office to inform her supervisor that she was ill and could not report to work. She again called in on September 22 to report that she would be absent due to illness. She also left word for the staff coordinator of nursing to return her call.

When the staff coordinator returned the call, Moody informed her that she was requesting an unpaid leave of absence in order to take care of severe family problems that she was having with two of her children. The coordinator informed Moody that because of staffing problems at the hospital and her poor attendance record, her request probably would be denied. Moody submitted a formal request in writing for a leave of absence because of "personal family problems." The coordinator then discussed her request with the assistant personnel director, who confirmed denial of the request.

Starting September 23, Moody did not report for work, although she telephoned her supervisor on each day of her intended absence for reasons of "sickness" or "family sickness." On October 11, she was informed of a hearing to be conducted on October 13 concerning her absences. She attended the hearing with her union representative, after which she was given a termination notice based upon her "continual absence."

Mary Moody and the union immediately filed a grievance protesting her discharge, which eventually was carried to arbitration.

POSITION OF THE HOSPITAL

The hospital contended that Moody's attendance for her entire period of employment was extremely excessive. No matter how good the causes or excuses for her absence, the hospital was entitled to her regular attendance. When an employee is absent as much as 10 percent of her scheduled work time, even for good reason, her services become of little value to the hospital and she should not expect to remain in its employ. Regular and prompt attendance is especially critical in this case because of the New York state accreditation requirements as well as the safety and health of patients.

The hospital acknowledged its responsibility to assist troubled employees; however, there were limits to the assistance it was able to afford. The hospital had already endured 21 months of undependable performance by Moody, and there was no indication that Moody's performance would improve in the future.

The hospital urged that the arbitrator uphold the discharge, since the hospital had ample just cause to terminate Moody as required by the labor agreement for disciplining and discharging of employees.

POSITION OF THE EMPLOYEES ASSOCIATION

The association (i.e., union) pointed out that the hospital's basis for terminating Moody was "continued absence" and not her past record; her past record should not be considered. Only the reasons for her present absence and its duration should be considered by the arbitrator.

The association argued that the hospital should have given special consideration to Moody's unique situation. She was the sole support of five minor children, including Eileen, aged 14, who had caused her grievous problems. On September 19, 1978, Eileen had been suspended from school for potentially violent behavior. Trained counselors had urged Moody to take a leave of absence from work so that she could devote full time and attention to the care and cure of her sick daughter. During the period of her absence from September 23, her daughter had undergone physical and psychological tests and examinations at the University of Rochester Medical Center to determine the cause of her abnormal behavior. She had also received treatment from a private physician and a psycho-educational evaluation at the Strong Memorial Hospital. And upon the initiative of the Rochester Board of Education, Eileen was assigned to the Neighborhood Achievement Center where an individualized educational and counseling program had been designed for her. During this time, Mary Moody had received counseling and psychological aid for more effective supervision of Eileen.

The association argued that in cases such as this, society should recognize individual problems of employees and attempt to help resolve them. The hospital could and should help Moody by making it possible for her to minister to the special needs of her child in this time of crisis. According to the association, Mary Moody was now ready to resume her full employment responsibilities, and she would again be a responsible and dependable employee.

The association urged that Mary Moody be restored to her job and be made whole for all monies, rights, and privileges lost as a result of her unjust termination.

QUESTIONS

1. Did the hospital have ample just cause to terminate Mary Moody for "continual absence"?
2. Should Mary Moody's past record be considered by the arbitrator, or only the circumstances surrounding the situation leading to her discharge? Discuss.
3. To what lengths should an employer attempt to balance the stress of personal problems experienced by an employee against its own demands for work attendance?
4. Why is a case of this nature difficult from a public relations point of view, particularly since this is a public sector employer?

56. TERMINATED AT 59 DAYS

Company: Paccar, Inc., Kansas City, Missouri
Union: United Automobile, Aerospace and Agricultural
Implement Workers of America, Local 710

Robert White[1] was employed by Paccar on March 20, 1978, and was terminated on May 24, 1978, after 59 days of total service. He would have completed his probationary period after his 60th day.[2] Normally, his termination would not have been subject to the grievance procedure; however, Wright was black, and the union charged that he lost his job as a result of discrimination.

BACKGROUND

Paccar, Inc., manufactured heavy equipment such as front loaders, log stackers, refuelers, and coal haulers. The company employed approximately 43 machinists in its machine shop. There were about 30 different types of machines of all sizes in the shop, including vertical and horizontal lathes, turret lathes, vertical and horizontal milling machines, drill presses, internal and centerless honing machines, and shapers.Some of the equipment was very sophisticated, being computer controlled.

Elton Davisson, the general foreman, was responsible for the machine shop. He supervised two foremen, one on the day shift and one on the night shift. Machinists were expected to perform their work with little technical supervision. Each machinist performed a variety of jobs and was required at a minimum to operate several machines. Job assignments varied in length from a half hour to a day

---

[1] The names of all individuals have been disguised.
[2] See Appendix to this case for relevant clauses of the contract.

or two, with most jobs requiring less than a day to complete. Machinists determined what operations were to be performed on a job assignment from a document known as the hard copy. In sequence, their jobs normally required them to (1) obtain the appropriate blueprints, (2) determine the machines and tools required, (3) set up the machines to perform the required operations, (4) operate the machines by setting the proper speeds and feeds, and (5) complete the required parts to specification, using micrometers and other precision measuring devices.

Davisson was responsible for interviewing applicants for machine shop positions to determine their overall knowledge, skills, and experience. After an applicant was hired, the foreman, in this instance Keith Hellwig, was responsible for the indoctrination, supervision, and performance appraisal of the new employee during the 60-day probationary period. In evaluating a new employee's performance, the foreman followed a well-developed procedure of assigning each new employee to a standard series of job assignments.

During the five years that foreman Hellwig had supervised new employees, approximately 25 probationary employees had been assigned to him. Six of these were terminated for failure to pass their probationary period. Wright was the only one of these six failing to pass the probationary period who was black; the others were white.

POSITION OF THE UNION

The union contended that the primary reason Wright was terminated during his probationary period was that he was black. The union charged that while the company had professed to subscribe to Article V of the collective bargaining agreement, in practice it had not done so.

The union held that no minority employee had ever successfully made it through the probationary period under Hellwig's supervision. According to the union, it was not unusual for the company to hire machinists "off the street" with little or no experience. Even experienced machinists made mistakes, and the company did not require all machinists in the shop to be able to perform on all the machines. The union contended that not more than two or three machinists in the shop were competent to perform job assignments on all of the machines. The union claimed that the company's allegations of lack of job abilities concerning Wright were used as a pretext against Wright because he was a black man.

The union pointed out that Wright had had about four years' prior work experience in several other metal fabricating plants working as a machine operator, machinist's helper, and assistant machine repairman. On those jobs he had operated several of the same machines on which he had been working at Paccar. In other words, he was not inexperienced at the time he came to the company, and he had performed capably at his previous employers.

The union produced three witnesses on behalf of Wright. The first was the business representative of the international union who stated that he felt that the company did not employ enough minorities. Only one black currently was employed in the machine shop. On the other hand, the business representative had no personal knowledge of Wright's own job performance and ability. A second witness was an employee who had worked as a machinist for the company for 10 years and who was the fair employment practices chairman in the union. He stated that the company had not employed sufficient minority workers; but he did not charge that the company had discriminated against Wright. The third union witness was also a machinist and a member of the union's bargaining committee which represented Wright at the third step of the grievance procedure. He also made no specific charge of discrimination. However, he disagreed with the company on Wright's performance, holding that his work as a probationary employee was satisfactory. He stated that while he made this evaluation of Wright's performance, he had little occasion to observe his work. However, he said that he had spoken with several machinists in Wright's department, all of whom said that Wright's work met at least minimum standards, and some of whom said that it was about average. All three witnesses held that in their opinion, Wright was a qualified machinist who had been unjustly terminated during his probationary period for alleged "poor performance." Although none made any specific allegations of discrimination, they believed that Wright deserved to be retained as a machinist since they felt he was as capable as other men who had passed the probationary period.

Wright testified on his own behalf. He contended that he was a qualified machinist, that he met at least the minimum standards of performance on his job assignments, and that he performed as well as other probationary employees. He made no allegations of specific acts of discrimination against him, but he insisted that he was qualified to do the work of a machinist in the company. He felt that he had been unfairly terminated because he was black.

The union sought reinstatement of Robert Wright with full back pay, seniority from the date of hire, and all other benefits and rights he would have accrued, had he not been terminated discriminatorily by the company.

POSITION OF THE COMPANY

The company argued that the union had failed to prove that Wright's termination was the result of discrimination. According to the company, the union did not demonstrate that Wright's job performance satisfied the company's normal work requirements for either a probationary or permanent machinist. The company held that Wright's work performance during his probationary period was unsatisfactory. Hellwig stated that Wright was unable to take a job from start to finish and produce acceptable parts. According to Hellwig, Wright seemed unable to operate the machines at safe speeds and with proper feeds. Wright was responsible for scrapping several valuable parts on which he had worked because he was unable to read the micrometers and work to close tolerances. Further, Wright had trouble reading blueprints, and he was unable to lay out a sequence of machine operations from a blueprint. Hellwig also stated that Wright required more help than other probationary employees in setting up his job. Wright's productivity was lower than that of other probationary employees, and more of his production required scrapping or reworking than that of other probationary workers. Because of all of this, Hellwig said that he decided that Wright could not handle the machinist's job.

The company pointed out that Hellwig had had the primary responsibility for probationary employees in the machine shop during the past five years. During that time, he had recommended termination of five white probationary employees. Wright was the first and the only black to be dismissed by Hellwig during that period. One other black had been hired into the machine shop; he had successfully completed the probationary period under a prior foreman to Hellwig.

The company introduced as evidence of Wright's unsatisfactory performance a copy of Hellwig's 25-day and 55-day written evaluations in support of the decision by Hellwig and Davisson to terminate him. These reports cited Wright's deficiencies, including his inability to read blueprints, to establish work procedures from "hard prints," a lack of ability to set up machines, a failure to operate machines at correct speeds and feeds, his inability to read micrometers and other measuring instruments accurately, and his production of abnormally large amounts of substandard work.

The company argued that its decision to terminate Robert Wright was based solely on his unsatisfactory performance as a probationary employee. Thus, the company had the right to terminate Wright under Article VI of the labor agreement. The company requested that the arbitrator deny the grievance.

APPENDIX

Relevant Provisions of the Contract

ARTICLE V—NONDISCRIMINATION

The Company and the Union subscribe to the principles of equal economic opportunity and nondiscrimination.

The provisions of the agreement will be carried out without regard to an employee's race, color, creed, national origin, sex, handicap, or age.

When reference is made to the masculine gender in this contract, it refers to male or female, whichever is applicable.

ARTICLE VI—SENIORITY

Section 1.   New employees shall be required to serve a probationary period of sixty (60) days during which the Company shall judge their qualifications. When an employee has accumulated sixty (60) days service with the Company, his seniority shall be established as of his original date of employment. The discharge or layoff of any employee during the probationary period shall not be subject to the provisions of the Grievance Procedure, unless during his probationary period the employee alleges the discharge or layoff was due to discrimination.

QUESTIONS

1. Evaluate the contentions of the union made on behalf of Robert Wright. Why is it sometimes difficult for a union and/or person to "prove" discriminatory intent in a case such as this?
2. Evaluate the position of the company. Why is it sometimes difficult for a company management to "prove" that it did not discriminate in a case such as this?
3. Is the fact that there was only one black machinist employee in the company a relevant factor in the arbitrator's decision? Why, or why not?
4. Might the Equal Employment Opportunity Commission (EEOC) use different standards in a case of this sort? Discuss.
5. Compare this case with Case 57, "No Date, No Job" for similarities and differences.

57. NO DATE, NO JOB?

Company: Paccar, Inc., Kansas City Division
Union: United Automobile, Aerospace and Agricultural
Implement Workers of America, Local 710

BACKGROUND

Sarah Sears[1] had been hired by Paccar, Inc., on March 27, 1978, as a frame shop assembler. Paccar, Inc., manufactured heavy-duty highway trucks. The company operated a plant in Kansas City which employed about 800 hourly employees; 12 employees were frame shop assemblers.

On May 24, 1978, after 59 days of total service, Sara Sears filed a grievance claiming that she was unjustly terminated one day before the conclusion of her probationary period because she repeatedly refused to date and party with her male foreman, John Tyler during nonworking hours.

Sears's job consisted of obtaining air tanks from a rack nearby and installing them. These tanks were attached to the frame of the trucks that passed on the assembly line in front of her.

John Tyler was hired two weeks after Sears. His supervisor was David Keldkamp, who was the general foreman of the frame line.

Five days before the conclusion of Sears's 60-day probationary period, Tyler and Keldkamp met to discuss Sears's job performance. They agreed that Sears did not satisfactorily perform her job; and on May 24, 1978, Tyler terminated her.

In her grievance, Sears alleged that the company had engaged in sex discrimination by firing her because she had refused to date or party with her supervisor. The union asked that Sears should be reinstated to her job with back pay and all other benefits, and that

---

[1] The names of all individuals have been disguised.

Tyler should be transferred and/or ordered to stop harassing and discriminating against her.

POSITION OF THE UNION

The union contended that Sarah Sears was terminated solely because she refused to socialize with foreman John Tyler after work. The union further took the position that the company had an obligation to make sure that male employees in managerial positions did not harass or exploit their female employees.[2]

Sears alleged that on several occasions Tyler telephoned her at home to make a date to go dancing or attend a movie. She always refused these requests. She added that on the day following his telephone calls, Tyler would confront her at work about her refusal to go out with him. Further, Tyler repeatedly offered to drive her home after work or tried to induce her to join him for a "quick drink" at a bar near the plant before going home. Sears said that she refused all his "overtures." She stated that following each refusal, Tyler would harass her on the job. He would sometimes step on the air hose which supplied power to her tools, hide her tools, touch her body, and make suggestive sexual remarks. She charged that his behavior caused her great emotional stress and interfered with her ability to keep pace with the work.

The union stated that whenever Sears refused to go out with Tyler, he went out of his way to impede her work performance. The union called two employees to testify about Tyler's behavior, Edward Jones and Clement Tomas.

Jones worked in the frame shop with Sears and testified that he saw Tyler step on Sears's air hose causing work problems for her on one occasion. He stated also that Tyler several times moved trucks on the assembly line while women were working in them but not when male employees were in them.

Tomas was a member of the union bargaining committee that investigated Sears's grievance. He stated that on one occasion he saw Tyler step on Sears's pneumatic hose causing a power wrench to be pulled from her grasp. He also testified that another female employee had complained that she was "having trouble" with Tyler.

The union pointed out that neither Tyler nor Keldkamp had notified the union steward that Sears was experiencing work problems during her probationary period. The union said that this "was customary, although not required." When the union learned that

---

[2] See Appendix to this case for relevant provisions of the contract.

Sears had been terminated, the union tried to obtain an extension of her probationary period, but this was refused.

The union urged that Sears's grievance be sustained in full by the arbitrator.

POSITION OF THE COMPANY

The company stated that this case involved the discharge of a probationary employee in which the company acted reasonably. It was not a case of wrongful discharge in which the company would be required to prove "just and proper" cause. The burden of proof was upon the union to show that the company acted unreasonably based upon the preponderance of the evidence, or that the company had engaged in illegal sex discrimination.

The company contended that the evidence did not support Sarah Sears's allegation that it had discriminated against her. When Sears was questioned about the specifics, such as time, place, and circumstances concerning the proposals made to her by Tyler, she could not provide them. John Tyler testified that he was engaged to be married and was seeing his fiancee on a daily basis during the time he was alleged to have been pursuing Sears. Tyler was married one month after Sears was terminated.

The company further argued that it could not be expected to take corrective action if it were unaware of the situation. What two people did off the job was not the legitimate concern of the company. If some of the trials and tribulations of an off-the-job courtship carried over into the workplace, there was little that the company could do about it. It would be unreasonable to expect an employer to police the workplace for "all signs of a courtship gone sour or revenge by a rejected suitor." If Sears was being harassed by Tyler, she should have informed her union steward who could have filed a grievance in accordance with the provisions of the collective bargaining agreement. This Sears failed to do.

The company contended that the testimony of both Jones and Tomas should be dismissed. Both admitted that they had no knowledge of Tyler ever having asked Sears for a date or having solicited her companionship in any way. While Tyler may have been guilty of some misconduct in stepping on her pneumatic hose, this should not sustain a sex discrimination charge.

The company stated that Sears was terminated because her work had been unsatisfactory. Keldkamp stated that he recommended that she be terminated because she was not mechanically adaptable. He testified that Sears had problems with the tools she was using on the job, including problems with recognition of wrench and socket sizes. She was often far behind in performing the tasks assigned her, she required frequent help to catch up, and she had caused the production line to be slowed on numerous occasions.

Finally, the company argued that under the contract, during an employee's probationary period a company could terminate marginal performers before they became regular employees with job security and seniority rights. The right of management to discharge probationary employees before they became full-time employees was protected by the labor agreement, and this was essential in order to maintain a productive labor force. This right should not be eroded because of an unsubstantiated sex discrimination charge filed by Sears.

The company requested that based on the facts of the situation, the grievance be denied.

APPENDIX

Relevant Provisions of the Contract

ARTICLE V—NONDISCRIMINATION

The Company and the Union subscribe to the principles of equal economic opportunity and nondiscrimination.

The provisions of the agreement will be carried out without regard to an employee's race, color, creed, national origin, sex, handicap, or age.

When reference is made to the masculine gender in this contract, it refers to male or female, whichever is applicable.

ARTICLE VI—SENIORITY

Section 1.   New employees shall be required to serve a probationary period of sixty (60) days during which the Company shall judge their qualifications. When an employee has accumulated sixty (60) days service with the Company, his seniority shall be established as of his original date of employment. The discharge or layoff of any employee during the probationary period shall not be subject to the provisions of the Grievance Procedure, unless during his probationary period the employee alleges the discharge or layoff was due to discrimination.

QUESTIONS

1.   Is the burden of proof on the union to "prove" Sara Sears's charge of sex discrimination? Discuss.

2. Could Sears also file charges of sex discrimination with the Equal Employment Opportunity Commission (EEOC) under the Civil Rights Act? Might the EEOC require a different burden of proof than would an arbitrator?

3. Why should a supervisor (in this case a male) generally avoid becoming involved in an off-the-job relationship with an employee of the opposite sex (in this case a female)?

4. Compare the issues in this case with those in Case 63, "A Weighty Problem," for similarities and differences.

58. TO PROMOTE, OR HIRE FROM THE OUTSIDE?

Company: Rotek, Incorporated, Aurora, Illinois

Union: Union Steelworkers of America, Local 8565

BACKGROUND

Rotek, Incorporated, employed approximately 60 bargaining unit employees at its Aurora plant and 51 employees at its Ravenna, Illinois, plant. Employees from both plants were in the same collective bargaining unit represented by Local 8565 of the United Steelworkers of America. The company manufactured large bearings used primarily in construction equipment and other industrial applications.

Under the labor agreement, the company had a system for posting permanent job openings for bids. On September 13, 1978, the company posted an electrician (maintenance) job (hereafter to be called electrician) for bid. James Snover[1] and 18 other employees bid on this job; Snover was the most senior bidder.

Snover and two of the other bidders held jobs which were classified as "general maintenance men." As a general maintenance man, Snover's primary duties consisted of piping, machinery setup, general repair, and electrical wiring. Snover had worked for the company for 10 years. Prior to that, he was employed for two years in home construction work, three years in industrial maintenance at a plant in Pittsburgh, and one year as an electrical repairman for a small plant.

The electrician job at Rotek required knowledge and training sufficient to install and maintain sophisticated machine tool equipment. Electricians also were required to maintain complicated heating and

---

[1] The names of all individuals have been disguised.

air-conditioning equipment and to be generally familiar with all phases of electrical work.

The job opening, as required by the job posting provisions of the agreement,[2] remained posted for three working days. Thereafter, the qualifications of all bidders were thoroughly reviewed. They were initially reviewed by Elaine Evans, personnel administrator, who pulled records of all the bidders and reviewed them for past experience and formal training. The records were then reviewed by David Shulman, manager of industrial relations, to determine if there were employees who were presently qualified or who could become qualified during a 45-day training period referred to in the labor agreement. In addition, Schulman consulted with the plant engineers of both the Ravenna and Aurora plants for their advice concerning whether any of the bidders were qualified through experience they had acquired on the job. Both plant managers said that none of the bidders were qualified. As a result of the review of the records and the consultations with the plant engineers, Schulman determined that none of the job bidders was presently qualified and none was trainable.

On October 3, 1978, Schulman notified the chairman of the union's grievance committee, Herbert Dart, that the company intended to fill the opening from the outside. Two days later, the local union president, Robert Bono, was so notified by Elaine Evans. James Snover, the senior bidder, was not notified.

The company then took the necessary steps to fill the opening from the outside, including conducting job interviews and reviewing job applications. It hired a new employee, Frank Borden, to fill the electrician's job; he reported for work on October 16, 1978. Snover did not know until that time that his bid had been rejected.

On October 18, 1978, Snover submitted a verbal complaint to the Aurora plant engineer, pursuant to step 1 of the grievance procedure outlined in the labor agreement. Subsequently, Snover submitted a grievance in writing on October 20, 1978, which was required at step 3 of the grievance procedure. Snover's grievance stated as follows:

> I, the undersigned feel I have been denied the opportunity according to Article 3, Section 3.3, Paragraph (b), and Article 6, Section 6.1. The company has unjustly denied me a benefit arising out of my job. The company has violated a specified, express term of this agreement.
> SETTLEMENT REQUESTED IN GRIEVANCE. To receive the job that was posted (electrician/maintenance) and retroactive back pay from 10/16/78 till this grievance is settled.

---

[2] See Appendix to this case for relevant provisions of the contract.

AGREEMENT VIOLATION Article 3, Section 3.3, Paragraph (b), and Article 6, Section 6.1.

At step 2 and all succeeding written answers, the company took the position that there was no violation of the labor agreement, but regardless, "In any event, the grievance was filed untimely." The grievance eventually was submitted to arbitration.

POSITION OF THE UNION

A. Timeliness

The union argued that the grievance was timely because the company's violation was a continuing one. The union contended that Snover's grievance was filed within the five-day limitation. It cited Article VI, Section 6.1, of the agreement, which used the phrase "after the rise thereof." The word *thereof* refers to the complaining person's "complaint." Thus, the question was: When was the "rise" of the complaint? The union maintained that it arose on October 16, when Frank Borden, the new employee reported for work; it was only then that Snover knew that his job bid had been rejected.

In contradiction of the company's claim that it was past practice not to notify employees that their job bids had been rejected, the union claimed that the company had been inconsistent on this. The union contended that the company did not always hire from the outside when it indicated that it was going to do so. Finally, the union pointed out that following the filing of this grievance, the company began posting its decisions on employee job bids.

B. Merits

As to the merits of the company decision to reject Snover's bid for the job, the union contended that the company had acted arbitrarily when it decided that Snover was not qualified and not trainable for the job opening of an electrician. Snover was the senior bidder with 10 years of service to the company. His past job experiences both with the company and prior to joining the company were similar in nature to the duties of the electrician/maintenance position. He had always been a good employee, and he had never received any disciplinary actions concerning his work performance.

The union claimed that Snover's seniority rights were being totally ignored by the company in this decision. The company had violated Snover's contractual rights by not affording him the training and trial

368

period prescribed in the labor agreement. Snover could possibly have met the company's job requirements had he been given the right to a trial period.

The union claimed that the company should be required to promote James B. Snover to the position of electrician retroactive to October 16, 1979, and be made whole for all wages, and other rights and benefits lost as a result of the company's failure to award the position to him, at least on a trial basis.

POSITION OF THE COMPANY

A. Timeliness

The company claimed that Snover's grievance was not timely, and that the matter, therefore, was not arbitrable. Schulman had notified the chairman of the union's grievance committee on October 3 that none of the candidates was qualified to fill the position of electrician, and that the company planned to hire an electrician from outside. In addition, Elaine Evans gave the same notice to the local union president on October 5. The company had fully met its responsibility to Snover by notifying the union of its plan to recruit an electrician from outside the company, since none of the interested employees were qualified or qualifiable within the 45-day training period specified in Section 3.2(b) of the contract. Since Snover did not grieve until October 18, the grievance was not timely and should be dismissed.

B. Merits

On the possibility that the arbitrator might rule for the union on the issue of timeliness, the company presented testimony and evidence concerning the merits of the case. The company pointed out that Section 3.3(a) of the labor agreement provided that a job bidder with the greatest seniority, previously meeting the provisions of Sections 3.2(a) and 3.2(b) would be awarded the bid. Section 3.2(a) provided that an employee was qualified for a particular job when he had worked that job for a specified period of time. Since Snover had not worked the electrician's job for the specified period of time, he was not qualified. Therefore, he was not entitled to the bid under the provisions of Section 3.3(a).

Section 3.3(b) provided that if the opening was not filled by a qualified employee, "an opportunity to train for the job will be given to the highest seniority employee bidding and *considered trainable for the job*" (emphasis added). The underlined words were the key words as far as the determination of this case on its merits was concerned. Snover was the highest seniority employee bidding, but was he "considered trainable for the job?"[3]

The company conceded that its decision as to whether Snover was or was not trainable for the job was a decision which was subject to challenge. The company attorney stated:

> It is uniformly agreed that under such language the employer has the right to make the initial determination subject to challenge by the union that the employer's decision was unreasonable, and that where the union challenges management's determination, it has the burden of proving that the employer's evaluation of abilities and qualification was incorrect.

However, the company argued that the position of electrician required an employee who was skilled in advanced applications of electrical and electronic principles. The job required more than just ordinary routine, elementary electrical experience. For example, the job description stated that part of an electrician's duties was to "install and wire centralized control panels." A single control panel might regulate many remote motors in different areas of the plant. The company had never permitted general maintenance personnel to wire centralized control panels. All new machines installed in the plant were equipped with solid state circuitry, and all electricians must "get in on the ground floor" with each machine in order to learn both its basic operation and its idiosyncracies. A high degree of sophisticated knowledge was necessary to perform both installation and maintenance work on new solid state equipment.

The company reviewed Snover's background at the company as a general maintenance man. Part of his duties included general electrical work, such as "trouble shooting" machines for electrical problems. He had performed a variety of tasks, including some electrical work on new machines, but not on any machines involving solid-state circuitry. His experience prior to being employed at the company was as a general house contractor, in finishing and maintenance work for a furniture company, in production and maintenance work for a manufacturing concern in Pennsylvania, and in maintenance work for a feedmill. None of the jobs entailed a great amount of electrical work, and none of them entailed the kind of intricate work that Snover would need to perform at the company as an electrician.

In contrast to the kinds of work that Snover had been performing

---

[3] The parties agreed that this term meant trainable within the time specified in Sections 3.2(a) and 3.2(b).

at the company, the employees who held the position of electrician had performed much more advanced work. The company gave several examples of machinery upon which electricians worked and the type of work they performed. For example, two electricians recently reworked a new German cutoff saw machine so that it would be compatible with American voltage. Another recent project of the electricians was the installation of a new air compressor. In the process of carrying out this assignment, the electricians determined that the compressor had two auxiliary pieces of equipment which were of different voltages, necessitating determining a transformer size able to operate all three pieces of equipment with the available 480 volts. The electricians were able to accomplish this and properly install the equipment. A third recent project involved a problem with a geartooth hardener at the Ravenna plant. The electricians were trying to assure that the machine would be more reliable and not turn out scrap material. They wanted to pick up every other tooth in the gear, and install a counter that would tell the machine that it was going to skip teeth. In order to get the machine to skip teeth, it was necessary for the electricians to cut into a circuit and put a counter into it.

The company admitted that James Snover had assisted the electricians on some of these projects. But his work on many of the machines appeared to be only peripherally involved with straight electrical work. For example, on the new German cutoff saw, he helped mount it on the floor, but it was the two electricians who determined how to rework the machine to be compatible with American voltage. In another instance, Snover helped the electricians in the addition of a 10-foot length of high voltage line within a special raceway located in the ceiling. He helped with the installation of that because of his experience with ironworkers; his experience had made him better qualified than the electricians to ensure that certain articles adhered to the ceiling. However, it was the electricians who determined what articles were needed to complete the project and how they would actually perform the final work on the project.

Finally, the company pointed out that Snover had agreed during discussions of his grievance that it would be necessary for him to take a course at Kent University in order to become adequately knowledgeable of solid-state circuitry and motor controls.

In summary, the company acknowledged that James Snover had been a good, dependable employee. But the company maintained that its managers had fairly assessed that Snover would not be capable of being trained to assume the electrician's job in a 45-day period. Absent any showing by the union to the contrary, the judgment of management should be affirmed and the union grievance should be denied by the arbitrator.

APPENDIX

Relevant Provisions of the Contract

ARTICLE III—SENIORITY, VACANCIES, REASSIGNMENTS, LAYOFFS, AND RELEASES

Section 3.2(a). An employee is qualified to do a particular job or operate a type of machine if the individual has worked at the job or operated the type of machine for forty-five (45) days of the employee's continuous working days, unless the company requests another extension of forty-five (45) continuous working days to qualify. (This extension will be granted in the following classifications: Maintenance, Electrician, Induction Fabricator, and Tool Maker/Machinist.)

(b) These forty-five (45) continuous working days shall be considered a trial period. If an employee shall fail to complete such trial period, either voluntarily or because of a company decision, the employee may return to the previous job in which said employee was qualified, provided an extension hasn't been granted as the provisions of Article III—Section 3.2, Paragraph (a), are fulfilled.

Section 3.3(a). If a permanent job opening occurs, the employee with the greatest seniority, previously meeting the provisions of Article III—Section 2, Paragraphs (a) and (b), and having bid the job, will be chosen over other bidders.

(b) If an employee bids for a permanent job opening and has not previously met the provisions of Article III—Section 2, Paragraphs (a) and (b), and such job is not filled by a qualified employee with more seniority, an opportunity to train for the job will be given to the highest seniority employee bidding and considered trainable for the job.

ARTICLE VI—GRIEVANCES AND ARBITRATIONS

Section 6.1 A grievance is defined as a complaint by any member of the union, covered by this Agreement, or by the union in its own behalf, that the company has violated a specified, express term of this Agreement, or that it has unjustly denied any employee his/her job contrary to the terms thereof, or has denied any employee any benefit arising out of his/her job. Such a complaint shall be treated in the following manner. With one (1) exception, suspensions pending discharge, such grievances shall proceed to step 4 of the procedure, after first lodging a complaint within the five (5) day period.

Step 1. The complaining party shall first lodge the complaint with his/her immediate supervisor within five (5) days after the rise thereof (wage claims excepted). . . . Failure to file a complaint within the time limitations set forth by this Article shall operate to nullify the complaint, without recourse.

QUESTIONS

1. Was the grievance filed in a timely fashion as required by the labor agreement? Discuss.
   On the assumption that the arbitrator would rule that the grievance was arbitrable:
2. Evaluate the facts and arguments presented by the union on behalf of grievant Snover.
3. Evaluate the facts and arguments presented by the company in support of its position.
4. Some arbitrators have advocated the use of the "head-and-shoulders concept" in deciding cases such as this. This concept suggests that a senior employee should be given an opportunity to fill a higher level job, unless the junior seniority employee or an outside person is significantly superior (i.e., head and shoulders above) the senior employee in merit, ability, and/or potential. Would this concept be applicable in this case? Why, or why not?
5. Compare the issues in this case with those in Case 44, "The Bypassed Senior Clerk."

59. WHO MUST PAY FOR THE SAFETY SHOES?

Company: Hater Industries, Inc., Cincinnati, Ohio

Union: United Steelworkers of America, Local 310

BACKGROUND

On May 17, 1978, Charles Mulhaney[1] filed the following grievance on behalf of Local 310 of the union:

> The United Steelworkers of America, Local 310, claim that the Company violated Article XV, Section 1—Safety and Health—of the Basic Agreement when it failed to furnish the safety equipment specified by OSHA.[2]

During steps of the grievance procedure, the company made the following reply to the union:

> Due to the fact that the Union agrees there is nothing in the collective bargaining agreement requiring the Company to pay for shoes, and that the Company has never in the past paid for safety equipment which employees are allowed to keep for their personal use, therefore, the Company has no obligation to pay for the shoes.

The parties were unable to resolve their differences and submitted the following statement of the issue to an arbitrator for final determination:

> Has the Company violated the Agreement between the parties by refusing to pay for safety shoes which employees must wear pursuant to the requirements of the Occupational Safety and Health Administration, and, if so, to what remedy, if any, are the grievants entitled?

---

[1] The names of all individuals have been disguised.

[2] See Appendix to this case for relevant clause of the contract.

Prior to the current agreement between the company and union, the company had always provided employees with certain safety equipment. During contract negotiations, the company agreed to continue this practice and to the provisions of Article XV of the agreement.

In January 1978, the Occupational Safety and Health Administration (OSHA) conducted an inspection of the company's facilities. As a result of this inspection, several citations were issued to the company for violations of federal requirements. One such citation was issued because safety shoes with metatarsal guards were not worn by employees working in the abrasive blasting area as a protection against foot injury. The OSHA regulation required that "safety shoes shall be worn to protect against foot injury where heavy pieces of work are handled."[3]

POSITION OF THE UNION

The union argued that the company must furnish the safety shoes required by OSHA regulations. The company's refusal to purchase safety shoes violated Article XV of the agreement between the parties, as well as past practices in the company. The agreement required that the company "must comply with applicable state and federal laws and regulations concerning the health and safety of its employees." In order to conform to the purposes and intentions expressed in Article XV, the company must purchase for its employees the safety shoes which OSHA mandated.

The safety shoes giving rise to this dispute were required by federal regulations. To be in compliance, the company was responsible to see that each employee in the affected areas possessed and used the required safety apparel. An employee's refusal to wear the required shoes would give the company grounds for discipline, including discharge. However, before the company could require employees to wear the required safety shoes, the company must furnish the shoes for the employees' use.

The union claimed that the company had always provided employees with necessary safety apparel in the past. For example, the company had supplied employees with aprons, gloves, rubber boots, safety glasses, and goggles. These items were paid for by the company at no expense to the employee. Where safety equipment was necessary, the company had also provided it. In the present instance, safety shoes had become necessary by law; thus it was the

---

[3] 29CFR19.0.94(a) (5) (v).

company's obligation to provide the shoes consistent with the agreement and long-standing past practices.

The grievance should be sustained.

POSITION OF THE COMPANY

The company maintained that the agreement between the parties did not require it to pay for employees' safety shoes. Further, neither the company's past practices nor OSHA regulations imposed this financial burden upon it.

The agreement between the parties required company compliance with all federal and state laws and regulations. However, the OSHA regulation for which the company received a citation required only that the company must assure that appropriate safety shoes were worn in compliance with the standard. But OSHA did not require that the company must pay for safety shoes to be worn by employees on the job.

In this regard, the company claimed that at no time was the company ever advised by OSHA that it was required to purchase safety shoes for its employees. Nor had the law ever been interpreted to require a company's purchasing of safety shoes. The company had been assured that its obligation was to make certain that safety shoes were worn by the employees working in specific areas of the plant. Thus, the company had no statutory nor regulatory obligation to purchase protective footwear for employees.

The company argued that the agreement between the parties did not require the company to pay for safety shoes which were required pursuant to OSHA regulations. Since the contract was silent concerning the purchasing of personal safety items, the company was not obligated to assume the cost of such items. The financial burden of protective wear was an item which was open for collective bargaining.

During previous contract negotiations between the parties, the union had proposed a provision to be added to the contract whereby the company would assume the cost of safety wear. However, the company rejected such a provision. The agreed-upon article (Article XV) did not require the company to purchase personal safety wear for its employees. Thus, it was clear that the company did not intend to be responsible for buying safety wear, and the union was clearly on notice of this position of the company.

Finally, the company contended that the practice of supplying certain safety items to the employees did not bind the company to supply safety shoes as well. The footwear required by OSHA was a personal item to the employee; these shoes could be worn at times which were of no benefit to the company. Supplying such an item differed greatly from the company's practice of supplying safety gloves, aprons, and glasses to employees. The company pointed out that it had consistently refused to be responsible for the purchase of personal safety items such as prescriptive safety glasses.

In summary, the company claimed that the union was attempting through this grievance to gain a benefit for the members which it had not been able to gain through negotiations. The company urged the arbitrator to deny the grievance.

APPENDIX

Relevant Clause of the Contract

ARTICLE XV—SAFETY AND HEALTH

Section 1. The company shall continue to make reasonable efforts to maintain its equipment and facilities in a safe operating condition. The company will also make reasonable efforts to maintain clean premises, and employees shall cooperate in keeping all facilities in a clean condition. Management alone may determine the specific means by which a safety hazard shall be corrected or eliminated, including closing such department or area. Employees must abide by management's health and safety rules, and misuse or disregard of safety devices or equipment are grounds for discipline including discharge. The company will comply with applicable state and federal laws and regulations concerning the health and safety of its employees.

QUESTIONS

1. Did Article XV of the agreement mandate that the company must pay the costs of the safety shoes under the circumstances of this case? Why, or why not?
2. Were the past practices in the company regarding safety equipment more supportive of the union's or the company's position? Discuss.
3. Was the union attempting to achieve through arbitration what it had failed to achieve at the bargaining table?
4. What are the precedent implications of the arbitrator's decision in this case?

60. WHO'S TELLING THE TRUTH?

Company: National Car Rental System, Inc., East Boston, Massachusetts

Union: International Brotherhood of Teamsters, Chauffeurs, Warehousemen and Helpers of America, Local 841

BACKGROUND

National Car Rental System, Inc., was in the business of renting out cars. The company operated a major facility near Logan Airport in East Boston, Massachusetts. Preparation of cars for rental took place in the firm's main car wash bay, which was a large building with a central heating system. During the winter months, employees often set the thermostat as high as 90°F. to keep the bay warm while they were working. This practice consumed a large amount of energy and kept the bay area warmer than necessary.

Because of the energy crisis which brought on a shortage and rapidly escalating cost of oil early in 1978, the company turned down the thermostat in the car wash bay to 72°F and requested employees not to change this setting. Some employees ignored this request and continued to turn the thermostat up to 90°F. Finally, on March 17, 1978, Peter Walton[1] the assistant manager, set the thermostat at 72°F and installed a lock box on the thermostat to prevent continued misuse. He also posted the following notice on several company bulletin boards:

> The lock box and thermostat in the bay are not to be touched. The heat is set at the proper temperature and must not be altered.
>
> If I find this unit tampered with again, I will shut off the heat altogether.
>
> Also, if I catch you touching the unit you will be terminated.

---

[1] Names of all individuals have been disguised.

This notice was posted and a locked plastic box placed over the thermostat to prevent vandalism to the thermostat.

At about 4:30 P.M. on December 27, 1978, Walton noticed that the doors to the main car wash bay were open and letting in the cold air. As he entered the bay through the open doors he observed two employees, John Bosworth and Melvin Ziegler, standing in front of the thermostat about 20 feet away. Bosworth was holding a straightened metal coat hanger, a newspaper, and other trash. Peter Walton then thought he saw Bosworth insert the hanger into the locked plastic box and tamper with the thermostat. Walton shouted at both men to stop tampering with the thermostat, whereupon they turned around and stared at him apparently startled by his voice. Walton then proceeded to walk toward them. When Walton got nearer, he noticed that the lock box had been cracked and the temperature setting changed to a setting of 85°F. Walton then escorted Bosworth to the shift manager's office and questioned him about the incident.

Bosworth stated that he had reported for work at 4:15 P.M. and immediately had started cleaning cars. He said that he and Ziegler had got to talking about the temperature in the bay, so they walked over to the thermostat to "check it out." Bosworth said he was still holding a coat hanger, a newspaper, and other trash that he had removed from one of the cars, when Walton walked into the bay. Bosworth claimed that he was merely checking the temperature, and that he did not insert the coat hanger into the locked box, did not break it, and did not change the thermostat setting in any way.

Bosworth admitted that he had read the notice dated March 17, 1978, prohibiting any tampering with the thermostat or its locked protective covering. He also stated that he knew that violators would be discharged.

John Bosworth was a 25-year-old high school graduate when he was hired in 1977. He had held various unskilled and semiskilled jobs in Boston and Hawaii before being hired as a service agent. His duties as a service agent included cleaning the interiors of rental cars, operating the mechanical car wash equipment, checking for certain deficiencies and defects, and checking gasoline, oil, water, and air levels.

His personnel records indicated the following prior disciplinary actions by the company: (1) June 27, 1977—verbal warning for being late for work on four days out of five during one week; and (2) October 27, 1978—three-day suspension for "screeching tires while exiting the bay."

Walton did not believe Bosworth's story, and after reviewing his employment record at National Car Rental, Walton discharged him. The discharge notice included the following reasons:

12/17/78.   Bosworth was observed using a coat hanger to lower the thermostat inside the service bay. Locks had been put on these thermostats so that no one would tamper with them.

Previous misuse of company property by Bosworth happened on 10/27/78.

The union filed a grievance on behalf of John Bosworth protesting his discharge and requesting reinstatement with restoration of full back pay, seniority, and any other benefits.

POSITION OF THE COMPANY

The company argued that Bosworth was "caught red handed" tampering with the lock box that covered the thermostat. Manager Peter Walton should be believed because there was no reason for him to fabricate such a story. Both Bosworth and Ziegler had a self-interest in denying that Bosworth had tampered with the temperature setting on the thermostat.

The company pointed out that Bosworth had a poor employment history including a warning for excessive tardiness and a suspension for misuse of company property. Bosworth was clearly aware of the regulation prohibiting tampering with the thermostat, which warned of termination for violation.

In response to Bosworth's and Ziegler's statements about their work activities, the company contended that there was no reason for Bosworth to be carrying the trash items which he held when Walton observed him near the thermostat. Trash items removed from cars were to be thrown on the floor or in a trash bin to be removed at the end of the shift. It was more logical to conclude that Bosworth deliberately carried the metal coat hanger (and other trash items) to the thermostat with the intention of using the hanger to crack the plastic box over the thermostat.

The company claimed that it had ample "just cause" to discharge John Bosworth, under a contractual provision which required that disciplinary actions taken by the company must be for "just cause." Bosworth was observed by a manager engaging in an act which he and other employees had been notified would lead to their termination. The discharge action should be sustained, and the union grievance should be denied.

POSITION OF THE UNION

The union did not contest the company's right to post the notice which Peter Walton had posted on March 17, 1978. The union acknowledged that the reason for this company action was to conserve fuel consumption and energy costs.

However, the union stated that the company had failed to meet the required burden of proof that Bosworth had violated a company regulation by tampering with the thermostat. Both Bosworth and Ziegler were doing nothing more than standing in front of the thermostat to check the temperature when Walton entered the car wash bay. Ziegler, who was standing next to Bosworth when the incident occurred, had a clear view of what was going on, and he testified that Bosworth did not tamper with the thermostat. Ziegler also confirmed Bosworth's statement that the clothes hanger was part of the trash removed from the rental cars, and that it had not been used to vandalize the lock box. The union claimed that Bosworth and Ziegler had told the truth, and the company should accept their statement of events as true. Obviously, someone else had tampered with the thermostat, not Bosworth as claimed by the company.

In addition, the entrance to the bay was 20 feet from the thermostat. Walton could not possibly have seen a thin metal hanger at that distance. It was even more unlikely that he could have seen the hanger inserted into the thermostat, since both Bosworth and Ziegler were standing in front of it with their backs to him.

In summary, the company did not adequately prove that Bosworth had tampered with the thermostat. Therefore, Bosworth should be returned to his job, and be made whole for all monies and benefits lost as a result of the company's action.

QUESTIONS

1. Discuss the burden of proof issue which is a central aspect of this case. Why do arbitrators generally place a heavier burden of proof requirement upon the management side in discharge cases?

2. How can the arbitrator resolve the conflict in testimony between the union and company witnesses?

3. If the arbitrator should resolve the credibility quesiton in favor of the testimony of Walton, was the infraction involved serious enough to sustain the discharge of Bosworth? Why, or why not?

61. A DISCIPLINARY WARNING TO THE UNION PRESIDENT

Company: Reichhold, Chemicals, Incorporated, Grand Junction, Tennessee

Union: United Rubber, Cork, Linoleum and Plastic Workers of America, Local 672

BACKGROUND

The management at the Grand Junction plant had watched employees gradually stretch their breaks to the point where the practice was affecting morale, costs, and productivity. In order to regain control over the length of employee breaks, the company instituted a rule requiring employees to punch out and in on lunch periods and authorized breaks. A petition had been circulated among the employees challenging the propriety of the rule. The union president, Rodney Jacobs,[1] appeared at the office of the foreman, Lenny Walker, with the petition fastened to a grievance on Monday, April 30, 1979, shortly before 3:30 P.M. when he was scheduled to start his shift. He requested an immediate grievance meeting. Walker contacted the plant superintendent, Robert A. Yehle, who reminded the union president that he had bypassed step 1 of the grievance procedure; but Yehle agreed to meet on Tuesday, May 2, at 3 P.M. Jacobs was not satisfied with this but went to his job at 3:30 P.M.

At about 3:35 P.M. Jacobs returned to Walker's office with Bill Sperry, vice president of the union. He demanded, "We want to have the meeting now." The plant manager, Edward Arnold, was tied up in a conference with two of his superiors from the headquarters office and was unavailable. After checking with all management personnel involved, Walker and Yehle told the union officers that no meeting could be arranged, and that they would have to abide by the contract by first having the employees take this matter up with their

---

[1] The names of all individuals have been disguised.

foremen. Jacobs replied that Yehle could go to the foremen for them. Yehle explained to Jacobs that he was mistaken. When Jacobs and Sperry then tried to push their way into the plant manager's office, Yehle instead directed them into foreman Walker's office. Yehle tried to convince Jacobs that he should follow standard procedures, to which Jacobs replied that he could confer with the plant manager any time he wished. After further discussion, Jacobs agreed to meet with Yehle on May 2, as had been originally planned. However, they then postponed the meeting to the next day, May 3, at 3 P.M. in order that they could also discuss a different grievance that had been filed by another employee, Willis Jones.

The May 3 grievance meeting began at 3 P.M. as scheduled. Although several members of the union grievance committee were present, Yehle was the only company representative in attendance. It was anticipated that the meeting would last only about 30 minutes and that Jacobs would be back at work as a "relief man" at the start of his shift at 3:30 P.M. A short time prior to the meeting, Jacobs's foreman, Lenny Walker, told him that his attendance at the grievance meeting had been approved. Walker did not obtain a substitute relief man, however, since he expected Jacobs to report for work at the start of the shift.

The Jones's grievance was quickly disposed of. Jacobs then asked Yehle to present the April 30 petition and grievance to the plant manager. Yehle informed the union committee members that he would not do so because the petition and grievance had not been properly presented through the established channels. At the close of the meeting, Yehle signed Jacobs's timecard, indicating that the meeting had ended at 3:30 P.M.

After leaving Yehle's office, Jacobs talked briefly with the other members of the union grievance committee, and then went to the plant manager's office. He presented the April 30 grievance to Arnold, explaining that Yehle had refused to do so. At that point, Yehle entered Arnold's office looking for Jacobs. Upon seeing Jacobs talking with Arnold, Yehle told Jacobs that his foreman had expected him to be at work and was looking for him. Jacobs did not leave, but rather asked Arnold to give him a written acknowledgement of having either accepted or rejected the grievance. Arnold supported Yehle's position in stating that it had not been properly processed, and that he would not initial it. Jacobs left Arnold's office at about 4:10 P.M. and returned to his job.

Shortly after Jacobs reported for work on the following day, his foreman handed him a written reprimand for having absented himself from his job on the previous day without permission from 3:30 to 4:10 P.M.

The union immediately filed a grievance in which it requested that the company remove the written reprimand from Jacobs's records. The parties were unable to resolve their dispute, and the union carried the grievance to arbitration. The union and company were unable to agree upon a statement of the issue that they wished the arbitrator to resolve. The company proposed the following:

> Did the company violate the contract by giving Jacobs a warning on or about May 3, 1979? If so, what should the remedy be?

The union declined to accept the company's statement of the issue and offered instead:

> Was the disciplinary warning given Jacobs on May 3, 1979, just and proper? If not, what should the remedy be?

POSITION OF THE COMPANY

The company charged that Jacobs possessed a distorted notion as to his role in employee relations. The company claimed that the petition presented by Jacobs had been drafted and circulated by him as a means of challenging the company's authority. Company witnesses cited several examples of Jacobs's behavior to support the company's position. For example, on April 30 when his foreman warned him not to be off the job and said, "If you do, we will be forced to take disciplinary action," Jacobs retorted without hesitation, "We'll see." Similarly, on May 3, Jacobs told his foreman, "I can come up and see the plant manager anytime I want to." At the same meeting, when asked if he had permission to be off the job, he responded with, "No, I didn't think that it was necessary."

The company claimed that during the grievance meeting on May 3, Jacobs stated that he was personally going to "try" the company, and that he planned to pick out something he was assigned to do, and then refuse to do it. Then after Yehle refused to waive step 1 of the grievance procedure and to accept the list of names on the petition as a grievance, Jacobs announced that he was left with no alternative other than to go to Arnold. In fact, he had many alternatives, including going back to step 1 and following the orderly steps of the grievance procedure without interfering with normal plant activities. But this would have been too tame for Jacobs. He preferred to go to Arnold immediately and complain because Yehle would not waive the contractual rights of the company.

The company contended that the arbitrator possessed no basis for upholding the grievance. Article II, Section 1, of the contract stated that the company retained all the functions, powers, and authority not specifically abridged, delegated, or relinquished by the contract.

Except for the prohibition of discrimination contained in Article III, Section 6, the only limitation in the contract on the company's disciplinary authority was in Article V which required that suspensions (including layoff) and discharges be given justly. The contract contained no such standard for the issuance of a warning or reprimand. Further, Article III, Section 4, prohibited the arbitrator from adding to or altering any clause in the contract. Thus the arbitrator did not possess the authority to find that the company violated any clause in the contract in issuing a warning to Jacobs.

For all of these reasons, the company requested that the arbitrator deny Jacobs's grievance.

POSITION OF THE UNION

The union argued that all types of disciplinary action taken by the company against an employee could only be for just cause. The company was in error in contending that Article V required only that suspension or discharge must meet the standard of fairness. Verbal warnings or any other form of discipline which may subsequently become the foundation or justification for suspension or discharge must also as a matter of logic be only for just cause.

The union contended that the plant manager, Edward Arnold, had encouraged union officers, including Jacobs, to bring any problems that they could not resolve at lower levels to him for additional discussion and resolution. In several such statements to union leaders, Arnold had placed no limits on the type or scope of issues or problems that he would be willing to discuss with them in this manner.

The union claimed that Article XI, Section 17, included union representatives other than stewards, including the union president, when conducting union business with the company. The language of Article XI, Section 17, required only that a foreman be notified when a union representative must obtain permission from a foreman before leaving the job to investigate a grievance. The union opposed any change in the language of the section. Thus, it was clear that it was not necessary for Jacobs to obtain permission from his foreman to be absent from his work. It was only necessary that he notify his foreman of his need to be away on union business with the company. The company was using Jacobs and this grievance to obtain through arbitration that which it had been unable to obtain through negotiation.

The union pointed out that company rules listed "leaving assigned area, department, or job without foreman's permission" as constituting minor misconduct. However, this rule could not apply to instances where the union representative must leave the job to transact union business with the company. The conduct of union business was specifically covered by the contract language of Article XI, Section 17.

Finally, irrespective of all of the above, Jacobs did not leave his position without permission. His foreman, Lenny Walker, knew on the previous day that Jacobs would be in a meeting on union business at 3:00 P.M. on May 3, 1979.

For all the reasons cited above, the union claimed that the disciplinary warning given to Jacobs was unjust. The union requested that Jacobs's grievance be sustained, and that the written warning be removed from his records.

APPENDIX

Relevant Provisions of the Contract

ARTICLE I—RECOGNITION AND REPRESENTATION

Section 1. The Company agrees to recognize and bargain with the accredited representatives of the Union, and the Union shall be the sole and exclusive bargaining agency for all production and maintenance employees of the Company's Grand Junction, Tennessee, plant. . . .

Section 2. There shall be no discrimination in respect to any term or condition of employment because of race, creed, color, religion, national origin, sex, or age. . . .

ARTICLE II—MANAGEMENT RIGHTS

Section 1. All the functions, powers, and authority which the Company has not specifically abridged, delegated, or relinquished by the Agreement are and shall be retained by the Company.

Section 2. The Union agrees that (a) the management of the plant, (b) the direction of the working forces, (c) the operation of the plant and machinery, (d) the number and location of plants, (e) the nature of equipment or machinery, (f) the methods and processes of manufacturing, (g) the right, subject to the terms of this Agreement, to hire, promote, demote, suspend and discharge employees and to relieve employees from duty for lack of work and other causes, including the right to transfer employees from one department or job to another department or job, (h) the assignment of work, (i) the scheduling of work . . . is vested exclusively in the Company. The exercise of such authority shall not conflict with this Agreement.

ARTICLE III—A. GRIEVANCE PROCEDURE

Section 2. Step 1: In the event that any dispute or grievance shall arise between the employee and the Company as to the application of any of the provisions of this Agreement, this matter shall first be taken up with the foreman involved by the employee, or the employee and Union representative. . . .

Step 2: If the grievance is not settled within twenty-four (24) hours from the time it is presented to the foreman in step 1, above, it shall be put into written form and presented to the supervisor within two (2) working days after the Company's answer in step 1 or the Company's answer shall be final. The supervisor and/or a member of management and the foreman involved shall meet with a Union Grievance Committee of no more than three (3) employees. . . .

Step 3: In the event no settlement is reached in step 2, the grievance may be submitted to the plant manager of the Company or a representative of management designated by him, who will meet and discuss the complaint with the Union committee. . . .

Section 3. (c) As in any arbitration, the Arbitrator will first decide any questions as to timeliness or arbitrability before rendering a decision on the merits, but there will be a single hearing on the entire case.

Section 4. The Arbitrator shall have no power or right to add to, subtract from, or alter any clauses in this Agreement. . . .

Section 6. The Company will not discriminate against any representative or employee properly participating in grievance matters or arbitration proceedings.

ARTICLE V—DISCHARGE OR SUSPENSION

Any employee found to have been unjustly discharged or suspended (including disciplinary layoff) shall be reinstated into his former job with all rights and privileges including full seniority. . . .

ARTICLE X—SENIORITY

Section 2. For all employees, seniority shall be the governing factor in determining the filling of job vacancies, shift preference, job selection within a job classification, transfers, layoff, and recall in accordance with the provision of this Agreement, provided the employee possesses the skill and ability to do the job.

ARTICLE XI—MISCELLANEOUS

Section 17. The proper Union Steward will be permitted to investigate grievances provided it does not interfere with the normal plant activities. The Union Steward will notify his foreman when necessary to leave his job to investigate a grievance.

QUESTIONS

1. Why is the exact wording of the issue being arbitrated of significance to the positions of both parties?
2. Evaluate the company's position that the arbitrator possessed no basis for upholding the union grievance.
3. Evaluate the union's position that by consistent reasoning all types of disciplinary action (i.e., a warning) must be for just cause.
4. Irrespective of the contractual issues involved, discuss the handling of the union president, Jacobs, by management personnel under the circumstances of the case. How could some of the problems have been avoided (or at least mitigated) by more astute management approaches?

62. THE SLEEPY INSPECTOR

Company: City of Iowa City, Iowa

Union: American Federation of State, County and Municipal Employees, Local 183

BACKGROUND

Steve Edberg[1] was discharged from his job as a building inspector for the city of Iowa City on January 3, 1979, after Ed Koch, his supervisor, again found him asleep at his desk. This action followed a series of events which began during the latter part of 1977 when Edberg started to experience periods of "uncontrollable" drowsiness and sleeping while at work.

Koch had observed that Edberg was dropping off to sleep from time to time while sitting at his desk. After discussing the matter several times with him, Koch referred him to the city physician. A thorough medical examination revealed that Edberg was suffering from several medical problems including congestive heart failure, chronic obstructive lung disease, and obesity. These medical problems were so severe that he was hospitalized in the early part of January 1978. The city granted him a paid sick leave; when that was exhausted, the city granted him an additional unpaid sick leave.

Edberg returned to work on February 14, 1978. Both the city's personnel director, Sylvia Collins, and Koch counseled with him concerning personnel policies and practices. Edberg was informed that he would be unable to receive additional sick leave beyond his normally accumulated sick leave, which at that time had been completely expended. He was warned that he would be terminated from his job if further hospitalization were required. Collins informed

---

[1] The names of all individuals have been disguised.

Edberg that the city would be especially unsympathetic to his problem if further hospitalization were to result from his negligence in following the dietary suggestions of his personal physician and the city physician.

Edberg continued to have difficulty in remaining awake and alert at work. He was verbally warned on April 27, 1978, and was given a written warning on May 2, 1978. He was further advised on the latter occasion that he would be suspended for three days the next time he was found asleep on the job. On June 8, 1978, Edberg was again found asleep at his desk. For this he received a three-day suspension. Although he did not file a grievance concerning this suspension, Edberg stated that the reason for his drowsiness was that he had remained awake almost all night for the previous three nights helping his wife with her homework and visiting with his children who were home on vacation from jobs in Chicago and St. Louis.

However, when he was terminated on January 3, 1979, Edberg through his union filed a grievance protesting his "unjust discharge." The grievance eventually was carried to arbitration.

POSITION OF THE CITY

The city pointed out that it had followed all the procedural steps outlined in the collective agreement when it warned, suspended, and discharged Edberg.[2] He had been warned on April 27, 1978, and again on May 2, 1978. He had been advised of the consequences of his continued sleeping at work on each occasion. He was suspended on June 8, 1978, and finally discharged on January 3, 1979. The city had taken steps to counsel Edberg in order to help him minimize the effects of his illness, and to enable him to perform his work. But Edberg had ignored this counsel and had failed to improve.

For example, during this time both supervisor Koch and the personnel director, Sylvia Collins, periodically had counseled with him in an attempt to get him to control his obesity and to conserve his energy. But Koch observed that Edberg continued to snack on candy bars and cokes several times a day. Koch testified that he spoke with him about this, but apparently with no effect. Koch testified, too, that he had urged Edberg to take walks when he felt an urge to sleep, or to get some fresh air, or get out in the field and perform inspections. Edberg similarly ignored these suggestions.

The city stated that it had "leaned over backward" to protect Edberg's job interests. Two other supervisors testified that they had

---

[2] See Appendix to this case for relevant clauses of the contract.

observed him sleeping on several occasions, but they had taken no action since these observations had been made only by themselves and no corroborating witness could be produced before he woke up.

The city claimed that Edberg did not maintain his fitness for work. Both the city's physician and his personal physician had attempted to get him from overindulging at mealtime as well as between meals. His supervisor also counseled with him about his poor eating and sleeping habits. Thus, the city contended that it had afforded Edberg every opportunity to present himself in a fit condition for work. The city emphasized that Edberg had not been discharged for being obese, but rather because he could not stay awake at work. Such behavior made him unfit for work, and it constituted ample just cause for discharge as required by the labor agreement.

Finally, the city claimed that Edberg's behavior created a serious morale problem among other employees and citizen patrons. Other employees felt that they were being required to perform Edberg's work for him because he lost considerable time dozing and sleeping. Citizens visiting city hall would become angry to discover an employee sleeping on the job. They were already unhappy over their taxes. Discovering an employee asleep on the job would confirm their (unfounded) fears that the city was poorly managed.

For the reasons stated above, the city urged that the arbitrator uphold its discharge of Steve Edberg.

POSITION OF THE UNION

The union agreed with the city that willful sleeping on the job was a serious offense which could merit some form of discipline. However, the union argued that the termination employed in this instance was not merited and constituted unjust discharge. Edberg suffered from a medical condition that caused him to experience momentary periods of unconsciousness from a lack of oxygen in his blood. His periods of drowsiness/sleeping were uncontrollable, not a willful act on his part in defiance of work rules. Edberg's work performance was good, and his health problem caused no safety hazard to himself or to others. Edberg was not an irresponsible employee caught sleeping on the job. Rather, this was a case where an otherwise excellent long-service employee suffering from a medical problem was fired by the city, even though that problem neither interfered with his work performance nor presented a safety hazard to anyone. Edberg's periodic dozing should not be considered of sufficient harm to himself, his fellow employees, or the city to justify discharge. Rather, the city should be willing to accommodate Edberg as it would any other handicapped employee.

The union contended that the city was entirely unreasonable to discharge an employee with a medically related problem when it did not affect the employee's performance and did not affect the performance, health, or safety of others.

The union requested that Steve Edberg be reinstated with full back pay and benefits. It also requested that his personnel record be purged of all documents relating to the discharge.

APPENDIX

Relevant Provisions of the Agreement

ARTICLE II—MANAGEMENT RIGHTS

Section 1. Except as limited by the express provisions of this Agreement, nothing herein shall be construed to restrict, limit, or impair the right, powers, and authority of the city under the laws of the state of Iowa and the city's ordinances. These rights, powers, and authority include, but are not limited to, the following:

(a) To direct the work of its employees.

(b) To develop, implement and enforce work rules, safety standards, performance, and productivity standards.

(c) To hire, promote, transfer, assign, classify, schedule, and retain employees within the operation of the city government and to develop and maintain qualifications, standards, and procedures for employment, promotions, and transfers.

(d) To discipline, suspend, or discharge employees for just cause.

(e) To maintain the efficiency of the governmental operation and to determine and maintain the nature, scope, and definition of city organization.

(f) To relieve employees from duties because of lack of work, lack of adequate public financing, or for other legitimate reasons.

(g) To determine the amounts, methods, and procedures for compensating employees and the definition of necessity for, allocation of, and nature of overtime and the method of compensating overtime.

(h) To determine and implement the methods, means, tools, locations, equipment, and assignment of personnel by which its operations are to be conducted including but not limited to the right to contract and subcontract work.

(i) To take such actions as may be necessary to carry out its mission.

(j) To initiate, prepare, certify, and administer its budget.

(k) To exercise all powers and duties granted to it by law.

QUESTIONS

1. Did the city have just cause to terminate Steve Edberg, or was this a medical/health problem which should have been approached differently? Discuss.
2. Evaluate the arguments presented by both sides in this matter. Which arguments are most persuasive?
3. Refer to the Rehabilitation Act of 1973 (as amended in 1974), which requires certain employers to adopt affirmative action programs and make reasonable accommodations for handicapped people. Might Steve Edberg be considered a handicapped person in the context of this law? Why, or why not?

63. A WEIGHTY PROBLEM

Company: Bethlehem Steel Corporation, Sparrows Point Plant

Union: United Steelworkers of America, Local 2609

Mary Weber,[1] a factory laborer, was terminated by the company within her first 520 hours of employment. The union filed a grievance on Decmber 12, 1979, charging that Weber had been terminated because of her "physical structure," a euphemism for obesity in this instance. The union and company could not resolve their differences, and the case was submitted to an arbitrator for a final and binding decision.[2]

POSITION OF THE UNION

Union representative Fred Lewis stated that he had inquired of plant superintendent Jesse Dowell the reason for Mary Weber's discharge. According to Lewis, Dowell stated that, "Weber's physical structure was detrimental to her employment. Her job required a frequent need to climb up and down steep and narrow ladders and to crowd into and through narrow and low areas, but her physical structure caused her much difficulty in performing her assignments." However, Lewis testified as follows:

> We have many employees, male and female but mostly male, who outweigh Weber and are also as tall as she is; there are many others taller, too, if that's the way to say it. And we thought our investigation

---

[1] The names of all individuals have been disguised.
[2] See Appendix to this case for relevant clauses of ther labor agreement.

showed that her size was in no way detrimental to any of the jobs she was required to perform. So we felt it was discrimination just on that factor alone.

In response to a question by the arbitrator, "Discrimination based on what?", Lewis stated:

On her sex, because we have male employees the same weight who would not be considered to be put out on the street just because they weigh 250 or 260, but yet they look at a female in the same way and determine in their own opinion that she can't make it.

The arbitrator then asked:

Do you know of any cases during your investigation where Weber was assigned to do a particular job and she could not fulfill it?

Lewis answered:

Not one, not one. I tried to look for those, just one. I tried to look for just one and I couldn't do it. Every job duty she was given, she performed.

The union requested that Mary Weber be reinstated and made whole for all losses in pay, seniority, and other rights and benefits.

POSITION OF THE COMPANY

The company did not cross-examine Lewis, or attempt to refute or challenge his testimony at the hearing before the arbitrator. Superintendent Dowell stated, "According to the contract, if we want, we can discharge an employee who is a probationary employee because he or she has green hair." He added:

I was prepared to put on testimony as to why Weber was not a satisfactory employee, but I don't think that is necessary. The union has not established sex discrimination; all they've established was that one person said it was because of her physical structure. Well, I submit physical structure isn't one of the reasons for discrimination. And we say the record is completely devoid of any evidence of any sex discrimination, and we ask that the grievance be denied.

The company reiterated that since the union could not prove sex discrimination had occurred in this case, the company could discharge Weber as a probationary employee for whatever reason it felt appropriate. The company urged that the grievance be dismissed in its entirety.

APPENDIX

Relevant Clauses of the Contract

ARTICLE II—APPLICATION OF AGREEMENT

Section I. Purpose and Intent of the Parties. *(d) Nondiscrimination:* It is the continuing policy of the Company and the Union that the provisions of this Agreement shall be applied to all Employees without regard to race, color, religious creed, national origin, or sex. The representatives of the Union and the Company in all steps of the complaint and grievance procedure and in all dealing between the parties shall comply with this provision.

ARTICLE X—SENIORITY

Section 6. New or Reemployed Employee. A new Employee and one who shall be reemployed after a break in his continuous service shall not acquire any seniority until the expiration of 520 hours of actual work following his employment and shall not receive any credit for continuous service during such period. If he shall be continued in the employ of the Company after the expiration of such 520 hours of actual work, the length of his continuous service shall be computed from the date of his employment or reemployment in accordance with the provisions of Section 2, Section 3, and Section 4 of this Article. During the first 520 hours of actual work, he may be laid off or discharged as the Management shall determine and his layoff or discharge shall not be made the basis of any claim, complaint, or grievance against the Company; provided that this will not be used for purposes of discrimination because of race, color, religious creed, national origin, or sex or because of membership in the Union.

ARTICLE XIII—MANAGEMENT FUNCTIONS

The management of the Plants and the direction of the working forces and the operations at the Plants, including the hiring, promoting, and retiring of Employees, the suspending, discharging, or otherwise disciplining of Employees for just cause, the laying off and calling to work of Employees in connection with any reduction or increase in the working forces, the scheduling of work and the control and regulation of the use of all equipment and other property of the Company, are the exclusive functions of the Management; provided, however, that in the exercise of such functions the Management shall observe the provisions of this Agreement and shall not discriminate against any Employee or applicant for employment because of his membership in or lawful activity on behalf of the Union.

QUESTIONS

1. Did the union establish that the company had engaged in sex discrimination? Why, or why not?
2. Evaluate the company's contention that it had the right to terminate a probationary employee who "has green hair."
3. Why did the company choose not to present any testimony or evidence in support of its position? Is this approach apt to be persuasive to an arbitrator in this type of case situation? Discuss.

64. THE JURISDICTIONAL DISPUTE

Company: Rust Engineering Company, Chattanooga, Tennessee

Union: Tri-State Carpenters and Joiners District Council of Chattanooga, Tennessee, and Vicinity

On May 22, 1979, the Rust Engineering Company filed the following grievance against the Tri-State Carpenters and Joiners District Council in connection with a work stoppage on a construction project at the Bowater Southern Paper Corporation, Calhoun, Tennessee:

Subject: Contract 21-1840 B. Project "Smoky"

Bowater Southern Paper Corporation
Calhoun, Tennessee 37309
Grievance for Strike Damages

Dear Mr. White:[1]

This letter will serve as Rust's written grievance demand, pursuant to the Project Agreement at the Bowater Southern project in Calhoun, Tennessee, for the reimbursement to Rust for damages in the amount of $4,642 resulting from the illegal strike in breach of the agreement's "No-Strike" commitments by millwrights on May 17 and 18, and by carpenters on May 18, 1979. Our damages are computed as *(a)* direct extra expenses caused by the strike, *(b)* unproductive people directly assigned to millwright and carpenter work, *(c)* a pro rata share of overhead that is normally borne by production of the craftsmen who struck, and *(d)* legal fees to procure an end of the strike and resumption of work (but not legal fees for processing this grievance).

---

[1] The names of all individuals have been disguised.

The damages are:

Rental equipment	$ 445
Wages and fringes	2,053
Temporary facilities	144
Legal fees	2,000
	$4,642

We consider this matter as step 2 of Article 9 of the Project Agreement. A copy is being sent to the international union. We will be glad to meet within ten (10) days or we will be willing to proceed directly to arbitration if you desire.

Please let me know how you wish to proceed.

The grievance was eventually submitted to arbitration.

BACKGROUND

The Bowater Southern Paper Corporation awarded the Rust Engineering Company on a cost-plus basis the entire construction contract to expand and modernize its newsprint manufacturing plant at Calhoun, Tennessee. One of the conditions precedent to awarding the contract to Rust by Bowater Southern was that for this project only all building trades unions having jurisdiction over local unions in the Calhoun area would agree upon comprehensive no-strike provisions in their agreements with the company and the Rust Engineering Company. The Carpenters Tri-State District Council of Chattanooga, which also included millwrights,[2] was one of the signatory unions to an overall Project Agreement which was negotiated between Rust and a number of local unions whose members would be employed on the Bowater job.

As part of the arrangements for implementing the special commitments made by the unions in the Project Agreement,[3] the above union agreed to inform its members of the necessity to abide by the agreement. Each worker in this union as well as members of other crafts, prior to employment, executed a written document acknowledging that he or she had been informed of the terms of the Project Agreement. Such acknowledgements were also signed by Harold F.

---

[2] Millwrights are skilled craftsmen who install, dismantle, move, and assemble machinery and equipment according to blueprints, layout plans, and schematic drawings. They use hoists, lift trucks, rollers, and hand tools to move equipment. They work with all types of building materials, such as wood, plywood, cement, and steel.

[3] See Appendix A to this case for relevant clauses of the Project Agreement.

White, the business agent of the carpenters-millwrights and all other stewards and foremen designated by the various unions.

The Tri-State District Council was given the right to designate all craft stewards, including the millwright and craft stewards; it also designated the business agents and assistant business agents; and it determined the general foreman as well as all craft foremen. The Council was designated as the agency to receive from Rust all pension and health and welfare payments on behalf of workers employed under the contract. The effective date of the special Project Agreement was August 30, 1977.

On Thursday afternoon, May 17, 1979, at about 1:30 P.M., during their scheduled work hours, 52 millwrights, who were represented by the Council and were working at the Bowater Construction site for Rust, walked off their jobs because of a jurisdictional dispute between members of the millwrights and the ironworkers union. That morning a sheetmetal subcontractor for Rust had assigned to members of the ironworkers union certain drilling and tapping[4] work that the millwrights claimed as appropriately belonging to them. Representatives of both Rust and the subcontractor discussed the problem all that morning with Ralph Flint, a District Council business agent, who claimed the drilling and tapping work for the millwrights. Nothing was resolved, and they left the site at 12 noon.[5]

Rust's project superintendent, John Burgess, learned that the millwrights were walking out at about 1 P.M. He immediately notified his main office and sent a telegram to the Council notifying the union of the walkout. At about the same time, the millwright union steward came into his office and notified him that the millwrights were leaving.

The dispute had apparently begun before the·Thursday morning work assignment by the subcontractor. On Wednesday afternoon, May 16, business agent Ralph Flint, while in Chattanooga, had received a telephone call from a union steward at Bowater concerning what he described as "a jurisdictional dispute and other working conditions and problems, including only 8 toilets for 70 men, unsatisfactory drinking water facilities, and so forth."

While business agents Flint and White were eating lunch at about 1:30 P.M. on Thursday, May 17, at a diner down the road, they saw several millwrights pass the diner. They said nothing to them, al-

---

[4] Tapping is the mechanical process of forming threads for bolts or screws inside a hole drilled into metal.

[5] Most of the following "reconstruction of events" is based on testimony of various individuals during the arbitration hearing.

400

though Flint had received earlier a telephone call from a millwright still on the job telling him that the millwrights were "fed up and that they had walked off the job." Flint and White then drove to Chattanooga, about 50 miles distance, arriving at about 4 P.M., "hoping to hear from someone from Rust." When they heard nothing, Flint went home and White drove to Cleveland, Tennessee, a small city situated about halfway between Calhoun and Chattanooga, as part of his investigation of the walkout, because "a lot of fellows live in Cleveland and go to the Cleveland local union meetings there." The Cleveland local union was comprised of both carpenters and millwrights.

White said that at a union meeting that evening, he told the members to return to work. He said that he specifically told them that "if the union wanted them to walk off the job, he would let them know." There were only a few millwrights at the meeting, however. He left the meeting at about 10:30 P.M., and returned home without contacting any of the union officials or millwrights to insist that they return to work Friday morning. White returned to his Calhoun office at about 8 A.M. on Friday morning, May 18, and found three or four millwrights standing around. He said that after talking with them, he "found that the millwrights had left their jobs, again a confirmation that the walkout was about 100 percent." (Company personnel records indicated that 65 millwrights and 35 carpenters remained off the job on Friday.)

White told the three or four men who were present in the office to go back to work and use the grievance procedure. He said that he had not yet heard from Rust, and felt that the company had some responsibility to get in touch with him. A few millwrights including a shop steward eventually reported for work, but none went through the gate except for millwright general foreman, Henry Mays. White apparently did not find out until later Friday morning that some of the carpenters had not reported for work either.

White claimed that Flint had started calling some millwrights on Friday morning, telling them to report for work; however, he was vague as to exactly when the telephone calls actually were initiated and as to how many calls were made.[6]

White added that he was contacted by Rust's attorney Friday morning advising him that there would be a court hearing, whereupon he referred the attorney to the union's attorney. He then went to the Federal Court at about 12 noon and remained there until 5:30 P.M.

---

[6] White later admitted that he did not start telephoning millwrights to return to work until after being ordered to do so on Friday afternoon by the Federal District Court.

He and other union officers began telephoning the millwrights Friday shortly after 5 P.M. immediately following issuance of a Temporary Restraining Order by the judge of the Federal District Court in Chattanooga, instructing them to return to work on Monday morning.[7]

Millwright general foreman Henry Mays attempted also to reconstruct the sequence of events on that Thursday and Friday. He recalled that at about 1:30–2 P.M. Thursday afternoon, he "had no millwrights." At about that time he had a conversation with a millwright steward about "where the men were," but this conversation was interrupted by an urgent message to report to the project superintendent. He claimed that he could not recall what was said at that meeting.

As was customary for him, Mays reported for work early before the other men arrived. He talked about the situation with the carpenters' general foreman, Tom Burton. The arbitrator and Mays discussed that conversation:

Mays: Well, Burton said that he looked for something like that to happen before then, see? In other words, before Thursday. He said there had been lots of mouthing around on the job for several days prior to Thursday.

Arbitrator: Did he say what the mouthing had been about?

Mays: Oh, just different things. They were squawking about one thing or another all the time. They would cry about the water and about materials and such as that.

Arbitrator: I believe that you were the only millwright and Mr. Burton was the only carpenter to show up on Friday?

Mays: I believe that's right, to the best of my knowledge.

Arbitrator: Why did you decide to leave, after you had been there an hour?

Mays: Well, I didn't know but that the boys would all be in, you see? And it was payday, also. I got my check and left.

Arbitrator: All right. Later on that day, did you have any conversations with any of the other workmen, or other millwrights or carpenters about the walkout?

Mays: No, sir.

Arbitrator: Did you receive any calls from anybody in the union about the walkout?

Mays: I did on Sunday. Actually, my wife received the call. I had already left home. We live in Alabama, and I was already on my way back up to Calhoun. When I telephoned her from a service station, she told me she

---

[7] On the company's motion, the Federal District Court issued a temporary restraining order on May 22, 1979, requiring that the union abide by its agreement with the company and order its members to return to work.

402

got a call for me to report back to work on Monday, which I was going to do anyway.

A second millwright general foreman, Frank Bowers, also discussed his role in the walkout. Bowers, as all the craft foremen and general foremen, was a member of a union. In this case, he was a member of Carpenters Local 654, which was associated with the Tri-State Carpenters District Council. He said that he was working at the finishing end of the paper machine when he learned from some of the millwrights that "several of the fellows were leaving." He also indicated that quite a few millwrights voiced considerable dissension as to working conditions before they left. The arbitrator queried Bowers:

Arbitrator: Well, the millwrights who told you that they were walking off, did they ask you to walk off?

Bowers: No, absolutely not. Nobody ever asked me to walk off. I met Mr. Peters, the mechanical superintendent, up in the building. And I said, "Looks like most of our men have left us," and he kind of laughed, and he said, "Yes, it looks like we might as well go with them."

Arbitrator: Did Mr. Peters leave?

Bowers: I don't really know.

Arbitrator: Did you interpret Peters's comment to mean that you should leave, or did you join the walkout?

Bowers: I didn't join the walkout. Me and one other fellow, one of my foremen, walked out together. But I never did see a mass walkout. I saw them trickling out one or two at a time through an opening in the building.

All millwrights and carpenters reported for work on Monday morning, May 22. None of the union members engaged in the work stoppage were fined for violating their no-strike agreement nor given disciplinary action by the union.

THE QUESTION OF TIMELINESS

The defense of "untimeliness" to the company's grievance was raised by the union.

On May 22, 1979, the company wrote the business agent of the Council and sent a copy of the letter to the international union. This letter was the grievance or complaint filed by the company. On May 24, 1979, business agent White wrote the project superintendent acknowledging receipt of the company's letter of May 22, 1979, as set out as the company's grievance. In the letter he questioned whether the walkout was grievable under the Project Agreement. He added that he would not be able to meet with the company representatives until 10 A.M., May 30. The company, by telegram, advised White of its acceptance of the date and time for a meeting.

There was no agreement at the May 30 meeting, and another meeting was held on June 11, which the company considered the "step 2 level." Again, there was no resolution of the company's grievance. By letter of June 13, the company exercised its right to proceed to step 3, and demanded that the grievance be submitted to arbitration.

The issues as stipulated by the company were:

1. Whether the arbitrator has jurisdiction over a strike damage claim where the work stoppage occurred as a result of a jurisdictional dispute.

2. Whether the union breached its no-strike commitment when all employees represented by it, including job stewards, struck in support of jurisdictional demands made by its business agent.

3. Whether Rust's alleged failure to follow the steps of the grievance procedure outlined in the Project Agreement has any effect on its right to bring claims before the arbitrator.

The issue stipulated by the union was:

Is Tri-State liable for the walkoff of millwrights for approximately two hours on May 17 and the refusal of the carpenters and millwrights to work on May 18. If so, what is the appropriate remedy?

POSITION OF THE UNION

The union contended that it gave its best and under the circumstances reasonable effort to get its members back to work. The company must bear a portion of the blame for the union not acting sooner. The company failed to call or notify the union on May 17, as it had previously done in the past concerning even the most minor incidents.

According to the union, the rule followed by some arbitrators is that the union must make a prompt, reasonable, and sincere effort to get the employees back to work. At least half of the arbitrators, if not the majority, have held that in a wildcat strike situation, the union is not liable unless it instigated, encouraged, or prolonged the strike. The union did not instigate, encourage, or prolong the strike. Further, it took prompt action to attempt to return the strikers to their jobs once the strike occurred.

The union argued that the only applicable language in the Project Agreement was contained in Article 16, which declared that all crafts shall cooperate with Rust and with each other in the performance of any reassignment of duties that may become necessary because of the refusal by any craft to staff the project, until such time as the uncooperative craft ceases to be in violation of the agreement. There was no evidence whatsoever to show that the District Council did not cooperate with the company, or that it had attempted to block any reassignment of duties. However, the union charged that Rust failed to cooperate with the union by failing to notify it immediatley about the walkout; and then when the company finally notified the union, it did everything possible to get its members back on the job. It accomplished this within 10 hours after they left their jobs.

The union pointed out that the grievance procedure established clear time limits. The Project Agreement provided that the impartial arbitrator be selected within five days from June 11. This language, drafted by Rust, does not state five working days, but just five days. In any event, even if the agreement were interpreted to mean "five working days," the time would have expired on June 18. It was not until June 19 that Rust's attorney even wrote for a panel of arbitrators. This is simply a case wherein Rust drafted an arbitration procedure aimed at preventing final arbitration for employees, and it overlooked the fact that it might want to use the arbitration procedure someday. The arbitration procedure backfired on the company.

The union next contended that the Project Agreement specifically provided under Article 11 that jurisdictional disputes will be settled through the Impartial Jurisdictional Disputes Board.[8] In this regard, the union held that a specific provision of an agreement has the effect of overriding a general provision. Article 11 provided the procedure for settling all union jurisdictional disputes arising on the construction project, which procedure included final and binding arbitration by an Impartial Jurisdictional Disputes Board located in Washington, D.C. The contract language was direct and clear on this. The union conceded the strike was over a jurisdictional dispute, but claimed that the matter should have been resolved by the Impartial Jurisdictional Disputes Board.

The union also contended that there was no contract language

---

[8] This refers to the Impartial Jurisdictional Disputes Board of the AFL–CIO. All labor organizations affiliated with the Building and Construction Trades Department of the AFL–CIO and various employer associations who employ their members have signed a stipulation to be bound by decisions of the Impartial Jurisdictional Disputes Board. In essence, when there is a dispute or potential jurisdictional dispute following an assignment of work, either the contractor(s) or labor union(s) involved may refer the issue to the Impartial Jurisdictional Disputes Board for a decision. There is a rather detailed procedure for both filing complaints and appealing rulings of the Board. See *Procedural Rules and Regulations of the Impartial Jurisdictional Disputes Board and Appeals Procedures*, a pamphlet published by the AFL–CIO Building and Construction Trades Department (June 1973).

providing for damages. The only means of resolving a jurisdictional dispute was to go to the Impartial Jurisdictional Disputes Board in Washington, D.C. The union further argued that Rust had the contract on a cost-plus arrangement and had lost nothing on which to base its claim for damages.

Finally, the union argued that the company was mistaken in regard to the law. The Supreme Court in the *Carbon Fuel Company v. United Mine Workers of America* case[9] took the position that the international union and its district and local unions could not be held liable for damages as a result of a wildcat strike.

In view of all the facts of the case, the union requested that the grievance be denied.

POSITION OF THE COMPANY

The company contended that the union had breached its no-strike commitment, when all employees represented by it including the union stewards struck in support of the jurisdictional demands made by the business agent.

In the instant case, the Tri-State District Council did nothing to force its members to return to work until after the Federal District Court issued a temporary restraining order. Subsequent to the issuance of the order, no disciplinary measures were ever taken against any strike participants, although discipline was the function of the District Council. The conduct of the union in this case clearly showed the ratification of the actions of its members, and damages may be imposed against the union consistent with the rulings of the Court.

The company further contended that where a contract provides for the determination of jurisdictional disputes by the Impartial Board, the only issue to be decided by that Board is which union is entitled to the disputed work. As to damages that had been incurred by the company as a result of this illegal strike, that question had been appropriately submitted for arbitration despite the fact that the illegal walkout occurred as a result of a jurisdictional dispute. Therefore, Rust's submission of the jurisdictional dispute to the Impartial Board in no way would act as a bar to seek strike damages through the arbitration procedure.

Rust maintained that it was entitled to an award of compensatory damages which should include the additional costs incurred for overtime hours worked in order to have the project completed on

---

[9] 444 U.S. 212, 62 Led. 2d 394, 102 LRRM 3017 (1979)—see Appendix B.

schedule, and a reasonable attorney's fee incurred in effecting a resumption of work on the project. In this regard, the company argued that the Carbon Fuel Company case was not applicable to this situation, for unlike that instance, the District Council, the local unions, and each individual member of those unions employed with Rust were signatories to the Project Agreement.

The company maintained that it could process its claim for damages even though it was operating on a cost-plus contract with Bowater Southern. In fact, it had a duty not to incur unnecessary costs in order to inflate its fee.

The company pointed out that any delays in the procedure for seeking arbitration should be charged to the union, and that the grievance was timely under provisions of Article 9, Section 3, of the agreement. The company within two days of the step 2 level meeting notified the union of its intention to proceed to arbitration. It also requested in its letter to the union that its attorney contact the union attorney "to obtain a panel of arbitrators and proceed to hearing." According to the company, its request was not honored by the union.[10] Therefore, on June 19 the company attorney requested that the Federal Mediation and Conciliation Service provide a panel of arbitrators. The company argued that it had attempted to make arrangements for the selection of an arbitrator within the five-day period set out by the contract. If the company failed specifically to obtain a panel within the five-day period, so did the union fail to get in touch with the company with reference to securing a panel of arbitrators, as requested in the company's letter of June 13.

Finally, the company took the position that the arbitrator had jurisdiction of its strike damage claims. The company requested that it be compensated for the costs incurred as a result of the walkout by the millwrights in violation of the collective agreement. The company submitted an amended claim for damages which was more than the amount stipulated in its original grievance letter of May 22, 1979. In making this claim, Rust emphasized that it did not seek punitive damages against the union for its actions; it only wished to be made whole for the damages it suffered because of the strike. Rust requested that it be awarded the sum of $3,625.25 representing the cost of overtime premium pay necessary to make up for production lost during the strike. Rust also requested that it be awarded the sum of $4,088.31 as attorney's fees expended to get the union members back on the job.

---

[10] The company attorney claimed that he had talked with the union attorney within the five-day period of step 2, but this was denied by the union attorney.

APPENDIX A

Relevant Clauses of the Project Agreement

ARTICLE I—INTENTION OF THE PARTIES

The purpose of this Agreement is to set out the conditions for the efficient prosecution of all work performed by Employer at the Bowater Southern Paper Corporation project being constructed at Calhoun, Tennessee, hereinafter referred to as the "Project," to establish and maintain harmonious relations between all parties to the Agreement, to secure optimum productivity and to eliminate strikes, work stoppages, lockouts, slowdowns, or delays in the prosecution of the work undertaken by the Employer.

The parties hereto agree and do establish and put into practice effective and binding methods for the settlement of all misunderstandings, disputes, or grievances that may arise between the union and its members and the Employer to the end that the Employer is assured of complete continuity of operation, without slowdown or interruption of any kind, and that labor/management peace is maintained.

ARTICLE 3—SCOPE OF THE AGREEMENT

(5) This Agreement represents the complete understanding of the parties. Any provision of local and national collective bargaining agreement contrary to or in conflict with this Agreement or contrary to the intent and meaning of this Agreement shall not be enforced as to the Employer working under this Agreement.

ARTICLE 9—GRIEVANCE PROCEDURE

Any controversy arising out of the interpretation and application of terms and conditions of this Agreement other than those pertaining to craft jurisdictional disputes shall be processed in the following manner:

(1) All controversies shall be referred to the appropriate craft business representative or his authorized agent and to the Employer's representative at the project site or his designated representative for adjustment.

(2) If the grievance cannot be settled it shall, within three (3) working days of occurrence, be reduced to writing and submitted to the appropriate International Union and the designated representative of the employer for consideration and settlement.

(3) If the grievance is not settled within ten (10) working days under step 2, it may be referred by either party to an Impartial Arbitrator for settlement. The Impartial Arbitrator will be selected

within five (5) days and shall be selected from a panel of arbitrators submitted by and in accordance with the rules and regulations of the American Arbitration Association.

The decision of the Impartial Arbitrator shall be final and binding upon all parties.

The expense of the Impartial Arbitrator shall be borne equally by the disputing parties.

ARTICLE 11—JURISDICTIONAL DISPUTES

(1) There will be no strikes, no work stoppages or slowdowns, or other interferences with the work because of jurisdictional disputes.

(2) Work shall be assigned by the Employer in accordance with the procedural rules of the Impartial Jurisdictional Disputes Board, and jurisdictional disputes will be settled in accordance with the procedural rules and decisions of such Board or successor agency.

(3) Where a jurisdictional dispute involves any union or employer not a party of the procedures established by the Impartial Jurisdictional Disputes Board and is not resolved between the unions, it shall be referred for resolution to the International Unions, with which the disputing unions are affiliated. The resolution of the dispute shall be reduced to writing signed by representatives of the International Unions and the Employer. The disputed work shall continue as assigned by the Employer until the dispute has been resolved. The provisions of Paragraph 1 will apply to disputes covered by this paragraph.

ARTICLE 16—NO STRIKE–NO LOCKOUT

The unions agree that there will be no strike (which term shall include any collective action which will interfere with, or stop, the efficient operation of construction work of the Employer) for any reason whatsoever during the term of this Agreement. Participation by an employee, or group of employees, in an act violating the above provision will be cause of discharge by the Employer. If there is a strike, work stoppage, or picket line in violation of the Agreement by any craft, it is agreed that the other crafts will be bound to ignore such action and continue to man the Project without interruption. Further, it is agreed that all crafts shall cooperate with the contractor and with each other in the performance of any additional assignments of duties resulting from the refusal to man the Project by any craft until such time as the involved craft ceases to be in violation of this Agreement.

There will be no work stoppage on the Project due to local negotiations. In the event of the expiration of a local agreement, the Employer will continue to recognize those terms and conditions of the expired agreement, not in conflict with this Agreement, until a new agreement is consummated between the union and the recognized bargaining agents. The Employer will recognize those terms and conditions of the new agreement not in conflict with this Agreement on the effective date of the new agreement.

The "No Strike-No Lockout" commitment is based upon the agreement by the parties to be bound by the grievance and arbitration procedure of this Agreement.

APPENDIX B

Decision of the US Supreme Court in Carbon Fuel Company v. United Mine Workers of America (444 U.S. 212; 102 LRRM 3017)

The Carbon Fuel Company and United Mine Workers of America (UMWA) were parties to the National Bituminous Coal Wage Agreements of 1968 and 1971, covering several of the employer's coal mines in West Virginia. Three local unions had engaged in 48 wildcat strikes in the employer's mines from 1969 to 1973. Efforts of both the international union and District 17, a regional subdivision of the international, were uniformly unsuccessful in persuading the miners not to strike and to return to work in each instance. The Carbon Fuel Company charged that the UMWA and District 17 were liable under Section 301 of the Labor Management Relations Act (LMRA) for the actions of the three locals.

The company charged that the international union and District 17 were obligated to use all reasonable means to try to control the locals' actions because the UMWA had agreed in the contract to resolve all disputes through the grievance procedure, and to arbitrate disputes as a last resort. The company further charged that the locals were agents of the UMWA, and that as a principal the parent organization was liable for the actions of the locals.

In December 1979 the Supreme Court ruled as follows:

1. The international union and District 17 were not liable for the actions of the locals under Section 301 of the LMRA. Section 301(b) provides that a union "shall be bound by the acts of its agents"; and Section 301(e) provides that the common law of agency shall govern "in determining whether any person is acting as an 'agent' of another person." This means that the principal (the international union and District 17) is liable for the wrongful acts of the agent (the three locals) only so long as the agent is acting within the authorized limits of the relationship, as established by the principal. Under the constitution of the UMWA, the local unions lacked authority to strike

410

without approval from the international union and District 17. The locals did not obtain such authorization. Moreover, both the international union and District 17 had repeatedly expressed opposition to wildcat strikes.

Failure of the international union and its district subunit to use "all reasonable means" to prevent "wildcat" strikes by the local unions in violation of the collective bargaining contract does not make the international union and District 17 liable for damages to the employer, even though the contracts contained an arbitration provision. The international and district unions did not instigate, support, ratify, or encourage the work stoppages by the locals. They, in fact, consistently expressed their opposition to the stoppages and took measures to get the workers to resume work. The employer failed to prove agency as required in Sections 301(b) and 301(e) of the LMRA.

2. An agreement by an international or district union to arbitrate employee grievances does not impose an obligation upon them to use "all reasonable means" available to them to control the actions to their affiliated locals' actions that are in violation of the collective bargaining contract.

QUESTIONS

1. Why is it unusual for a company to file a grievance against a union as happened in this case?
2. Evaluate the issue of untimely handling of the grievance. Are the arguments of the union persuasive that the grievance was not admissible because the procedural time limits were not followed exactly? Discuss.

If the grievance was ruled to be timely by the arbitrator:

3. Evaluate the various arguments presented by the union. Which are the most compelling?
4. Evaluate the various arguments presented by the company. Which are the most compelling?
5. Would the arbitrator possess authority to order monetary damages in the event the arbitrator found that the union had violated the Project Agreement? Why, or why not?
6. To what degree are the issues in this case relevant or inapplicable to the *Carbon Fuel Company v. United Mine Workers* Supreme Court decision cited in Appendix B?

65. THE WASTEBALER AND THE CUSTODIAN

Company: St. Regis Paper Company, Consumer Products Division, Vernon, California

Union: Printing Specialties and Paper Products Union, District Council No. 2

At about 6 A.M. on September 25, 1979, Melanie Castle[1] and her co-worker, Doris Duncker, walked into production manager Earl Holt's office to report an alleged threat made against Castle by Henry Mangrum. Castle said that shortly after the 4 A.M. lunch break, Mangrum strode up to her and announced, "I'm going to get you; I'm going to rape you."

The "threat" was later denied by Mangrum; and of course there were several events leading up to the incident.

BACKGROUND

As of the date of this event, Henry Mangrum had been working as a wastebaler on the graveyard shift at the company plant in Vernon, California. He was 22 at the time and had been employed by the company for 13 months.

Sometime during the first half of the shift on September 25, Mangrum had an argument with Melanie Castle, who was 19 and had been working for the company about two months as a custodian. Her job entailed delivering waste paper to the baling machine where Mangrum was stationed. The nature of their argument was never clearly established, but it was either about whose job it was to throw the paper into the baler or about whether the paper she brought was the right kind to be put into the machine. Castle claimed that in the course of the altercation, Mangrum grabbed her

---

[1] The names of all individuals have been disguised.

by the collar and poked her in the chest with his finger, causing a coke in her hand to spill and wet her clothes. Mangrum later claimed that he merely "nudged" her, while John Woodson, who observed the incident and later testified for Mangrum, stated that Mangrum "pushed her away." Castle admitted that she threw the rest of her coke at Mangrum and kicked him in the leg. She also said to Woodson, "I'm going to get him fired." Mangrum was unable later to recall either having been kicked in the leg or hearing Castle speak to Woodson.

Castle promptly told her long-time good friend, Doris Duncker, what had transpired. Duncker had previously urged Castle to report to management some earlier encounters with Mangrum, but as Castle put it, she "didn't want to get him fired," and was afraid "different things would happen." Duncker insisted that this was the "straw that broke the camel's back" and went with her to meet with production manager Earl Holt.

Castle told Holt what Mangrum had said and done that day, as well as what he had done on three previous occasions. She told him that Mangrum had come up behind her about a month before and "felt my butt"; another time he lifted her up, but put her down when she started kicking; and he once put his arms around her waist from behind and tried to kiss her cheek.

Holt told Castle and Duncker to go to the stockroom and lock the door. Then he called Mangrum and the shop steward, Lloyd Roberts, into his office. Holt told Mangrum that he was "not going to tolerate any more of his threats."

Holt's comment about Mangrum's threats resulted in part from a three-day suspension levied on Mangrum for threatening to "knock a supervisor down." (An arbitrator had sustained the company's disciplinary action a few weeks earlier.) Several other employees had also complained about having been threatened with bodily harm by Mangrum, but all had refused to follow through on their complaints. Mangrum's work performance had been only marginal during his employment with the company; and he had received a number of written warnings for unsatisfactory work and absenteeism. Although he had been promoted to wastebaler only two weeks earlier, he also had been the only bidder; the union had urged his promotion on the ground that he would perform better as a wastebaler than as a custodian.

The meeting between Holt, Mangrum, and Roberts did not go particularly well. Holt refused to identify the complainants, including Castle and Duncker, fearing repercussions, especially since both women were still on the premises. The shop steward seemed to have known of the dispute that had occurred less than two hours earlier;

without mentioning Castle's name, he charged that Holt seemed to be accusing Mangrum of threatening a single "employee" whom he would not name.

Holt discharged Mangrum at the close of the meeting. Holt alleged that later when he and Mangrum were leaving the plant, Mangrum said, "I'm not finished with you yet," a statement that Mangrum later denied.

Subsequently, the union filed a grievance protesting Mangrum's "unjust discharge," which eventually was carried to arbitration.

POSITION OF THE UNION

The union argued that Holt, the production manager had, "summarily" discharged Mangrum "without any thorough investigation of the facts and without allowing him to give his version of what had occurred on and before September 25." Holt had conducted a "kangaroo court" by calling in Mangrum and reading him the "riot act" about various threats he had allegedly made against various unnamed employees. Mangrum was given no opportunity to defend himself or confront his accusers.

The union also contended that Mangrum's language constituted nothing more than "shop talk" and that his behavior was no more than what is customary in a shop employing both males and females. Mangrum's earlier encounters with Castle—"if they did, in fact, occur"—amounted to "harmless horseplay."

Several male witnesses testified for the union that Castle "likes the attention of men," has a "sexy walk," and so forth. The union noted that Castle's "handling" of those incidents "would lead Mangrum to wonder whether she really minded his alleged advances." The union pointed out that Castle apparently was unafraid of Mangrum, as evidenced by her having thrown her coke at him and kicking him.

The union also charged that her complaint arose out of "sheer vindictiveness" that had been supported by Duncker. Castle was obviously very angry after Mangrum had pushed her and caused her to spill her coke and get wet. In fact, she had on at least one previous occasion threatened to a few of her co-workers to "get him fired"; yet she did nothing on this occasion until almost two hours after he had allegedly threatened to rape her. It was only after she had spoken with her friend, Doris Duncker, that she complained to Holt.

Finally, the union pointed out that while the company had made many accusations about Mangrum's threats against his fellow employees, only Castle had identified herself as a complainant. The company had a duty to substantiate its charges of intimidation.

The union requested that the arbitrator reinstate Henry Mangrum

414

with full back pay and all other benefits and rights he might have accrued had he not been unjustly discharged on September 25, 1979.

POSITION OF THE COMPANY

The company stated that Holt had not acted hastily in discharging Mangrum on the morning of September 25. First, he had called in the shop steward, Lloyd Roberts, before talking to Mangrum, even though the labor agreement did not require that safeguard. Second, Holt had acted upon firsthand reports of Castle, Duncker, and others who had refused to be identified. Third, both Castle and Duncker subsequently testified at a formal grievance meeting conducted a few days later to hear Mangrum's appeal. Finally, both Castle and Duncker were still on the premises on September 25 at which time Holt spoke with Mangrum. Holt was so apprehensive about their safety that he had even requested that they lock themselves in the storeroom.

The company pointed out that Holt's actions on September 25 were not those of an impetuous and inconsiderate manager. The company cited the previous occasion on which Holt had levied a three-day suspension on Mangrum as an example. On that occasion, Mangrum's supervisor reported that he had been threatened with bodily injury by Mangrum. When Holt questioned Mangrum about the threat, he denied having made it. At that point, Holt removed Mangrum from the job and arranged for a formal meeting to take place as soon as all the parties and evidence could be assembled, which was several hours later. Holt's action on that occasion, as on this, was deliberate and thoughtful, and gave full consideration to the safety and rights of everyone concerned.

The company noted that in making these procedural objections against the company, the union did not claim surprise. The union seemed to have already received all the facts, as the company detailed them, and was quite prepared to meet and counter the company's arguments and evidence.

The company argued that Mangrum's threat to rape Melanie Castle was only one of many evidences that Mangrum was an unsatisfactory employee. He had already received several written warnings for unsatisfactory work performance and excessive absenteeism. Several employees had already complained of having been threatened by him. He had been suspended for three days for threatening a supervisor. And following the threat of rape against Melanie Castle, he threatened Holt with some sort of retaliatory action for having discharged him.

The company requested that the arbitrator sustain its decision to discharge Henry Mangrum on September 25, 1979.

QUESTIONS

1. Was the statement about rape made by Mangrum to Castle a serious threat, or was it "harmless horseplay" or "shop talk" as claimed by the union? Discuss.
2. Did company manager Holt follow proper procedures in reaching his decision to discharge Mangrum? Should this aspect of the case make any difference in the arbitrator's determination?
3. To what degree was Mangrum's behavior influenced by the behavior of Castle? Why is this area of male/female relationships often a gray area in acting upon charges of sexual harassment?
4. Did the company have just (proper) cause to terminate Mangrum? Why, or why not?

66. THE REFUSED ASSIGNMENT

Company: Interstate Brands Corporation, Springfield, Illinois

Union: International Brotherhood of Teamsters, Chauffeurs, Warehousemen and Helpers of America, Local 916

BACKGROUND

On February 15, 1980, Teamsters Local 916 filed the following grievance on behalf of Donald K. Rebstock,[1] a driver-salesman employed by Interstate Brands.

> On Monday, February 11, 1980, the Interstate Brands Company apportioned the business of my route to other routes without taking into consideration my seniority with the Company.
>
> The working agreement between Teamsters Local 916 and the Interstate Brands Corporation, Section 1, of Article 4, provides that seniority shall prevail.
>
> The unilateral action by the Company in apportioning the business of my route to other routes and not giving me the opportunity to have one of the routes is a violation of my seniority with the Interstate Brands Corporation.
>
> I am requesting assignment to one of the routes affected consistent with my seniority.

On February 20, 1980, Ronald Schuessler, general manager of the Springfield plant, sent Jack Belding, president of Local 916, a reply denying the grievance. The essential portion of his letter stated:

> Received the letter on Mr. Donald K. Rebstock.
>
> This route was eliminated because it was geographically located so all accounts could be put on other routes with the least amount of miles and man-hours.
>
> As the contract states Article 4, Section 3 (in case of reduction in

---

[1] The names of all individuals have been disguised.

force the youngest man in seniority shall be laid off first), which is what we did, and placed Don Rebstock in his position. If and when a route becomes open for bid, Mr. Rebstock will have the opportunity to bid on it.

Our position is that we followed the guidelines of the contract as stated in Article 4, and it is the company's position that this grievance is unwarranted and should be retracted.

Rebstock was very displeased with the company's reply to his February 15 grievance. He was even more displeased when his supervisor, Tom Costello, informed him on Friday, February 22, 1980, to report for work on Monday, February 25, at 5:30 A.M. at the company's Litchfield terminal to work temporarily on a route there. He refused the assignment. On March 17, 1980, he filed the following second grievance.

I was suspended for ten (10) days because I refused to accept work out of the Springfield Area and Teamsters Local 916's jurisdiction, where I hold my seniority.

I am requesting that I be paid for all time lost as a result of that suspension.

The parties were unable to resolve their differences, and the union invoked its right under the collective bargaining agreement to refer both grievances to an impartial arbitrator whose decision would be final and binding upon both parties.

TESTIMONY AND EVIDENCE PRESENTED
AT THE ARBITRATION HEARING

Interstate Brands in the Springfield, Illinois, area had been experiencing severe competition from other large baking companies, especially price competition from manufacturers of private brand merchandise. Early in January 1980, the general manager, Schuessler, decided that eliminating the least effective route by combining it with other routes would be one of several steps taken to reduce costs. It was Rebstock's route that was selected for elimination.

Donald K. Rebstock was a driver-salesman who had worked in that capacity for some 23 years for Interstate Brands. His major duties included loading his truck with bread and other bakery goods, driving to retail stores on his route, taking orders, placing merchandise on the store shelves, removing stale bakery goods to be returned to the Interstate distribution depot, and making collections for merchandise sold. He could also solicit new grocery outlets, as time permitted, and set up special displays for company promotion of special and seasonal items. He had a very good work record. He was an excellent driver, never having been involved in a driving accident. No disciplinary action had ever been levied against him for any aspect of his work or behavior.

Rebstock normally worked out of the Amos Street Depot in Springfield, although there is a second depot (also known as a terminal) in Springfield identified as the Clearlake Terminal. Approximately 14 employees were in the bargaining unit. At the time of these grievances, Rebstock was operating a route in the west part of Springfield. It encompassed a three-mile area, and included some 26 stops. Rebstock was told early in January 1980 by his supervisor, Tom Costello, that the general manager had decided to eliminate his route. The actual elimination of Rebstock's route occurred during the first week of February.

Rebstock's previous route was allocated among those of a number of other drivers. Some of his previous stops were given to drivers who were senior to him, but six of his stops were assigned to James Flanagan, who was junior in seniority to Rebstock.

Rebstock was compensated at a rate of $122.50 per week, plus a 10 percent commission on all net sales over $450. Junior seniority sales-drivers hired after July 23, 1968, received $161.50 per week, plus a 7 percent commission on net sales over $475.

Schuessler and Costello met with Rebstock during the last week in January to explain the company's decision to eliminate his route. They also told him that he would be assigned to the swingman's route, currently held by Dave Hawley. Hawley was the most recently hired driver-salesperson with only a few months seniority and service with the company. Rebstock protested against taking the swingman's route, and claimed that he should be able to "bump" Flanagan who held 12 years seniority, the next highest seniority rank among the drivers, or any other driver with less seniority than himself. Schuessler would not agree with him on his proposed reassignment, and Rebstock went to work as a swingman on Monday, February 11. Swingmen are driver-salespersons who perform all the regular duties of that position; however, they have no regular route. They fill in when regular drivers are on vacation, ill, on jury duty, and so forth. They may also ride with a regular driver whose route required temporary additional time and attention. Rebstock immediately filed a grievance.

On Friday, February 22, Costello told Rebstock to report on Monday, February 25, at 5:30 A.M. at the Litchfield terminal located 50 miles from Springfield, to work for a few days on a route with the regular driver who was returning to work following surgery. Sales on the Litchfield route were very large averaging about $3,000 per week, as compared with $2,200–$2,400 per week on Rebstock's previous route. He would receive his full commission on all sales while assisting temporarily on the Litchfield route. He spoke immediately with his shop steward, Sam Montaldo, and his union president, Jack Belding. Both informed him that "he didn't have to go to Litchfield," and they assured him that the union would back him fully if he chose to file a grievance.

While Springfield drivers in the past had always accepted assignments at the Litchfield terminal, the union had always taken the position that they need not accept such assignments, since Litchfield was within the collective bargaining jurisdiction of a different Teamsters local union.

Rebstock refused to accept the Litchfield assignment. He was away from his job for 10 days, returning to work on Monday, March 10. He filed a second grievance on March 17.

The company and the union did not agree as to whether Rebstock had been suspended for 10 days, or had simply failed to report to work for that period. Rebstock claimed that at first he was told that if he did not report to the Litchfield terminal, he should not come in. According to him, he was first "terminated," but that action was later changed to a 10-day suspension. On the other hand, both Schuessler and Costello maintained that Rebstock was never told that he should not report for work, or that he was suspended or terminated. He simply failed to appear.

POSITION OF THE UNION

The union argued that the company ignored the seniority requirements of the collective bargaining agreement when it demoted Donald K. Rebstock from a driver-sales employee to a swingman. According to the union, Article 1, Section 4, of the agreement[2] recognized that the two positions are different; and, Article 2, Section 2, indicated that the position of swingman is below that of driver-sales employee in the job hierarchy by expressly stating that the former "shall have the opportunity to fill route job vacancies by the bidding procedure." Swingmen work under less favorable conditions than the regular drivers. The company acted correctly in following Article 4, Section 3, when it laid off Hawley, the employee with least seniority. However, it erred in assigning Rebstock, an employee with 23 years experience and who held number three rank among all driver-salespersons, to Hawley's swingman position. Rather, the union contended, "the number three man in seniority should be able to 'bump' any driver-sales employee less senior than himself, and take that less senior employee's route." In fact, the union argued, Article 4, Section 1, provided that "Seniority shall

---

[2] See Appendix to this case for relevant contractual clauses.

prevail, dated from the date of employment in the sales department."

Rebstock had 11 more years seniority than Flanagan, and should have been permitted to bump into the latter's job, or that of any driver-sales employee with less seniority. Flanagan, in turn, should have been able to bump into the route of any other driver-sales employee with less seniority than he.

The union reinforced its claim for Rebstock by adding that the application of the seniority principle was not qualified in any way in the collective bargaining agreement. For example, the contract did not say that the company "may take into account seniority," thereby making seniority discretionary with the company; nor did it say that seniority was a factor to be considered in conjunction with other factors, such as versatility, educational level attained, physical capacity, and so forth. The language of Article 4, Section 1, made the seniority clause a "strict" seniority clause.

The union noted that Flanagan's commission rate was less than that of Rebstock. The company's motive in eliminating Rebstock's route was simply that of replacing a 10 percent commission with a 7 percent commission. As swingman, Rebstock's sales would fluctuate from week to week according to the amount of sales of the particular route he was working.

The union further argued that the company acted in an arbitrary and unreasonable manner in directing Rebstock to report to Litchfield on Monday, February 27, 1980, to run a route as a swingman. It held that the company compounded its previous action when it suspended him for 10 days when he refused the assignment. The hardships of the two-hour drive, the cost of gasoline, and the stresses of an unfamiliar route were great. The company treated a 23-year employee inconsiderately, and his response to the order should have come as no surprise. The union noted, too, that Interstate Brands had no contract with Local 916 in Litchfield. Since Rebstock held no seniority in Litchfield, the purposes of collective bargaining were subverted if the company was able to assign an employee to Litchfield, or some more distant city, and then discipline him or her for not accepting the assignment.

The union contended, finally, that the company had chosen to assign Rebstock to the Litchfield terminal in retaliation for his having filed a grievance on February 11, protesting against a demotion from position of driver-sales employee to that of swingman. In fact, on February 26 the union and Rebstock chose to file the following charge with the NLRB.

I have been a driver for the above-named employer for 23½ years. The employer is under a contract with Teamsters Local 916, which expires August 3, 1980. I am one of the senior drivers. Recently the employer did away with my route and assigned coverage to other routes. Under Article 4 of the contract, I am entitled to another route. See Article 4 of the contract attached. The company refused to give me another route. I filed a grievance on this matter about one week ago. The grievance has not been disposed of yet. Today the employer attempted to assign me to a different area, different unit, and outside the jurisdiction of the current contract. The other assignment would be in Litchfield, Illinois. His action, in making this assignment in derogation of the contract, is motivated by my having filed a grievance. The current attempted assignment is in fact a discharge. This action by the employer is discriminatory toward me because of my union activity and my filing a grievance, all in violation of the Act.

The union requested that Rebstock be restored to his position of driver-sales employee according to the principles of seniority, and that he be made whole for full pay and all other rights and privileges lost during his two weeks of suspension.

POSITION OF THE COMPANY

The company stated that its decision to eliminate Rebstock's route by incorporating it into those of other driver-salespersons was purely an economic one. Eliminating his route substantially reduced the mileage driven because a number of stops were located close to other routes. And the elimination of his route would produce considerably greater savings than the elimination of any other route. Schuessler pointed out that routes had been realigned on various occasions in the past, sometimes adding stops and sometimes deleting stops. The union had never previously protested this action by the company. In fact, the net effect of increasing the efficiency of the routes had always been to increase driver earnings by increasing sales on each route.

The company argued that to have granted Rebstock's grievance of February 15 would have resulted in wholesale bumping of employees. This would have reduced the efficiency of the sales program, required extensive retraining, and reduced the personal relationship of drivers with the grocers. Every driver potentially could have ended up with a different route.

The company contended that its treatment of Rebstock was consistent with both the terms of the contract and past practice. In fact, it held that during the most recent contract negotiations of January 1977 the union attempted to amend Article 4, Section 3, as follows:

> In the event a route is abolished, the driver-salesman effected shall be allowed to bump to whatever route his seniority will allow. Such

displaced routeman shall be allowed same privilege until down to youngest man who shall take the layoff.

The company refused to accept this union proposal for the reasons cited above. The company held that the February 15 grievance, which was designed to permit chain bumping, was nothing more than an attempt to obtain through arbitration that which the union had proposed and failed to obtain in negotiations.

The company noted that nothing in the contract permitted Rebstock to bump any driver with less seniority when his route was eliminated. The only contractual limitation upon the company in managing any reduction in force is the provision of Article 4, Section 3, which required it to lay off personnel according to seniority. After abiding by Article 4, Section 3, the company's options regarding the operation of its business in a reduction of force were not limited by the contract. It chose among all the available options the one which was least disruptive; it reassigned Rebstock. The company cited the last sentence of Article 4, Section 4, as evidence of the high value it has placed upon minimizing changes of routes by driver-sales personnel.

The company further noted that the union knew that chain bumping was not required by the contract; otherwise it would not have tried to negotiate a change in the wording of Article 4, Section 3, in 1977.

The union's reliance upon Article 4, Section 1, to support its argument for strict seniority was misplaced, according to Schuessler. If the union's position were correct, there would be no need for Sections 2 and 3 of that article. Furthermore Section 4 of that article provides that "merit" and "capability" override seniority in the determination as to who will be awarded a job bid. The contract did not require a strict application of seniority. In fact, it made specific provision for other considerations.

As to Rebstock's grievance of March 17, the company took the position that he should have followed the important labor relations rule, "work now and grieve later." That is, what he did when reassigned on February 11 was what he should also have done on February 25. He had a duty to follow his supervisor's instruction to report for work at the Litchfield terminal. He also had the right to file a grievance concerning that assignment. Costello's job assignment was reasonable and proper. Even if Rebstock and the union believed that it was improper, both were bound by the contract to pursue their remedy through the grievance procedure, and Rebstock was bound to work until an arbitrator ruled otherwise. The union erred in telling Rebstock that he need not report for work at Litchfield.

The company pointed out that the contract contained no definition of a geographical area for any purpose. If a union for internal purposes restricts itself to a certain geographical area, that restriction had no effect upon the company. Furthermore, it was unreasonable for a local of the Teamsters union to argue that its drivers were not permitted to work beyond that local's claimed geographical boundaries. It seemed even more unreasonable for a union to want to reduce job opportunities for its members.

The company denied that it assigned Rebstock to the Litchfield route in retaliation for the February 11 grievance. The assignment was reasonable and proper, and other employees from Springfield had accepted these assignments in the past. All Rebstock was required to do was assist an ill driver-salesperson perform his job. Rebstock was not harmed in any way; his compensation would have been larger in Litchfield; his job duties would have been the same; he would have been working in an area in which the company recognized the Teamsters as bargaining agent. The claim of retaliation was entirely unfounded.

The company requested that the arbitrator deny both of the grievances in their entirety.

APPENDIX

Relevant Clauses of the Contract

ARTICLE 1—EMPLOYING UNION DRIVERS

Section 1.   All workers employed by the Employer and coming under the Union purely by reason of this Agreement shall be employees in good standing with the Union as long as the terms of this Agreement are in effect.

* * * * *

Section 4.   It is understood and agreed that driver-sales employees and swingmen come under the jurisdiction of Local 916, and shall become members of this Union as provided for in Article 1, Section 1.

ARTICLE 2—NEW EMPLOYEES

* * * * *

Section 2.   Employees hired as swingmen shall be paid $151.50 per week while being trained. When trained and able to operate routes unassisted, he/she shall be paid the applicable base pay as stated in Article 2, Section 1, plus 7 percent commission on the net weekly average route sales of the depot where he/she is domiciled. It

424

is further agreed that swingmen shall have the opportunity to fill route job vacancies by the bidding procedure.

ARTICLE 4—SENIORITY:
DRIVER-SALES EMPLOYEES

Section 1. Seniority shall prevail, dated from the date of employment in the Sales Department.

Section 2. Driver-sales employees shall pick their vacations by order of seniority.

Section 3. In case of reduction in force, the youngest man in seniority shall be laid off first.

Section 4. In the event a route is open, or a new route created, that such opening shall be posted and any driver-sales employee can ask for the opportunity to advance providing:

(a) The driver-sales employee has been a routeman with the Employer for one (1) year.

(b) Such advancement is based on merit.

The Employer agrees to give such request fair consideration on the basis of seniority, and comply with the same if the driver-sales employee is capable. Should such move be made, it shall be the only change and the driver-sales employee making such a change shall make no further bids for advancement for a period of two (2) years.

QUESTIONS

1. Evaluate the union's arguments that Donald Rebstock should have been allowed to bump junior seniority employees to choose a preferred route.

2. Evaluate the company's arguments that the union was attempting to achieve through arbitration what it could not achieve through negotiations.

3. Did the company have the right to assign Rebstock to work out of the Litchfield terminal which was not under Teamsters Local 916's jurisdiction? Why, or why not?

4. Does the arbitrator's decision depend in any way upon the determination of the NLRB in regard to the union's filing of unfair labor practice charges?

5. Evaluate the company's position that Rebstock and the union should have "worked now and grieved later." Surmise why Rebstock and the union did not follow this principle in this case situation.

67. EMERGENCY LEAVE PAY

Company: Basin Electric Power Cooperative, Bismark, Minnesota

Union: International Brotherhood of Electrical Workers, Local 1593

In July 1983, employees Melvin Kane and Roger Field[1] each filed separate requests for emergency leave without payroll deduction because of medical emergencies within their immediate families. Their claims were denied and each filed a grievance. The parties failed to settle their differences, and the union requested final and binding arbitration as provided in the agreement. They agreed that the issue to be resolved was:

> Did the company violate Article XI, Section 4(c) of the Agreement when it denied emergency leave pay to Melvin Kane for June 8, 9, and 10, 1983, and to Roy Field for July 5, 6, and 7, 1983, and if so, what is the appropriate remedy?

BACKGROUND

The Field Case

On June 21, 1983, Roy Field was on company business in Duluth, Minnesota, when his wife phoned and informed him that their daughter had a brain tumor. He immediately returned home and conferred with their physician for one and a half hours that afternoon. He was advised that there should be two operations, the first to relieve the pressure within the cranial cavity and about a week later the second would be performed in an attempt to remove the tumor. The first operation was performed on June 23. Field was paid

---

[1] The names of all individuals have been disguised.

425

one and a half hours emergency leave for June 21 and eight hours for June 23.

The daughter remained in the hospital and the pressure subsided to the point that the second operation was scheduled for July 5. She was, however, permitted to return home for the preceding weekend as her physician thought she would be more relaxed there. After the operation she remained in intensive care on July 5 and 6. She continued to be in serious condition and under strict observation through July 7. At Field's request, his daughter's physician gave him a letter stating that the daughter had undergone emergency surgery and that her father was with her on July 5, 6, and 7.

The Kane Case

On April 4, 1983, Melvin Kane's daughter suffered an attack of asthma. She was admitted to the local hospital where she received emergency treatment; she was released the same day. Following that episode she remained under the care of her physician, and she was "in and out" of the emergency room of the hospital in Bismark on several occasions. Kane was paid emergency leave for April 4.

During the course of her treatment, her physician and parents decided that she should be admitted to the University of Minnesota Hospital in Minneapolis for examination and consultation; an appointment was arranged for June 9. She was taken there by automobile on June 8. During that 450-mile trip she was on a life support oxygen system, and four or five stops were made to activate the system. She remained in the hospital for several days. The daughter's physician in Bismark wrote a letter to the company in which it was stated that "this referral to the University Hospital was of the utmost urgency and was accomplished at the only time available. Mr. Kane's time should be covered as if it were an emergency situation."

Testimony of the Company

Both Field and Kane worked under George Connors, chief of transmission. He said that he denied both claims because he did not believe that they involved an emergency. He expressed the view that a medical emergency must involve major surgery or a serious accident or illness, and that it must be unforeseen and require immediate action. He stated that he had followed that definition in ruling on other employee requests for emergency leave pay. Connors discussed both cases with the director of personnel who agreed because these events were "scheduled, not unforeseen."

POSITION OF THE UNION

The union held that both the Field and Kane cases constituted an emergency within the meaning of Article XI of the Agreement.[2] The union cited a definition from the *World Book* dictionary to substantiate its claim. The dictionary defines an emergency as "a sudden or unexpected happening or situation that calls for action without delay." It also states that it means a crisis that is a "trying or dangerous time or state of affairs." The union argued that the situations in both cases were trying or dangerous and a crisis of life or death nature. They were of a continuing nature, fraught with uncertainty and renewed by the dangerous aspects of the treatment. The union argued that "emergencies can be created by man in quest of corrective treatment."

The union urged that the arbitrator sustain the grievances of Field and Kane.

POSITION OF THE COMPANY

The company took the position that the claims of Melvin Kane and Roger Field were properly denied, because the events were scheduled in advance, and therefore there had been no need for immediate action and no emergency. The company had consistently followed a policy of allowing emergency leave pay only when a true emergency existed which had been unforeseen and which required immediate attention. This was not the case in these situations, and the company requested that the arbitrator deny the grievances of both Field and Kane.

APPENDIX

Relevant Provisions of the Contract

ARTICLE XI—SICK LEAVE

Section 4(c). Emergency leave, without payroll deduction, will be allowed for medical emergencies within the immediate family for the time necessary for such occasions, but not to exceed three (3) work days. Emergency leave shall be limited to serious accidents, illnesses, or major surgery. Doctor, dental, or eye appointments, or physical checkups will not be permitted. Immediate family shall mean those members of the employee's household and the following

---

[2] See Appendix for this provision.

relatives who may not reside within the employee's household: Husband, wife, son, daughter, father, mother, sister, brother, father- and mother-in-law. Upon request, emergency leave for family members not residing within the employee's household must be supported by a medical certificate which statement shall certify to the nature of the medical emergency.

QUESTIONS

1. According to the Company, what is an emergency?
2. Is the Field case different from the Kane case? If so, how?
3. According to Article XI of the collective bargaining agreement, does either of the two cases constitute an emergency? Discuss.
4. Do you agree with Connors' interpretation of the concept of emergency? Why, or why not?

68. THE DISPUTED TEST

Company: Star Manufacturing Company, St. Louis, Missouri

Union: International Brotherhood of Teamsters, Chauffeurs, Warehousemen, and Helpers of America, Local 688

On April 14, 1982, Roy Camp,[1] a setup operator at Star Manufacturing Company, submitted the following grievance to his supervisor:

> The company has disqualified me from the model template and sample maker job. I feel that I can effectively perform the duties outlined in the job description.
>
> Settlement Requested: Granted a 90-day trial period as described in the job bid.

On April 21, plant superintendent Robert Decker replied to Camp and the union as follows:

> After considering testimony given in the grievance hearing of April 20, 1982, with regards to Roy Camp's qualifications for a model maker position, please be advised of the following:
>
> Consideration was given to Camp's work experience, along with the results of job-related tests that were administered by the company. These were then compared with the qualifications required to be able to perform the duties of the position in question.
>
> It has been concluded that the grievant lacks the overall ability to fulfill all the requirements of this job. This lack of ability includes areas that are critical to the basic performance of the job.
>
> Therefore, the grievant's job bid and grievance are being denied.

The parties were unable to resolve the dispute, and as provided in the collective agreement, they submitted the case to an arbitrator for

---

[1] The names of all individuals have been disguised.

a final and binding decision. The parties agreed that the arbitrator should address the following issue:

> Did the Company violate the Agreement by not awarding Mr. Camp the position of model maker on which he was senior bidder and by not giving him a reasonable trial period on this job? If so, what should be the appropriate remedy?

BACKGROUND

Roy Camp had been employed by the company since 1973 and had been a setup operator since 1979. In describing his job he stated that it included such functions as reading and interpreting engineering blueprints, making setups on machines, and operating a number of machines such as the shearing machine, punch press, and brake press machines. Camp had a good work record with no disciplinary problems. He also received extra compensation as a "lead man." He was one of 12 setup men performing duties similar to his.

The job of model, template, and sample making[2] is located in a laboratory area separate from production operations. Camp stated that he had worked in the lab area on a number of occasions and that he had assisted several model makers whom he had known down through the years. While the model maker's job paid the same wage rate as the setup operator's job, Camp had bid on the former job in order that he "might learn something new and different." He said that the model maker operated many of the same machines and tools as that of a setup operator, but that it would not be difficult to learn the additional machines on which model makers work. He added that he had already operated much of the equipment in the lab. According to Camp a model maker primarily makes the templates (patterns) used in making the production items and from which a setup operator works in setting up and adjusting machines in the manufacturing process. The model maker develops a "prototype of what is manufactured in the plant."

Camp bid on the model maker's job in April 1982. He was the senior bidder on the list of those who bid on the position. Several days later he was administered a written test by the chief engineer, Joseph Shell.

Shell described the test as one requiring applicants to answer questions about various prints, reading caliper and micrometer measurements, and the like. The test placed special emphasis upon visualizing and conceptualizing three dimensional drawings. There

---

[2] See Appendix for job description and relevant contractual provisions.

were 10 questions requiring about 45 minutes to complete. Camp failed the test and was so notified about a week later. Shell later reviewed the test results with Camp, who felt that he had answered 7 of the 10 questions correctly. Shell, however, informed him that he lacked an essential skill in that he didn't have "the visual concept."

At the request of the union, Shell administered a second test to Camp. This test included a number of exercises in which he was required to make forms, shapes, and items from drawings. Shell informed Camp that he had also failed the second test and that he had "no visual concept for form or views." Camp disagreed with Shell's evaluation of his abilities because he had "to work from blueprints as a setup person." He stated that he did have to visualize three dimensions from drawings in his present job. Further, as a setup operator it was necessary for him on occasion to make new parts or modify existing parts and dies. He claimed that a setup operator must be able to visualize and that he could learn the visualization that was necessary for the model maker's job.

TESTIMONY AND POSITION OF THE UNION

The union contended that the positions of setup operator and model maker were quite similar although there were some important differences. For example, the model maker works from "beginning to end on each new model, puts the parts together, and tests the model to ensure that it functions as originally conceived." The union steward, Gino Bertelli, argued that the best experience for becoming a model maker would be to work as a setup operator. He also stated that to his knowledge, no black employee, such as Camp, had ever risen to the position of model maker. Bertelli stated that he had reviewed Camp's test results and felt that he had performed adequately to warrant a 90-day trial in that position. He also reviewed the test results of Robert Peters, the second most senior setup operator who successfully passed the test, and felt that he had done "only about equal" to the test performance of Camp. The steward noted that a model maker could readily obtain assistance and help from the engineers and inspectors if a model maker had a problem with a job assignment. While he minimized the significance of the test results, he acknowledged that tests had been used for many years for the model maker's job. Bertelli pointed out that the company had also used a similar test for the position of inspector since 1968. Camp had taken that test in 1975 when he had bid on the job of inspector. He failed that test; the company, nevertheless, gave him a trial period to qualify for the job. He successfully completed the probationary period for the position of inspector. And, subsequently, he was promoted to the job as a fully qualified inspector. Bertelli argued that Camp would qualify as a model maker, if given the 90-day trial period, in the same fashion as he had earlier qualified for the inspector's position. He claimed that Camp had earned the opportunity to try out for the position of model maker and should not be denied that opportunity because of race.

The position of the union was summarized in a post-hearing brief. Relevant excerpts from this brief follow:

> Roy Camp was the senior qualified person bidding on the model maker job. The company's entire case is based on the subjective opinion of Joseph Shell that Camp was unqualified because he failed to prove on the tests to Mr. Shell that he had the ability to "visualize" properly. They did not in any manner contend that "relative" ability played a part in the management's decision to place the recently hired Leo Kelly in the model maker job since the collective bargaining agreement clearly is of the modified type which provides that the senior employee shall be given preference if he possesses sufficient ability. Under this clause the question simply is, "Can the employee in fact do the job?" In this case the company has admitted that no employee can step immediately into the model maker job and perform it. Training is necessary.
>
> The union strongly believes that the company violated the intent of Article VIII by *solely* relying on the test results to determine that Camp was not qualified. The union has never contested the right of the company to administer a test to employees to aid management in determining an employee's ability to do a job. The key is that the test results must be *only one* of various methods and means of determining the issue of ability. In the instant case the company *solely* relied on the test results as judged by Mr. Shell.
>
> Elkouri and Elkouri in *How Arbitration Works* (1973 edition) state: "It must be kept in mind that arbitrators generally take the view that while the test may be used as an aid in judging ability or as a "verification" of ability, the employer may not base his determination of ability solely upon the results of a test but must consider other factors and other evidence."
>
> The union believes that the company failed to consider the grievant's excellent past performance in the job of "setup" which admittedly is one of the best training grounds for a model maker job. Mr. Camp's past experience was not given due consideration. Because the grievant on a couple of questions failed to convince Mr. Shell that he had the "visualization" ability, the company has unfairly prevented him from expanding his job future. The evidence is clear that the model maker position is a stepping stone to a management position. Mr. Camp believed he had all the qualities and abilities to become a good model maker just as he had become a good setup person. Undoubtedly had Mr. Camp been required in 1975 to pass a test for

"setup" he would have failed, just as he failed an identical type test for the inspector's job.

Elkouri and Elkouri in their book *How Arbitration Works* state on page 583: "Agreements sometimes provide for a trial or break-in period on the job to determine ability, and questions in connection with the interpretation and application of such provisions are frequently arbitrated. In the absence of contractual provision, the question arises as to whether management must give the senior employee a trial. Obviously, ability to perform the job, or the lack of it, may be demonstrated by a trial or break-in period on the job. As stated by arbitrator Carl A. Warns, "The best evidence as to whether an employee can do a job is to give him a fair trial on it." Arbitrator Vernon L. Stouffer stated that "The purpose of a trial period is to afford an employee the opportunity to demonstrate that he has the ability for the job in question or can with some familiarization therewith achieve the necessary skills within a reasonable period of time to perform the job in an acceptable manner."

The grievant and the union have from the very beginning of this dispute only asked that the company give Mr. Camp a trial period. Article VIII, Section (e) of the contract clearly protects both parties and contemplates the use of such a trial period. The union urges that the company has been unfair in not utilizing the trial period provision.

Thus, arbitrators generally are inclined to the view that if there is a reasonable doubt as to the ability of the senior employee and if the trial would cause no serious inconvenience, it should be granted, but that a trial should not be required in all cases.

In order for management to fairly use test results, the test itself must be prepared, administered, and graded fairly and objectively. It is the union's belief that in the instant case the company has failed to prove that the above criteria were observed. Mr. Shell continually used the phrases "lack of ability to visualize" or "no visual concept" as demonstrating why he considered that Mr. Camp failed the test. But this observation by Mr. Shell is his subjective *opinion*.

For all of the above reasons, the union strenuously urges the sustaining of this grievance.

TESTIMONY AND POSITION OF THE COMPANY

The company first made considerable effort to establish the credibility and testimony of chief engineer Joseph Shell by pointing out that he had been employed by Star for 26 years; that he was an electrical engineer; that he had served as plant manager for several years; and that he had been "accepted as an expert in numerous federal and state trials as a professional engineer."

In discussing Camp's performance on the test, Shell described the test as being made up of 10 questions. Six of the questions were concerned with flat planes; Camp answered five of the six correctly. Three of the questions involved three-dimensional drawings and prints; Camp answered all three incorrectly. He stated that from the test results, he concluded that Camp was unable to "visualize parts in total and accumulate the kind of information necessary to perform the model maker's job adequately."

Shell stated that the model maker's job was different from the setup operator's job in three major respects: (1) the model maker must take sketches, prints, and verbal instructions from an engineer and convert these into parts (including their assembly) which had never before been produced; (2) a model maker must be able to make templates from a part and convert these to flat view sketches from which setup men adjust and set up various machines to produce items for production; (3) the model maker on occasion must also test various items produced from the sketches and drawings for electrical, chemical, and other properties. The test administered to Camp primarily addressed the first area, not the other two, which Shell claimed contained the primary differences between a model maker's and setup operator's job. The test primarily attempted to determine whether or not the applicant possessed the basic visualization skills necessary to perform the job. Management felt that it lacked the expertise to train a person to acquire conceptual skills and felt that this type of skill would be most difficult to teach under the best of circumstances.

Shell stated that after Camp and the union complained about the results of the first test, he agreed to give him a second test which he had never done before in this kind of situation. The second test contained five problems, of which Camp correctly answered two and correctly answered a third in part. Shell stated that the results of the second test confirmed those of the first—that Camp could not "visualize spatial dimensions," an ability that was absolutely essential for a model maker.

The company stated that Shell had administered basically the same test or tests to all other model makers in the plant since 1968. Those who were awarded the job of model maker had all passed the same test or tests as those given to Camp. These tests are "very practical and directly job related;" they included several blueprints and sketches typical of the work performed by a model maker.

Shell stated that applicants who failed the test were not promoted to the position of model maker. No one who had failed the test had ever filed a grievance in the 14 years that the testing procedure had been in effect.

The company pointed out that as a result of Camp's grievance, it employed an outside consultant to review the procedures and tests involved in this case. The consultant's report stated:

> In my opinion the testing procedure covers the various phases of the work which is to be accomplished, particularly since test questions are based upon common production parts and is therefore fair.

Shell testified that Robert Peters, the second most senior setup operator, was awarded the vacant position of model maker but he stayed on that job only a week before deciding to return to his former job as setup operator. Subsequently, Leo Kelly who was also on the bid list, was given the same two tests as Camp and Peters. Kelly passed both tests successfully and is currently a model maker.

The position of the company was summarized in a post-hearing brief. Relevant excerpts from this brief follow:

> The contract is clear that this position is to be awarded, not on strict seniority, but to the senior "qualified" bidder. Consistent past practice has given this provision the meaning that, for the model maker position, the bidder "qualifies" by passing a test. This same practice has also consistently applied to the inspector position and was in 1980 extended to the setup position. On these facts it is difficult to see how the union can challenge the company's right to test model maker bidders.
>
> Therefore the union must be challenging, not the company's right to test, but the result in the particular case of grievant Camp. Fundamentally the integrity of the tests depends upon the competence and integrity of the tester. The qualifications of Shell as an expert engineer were unrebutted and his testimony was unchallenged by any union witness with similar expertise. Normally judges and arbitrators accept the testimony of lay witnesses only as to what they saw or heard but not as to what they opine. The point of qualifying someone as an expert is that a tribunal is entitled to rely on that expert's opinion. The company submits that in an industrial setting both it and the arbitrator are entitled to rely on an engineer's opinion as to whether Camp passed tests within the engineer's competence to devise and judge. The union offered no expert testimony to the contrary.
>
> The union noted that Camp failed the test for the position of inspector, at which he ably performed. But this does not show that the tests are unreliable. Camp's inspector test was taken in May 1975, over a year and a half before he was awarded the inspector position on January 20, 1977. Apparently he learned enough in that year and a half to become a successful inspector.
>
> The union also argues that Camp's performance was similar to that of Peters, who passed. First, the company feels that it and the arbitrator are entitled to rely on the judgment of chief engineer Shell that Peters passed and that Camp failed. Moreover, we wish to point out

that Peters did not exhibit the same consistent deficiency as Camp had. We concede that Peters' results were closer to those of Camp than to those of Kelly. Perhaps this is why Kelly is still on the job and Peters begged off after a mere week. If Peters, who tested better than Camp, lasted but a week, surely Camp was unqualified.

The union argued that Camp does not test well but he worked well. But chief engineer Shell took the test procedures from day-to-day work performed at the company. Therefore if you can't do the test, you can't do the work. If Camp could not do the relatively simple visualization required on common production parts used in the test, how could he produce parts from more complex prints? An independent industrial engineer validated the job relatedness and fairness of its tests. The union offered no such evidence to the contrary.

Chief engineer Shell's tests and judgment of them were considered fair by all employees who passed and failed them since 1968. At least no one grieved until now. Moreover when the union in 1980 agreed to testing for the setup position, they knew that chief engineer Shell would conduct these tests as he had all others. If he or his tests had been considered unfair, the union would never have agreed to expanding his testing jurisdiction to yet another position.

The union made an unworthy effort to claim racial discrimination. The truth is that these same tests have been given to employees, black and white, for years. When a black passed the test, no white grieved his being awarded the position. When a white failed the test, he accepted this result. Only Camp has grieved. In fact the only racial discrimination here is that, for the first time in its history, the company gave a bidder (Camp) two tests, something it had never done for a white employee. Instead of discriminating against Camp, the company bent over backward for him.

Moreover if one compared the union's description of the model maker's duties with Shell's description, one would never guess they were the same position. For purposes of this grievance the union protrayed the model maker as a glorified setup man. If that is all the model maker was, there would be no separate classification. Shell's description of the model maker's duties shows both the importance of the position and the reason for testing.

Finally, the union bore and failed to carry its burden of proof that the company violated the contract.

The company urged the arbitrator to deny the grievance.

APPENDIX
_____

Relevant Provisions of the Contract

ARTICLE VIII—JOB VACANCIES

(a) All job vacancies or new positions and the number thereof shall be posted for a period of two (2) working days. Eligible employees not at work at the time of posting shall be notified by registered mail or telegram of the opening and will have two working days after receipt of such notice in which to notify the company of their intention to bid for such opening, provided that they return to work within 30 calendar days of the original posting of such an opening.

* * * * *

(c) Employees shall be entitled to bid on such jobs, and the job shall be awarded to the senior qualified employee bidding therefore within a period of five (5) working days and shall be paid at the appropriate rate of pay. If the senior employee bidding for the opening is not qualified to perform the work satisfactorily, the job shall be awarded to the next senior qualified employee who has bid for the job, subject to the grievance procedure. No employee's bid for an opening will be considered unless it would represent a movement to a job of the same or higher rate of pay, except by mutual agreement of the parties.

* * * * *

(e) An employee awarded a job through the foregoing bidding procedure shall be given a fair trial for a period not to exceed 90 days, but it shall at the end of a fair trial be decided by the Employer (subject to the grievance procedure) that such employee cannot adapt to the new position, or if the employee desires, he or she shall be returned to his or her former position at the rate of pay for that position.

Relevant Job Description

Model, Template and Sample Making. Under the direction of his supervisor, the model, template and sample maker performs duties including, but not limited to, the following:

1. Uses hand tools, power tools, power machinery, spot-welders, grinders, etc. and employs soldering and brazing and other techniques to produce models, templates and samples as required.

2. Reads drawings and is able to make parts and templates from prints, sketches and verbal instructions or sample parts.

3. Performs other experimental and testing work as directed by the Chief Engineer and his assistants.

4. Must furnish and be proficient in the use of his own tools.

5. Keeps daily time card.

6. Maintains orderly working area.

The Job Bid Posted on the Company Bulletin Board

JOB BID

DATE POSTED _____4-06-82_____
TIME POSTED _____11 A.M._____
If qualifications are in doubt test will be given.
PROGRESSION RATE SCHEDULE
$6.67–$8.31
HOURS OF WORK * Unless otherwise stated, the hours of work will be the same as those worked by the general factory work force.
TRIAL PERIOD * Unless otherwise stated, the trial period will be from five (5) to ninety (90) days.
BIDS ARE TO BE TURNED IN TO A FOREMAN OR TO THE PRODUCTION OFFICE.

QUESTIONS

1. Is the job of model maker different form that of setup operator? If so, how? Are these differences significant to this case?
2. What was the skill that the company contended that Camp lacked?
3. What is the "head and shoulders" principle? Why is this an important concept in cases of this type?
4. Did the company have a duty to grant Camp a 90-day trial period? Why or why not?

69. THE FORBIDDEN NUPTIALS

Company: Distribution Center of Columbus, Inc., Columbus, Ohio

Union: Columbus Warehouseman's Union, Local 102

Mark Fuller[1] was hired by the Distribution Center of Columbus in February 1978. He was terminated on November 22, 1983, because on October 22, 1983, he had married a fellow employee, Irene Fraser. Fraser was hired by the company in June 1976; on November 22, 1983, she had seven years and five months seniority, while her spouse had five years and nine months seniority. The company terminated Fuller, the less senior of the two, for having violated an administrative policy[2] prohibiting the employment of related persons.

BACKGROUND

Fuller and Fraser met while both were employed by Distribution Center. They began dating, and in April 1983 they began living together with the full knowledge of the company. This knowledge was both informal in that their supervisor knew of it, and formal by reason of Fraser changing her address on company personnel records to the address of Fuller.

The administrative policy in question was an internal management document. It was not collectively bargained; nor was it part of the published work rules which were made available to employees when hired and which were posted. The administrative policy was not posted but its existence had been rumored among employees including Fuller and Fraser. However, it had never been seen in

---

[1] The names of all individuals have been disguised.

[2] See Appendix for relevant provisions of both the contract and the administrative policy.

written form by any of the employees, nor by any union official, until Fuller made a formal inquiry to his supervisor. He was furnished a copy on October 19, only a few days before the couple was married.

Both Fuller and Fraser were classified as warehousemen B. Neither supervised the other. Both had received awards for attendance for the first six months of 1983, and neither presented any disciplinary problems. Both were considered very good employees during this time. If Fuller had not married Fraser, he would not have been terminated by the company.

POSITION OF THE UNION

The union argued that the company had no right to enforce its policy when that policy had not been clearly communicated to employees. The union also argued that the policy was unreasonable, unjust, and contrary to public policy. Fuller and Fraser did not learn of the policy until they made formal inquiry and even then they received a copy only three days before their marriage.

The right of management to make reasonable rules does not override the "just cause" protection provided in the collective bargaining agreement.

The union urged the arbitrator to order the company to rehire Fuller with full back pay and seniority, to restore any rights and privileges lost as a result of the company's action, and to remove all reference to this disciplinary action from his personnel records.

POSITION OF THE COMPANY

The company contended that the discharge of Fuller was for "just cause," because he had knowingly violated the company's long-standing "no-spouse," antinepotism policy. The policy was a reasonable one and was supported by substantial business considerations. Further, the policy had been enforced in the past and should also be enforced in this instance. The labor agreement itself provided that the company could make and enforce reasonable rules and regulations.

Finally, the company argued that if the union's position were sustained in this case, this decision would abrogate the policy with respect to all present employees. This would seriously jeopardize the company's ability to protect itself against the detrimental effects which result from spouses working together.

The company urged the arbitrator to deny this grievance in its entirety.

APPENDIX

Relevant Provisions of the Contract

ARTICLE III—MANAGEMENT RIGHTS

The company retains the right to make and enforce reasonable rules of conduct and regulations not inconsistent with the provisions of this Agreement. However, such rights can only be exercised to the extent that the express provisions of this Agreement do not specifically limit or qualify this right.

The company agrees that disciplinary action, including discharge, shall be only for just cause.

Relevant Provisions of the Administrative Policy Manual

Distribution Centers, Inc. has a policy which prohibits the employment of anyone who is related to another Distribution Centers Associate. This policy is a common practice which many companies adopt for a number of sound reasons, some of which are as follows:

1. Avoiding difficulties in scheduling work where two relatives desire the same hours of work.
2. Preventing family matters from distracting Distribution Centers Associates from their job duties.
3. Minimizing absenteeism, where one relative must take time off to care for another.
4. Avoiding conflicts involving the Associate's loyalties to the spouse or other relatives and his obligation to the Company.

This policy was initiated in January of 1970 and exceptions were made for any relative on the payroll at that time.

For these reasons, the company will not hire or continue the employment of relatives of any existing Distribution Centers Associates or of their spouses regardless of location or facility involved excepting those hired prior to January 1970, as indicated above. The term relatives includes those related by blood or marriage, and if used in this policy, means spouse, parent, children (including foster and adopted), brother, or sister. Should two Distribution Center Associates become related to each other, whether by marriage, adoption, or otherwise, one must resign within 30 days thereafter. If neither employee resigns the one with the least seniority with the company will be discharged.

QUESTIONS

1. Why did the company enact a rule prohibiting the employment of related persons?
2. Do you agree with the Company's position on this issue? Why, or why not?
3. Were Fraser and Fuller adequately advised of the rule?
4. Regardless of its outcome, why is a case of this type difficult to management from a policy point of view?

70. THE FRUSTRATED BUS DRIVERS

School District: Des Moines Independent Community School District, Des Moines, Iowa

Union: American Federation of State, County, and Municipal Employees, Local 2048

On June 22, 1983, Patricia Abbey, Jean Bass, Carol Real, Linda Sims, and Dana Tebo each filed a grievance alleging that the "grievant has relatively equal qualifications, if not superior qualifications, and has greater total seniority within the unit" than the five persons selected for the position of transportation driver, class 2.[1] Linda Sims filed a concurrent complaint with the Des Moines Human Rights Commission. The five employees were currently employed in the position of transportation driver, class 1, and each had bid on the class 2 position which had been announced in School District Bulletin 26, dated February 28, 1983.[2]

The grievances were processed through the grievance procedure to arbitration. The parties agreed that the issues to be resolved by the arbitrator were:

1. Is the grievance of Linda Sims arbitrable?
2. Did the employer violate the comprehensive agreement when it eliminated the grievants from consideration for the class 2 driver positions announced on February 28, 1983? If so, what is the appropriate remedy?

BACKGROUND

The collective bargaining agreement provided for three classifications of transportation drivers. Class 1 drivers work less than six

---

[1] The names of all individuals have been disguised.

[2] See Appendix for relevant provisions of the contract, state statutes, and job descriptions.

hours per day and may be assigned daily routes or they may be unassigned. Class 2 drivers work more than six hours per day for 10 or 12 months per year and are assigned to specific routes. Class 3 drivers are at the highest classification and work full time but are unassigned.

Forty-five applicants filed for the five positions that were announced to be open on February 28, 1983. The employer (Des Moines Independent School District) reviewed the applications of all those applying and selected Sheryl Smith, Daniel Wesley, Joseph Rohn, David Knox, and Lance Cary to fill the vacancies. The five grievants had greater seniority than those selected by the employer and grieved to be placed in the class 2 driver positions with full back pay.

On July 6, 1983, Linda Sims filed a racial discrimination complaint before the Des Moines Human Rights Commission. She recited essentially the same facts that she offered in her grievance to the employer.

Testimony of Linda Sims

Sims testified that she was a class 1 driver and had been with the School District since March 1, 1978. She stated that this was her seventh or eighth driving season and that she had applied five or six times for a class 2 driver position. In each instance, she was refused on the grounds that her qualifications "were not deemed equal." She alleged that many other positions were automatically filled by seniority but that the employer consistently discriminated against her. She affirmed that she had been convicted of speeding in February 1982, that she had several nonchargeable accidents, but that in 1981 she did not have a chargeable accident. She further acknowledged that she had received a written reprimand and that she had also been cited for insubordination by the School District. She reported that her absences were principally for surgery and maternity reasons and for injuries suffered in an automobile accident in which she had been involved. All of these, she claimed, were "excusable."

Sims stated that her claim pending with the Des Moines Human Rights Commission was separate from her grievance. She said that she filed it because there was a 180-day time limit in which to file a claim; she could not wait until after this grievance had been resolved to file a claim.

Testimony of Jean Bass

Jean Bass testified that she was a class 1 driver and had worked for the employer since September 1978. She stated that her performance evaluations had been good and that she had received commendations. She reported that her attendance was average and that she had no chargeable accidents. She further alleged that her absences were due to bronchitis and pneumonia. She affirmed that she was presently on maternity leave. She admitted that she had been off from her work for almost a year on approved leave and that even if she had been earlier selected as a class 2 driver, she could not have performed those duties until the present time. She stated that she had had her baby and that she was now available. She further acknowledged that she had not informed the School District of her present availability until this time.

Testimony of Patricia Abbey

Patricia Abbey testified that she had been a class 1 driver for the school since August 1979. She stated that her application for a class 2 position had been denied. She acknowledged that she had a high rate of absenteeism.

Testimony of Carol Real

Carol Real testified that she had been a class 1 driver since August 1979. She stated that she had applied for a class 2 position on four previous occasions and had been rejected in each instance. She pointed out that she had two letters of commendation in her file and that she had no chargeable accidents on her record. She affirmed that she had received a low rating on her personal evaluations by her supervisor, Sharon McCloud, but she claimed that these evaluations were unfair.

Testimony of Dana Tebo

Dana Tebo testified that she had been a class 1 driver for the employer since September 4, 1979. She alleged that the School District had used her 1980 evaluation in finding her not qualified for the position of class 2 driver instead of her 1981 evaluation. She acknowledged that she had had a change in name during this period. She also acknowledged that the low ratings she received for poor attendance in both 1980 and 1981 were correct.

Testimony of Peter Ellis, Chief Union Steward

Peter Ellis testified that he was the class 3 lead driver for the school district. Along with driving, he also trained drivers and assisted in their evaluation. He reported that he also held the position of chief union steward.

Ellis argued that the employer was unfair in its selection process. First, he criticized the selection of an applicant, David Knox, who had no previous experience driving a bus. This applicant's prior driving experience had been as a food truck driver. All other applicants with bus driving experience should have been recognized as better qualified. Second, Ellis alleged that the employer gave inadequate consideration to seniority. Seniority is important to workers; it should be given primary consideration; junior applicants should be given preference only when the employer can clearly establish that their performance, abilities, and qualification are "head and shoulders" above that of the senior candidates. He claimed that, in his opinion, all of the grievants had more than equal ability to those selected. They also had greater seniority. The criteria used by the employer were neither consistent nor fair.

Ellis spoke to the issue of the arbitrability of the Sims grievance. He argued that her grievance was filed to establish her "relatively equal" qualifications and greater seniority, whereas her complaint before the Des Moines Human Rights Commission alleged a different problem—that of continuous "racial discrimination."

The chief union steward also criticized the use by the employer of attendance records. This factor inherently was included in the factors of discipline and personal evaluation. Thus, attendance had been weighted much too heavily in evaluating the relative performance of the candidates.

Testimony of John Enders, Supervisor of Transportation

John Enders stated that he had been employed with the school district for 18 years and he had served as the director of transportation for four years. He also indicated that he had driven buses, repaired them, and had extensive experience and training in the management of a school transportation department.

Enders testified that he gathered complete and accurate data on each of the 45 applicants on the following categories: seniority, driving records, attendance, discipline, and personal evaluations. He said that he prepared a chart on which he listed each applicant according to seniority. In separate columns he summarized the applicant's driving record, attendance, discipline, and personal evaluations.

Enders reported that he collected and analyzed the information on each applicant in an attempt to comply with an arbitration ruling rendered by John M. Gradwohl, arbitrator, on July 23, 1982. This earlier grievance concerned a similar dispute between the parties. It had been filed by other grievants who had been eliminated from consideration for class 2 driver positions that were posted by the employer on October 26, 1981.[3]

Enders explained that shortly after the Gradwohl decision, he and Dr. David Prince, assistant superintendent for personnel management, developed those five categories used in evaluating applicants for the position of class 2 driver.

He further explained that he assigned each applicant a point value on each of the four factors (driving record, attendance, discipline, personal evaluation), following guidelines established by Prince and himself. From this, he obtained a total point value for each applicant. He and Prince had established a minimum acceptable score on each of the four factors, as well as a minimum total score. From those who met the minimum established standards on each factor and who also met or exceeded the minimum total score, Enders prepared a list of acceptable candidates listed according to seniority. Those achieving satisfactory scores were further reviewed. Where the composite scores of applicants were equal or nearly equal, the senior applicant was selected. The five candidates selected by Enders and Prince were the most senior of the group considered to be clearly most competent.

Enders said that the applicant's driving record was relevant because of the safety factor associated with the transportation of students. He indicated that regular and prompt attendance was essential in order to let both parents and students know that the bus system operated on a dependable schedule and in order to maintain good discipline among those riding the buses. The disciplinary record of applicants was considered to be important because it related to their behavior, to the type of example they set for students, and to their eligibility for promotion. Enders stated that he reviewed the personal evaluations by the supervisors of the applicants, along with his own personal observations and opinions of each applicant based upon his observations of their personal behavior and work performance.

Enders stated that after going through this evaluation process, he reviewed the entire process with Dr. Prince. The final selection of the five new class 2 drivers was made after careful deliberation by both of them. He stated that they were particularly careful to comply with the requirements of the Gradwohl decision.

---

[3] See Appendix for relevant text of the Gradwohl arbitration decision.

Testimony of Dr. David Prince, Assistant Superintendent for Personnel Management

Dr. Prince reaffirmed Enders' testimony to the effect that they had worked together in setting up the evaluation process. He stated that the criteria and the charts used to review the applicants were as fair and objective as circumstances permitted. He further stated that he was satisfied as to the propriety and fairness of the procedure utilized; and he felt confident that he and Enders had selected the right candidates.

POSITION OF THE UNION

The union argued that the employer's selection policies and procedures had not been consistent. Prior to the most recent instance of selecting class 2 drivers, the school district required that the applicant must have had previous experience with driving a bus. In the current instance, truck driving experience was deemed adequate. The employer erred in awarding a class 2 position to a food truck driver; all experienced bus drivers should have been evaluated as better qualified.

The union further argued that the school district gave inadequate regard to the factor of seniority. Repeating the testimony of the chief union steward Ellis, the union contended that the senior employees must be given preference, except where the employer could prove that the junior employee was "head and shoulders" above the senior employee. The school district did not prove this; therefore, the five grievants should be promoted to the position of class 2 driver over the five others recently promoted.

The union asserted that the Linda Sims grievance was arbitrable and that it did not conflict with Article XVIII of the collective bargaining agreement. The issue before the Des Moines Human Rights Commission involved racial discrimination while the issue presented to the arbitrator concerned relative ability and seniority.

The union urged the arbitrator to direct the school district to transfer and promote the five grievants to the position of class 2 transportation driver and to make them whole for any back pay and rights to which they would have been entitled if they had been promoted to class 2 positions at the time of the original selection.

POSITION OF THE SCHOOL DISTRICT

The school district contended that the Linda Sims grievance was not arbitrable under Article XVIII of the collective bargaining agreement. The wording of the complaint filed with the Des Moines Human Rights Commission was almost identical to that of the grievance filed with the employer. By the terms of the collective bargaining agreement, the arbitrator was barred from hearing her grievance.

The school district claimed that the selection criteria and process developed and utilized by John Enders and Dr. David Prince in the selection of the class 2 drivers from the applicants generated from the February 28, 1983 notice complied with the decision of arbitrator Gradwohl. The employer's selection system was designed properly and administered fairly in the consideration of each applicant for a class 2 driver position.

The district took the position that seniority was given primary consideration, but that the other factors were also properly assessed in making the selection decisions. Article IV of the collective bargaining agreement gives the employer the right to transfer employees and Article VIII provides that the needs of the employer, as well as of the employee, shall be considered in making transfers.

The school district requested that the arbitrator rule that the Linda Sims grievance be declared unarbitrable under the terms of Article XVIII of the collective bargaining agreement and that the arbitrator sustain the school district's action on the four other grievances.

APPENDIX

Relevant Provisions of the Contract

ARTICLE IV—MANAGEMENT RIGHTS
PUBLIC EMPLOYER RIGHTS

Consistent with this Agreement, the public employer shall have, in addition to all powers, duties, and rights established by constitutional provision, statute, ordinance, charter, or special act, the exclusive power, duty, and the right to:

*   *   *   *   *

2. Hire, promote, demote, transfer, assign, and retain public employees in positions within the public agency.

*   *   *   *   *

4. Maintain the efficiency of governmental operations.

*   *   *   *   *

6. Determine and implement methods, means, assignments and personnel by which the public employer's operations are to be conducted.

7. Take such actions as may be necessary to carry out the mission of the public employer.

* * * * *

9. Exercise all powers and duties granted to the public employer by law.

ARTICLE VIII—TRANSFER PROCEDURE

Transfer shall mean movement of any employee to another job classification, or location within the District. A vacancy exists as a consequence of an employee's action or the creation of a new position.

Notice of such vacancy will be posted in the "Superintendent's Bulletin" and within seven working days of the date of the "Superintendent's Bulletin" employees may apply for the vacancy by filing a written statement with the office of the Executive Director of Personnel. The notice of the vacancy shall include job qualifications deemed necessary, hours of work, and location of the opening. The Executive Director of Personnel shall acknowledge to the applicant the receipt of such application, and shall notify the applicant when the position is filled.

The Employer shall consider the needs of the District and each applicant's qualifications. When two or more applicants have relatively equal qualifications, the employee applicant with the greatest total seniority within the unit will be given priority.

ARTICLE XVIII—GRIEVANCE PROCEDURE

* * * * *

B. Rights of employees to representation

* * * * *

It is understood and agreed by the parties that the grievance procedure and the steps outlined in the grievance procedure are the appropriate method of resolving grievances which may arise during the term of this Agreement. If an employee formally files an alleged violation of this Agreement other than under the grievance procedure, then the Employer shall not be required to process the said claimed set of facts through the grievance procedure.

C. Steps in grievance procedure

* * * * *

Step IV   Binding Arbitration

*   *   *   *   *

The arbitrator, in his/her opinion, shall not amend, modify, nullify, or add to the provisions of the Agreement. His/her decision must be based solely and only upon his interpretation of the meaning or application of the express relevant language of the Agreement. He/she shall be asked to issue his decision within 30 calendar days after conclusion of testimony and argument.

Relevant State Statutes

Section 20.7, Code of Iowa (1983) Public employer rights.   Public employers shall have, in addition to all powers, duties, and rights established by constitutional provision, statute, ordinance, charter, or special act, the exclusive power, duty, and the right to:

1. Direct the work of its public employees.
2. Hire, promote, demote, transfer, assign and retain public employees in positions within the public agency.
3. Suspend or discharge public employees for proper cause.
4. Maintain the efficiency of governmental operations.
5. Relieve public employees from duties because of lack of work or for other legitimate reasons.
6. Determine and implement methods, means, assignments and personnel by which the public employer's operations are to be constructed.
7. Take such actions as may be necessary to carry out the mission of the public employer.
8. Initiate, prepare, certify and administer its budget.
9. Exercise all powers and duties granted to the public employer by law.

Section 20.17(6), Code of Iowa (1983), as follows:
No arbitrator's decision shall be valid or enforceable if its implementation would be inconsistent with any statutory limitation on the public employer's funds, spending or budget or would substantially impair or limit the performance of any statutory duty by the public employer.
Section 20.18, Code of Iowa (1983);   An arbitrator's decision on a grievance may not change or amend the terms, conditions of applications of the collective bargaining agreement.

452

Job Description Published February 28, 1983.

TRANSPORTATION DRIVER
Class 2 (10 months)

Hours of work: to fit District's need

Required experience/training: Valid chauffeur's license; driving record void of moving violations, convictions or suspensions; demonstrable leadership, communications and organizational ability; good personal attributes and physical qualifications.

Desired experience/training: High school diploma; previous bus or truck driving experience.

Special requirement of the position: Must qualify for State School Bus Driver Permit; physical attributes sufficient to meet the demands of the position—vision, lifting, climbing, etc. (physical examination on file); personal attributes—alertness, normal intelligence, capable of managing students and retaining their respect; safety oriented and responsible driver; disciplined with an adherence to the rules and regulations of the Iowa Department of Transportation, Iowa Department of Public Instruction, and the District concerning driving, driving habits and conditions of continuing employment; competitive rating on employee evaluation criteria as established by the District.

Qualified applicants should write to Dr. David Prince, Assistant Director of Personnel. Applications close March 9.

Relevant Sections of Text of Decision of Arbitrator John M. Gradwohl (July 23, 1982).

The Comprehensive Agreement states plainly in the Transfer Procedure Article:

The Employer shall consider the needs of the District and each applicant's qualifications. When two or more applicants have relatively equal qualifications, the employee applicant with the greatest total seniority within the unit will be given priority.

It is equally plain from the prescreening criteria and from the testimony at the arbitration hearing that the School District did not give effect to the contractual language "When two or more applicants have relatively equal qualifications, the applicant with the greatest total seniority within the unit will be given priority." The preceding sentence allows the School District to "consider the needs of the District and each applicant's qualifications." The safety and regular reliable attendance considerations are certainly important qualifications. The parties have agreed in the Comprehensive Agreement that, additionally, the School District will apply a seniority factor which gives a priority to the employee with the greatest total seniority within the unit when two or more applicants have relatively equal qualifications. The School District simply did not carry out its contractual obligation to take seniority into account in the present instance.

QUESTIONS

1. Assess the "qualifications" of each of the grievants for the position of transportation driver, class 2.
2. Does it make any difference that Linda Sims concurrently filed a grievance with the district and a charge with the Des Moines Human Rights Commission? Why, or why not?
3. Did the district simultaneously comply with the terms of the collective bargaining agreement and the terms of the decision of Arbitrator John M. Gradwohl? Discuss.

71. NO BREAD IN THE STORE

Company: Wolf Baking Co., Inc., Baton Rouge, Louisiana

Union: International Brotherhood of Teamsters, Chauffeurs, Warehousemen and Helpers of America, Local 568

BACKGROUND

Route salesman Kevin Holt[1] was discharged by the Wolf Baking Company on October 6, 1983. The company charged that Holt's unsatisfactory work performance in antagonizing an important customer justified his summary dismissal without either previous warnings or without a written statement to either him or the union at the time of discharge.

Holt had been with the company for five and one-half years and was responsible for the delivery of the company's baking products to customers on his route. He was compensated in part by a commission from sales. Routes were subject to bid and were awarded on the basis of seniority. His route included four convenience stores of the Little General chain.

On the morning of October 6, 1983, Holt was making his usual stop at the Little General store on MacArthur Drive in Alexandria, Louisiana. The store was in the process of being remodeled, and the display gondolas (including the bread racks) had been disassembled and taken outside. Despite the disarray and confusion, the store manager, Helen Jackson, had decided to remain open for business in the expectation that the remodeling would be completed later in the day.

Holt picked up the stale items and asked the store manager if he should make his delivery of fresh products. Jackson was not certain and asked her division manager, Barbara Bauer, who had come into

---

[1] The names of all individuals have been disguised.

town to supervise the remodeling. Bauer instructed her to tell Holt to come back in two hours by which time it was expected that the gondolas would be back up. However, Holt replied to her request that he would be tied up in a delivery to Oakdale, some 40 miles round trip, and could not be back at the requested time.

Bauer then came over to talk to Holt about the problem and again requested that he make some arrangement to have the bread delivered in about two hours. Holt offered to leave the products on top of a video game machine or to come back after completing the rest of his route, but neither of these alternatives were satisfactory to Bauer. She became irritated at what she perceived to be Holt's lack of cooperation. She then telephoned the company's offices in Baton Rouge and talked to Peter Larson in sales and marketing, telling him that Holt had "refused" to make the delivery and that the company had better get the merchandise out to the store or lose the entire business of the entire Little General chain. Then, Bauer told Holt to leave and not come back.

Larson reported his telephone conversation with Bauer to his superior, Jack Helwig, who began to try to contact Carl Day, sales manager of Wolf Baking in Alexandria. Day was located a short time later in Natchitoches and drove immediately to Alexandria to see what was going on at the Little General store. He talked to Bauer who was adamant that she did not want to allow Holt to continue serving her stores. Day promised to arrange for an immediate delivery.

In the meantime, Holt had attempted to contact his superior for instructions as to what he should do. He knew that his immediate supervisor, Clement Peyton, was at Fort Polk and unavailable, so he phoned the Alexandria office to try to reach Day. Day was out; the only person in the office was an employee who operated the company's thrift store on the premises. She told him that she did not know where he could locate Day. It did not occur to Holt to phone the Baton Rouge office. He decided, at that point, to go on to Oakdale and complete his route.

Holt returned to Alexandria at about 3 P.M. where he was making a delivery to the A&P Store when Day, who had been looking for him, drove up. Holt and Day drove directly to the Little General store to attempt to make the delivery. Bauer was still there; she refused to allow Holt to enter the store.

After returning to the office, Day phoned Jack Helwig in Baton Rouge to discuss the problem. They concluded that it would be necessary to terminate Holt because he could not service his route. The union steward offered a compromise solution which would allow Holt to exchange part of his route with another salesperson who was overextended. The company refused to accept this proposal. It made no other attempt to persuade the management of the Little General stores to rescind the ban on Holt.

On October 7, 1983, the union filed a grievance in behalf of Holt. It was processed through the grievance steps to arbitration.

POSITION OF THE UNION

The union argued that the discharge of Holt was procedurally deficient because it violated the express requirements of Article X of the contract.[2] This article required the company to give at least two written warnings, except for a specific list of offenses which require no warning notices. None of the items listed included the offense for which Holt had been charged. Thus, Holt should have received a written warning at most.

The union also contended that Holt was the victim of an unreasonable demand placed upon him by a customer, which, in order to satisfy, would have required him to delay service to his customers in Oakdale and which would possibly have antagonized them as well.

The union pointed out that this is not the only occasion that customers and salespersons have had a confrontation. This same thing had happened at Natchitoches several months earlier with a salesman named Smith. In that instance the company interceded with the customer to let the salesman back into the store. The company made no effort to persuade the management of the Little General store to reconsider its hasty action.

Finally, the union stated that it had proposed a viable alternative to switch part of Holt's route with that of another salesman. This would have cost the company nothing in extra commissions or downgraded service.

The union urged that the arbitrator restore Kevin Holt to his position of salesman and make him whole for all financial losses and benefits lost as a result of the company's action.

POSITION OF THE COMPANY

The company argued that Holt had disqualified himself from continuing as a route salesman by refusing to service his accounts. The company's business was extremely competitive, and its very survival in business depended on the good will created by its route salesmen in servicing their accounts; thus, any action which antagonized a customer had to be treated with the utmost seriousness.

---

[2] See Appendix.

The company asserted that there were situations where issuing a warning notice would be unwarranted. This was one of them. There was no way to resolve this conflict without either terminating Holt or losing a large and valued customer. It was not necessary for an offense this serious to be specifically listed in Article X any more than would be necessary to list a large number of other offenses, such as fighting, thievery, and so forth.

Finally, the company contended that it was under no obligation to switch routes among salesmen, even if the union and other salesmen agree to the switch. Furthermore, such a switching of customers might have given rise to a grievance by the other salesmen.

The company urged the arbitrator to deny the grievance and sustain the discharge of Kevin Holt.

APPENDIX

Relevant Provisions of the Contract

ARTICLE X

The employer shall not discharge or suspend any employee without cause, and shall give at least two (2) warning notices in writing of the complaint against such employee to the union. . . . No warning notice need be given to an employee before he is discharged if the cause of such discharge is for dishonesty, drunkenness, drinking on the job, reporting to work while under the influence of drugs, narcotics, or drink, carrying unauthorized passengers, failure to report an accident, or for recklessness in damage to equipment, carrying firearms or dangerous weapons on company property, possession of habit forming drugs on company property, fighting on company property, commission of criminal acts on company property. Discharge must be by proper notice.

QUESTIONS

1. Was the discharge of Holt by the company procedurally deficient? Why, or why not? If so, would this justify his continued employment under the circumstances?
2. Had the company taken reasonable measures to intercede with the customer in behalf of Holt? Discuss.
3. Is the discharge of Holt justified? If not, how should the company have handled the problem?

72. ONE LAST CHANCE?

Company: Ohio River Company, Cincinnati, Ohio
Union: United Steelworkers of America, Local 14262

At approximately 6 P.M. on December 13, 1983, the towboat *Jennifer Leigh* was passing through a lock on the Ohio River. Henry Thompson[1] and two other deckhands were called to the deck to "lock the barges through." This procedure required that the deckhands leave the vessel and work at the side of the lock. As the three men were returning to the vessel, Thompson fell overboard. He was rescued and admitted to the hospital. The admitting diagnosis read as follows:

ADMITTING DIAGNOSIS

1. Blunt abdominal trauma.
2. Multiple rib fractures, bilateral. Rule out fracture of the right wrist.
3. Acute alcohol intoxication.

Upon investigation the next day, Thompson admitted to two company representatives that he had been drinking. Thompson was immediately discharged for violation of a posted company rule prohibiting drinking and intoxication on the job.[2]

BACKGROUND

Henry Thompson was hired as a deckhand on December 30, 1969, by the Ohio River Company which conducts barge operations on the Ohio River.

---

[1] The names of all individuals have been disguised.
[2] See Appendix for relevant provisions of the contract and the company rule.

The work schedule of the crews is 25 continuous days of work on board a towboat followed by 25 days off the vessel.

The *Jennifer Leigh* carried a crew of 10 which was divided into two teams of four each with the remaining two members being a cook and a floating deckhand. Each crew worked six hours on and six hours off during the time they were on the vessel. Vessel crews did not remain together when crewmen were transferred from one vessel to another. The individual crewmen received new monthly assignments following their 25-day rest period.

Thompson joined the *Jennifer Leigh* at 2 A.M. on December 13, 1983. It was a company rule that when an employee boarded a vessel, he was required to sign a "boarding report." Thompson did not sign this boarding report as he was assigned immediately to the loading of stores. Thompson asked the captain if he could use his seniority to displace another employee in the position of the swing man deckhand. This was agreed, and Thompson then went to bed.

During the night, Thompson went up to the pilot house and told the pilot that he had forgotten his glasses and did not complete his boarding report. He subsequently located his glasses and completed the report at 12 noon on December 13, 1983. The relevant portion of the report read as follows:

1. Have you been treated by a physician for an injury or illness during your accumulated time off? (Answered NO)
2. Have you (in the last 24 hours) or are you now taking any drugs or medications prescribed by a physician or bought over the counter? (Answered NO)
3. Are you aware of any condition that may impair your ability to perform all duties of your job classification? (Answered NO)

During the investigation following Thompson's accident and hospitalization, it was learned that at least some of the crew suspected that he was under the influence of alcohol when he came on board the vessel early that morning and also that he had been drinking later during the day. They did not convey their suspicions to the vessel's officers. There was also evidence that some of the vessel's officers suspected that Thompson had been drinking while on board; however, no one followed up on these suspicions.

POSITION OF THE UNION

The union stated that Thompson admitted that he had an alcohol problem, that he was drinking on the vessel, and that it was wrong to do so. He had not had a drink since the accident and had joined and had become a continuing member of Alcoholics Anonymous— going to meetings three to five times per week.

460

Thompson began serious drinking when a three-month strike occurred in 1983. Prior to that time he had quit drinking and had his problem under control. He lived alone and, therefore, had suffered with the problem when he was off the vessel for the 25-day period. This accident impressed upon him the seriousness of his illness. On his own initiative he sought out and joined AA. He should now be considered a cured alcoholic.

The union alleged that the company had not enforced consistently its no-drinking rule. The union spokesperson testified that it was well known that on several occasions employees had come on board the vessel in an intoxicated state without the company taking any disciplinary action against them. It was also well known that the crew had put intoxicated crew members to bed to sleep off their drunken condition; the company took no disciplinary action in those situations either. Furthermore, in Thompson's case at least one of the vessel's officers knew, or should have known, that he had been drinking on board.

The union also contended that, since Thompson had admitted that he had an alcohol problem, had joined AA, and had not had a drink since the accident, he should be given one "last chance." The company should also consider his long and good service with no disciplinary record. Other employees in the past had been given "one last chance," and, following past practice and practicing fair and equal treatment to all, Thompson should also be given another chance.

The union strongly urged that the arbitrator reduce the penalty of discharge to that of suspension.

POSITION OF THE COMPANY

The company pointed out that Thompson was found to have an alcohol content of .3034 percent which, according to the attending physician, was high enough to render a normal man unconscious. The company pointed out that most states consider a person with .10 percent alcohol in the bloodstream to be legally intoxicated.

Thompson had been drinking on the vessel—a clear violation of the rule against drinking posted on the bulletin board, given to him in a copy of the work rules, and included in a copy of the deckhands' manual.

In order to protect the safety of the employees and the safety of the equipment, the company had the right to enforce reasonable rules. The rule against drinking was reasonable and had been enforced on numerous occasions. The accident severely jeopardized Thompson's life and the safety of others and constituted an unnecessary expense to the company. The company had the right to terminate Thompson under the terms of Article 5 of the contract. In addition, the union had agreed in Article 12(b), that the "safety of operations and precautions against all hazardous conditions shall be a joint effort and mutual aim of the company and the union." Therefore, the union was required, by contract, to accept this reasonable safety rule.

The union also agreed in Article 13, Section 3, that "it will not oppose the efforts of the company to obtain a normal day's work" and will combat employee practices which restrict or limit efficient operations. Being under the influence of alcohol and drinking on board the vessel restricts or limits efficient operation. The union should support the company in this discharge.

As to the union allegation that the company had not applied the rule consistently, the company claimed that the situations referred to by the union occurred more than three years previous. The company had been conscientiously endeavoring to tighten disciplinary standards. It did not condone either coming on board a vessel in an intoxicated condition or drinking alcohol once aboard. All of the situations referred to by the union involved coming on board in an intoxicated condition, and not to drinking on board as Thompson had done.

The company argued that Thompson's plea to the effect that he no longer was an alcoholic revealed that he did not understand the philosophy of Alcoholics Anonymous which states that "once an alcoholic, always an alcoholic." For example, when questioned during the investigation, he was asked:

Q. Do you regard yourself as an alcoholic?
A. Well, I would say I was. But I ain't now.
Q. You aren't one now?
A. No, I ain't.

Thompson did not understand his problem; he was still an alcoholic; he would certainly drink again.

The company urged that the arbitrator sustain the company's position and uphold the discharge of Henry Thompson.

APPENDIX

Relevant Provisions of the Contract

ARTICLE V—MANAGEMENT

Nothing herein contained shall be construed to limit the authority of the Master, Pilot, Chief Engineer, Company Officers or Designated Representatives in the discharge of their lawful duties. The management of properties, including boats, the direction of the

462

working force, the right to hire and discharge and/or transfer are vested exclusively in the Company, and the Union shall not abridge these rights. The Company shall not discriminate against employees because of membership in the union.

ARTICLE XII—SAFETY & HEALTH
(Boats and Terminals)

Safety

(b) Safety of operations and precautions against all hazardous conditions shall be the joint and mutual aim of the Company and the Union, and every effort on the part of each party shall be directed to this end.

ARTICLE XIII—MISCELLANEOUS
(Towboats and Terminals)

Efficiency

The Union agrees that it will not oppose the efforts of the Company to obtain a normal day's work on the part of its members and will combat absenteeism and any other employee practices which restrict or limit efficient operation. The Union further agrees that it will not oppose the Company in the Company's efforts to eliminate waste; conserve materials and supplies; improve the quality of workmanship; prevent accidents; and strengthen the good will between the Company, the employee, the customer and the public.

Company Rule Posted on All Bulletin Boards

POST ON BULLETIN BOARD

TO: ALL VESSEL EMPLOYEES, OHIO RIVER COMPANY—OHIO DIVISION
RE: DRINKING AND INTOXICATION WORK RULE

Boarding any company vessel or being on any company property under the influence of alcoholic beverages is prohibited. Bringing alcoholic beverages on company property, including vessels is prohibited. The consumption of alcoholic beverages on company vessels or property is also prohibited.

Any violation of this rule will result in an immediate suspension, possibly resulting in discharge.

Intoxication and the possession of alcohol aboard our vessels and property endangers not only the safety of the offending party, but also the safety of the crew. Therefore, the company cannot and will not tolerate any exceptions to this work rule and hereby gives advance warning to all employees that any violation of this work rule will be considered a matter of the utmost seriousness. It is the Master's and/or Pilot's responsibility to enforce this work rule.

s/John J. Egan, Jr.
Port Captain
June 17, 1958 (Original Date)
January 22, 1968 (Revised Date)
August 6, 1969 (Revised Date)
March 23, 1973 (Revised Date)
August 16, 1982 (Revised Date)
September 20, 1982 (Revised Date)
November 17, 1983 (Revised Date)

In addition, on the grievant's employment application, he had signed the following statement:

I also understand that the use of intoxicants or being intoxicated or illegal use of narcotics during company time is sufficient cause to terminate my employment with the company. (November 17, 1983)

QUESTIONS

1. What is the fundamental issue in this case?
2. If the company had permitted crewmen to come to work drunk in the past without having taken any action, would this have any bearing on this case? Does the fact that the company had been attempting to tighten disciplinary standards have any bearing on this case? Discuss.
3. How important is the issue of safety?
4. How important is the fact that Thompson had become a member of Alcoholics Anonymous and had abstained from the use of alcohol for a considerable period of time after this incident?
5. Does Article 12(b) require that the union support the company's action? Discuss.
6. Was the discharge of Thompson warranted under all of the circumstances? Why, or why not?

73. THE PAYROLL ERROR

Company: Hermann Oak Leather Company, St. Louis, Missouri

Union: International Molders and Allied Workers Union, Local 59

BACKGROUND

On December 7, 1982, foreman Charles Johnson[1] received written notices of a grievance from John Coffman which stated:

> Company said they overpaid me for 22 weeks. They said I should have caught it and reported it to them. I feel that they fired me unjustly. I want to be paid average for all time lost.

And on the same date, Johnson received an almost identical grievance from Roger Bickford:

> Company said they overpaid me for 24 weeks. They said I should have caught it and reported it to them. I feel that they fired me unjustly. I want to be paid average for all time lost.

Both employees worked within the shipping area of the finishing department of Hermann Oak. Their jobs included the measuring, rolling, binding, and shipping of leather that had been processed from raw hides to finished leather.

The company primarily was involved in tanning and finishing leather for sales to manufacturers. It employed about 50 persons in the tanning and finishing departments.

On Thursday morning, December 2, 1982, Anne Beck, payroll manager, informed plant manager Jack Rand that there had been a

---

[1] The names of all individuals have been disguised.

major error in piecework rates paid to two employees in the shipping department. This was discovered because new piecework rates, to be effective in January 1983, were being programmed into the computer. Five different piece rates involving Bickford and Coffman had been programmed in error resulting in overpayment to them. On the following day Beck reported to Rand that the overpayment had extended from June 1982, through the remainder of the year. These overpayments averaged $35 per week but were as large as $67. Bickford had been overpaid a total of $840.88 during the 24-week period, and Coffman $780.64 during the 22-week period. (Coffman had been on two weeks vacation during that time.)

Rand met with both Bickford and Coffman later that day; he informed them that they had been overpaid and that they would be told later what would be done. According to Rand, Bickford then turned to Coffman and said, "I told you so." Neither man denied receiving the overpayment. On the following Monday, both men were presented copies of a compilation that had been prepared by Beck.

Subsequently that day, Rand and Beck met with Robert Henkle, president of Hermann Oak, and the company attorney to determine what action should be taken. A decision was made to terminate both Bickford and Coffman because both were considered to be guilty of major dishonesty.

The union appealed the company's action through the established grievance procedure without agreement. The case was submitted to arbitration. The parties agreed that the issue to be decided was as follows:

> Were the grievants, Coffman and Bickford, discharged for just cause? If not, what should be the appropriate remedy?

TESTIMONY OF THE GRIEVANTS

Coffman testified that he had been employed by the company for 14 years, during 12 of which he had served as a union committee person and steward. He indicated that during those years he had been involved in contract negotiations and grievance meetings, and that he had engaged in many "heated discussions" and "yelling contests" with management. However, he claimed that he had never received any disciplinary actions for his work. He felt that the company had terminated him for his union activity. To support this contention, he claimed that on one occasion Rand had said "he'd get me" following a heated grievance meeting.

Coffman admitted that he had pleaded guilty of embezzlement of union funds in the U.S. District Court and had been placed on probation in return for 200 hours of community service and restoration of the monies to the union.

According to Coffman, he "didn't know anything" about being overpaid for 22 weeks in 1982 until he was informed by the plant manager to this effect on December 3, 1982. He acknowledged that he had lodged several complaints during the earlier months about not being paid enough. But he said that he and Bickford had checked their pay only for about the first five months of 1982; since most of the time company calculations were correct, both he and Bickford stopped challenging their paychecks rather than engage in "aggravating" the company.

He claimed that during the meeting with Rand on December 3, the plant manager said that "the company would figure out some plan of restitution," but that this opportunity had never been offered to him and Bickford. He further claimed that during a grievance meeting protesting his discharge, he offered to pay the money back on a weekly installment basis if he could get his job back, but that his offer was not acceptable to the company.

Bickford stated that he had been with Hermann Oak for 16 years, during 10 of which he had served as a union committee person and steward. He, too, felt that he had been treated unusually harshly by management because of his union activities. He said that he had participated in many heated arguments during grievance meetings, and that he was not liked by several members of management because of his assertive behavior on behalf of his fellow union members. He stated that he had a good work record with the company.

Bickford testified that he had never been indicted nor charged with a crime by the grand jury, although he had been investigated by the U.S. Department of Labor for allegedly claiming and receiving more money from the union for negotiating time than he was entitled to collect.

He testified that he kept "a little black book" in which he kept detailed records of his piece rate earnings, but that he kept such records only at the beginning of each year until such time that he felt assured that the company was correctly calculating piece rates. In 1982 he stopped keeping records after satisfying himself that the company's calculations were generally accurate. He said that he was "not a good mathematician" and that his paychecks varied by as much as $50 from one week to another. It was only reasonable that he attempted to determine his earnings on a daily basis, especially when errors by company records were likely to occur.

He claimed that he had stopped maintaining accurate records of daily earnings late in May 1982, and that he had no personal knowledge of the overpayments from June through December. Like Coffman, Bickford stated that during his first meeting with Rand on December 3, the plant manager suggested that he would be allowed to make some form of restitution. However, subsequently the company refused to offer him this opportunity in exchange for reinstatement to his former job.

POSITION OF THE UNION

Lester Norvell, international union vice president, argued on behalf of Coffman and Bickford, as well as for the interests of all other members of the union. He pointed out that two other employees were also overpaid during the two weeks that Coffman was on vacation, but that they had not been either asked to refund the overpayments or disciplined in any manner.

He further argued that neither Coffman nor Bickford had falsified their time cards. The principal problem with the miscalculation of their pay was because of the incompetence of management in programming the computer and with the failure of the company to monitor the operation of its bookkeeping system. This was not only a classic case of "garbage in, garbage out" but also of slovenly attention to what was happening in the bookkeeping department. Neither Coffman nor Bickford was either a computer expert or an accountant. They kept track of their earnings during the first few months of 1982, but did so with difficulty and the devotion of much time to the activity. They uncovered several errors in payroll calculations, one as small as $1.33, but usually in the $5–$10 range; after all, even $1.33 was important to a working man. However, after determining that their pay was being accurately calculated, they were only too happy to stop keeping detailed records, which they did toward the end of May 1982.

Norvell also pointed out that the collective bargaining agreement contained no provision, or even an implication, that required an employee to either compute his own pay or report an overpayment if such occurred.

Norvell argued that the company discharged Bickford and Coffman because of their tenacious defense of the rights of their fellow union members under the terms of the collective agreement.

The union urged that both Bickford and Coffman be reinstated to their former jobs, that they be paid for all time lost, that all references to the company's unwarranted disciplinary action be removed from their personnel files, and that their seniority remain uninterrupted.

POSITION OF THE COMPANY

The company charged that both Bickford and Coffman were guilty of major dishonesty because both men clearly knew for an extended period of time about the overpayments. In support of the company's contention, Thomas Howell, assistant plant manager and superintendent of the finishing department, stated that he had observed both Coffman and Bickford figuring and maintaining a record of their pay. According to him, they maintained a "little black book" in which they recorded their pay; he had seen this book in discussions with them. He said that they calculated their pay each day at the end of their shift and that they knew what pay was due them "to the penny." He stated that both men had discussed discrepancies in their pay at least a dozen times, and that when they did so, they always claimed underpayment. These discussions were during the period of January-June, 1982. During the period June-December, 1982, they raised questions about wages paid to other employees, although they did not question him about their own checks during those months. Howell indicated that he heard Bickford tell a fellow employee following the meeting of December 3, "Didn't I tell you that I was being overpaid?"

Payroll department manager Anne Beck also indicated that she had discussed payroll matters with both Bickford and Coffman at least a half dozen times during the past year. She claimed that both men calculated their pay on a regular weekly basis, and she cited several examples from payroll records where they contested alleged payroll errors prior to June 1982. All of the amounts were less than $10. Three examples were:

  a. April 1979: $1.33 due Bickford
  b. October 1979: $8.26 due Coffman and $8.54 due Bickford
  c. April 1981: $6.40 due Bickford and $6.25 due Coffman

Beck also claimed that on many instances they brought payroll matters to her attention in which they were proven wrong. These, too, were minor discrepancies usually involving less than $10. Beck stated that she was not sure who made the computer error, but she held that it was an "innocent mistake." Coffman and Bickford were the only two persons who were overpaid excessively during this period.

The company supported its contention that both men were dishonest in citing that Coffman had been found guilty of embezzlement of union funds in U.S. Circuit Court. And Bickford was under investigation by the U.S. Department of Labor for allegedly padding his expense account, thereby potentially defrauding the union of a considerable amount of money; the charge was that he claimed payment for more time spent in negotiations than he actually devoted to that union activity.

The company stated that only Bickford and Coffman had been disciplined because they were the only persons who knew that they were being overpaid over a long period of time. Two other employees who served as vacation fill-ins, for one week each, had no reason to know of the overpayments. Thus, the company considered them innocent of dishonesty.

The company acknowledged that both Coffman and Bickford were union officers, and that management found both men to be somewhat contentious in arguing the terms of the collective bargaining agreement and aggressive in supporting their perceived rights of other union members. However, plant manager Rand stated that on no occasion had he or any other member of management ever said to either man, "I'll get your job." On the other hand, Rand admitted that he had written an official warning to Bickford dated March 15, 1976, which placed him on final warning for his part in supporting a work stoppage. The company maintained that dishonesty, not union activity, caused the company to terminate both employees.

Finally, the company argued that it was absolutely essential that employees in the shipping area be honest in their actions, since these men measured and weighed valuable materials shipped to customers. Both men were responsible for reporting rate figures to the company on which the company relied; and both men also calculated their own pay on a regular basis and had challenged the company on numerous occasions for errors. They knew how to calculate their pay; they regularly did so; and they knowingly accepted for many months overpayments to which they were not entitled. Such gross dishonesty could not be permitted in such responsible positions as held by both Bickford and Coffman.

The company urged the arbitrator to find the company's action reasonable, the discharge to be for just cause, and to uphold the termination of both Bickford and Coffman.

APPENDIX

Relevant Provisions of the Contract

ARTICLE VI—MANAGEMENT RIGHTS

The direction of the work and the selection, promotion and transfer of employees, except as limited in this Agreement or by law, shall lie with the Company. All employees shall observe rules and regulations made by the Company for the conduct of its operations. Any employee shall perform any service at any time in the Company's operations which he is required to and is in the opinion of the Company qualified to perform. Except as herein limited, the hours of labor, the assignment of duties and tasks and the general conduct and management of the Company and of its production processes and facilities, rest with the Company. Nothing herein shall be so construed as to impair or abate the right of the Company to change, modify or cease its operations, processes, or production in its discretion; and in the event of such change, modifications or cessations, the Company shall be the sole judge of all factors involved, including, but not limited to, the efficiency, usefulness and practicability of machinery, processes, location of business, and personnel required by it. The Company will, however, discuss with the Union, on its request, any such change, modification or cessation which would affect the wages, hours or working conditions of the employees. The Union will not interfere with the sales policies of the Company or with its source of supplies of raw materials, equipment, supplies, power, services, or other articles and services required by it in its unlimited discretion.

ARTICLE VII—SENIORITY

4. Seniority shall be lost and employment may be terminated for any of the following:
A. Discharge for cause.

QUESTIONS

1. Did Coffman and Bickford knowingly accept monies to which they were not entitled? Discuss.
2. Should the responsibility for these payroll errors be attributed to the payroll manager? To Coffman and Bickford?
3. Are the past backgrounds of Coffman and Bickford of any direct relevance to the issues in this case?
4. Were the discharge actions justified? Why, or why not?

74. THE UNRECORDED PURCHASE

Company: Furr's, Inc., Albuquerque, New Mexico

Union: United Food and Commercial Workers Union, Local 1564

Jane Eyer[1] was employed as a food clerk by Furr's, Inc., from October 25, 1973 until her suspension on March 24, 1984 and her discharge on April 2, 1984. She was discharged for a violation of the company's "Failure to Ring Up Purchases" policy.

The union filed a grievance in behalf of Eyer. It was processed through the grievance procedure to arbitration. The parties agreed that the question before the arbitrator was as follows:

1. Did the company have just cause to discharge Jane Eyer for violation of the "Failure to Ring Up Purchases" policy?

2. If not, what is the appropriate remedy?

BACKGROUND

Jane Eyer reported for work on March 23, 1984, having missed the previous two days because of illness. At approximately 11:20 A.M., a customer named Celia Tamm approached Eyer's checkout station with her baby, pushing a grocery cart filled with grocery items which she desired to purchase. Tamm had divided the groceries into two groups. The first group included items to be paid for with a "Women, Infant, and Children Nutrition Program" check ("WIC" check); and the items in the second group were to be purchased with Tamm's personal check. The WIC program was conducted by the State of New Mexico; it provided certain grocery items to qualified

---

[1] The names of all individuals have been disguised.

471

persons at no cost. The mechanics of a purchase under the program provided that a qualified person, such as Tamm, was entitled to purchase certain specified food items with a WIC check drawn on the State of New Mexico.

According to Eyer, she noted the items which were being purchased by Tamm with the WIC check and compared them with the items which Tamm was authorized to purchase. Tamm completed the name and address portion of the WIC check and gave it to Eyer. Eyer did not, at that point, complete the transaction on her cash register and place the WIC check in the register drawer. Eyer then rang up the other items which Tamm paid for with her personal check and which Eyer deposited in the register drawer. During that time, Tamm's baby was crying very loudly which disturbed both the baby's mother and Eyer. (Tamm corroborated Eyer's recollection of the details of the transaction.)

After Tamm left the store with her purchases, Eyer waited on two or three additional customers before realizing that she had not either rung up the purchases for the WIC check or deposited the WIC check in the register drawer. In attempting to rectify this mistake, she first made an error in the proper amount of the WIC check. She stated that she confused the proper amount of Tamm's WIC check with the dollar amount of the purchases of one of the subsequent customers she had waited on in the meantime. Further, she claimed to have had difficulties in getting the register to function properly.

Each cash register had a transaction number that identified each transaction. Tamm's personal check was identified as transaction number 4239. The last transaction involving the WIC check was number 4255. If Eyer had followed company procedure precisely, the WIC check would have been deposited before the purchase involving Tamm's personal check and would have been recorded as number 4238.

At some time between transaction 4239 and 4255, the head clerk noticed that Eyer was experiencing a problem with her register, asked her about it, and upon receiving an affirmative response, pushed the "clear" key on the register to clear the machine.

At the end of the day management personnel examined the "detail tape" which recorded each transaction on the register. The next day company security personnel conducted an investigation of Eyer's failure to ring up the WIC check. At the end of her work shift on March 24, Eyer was suspended; and she was discharged on April 2, 1984.

An audit of Eyer's transactions on March 23 revealed that there was no shortage; instead, there was an overage of $1.34.

Furr, Inc., had a "Failure to Ring Up Purchases" policy for more than 10 years prior to this incident. Each new employee was advised of the policy at the time of hire and was required to read and sign the written policy statement when first employed. Each time the policy was changed or revised in any way, a copy of the new version was issued to all employees to be read and signed. The last revision occurred in August 1978, and it had been read and signed by Eyer.[2]

POSITION OF THE UNION

The union contended that Eyer attempted to ring up the WIC check within 10 rings but was unable to do so because of a malfunction of the cash register. She became quite nervous upon discovering that she had failed to ring up the WIC check properly. The malfunction may have been caused, at least in part, by some misstep on her part, but it did occur.

The union also pointed out that the acts of Eyer were not willful, deliberate, or intentional violations of the "Failure to Ring Up Purchases" policy. As soon as she discovered her error, she immediately attempted to rectify it. She was not attempting to defraud the company; she ultimately recorded the transaction properly; the company lost nothing.

Eyer had a long record of excellent service. She was a loyal and competent employee with no prior disciplinary record for any reason. The company had no just cause for discharge.

The union urged the arbitrator to restore Jane Eyer to her position of food clerk with full back pay and restoration of all benefits.

POSITION OF THE COMPANY

The company argued that the penalty for a violation of the "Failure to Ring Up Purchases" policy had always been discharge on the first offense without any prior warning. The policy had been invoked consistently and without exception. The penalty was appropriate because of the serious nature of the offense.

The company cited the text of an earlier decision by arbitrator Donald Daughton who had heard a similar case involving a violation of the company's "Failure to Ring Up Purchases" policy:

> First, in the judgment of management the company's policy on "failure to ring" is essential to maintaining inventory and cash control at the retail store level. Second, the establishment of such a policy by other retail grocery chains is the norm rather than the exception. Third, the employees of the company were specifically advised of the

---

[2] See Appendix for copy of the "Failure to Ring" policy.

policy, and that a violation of the policy would result in discharge on first offense. Fourth, the policy had been uniformly applied by the company.

Food clerks play a vital role in the operations of the company inasmuch as all the payments for purchases must go through their hands. Consequently, it is necessary that the company policy governing the receipt of monies be meticulously adhered to. Given the crucial role which food clerks play in the operation of a retail grocery business, arbitrators have uniformly acknowledged the right of the company to impose the penalty of discharge for a first violation of a company policy of the kind involved in this arbitration.

The company urged that the arbitrator sustain the discharge of Jane Eyer.

APPENDIX

Relevant Clauses of the Contract

4.2—DISCIPLINE—The employer shall have the right to discharge, demote or suspend any employee for just cause. However, prior to such action being taken, at least one (1) written corrective action notice on a related or similar offense must be given to an employee, except in those cases where there is just cause based upon a particular offense.

Relevant Company Policy Read and Signed by Employee Jane Eyer

FAILURE TO RING UP PURCHASES
Revised Rule 8–78

The primary responsibility of every checker is to make an accurate record, by use of the cash register, of all purchases made by a customer to receive correct payment for same and to place all money, checks, food stamps, and coupons received into the cash register.

Money or legal tender is to be placed in the register immediately after each complete customer transaction. Failure to do this shall constitute failure to ring and the penalty for violation of this rule is DISCHARGE WITHOUT WARNING.

An employee will be discharged on first offense if he/she fails to ring up money received by a customer for a purchase whether or not the money so received is placed in the cash register.

If an additional sale is made to the same customer, it will be treated as a separate sale and handled by ringing up the purchase, placing the money in the cash register, and issuing the customer receipt and tape to the customer.

In the event that a customer gives you, or leaves you the correct amount for a purchase while you are recording another sale, the money will be placed on the change plate of the cash register. This sale must then be recorded as the next immediate transaction even if other customers are in line. The money received in this type of sale must be recorded on your register and not issued to another checkstand.

Customer's money or the company's money, saving stamps, coupons, or food stamps shall not be mixed with personal funds or kept on your person. Violation of this rule shall result in immediate discharge.

Professional shoppers are retained by Furr's who act as customers to shop employees periodically to determine if the above rules are being followed. A typical examination of this kind is conducted by two or more shoppers working in conjunction so that at least one shopper can observe or identify the transaction of the other shopper who will tender exact change for a purchase and not wait for a detail tape. Employees who fail to record monies received in this manner will be discharged for failure to ring.

The detail tape will be used to identify the transaction and if the money so tendered is not indicated on the detail tape within 10 transactions it shall be defined as failure to ring.

If you have any questions on the above procedures, please ask your immediate supervisor.

I have received, read, and understand these procedures.
/s/ Jane Eyer 11/18/78 #22
(Signature   Date   Store No.)
Each checker should keep the first copy for his/her personal file and return the second copy to his/her store manager signed and dated.

Employee's Name: ___Jane Eyer___
(Please Print)

QUESTIONS

1. Should the fact that Eyer had been employed as a food clerk for over 10 years influence the arbitration decision?
2. Do the circumstances surrounding her failure to ring up the purchase have any influence on the arbitration decision?
3. Was the company's rule on ringing up purchases reasonable? Why, or why not?
4. How has the company enforced the rule in the past?
5. Had Eyer been adequately informed of the rule? Discuss.
6. If you had been the manager of this store, how would you have handled this case?